# THE FAIR VALUE OF INSURANCE LIABILITIES

The New York University Salomon Center Series
on Financial Markets and Institutions

VOLUME 1

*The titles published in this series are listed at the end of this volume.*

# THE FAIR VALUE OF INSURANCE LIABILITIES

Edited by

IRWIN T. VANDERHOOF

and

EDWARD I. ALTMAN

*Stern School of Business*
*New York University*

KLUWER ACADEMIC PUBLISHERS
BOSTON / DORDRECHT / LONDON

A C.I.P. Catalogue record for this book is available from the Library of Congress

ISBN 0-7923-9941-2

Published by Kluwer Academic Publishers,
P.O. Box 17, 3300 AA Dordrecht, The Netherlands

Sold and distributed in the U.S.A. and Canada
by Kluwer Academic Publishers,
101 Philip Drive, Norwell, MA 02061, U.S.A.

In all other countries, sold and distributed
by Kluwer Academic Publishers Group
P.O. Box 322, 3300 AH Dordrecht, The Netherlands

*Printed on acid-free paper*

All Rights Reserved
© 1998 Kluwer Academic Publishers
No part of the material protected by this copyright notice may be reproduced or
utilized in any form or by any means, electronic or mechanical,
including photocopying, recording or by any information storage and
retrieval system, without written permission from the copyright owner.

Printed in Great Britain

# Table of contents

|   | Introduction<br>Irwin T. Vanderhoof | vii |
|---|---|---|
|   | Welcome<br>Frederick D.S. Choi | xvii |
| 1. | Background on fair value accounting of insurance company assets and liabilities<br>Robert C. Wilkins | 1 |
| 2. | Comparison of methods for fair-value life insurance liabilities<br>Arnold A. Dicke | 7 |
| 3. | Fair valuation of life insurance company liabilities<br>Douglas C. Doll *et al.* | 21 |
|   | *Discussion*<br>David F. Babbel | 115 |
| 4. | Experience in implementing fair value of insurance liabilities<br>Dennis L. Carr | 127 |
|   | *Discussion*<br>J. Peter Duran<br>Joseph E. Crowne | 133<br>137 |
| 5. | Allowing for asset, liability, and business risk in the valuation of a life company<br>Shyam J.B. Mehta | 143 |
|   | *Discussion*<br>Phelim Boyle | 197 |
| 6. | A market-value accounting framework for insurance companies<br>Mark Griffin | 201 |
|   | *Discussion*<br>Joan Lamm-Tennant | 211 |
| 7. | Option adjusted value of the firm<br>David N. Becker | 215 |
|   | *Discussion*<br>Kim Staking | 289 |

vi  *Table of contents*

| | | |
|---|---|---:|
| 8. | The cash flow method for valuing liabilities in Canada<br>Allan Brender | 297 |
| 9. | The derivation and application of accounting standards to the market value of liabilities<br>Christopher D. O'Brien | 303 |
| | The indexed discount rate method for fair valuation of liabilities<br>S. Michael McLaughlin | 331 |
| | Is Paul vs. Virginia dead?<br>Krzysztof M. Ostaszewski | 351 |
| | Remarks<br>Joan Lamm-Tennant | 361 |
| | List of contributors | 363 |
| | Index | 371 |

IRWIN T. VANDERHOOF
New York University

# Introduction: fair value of insurance liabilities

The formal papers in this volume are responses to a call for papers on the subject of 'market' value of insurance liabilities sponsored by the Society of Actuaries. 'Fair value' and 'market value' are viewed as equivalent ideas by FASB. The discussions were prepared for a conference jointly sponsored by the Society of Actuaries and the Salomon Center at the NYU Stern School of business. Both the call for papers and the conference were inspired by the decision of the Accounting Standards Board and the SEC that at least some assets of insurance companies should be reported on a basis of market value rather than amortized cost. In addition, in the future mutual companies will have to make reports using generally accepted accounting principles (GAAP) rather than only using statutory accounting methods.

These new standards seem to require rethinking of the accounting and financial operations of insurance companies, banks, and other financial intermediaries, for they are all subject to the same requirements.

## A ROMANTIC VIEW OF ACCOUNTING

Characterizing this as 'romantic' is intended to absolve me from strict adherence to whatever facts may be pertinent.

Let us first consider the romantic history of accounting and its contribution to literature and science. It is generally accepted that the oldest written piece of literature still existent is the *Epic of Gilgamesh*, dating to the Sumerian civilization, but there are written records that predate even this ancient lay. These are scraps of parchment containing notes of items and prices. They are trade documents and accounting records. Sacred scripture could be, and often was, memorized. Accounting records keep changing and they may have to go from hand to hand rather quickly. Memories were inadequate for this purpose. Records of debt might be traded and records were needed so that a legal status could be attained. Only writing was adequate for these purposes.

The records of every civilization support the idea that writing was not developed to allow poetry or plays to be written. It was not developed to allow the writing of sacred texts. It was developed for accounting. The poetry and plays were just a side benefit.

Similarly, it seems unlikely that mathematics was devised so that people could develop number theory or Euclidean geometry. The basis of mathematics was counting and the reason for counting was the need for accounting records. Even one old meaning of the phrase 'to account for' is to give an explanation. Accounting has therefore been closely allied and behind the underpinning of mathematics and science.

Being the basis for literature, mathematics, and science should be enough to qualify accounting for some romantic treatment.

Let us consider a simplified history of accounting to see how we arrived at our present kinds of problems. Let's start with the situation of the Roman merchant Severius. He sells the jars called amphora for a certain number of the coins called denarii. He buys for one and sells for two, thereby showing a 1% [100%???] profit. (Percentage calculations were hard with Roman numerals). If the business owns only its inventory, then he can conveniently measure his profit in terms of the number of denarii in his safe hole. His concern with accounting at this stage is simply whether he is conducting his business properly and how to improve profits. He will measure his wealth in terms of denarii.

On the other hand, that may not work. If he has recently purchased a large number of amphora, then his denarii may be down even though his wealth has not decreased. He can measure his actual wealth only by taking into consideration the inventory as well as the amount of cash in hand. How should we measure the value of the inventory? One way would be to value the inventory at current market prices. In this case we would have to decide whether to use a seller's price or a buyer's price. When describing his wealth to his significant other, he might use the price at which he thought he could sell the jars. If he were optimistic, this might be much larger than the price at which he bought.

If he wanted to use his wealth as a basis for borrowing more money to allow the purchase of more inventory, then he would certainly use the higher price. On the other hand, the lender might reject this valuation. The lender might well say that the proper basis would be the price at which the items were purchased. At least that should be clearly determinable. This might be a basis for determining the ability to repay the loan. This conservative approach might be more comfortable for the lender. However, even this might fail. The wholesale market for amphora might have collapsed, and the more conservative value of market should be used. A current American approach to this problem would be to use cost if consideration of the market made it possible to believe that this would be recouped. In some countries the choice has been to use the lower of cost or the lowest market value ever observed.

Severius has now borrowed money for a radical expansion of inventory. He has found some Greeks that are charging prices that seem to make the sales a gift. He therefore borrows and buys all he can.

There is then a question as to what the market really is. His inventory now exceeds the demand for jars for the next several years. If he tried to sell, even at the buyer's price, there would be no buyers. There is now a real question as to what is meant by market price. However, despite the fact that there may be a question of the liquidation value of this inventory, if we can establish that the business is a going concern, that it will continue for a long period in the future, then we can treat the valuation of the inventory on that basis. We do not have to treat it as market value in a panic sale.

His next problem is to find a place to store all these items. He is able to borrow more funds to build a special purpose warehouse for the jars. He is now in a situation where the debts clearly exceed the market value of his possessions. In the case of the warehouse, there is not even a buyer available. How can the accountant look at this situation? Well, if he is still able to sell this product at a traditional price, then the warehouse can be valued at some version of cost. From the point of view of wealth this activity has not impaired the value of the business. We still, however, need to consider the expenses involved.

While the problem of too much inventory can be related to the 'going concern' view of a company, the problem of expenditures for fixed assets, like a building, require another insight. In this case, that is provided by the matching of revenues and expenses. The building will be used over many years; therefore, the expense of it must also be spread over many years in calculating the net income.

While it is nice that Severius was so easily able to find a lender to finance his expansion, that lender might also have some concerns and requirements. Obviously, the lender would be concerned about the honesty of the representations in the ledgers. He might require that someone independent check the books. The lender would also be concerned about the relative attractiveness of this loan vs. others that were also available to him. Because of this concern, the lender would try to impose some sort of consistency between the accounting treatment used by different borrowers. The worm in the accounting apple now appears. Unless great care is taken, borrowers will try to manage the accounts instead of managing the business. Accounting, which should help the management of the business and the understanding of the business by outsiders, becomes a driving force. Managing the appearance may become as important as managing the business.

The final great conceptual evolution of accounting took place in the Middle Ages. A monk, Brother Pacioli, wrote a book on double entry bookkeeping. An undigested piece of mutton and an extra glass of Benedictine are equally suspect in this. While the idea is surely a great step forward, when actually trying to implement it, there are often problems. The great advantage of double entry bookkeeping is that it is easier to find wrong entries, both accidental and intentional. Since every entry is made as both a debit to one account and a credit to another, income or asset or expense or liability, if the two totals are not consistent, we know there has been an error. Unfortunately, while it is easy to determine that there is a wrong entry, it may not be so simple to determine exactly where the error is.

Life insurance companies, prizing a reputation for eccentricity, often talk as if they use single entry accounting. They cite the fact that the reserve calculation is done on an inventory basis and a bulk adjustment made to income and liabilities. Lots of such adjustments are made. Life insurance accounting is like that of any other business from this point of view.

## Onward to FAS 115

The justification for the fanciful view of accounting is that it illustrates that the essential accounting approaches are understandable in terms of the smallest business. Matching revenue and expenses, the going concern principle, and the need for consistency are the principles that must guide our efforts. They can all be illustrated in terms of the simplest examples. However, what does that lead to in terms of life insurance accounting?

Life insurance accounting could be portrayed as a maverick kind of operation – hardly obeying the rules. I have already mentioned the double entry accounting question. There was supposed to be another crucial difference. It was that life insurance accounting was supposed to be based on liquidation values, not going concern values.

Well, this was clearly not true. If you were concerned with liquidating values, you would always use market values for assets. There was a clear methodology built up so that market values were practically hidden. The objective was not to provide a liquidating values statement. The objective was to provide a financial statement that would demonstrate the ability of the company to pay claims when due and to provide a gradual development of surplus. These accounting objectives would reduce the possibility of policy holder runs against the companies. This was always a significant danger when many of the assets were illiquid.

A second crucial objective was that the company should have significant hidden values. This would allow the regulators to take over the companies while there was enough embedded value to allow the policy holders to be paid off in full. This was accomplished by using low interest rates in the valuation requirements and by writing off expenses rather than amortizing them.

Two of the basic principles of accounting were being implemented in life insurance accounting. The statutory statements were on a going concern basis, despite industry protestations to the contrary, and there was excellent consistency between years and companies. Consistency was generally mandated by the laws of the states. Statutory accounting was not a total failure. Some companies are using it as the basis for both management and reporting because of the consistency factor.

A third principle was ignored, however. That was that there should be reasonable matching between the timing of revenue and expenses. The possible mismatch created by the use of a low valuation interest rate might have been tolerated as long as the differences were small. The difference caused by the writing off of acquisition expenses in the year of issue of a new policy was too much for investors to bear. The well-managed companies that were rapidly growing had terrible earnings statements while the companies that were practically going out of business looked great. One company was purported to have deliberately planned to hold down new business in a perverse attempt to improve earnings. The accounting system was once more taking control of the business. Managements became concerned with looking good instead of doing well.

As we would expect, investment bankers were quick to rush to the rescue. They invented a series of adjustments to statutory earnings to overcome the lack of reporting by management. While this was purported to overcome the problem of lack of proper accrual of revenue and expenses, the variety of adjustment factors and methods used allowed anyone to show how very well their favorite company was doing. The accounting profession was finally forced to take some action, and the DAC asset under GAAP came into being. There would now be some reasonable relationship between revenue and expenses during each period of time.

The development could have ended there. Managements tended to manage based on statutory accounting principles, while investors had GAAP and the IRS had their own system of developing taxable income. If the world had remained the same, we might have been able to get along indefinitely with these three systems. We could have even adjusted to a management accounting system that would be some sort of amalgam of the others to allow the company management to better operate the company and prove to the board of directors that existing company management was superb. Managements like such management accounting systems because they can be rigged to demonstrate this desired result.

The thing that upset this nice little arrangement was an unsettled environment. While interest rates were generally stable, the use of amortized costs as the stable values for assets could be tolerated. When the interest rates in the environment became unstable, the argument became less creditable. Even worse than the changes in the underlying risk-free rate were the changes in the risk premium for various assets. The accounting system allowed the assets that had depreciated to be carried at book value while the appreciating assets were sold to realize a booked capital gain. The result of these transactions was once again to 'paint the books' so that the company seemed to be operating more favorably than was the case. Management was once again managing the books and not the company.

It would be an error to believe that this was not widespread or that it was not a serious problem. The taking of capital gains and avoiding capital losses was common among banks and the S&Ls as well as insurance companies. In addition, the damage was not only to the pocketbooks of the investors who were misled. The more serious damage was to the companies. They were paying taxes on capital gains that did not correspond to a real change in their economic condition. The perverse result was that the companies looked better and paid more taxes but were economically weaker as a result of these transactions.

This management venality was at least partially responsible for the push of the SEC towards getting financial institutions to adopt market value accounting. It is also possible that there is some mystique in market value that attracted the regulators. In the case of the insurance industry, steps had already been taken toward preventing the kinds of abuse just described by using a combination of risk based capital and the interest maintenance reserve (IMR) to spread the investment results over the same period as the original investment.

In any case, a decision was made to require that a form of market value of some assets be used. Those assets were debt securities and equities. Debt securities included publicly traded bonds and private placements. The various forms of securitized mortgage obligations were included, but real estate and commercial mortgages were not. For many companies the inclusion of public and private bonds would constitute the major part of the investment portfolio.

Debt securities were to be classified into three groups: hold to maturity (HTM), available for sale (AVS), or trading (T). HTM could be carried at amortized cost. AVS would be kept at a best estimate of market value and changes in market would be carried through to the capital account directly. Such changes would not go through earnings. Finally, the T securities would be held at market and changes in market would be carried through to earnings.

This approach was resisted by the life insurance companies on the grounds that marking one side of the balance sheet to market would distort the equity and earnings of the company. The life insurance companies believed that adequate theoretical work had been done to allow the calculation of a consistent fair value of liabilities.

The decision made in the adoption of FAS 115 was clearly an attempt to address a problem in management created by accounting rules. Unfortunately, the cure may be as bad as the problem.

## THE PROBLEM WITH FAS 115

Let us look at the potential that FAS 115 has for the creation of problems from the point of view of Severius and his lender.

First, comparability between companies and with other industries is lost. Since two different companies with identical businesses could make different decisions with respect to the classification of the assets into the three categories, a comparison of earnings and stockholder equity would no longer be informative.

Second, the principle of a going concern would be violated. Marking the assets only to market and showing the liabilities at policy account values is consistent with liquidation, not a going concern.

Third, since gains and losses in market may not occur in the same accounting period as the realization of such gain or loss, we must conclude that the accrual principle is also violated.

If the underlying principles of accounting have any validity or usefulness, these violations by FAS 115 would be expected to compromise the usefulness of GAAP financial statements for the management, the investor, the regulator, and the policyholder. This has, in fact, happened.

The underlying objectives of statutory accounting are also violated. GAAP earnings and capital will be highly volatile, even if the company operation is smooth.

Finally, we will again be faced with situations where the accounting methods may encourage management to take incorrect action. The most serious example may be asset–liability management. Prudent management requires that judgment about the asset structure be made in a context where both assets and liabilities are carried at market. In a sense, the many simulations required in these calculations involve an internal market with consistent cash flows timed to occur under all market conditions. Actions that seem necessary in this context could conceivably produce very unsatisfactory statements for stockholders. We can guess whether prudent action or good-looking statements would control.

The simplest example of ill management would be a decision that, since privates cannot be easily sold anyway, we might as well have an illiquid portfolio classified as HTM. The loss of liquidity could be dangerous for the company and the policy holders.

## THE PAPERS

As was mentioned, the papers in this volume are largely the result of a call for papers on the subject of market value of insurance liabilities sponsored by the Society of Actuaries. They are largely written from the point of view of the mechanics of calculating such a value. Other papers were added to this group to assure that the final volume includes some input from FASB and the investment banking community.

In addition there were comments by a series of academics on the points developed in each of the papers. Finally, some material was included on the experience of those few companies that are actually already reporting fair value of liabilities to shareholders.

The purpose of the whole volume is to provide a summary of the thinking that needs to be developed to allow an improved solution to this problem.

## REMAINING QUESTIONS

One question that has not been well addressed by the papers is that of which liabilities should this sophisticated methodology be applied to. It seems that contracts that do not provide surrender values would be clearly appropriate for fair valuation. It is not so clear that liabilities that have some aspects of demand deposits should be treated identically. There should be some sensible way of establishing how this continuum should be handled.

A final consideration would be the hypnotic fascination that the SEC seems to have on market value. The accounting identity that 'equity equals assets less liability' can become misleading when assets are on a market value basis. Outside considerations can wreck the identity. Depending upon the original cost, the assets may have embedded tax liabilities. The solvency of financial institutions may be better measured and tested by the matching of cash flows than by market value discipline. Unfortunately, they become almost impossibly complex for stockholder reports.

It may be that the various problems which led to FAS 115 could be better settled by simple further adjustment of statutory accounting in terms of the IMR and risk based capital requirements. We can hope that these simpler possibilities will also be further explored.

There remains the final criticism of market valuation of liabilities. There seems to be a market crisis and collapse every generation or so. Since we know in advance that market discipline will not be enforced at those times since it would collapse the whole system, shouldn't we try to develop a more rugged methodology that would not need to be ignored when it was giving its loudest possible signal?

### A FINAL NOTE FROM THE INVESTMENT BANKERS

Perhaps the clearest call for a method of setting fair values for insurance liabilities was expressed by Derek Kirkland. At the conference luncheon he said that the use of fair value of assets without a corresponding fair value of liabilities seriously compromises the usefulness of GAAP equity (the difference between GAAP assets and GAAP liabilities) as a measure of the value of an insurance company as an investment. Since the implementation of FAS 115, GAAP equity can no longer be used as a factor in the investment analysis of insurance companies. Mr. Kirkland is a principal of Morgan Stanley with particular responsibility in the area of valuation of insurance companies as investments.

### ACKNOWLEDGMENTS

The success of the conference and this volume is based upon the work of many individuals and several organizations. The organizations were the Society of Actuaries, which made the original call for papers, and the Salomon Center of New York University, which set up the actual arrangements for the conference. Individuals who deserve special mention are Mary Jaffier of the Salomon Center, Warren Luckner of the Society of Actuaries staff and Douglas Doll of Tillinghast, who headed the Project Oversight Group on this Society of

Actuaries research project. Obviously, the main thanks are due the various authors, their efforts will be appreciated as the ideas in this volume become part of the literature and work of financial institutions.

Special thanks and appreciation are due to Deloitte & Touche LLP, Ernst & Young LLP, and Tillinghast-Towers Perrin. Their support of the conference, both financial and otherwise, was crucial in making it all come to pass.

FREDERICK D.S. CHOI
*New York University*

# Welcoming remarks

It gives me great pleasure to extend very warm greetings to everyone this morning on behalf of the Stern School, and to welcome you to this conference on Fair Value of Insurance Liabilities. To be sure that we get off to the right start, I will follow the advice of Oscar Wilde, who said, "To begin, be brief, be seated, and be gone." Actually, I added the last phrase, because I have a commitment very shortly and so I'm going to have to leave in just a little bit.

As one who has taught accounting for a number of years, this whole subject as is mentioned of today's conference very much interests me. And although I really searched this document, this brochure, for the word accounting, I couldn't find it. But this is, of course, very much an accounting issue. Now, when I talk to my first year accounting students about asset and liability measurement issues, I normally precede that discussion by asking a question and that is, what is the relationship between a firm's income statement and balance sheet? Anybody remember that? Accounting 101? Well, basically, the answer is that, assuming there haven't been any additional investments or withdrawals by the owners of the firm, that a firm's income statement explains in some detail, why owners equity changed during the period.

Now we can express that in terms of a very neat expression that goes something like this. "That a firm's net income ($NI$), is equal to revenues minus expense ($R - E$), which in turn is equal to the change in owners equity during the period, $\Delta OE$. Based on the accounting equation, we know that $\Delta OE$ is equal to the change in a firm's assets and liabilities. So if I substitute that back into the original expression, we have $R - E$ is equal to the change in $A - L$. So then the question is, well what does that imply?

Well, you know, my students never really give me the right answer, but it basically implies that you cannot separate the income statements and the balance sheet. Many analysts in the USA feel that of the two financial statements, income statement and balance sheet, the income statement is the most important statement as a basis for determining equity value. A lot of other people, especially European analysts, feel that the balance sheet is the more important determinant of equity value. So the question is, who is correct? Based on that equation that I took you through, they're both wrong: you cannot separate income measurement from asset and liability measurement; income determination is closely intertwined with asset and liability evaluation.

Now in terms of measuring assets and liabilities, this whole discussion of fair value measurements is not new. Formal debate on this issue, at least in the accounting literature, goes back to the early 1960s and even before that.

*I. Vanderhoof and E. Altman (eds.), The Fair Value of Insurance Liabilities, xvii–xviii.*
© *1998 Kluwer Academic Publishers. Printed in the UK.*

Raymond Chambers, produced the measurement framework called 'continuously contemporaneous accounting'. Basically he was advocating measuring assets and liabilities in terms of their current cash equivalence, as established by current markets. The reception to his proposal within the profession was very chilly. I don't think we had the measurement technology in place to do that very objectively, and so, we continued to have a relatively historical cost framework. However, after a number of years, we began to see some departures from historical cost, when accountants began to write inventories down to lieu of cost of market in order to be conservative. The problem with that is, marking to market was in a unique direction – we would mark *down* to market, never *up* to market. Ditto, for asset impairments, etc.

Today, with the improvements in measurement technology and financial technology, we have this whole birth of all these new financial instruments; it is now very popular to measure or mark assets to market. Again, if you come back to that expression that I introduced you to, today's discussion on valuation still ignores one element in that equation, which is liabilities. I very much applaud the efforts of Professors Altman and Vanderhoof and Lamm-Tennant, in putting together this conference, which concentrates on the measurement of liabilities. And although this conference is concentrating on the insurance industry, much of your discussion and conclusions that you reach today will have significant implications for other firms in the financial services industry, for market regulators and accounting standard setters.

So in conclusion, let me just extend my best wishes for a very successful, stimulating, interesting conference.

ROBERT C. WILKINS
*Financial Accounting Standards Board*

# 1. Background on fair value accounting of insurance company assets and liabilities

*Reading Mr. Wilkins' paper gives some idea of the efforts the accounting profession has made in trying to solve these problems. It also gives some indication of the problems they have had in reaching a conclusion. – Ed.*

I plan to provide you with some background on how the FASB has discussed the valuation of liabilities and how it has come up in conjunction with our project on Statement 115. I was the project manager on Statement 115.

We talked about the valuation of liabilities back in 1991 and 1992, so it is not a strange topic at the FASB. We did this as part of our marketable securities project, which was the general reference we used for the project that led to Statement 115. We also plan to discuss very shortly (in December 1995) this very same issue, the valuation of liabilities, in conjunction with our project on the accounting for derivatives and hedging.

Our marketable securities project resulted from concerns about the accounting for debt securities. We first discussed it with the Board in November of 1990, shortly after the Chairman of the SEC had made some comments about his views of thinking that that the depository institutions ought to report their investments at market value. That was also shortly after the American Institute of CPA's top technical body, the Accounting Standards Executive Committee, had decided to postpone some efforts they had in also addressing that issue. Board members did not want to merely commit themselves to undertaking a project. They first felt that they needed to understand better how entities use investments, both equity securities, but principally debt securities. They also wanted to reach some agreement among themselves about the direction that a project might take before actually adding it to its technical agenda.

We met with bankers and thrift representatives, as well as insurance company representatives. We met not only with the accountants; we also had the opportunity to meet with those that handled asset–liability management at various institutions. Board members were, therefore, well aware that financial institutions managed their exposure to interest rate risk by correlating the repricing or maturity characteristics of the assets with those of the liabilities. They understood that if we were going to be addressing the accounting for certain assets (investments in debt securities, and then we also thought we had to similarly address marketable equity securities) and if we're going to be marking to market, then we needed to also take a look at the liabilities, because obviously the one concern we had was that if we had certain assets at market value and there was a change in market interest rates, the valuation of the assets would change, but if we didn't do anything about the liabilities, then GAAP shareholders' equity had the potential then to show a volatility that was not representative of the institution's exposure to interest rate risk.

Consequently, the Board decided – and it took really well in excess of seven months before we actually decided to move ahead – to undertake the marketable securities project. The goal of the project at that time in 1991 was that investments and securities should be at market value, and the Board also threw in the 'and perhaps liabilities' reference because they realized that it would make sense to do both sides, or at least to permit both sides. They were not yet convinced that that was something that could be achievable, and it was June 1991 when we formally undertook the project that eventually led to Statement 115, and it was a pure market value project. Investments in securities were to be at market value.

Now when we discussed liability valuation with the Board in greater detail we really had two problems. First, since we were addressing only some assets, and not all assets, we needed to determine which liabilities needed to be reported at fair value. We didn't think it appropriate to say all liabilities should be at fair value because if we go with all liabilities at fair value, then we simply have an imbalance in the other direction. The problem was that some assets were going to be at fair value, and no liabilities at cost, and thus we say there's an imbalance, a potential for volatility in equity that's not representative. We felt that we had to, in some fashion, identify *which* liabilities should be at fair value, rather than have all liabilities at fair value.

The second problem was that there were certain difficulties with determining the fair value of just certain liabilities. Most of our efforts focused on the first issue; we had extensive discussions in the autumn of 1991, on the issue of how you determine which of the liabilities should be reported at fair value. The difficulty was that we couldn't just turn to companies and say "Your own asset-liability management will tell you that answer" because most entities did not correlate specific liabilities with specific assets, but managed their exposure to interest rate risk on an overall (or global) basis. There were certain limited areas, however, where a correlation perhaps did exist – a direct relationship where there was some linkage. That was true in some small parts of insurance companies and similarly, in certain areas in banks. Generally speaking, however, we could not really say report at fair value the liabilities that are directly linked to your investments in debt and equity securities because they didn't make that kind of linkage. They just looked at overall positions to manage their exposure to interest rate risk.

So we tried many different ways in which we could make this notion operational – to identify which liability should be there. We went through various designation methods or approaches where entities could designate liabilities just for purposes of this standard, and therefore, have those designated liabilities be reported at fair value. We had various constraints that we discussed about imposing on such designation approaches or methods.

The bottom line, though, was that the Board members felt that every one of our approaches was just not satisfactory; they felt each was either too artificial or too easily manipulated to basically give management complete discretion to report whatever it wanted, and there were a lot of problems. What happens if one side is liquidated? What do you do with the other side that's now at fair value? The bottom line was that the Board stumbled so hard on the very first issue, on how you determine which of the liabilities should be at fair value, that we never really got into an extensive discussion of the second issue. There was also a third, somewhat related issue – should the fair value of a liability be affected by a deterioration in the creditworthiness of the issuer (the debtor)? Obviously, if the issuer has deterioration in his creditworthiness, the fair value (at least as observed in the marketplace, if we're talking about public debt, or traded debt) the market value of the debt falls, so the market value of the liability falls and of course, in good old double-entry bookkeeping, that means an increase to shareholders' equity. Some Board members were troubled by that, even though one could say that perhaps that's the reality of it – that there is a sharing between shareholders and debt holders when the creditworthiness of the institution suffers. This reduction in fair value of the liability (and therefore, increase in shareholders' equity) is a fact in that the shareholder doesn't bear the sole brunt alone, that it's a sharing between debt holder and shareholder. In any case, that was an issue. Returning to the second issue, certain liabilities were posing problems: principally, the deposit liabilities of banks and thrifts and credit unions, and then insurance liabilities. With respect to the former, clearly we had bankers telling us that they thought it was most appropriate to consider deposit liabilities as a cheap form of financing and, therefore, they should compare the interest cost of their deposit liabilities with the interest cost related to the cost of replacement funds. They wanted to anticipate the forbearance of the depositor in withdrawing those funds. This led to their conclusion that it would be appropriate to say that the fair value can be, and in fact should be, less than what is payable on demand. If you have a $1000 savings account, it's okay for the bank to anticipate that you will not withdraw that for several years, and because that pays a pittance of a rate (2 or 3%, whatever it might be) and the cost of alternative funds would be much higher, that they should say the fair value of that $1000 deposit in the passbook account is perhaps only $950. Some Board members were very troubled by that and said "How can you say that the fair value of a liability is less than what is payable on demand?" There is the corollary situation, of course, in the insurance world, and that's with cash surrender values.

We hold regular liaison meetings with a number of organizations annually. We meet with various banking organizations. We also meet with the American Academy of Actuaries. When we met with that group, we would hear from them (as we heard in private meetings with insurance representatives) the idea that perhaps maybe the fair value of life insurance liabilities should be able to be less than the cash surrender value. Board members were troubled by that, saying that it didn't seem appropriate to say that if somebody can surrender a policy and demand a payment, that you should in essence show a loss simply because they exercised a pre-existing right. They felt that there ought to be a floor on the valuation of liabilities comparable to the amount payable on demand.

We had a lot of problems, and this is what really led us then to not be able to make progress on the liability side. They decided at the end of 1991 that the valuation of liabilities just was not workable and that they were going to set it aside and have the project focus only on investments in assets.

At that time, we had only six Board members and we normally have a full complement of seven. We require a two-thirds majority to reach any conclusions and, because a new Board member was starting on March 1, 1992, we decided to hold in abeyance our conclusions and to redeliberate the issue again in 1992, with the full complement of seven Board members. We went through the exercise a second time, and again the Board decided that, as an organization, we could not reach a satisfactory answer with respect to the valuation of liabilities. There were too many problems and this is why, when we then finally came out with Statement 115, you see no reference to liabilities.

Now, I also might comment that regarding Statement 115, you might notice that it bears no relationship to the original goal – the target, the objective that the Board set out when they first undertook the project – because it's not a mark-to-market answer. We still permit the use of amortized cost for certain debt securities. And because we were permitting the retention of cost, the Board members viewed it more as a clarification of what some of the existing literature requires. Our Statement 60, which is a long-standing document, does require that there be the ability and intent to hold to maturity in order to use amortized cost. So really 115 can be viewed as an articulation or rearticulation of what was already the rule, even though we might acknowledge some people applied it perhaps more loosely than 115 would permit.

In my comments, you might notice that I have not made any attempt to use just one term or another. Back in 1991, we were using the term 'market value'. In Statement 115, we used the term 'fair value' and that was commented on this morning. Really, at the FASB, we have viewed those terms as synonyms. We also had a project (which led to Statement 107) dealing with the disclosure of market value. When we put our proposal out for comment in the form of an Exposure Draft, we received a lot of feedback disagreeing with our definition of market value; we felt that market value should include estimates when there was no active ready market. Some people clearly were using the term *market value* in a more restrictive sense. And so, for purposes of 107 and subsequent documents, we decided to switch over and use the term 'fair value'. We didn't change the definition at all. The definition of fair value in the final document is the same as the definition of market value in the Exposure Draft because we were using them as synonyms.

There was another reason for the use of the term 'fair value' and that is in the interest of international accounting standard harmonization, because other standard setting bodies internationally have tended to use the term 'fair value', not 'market value'. At the time, 'fair value' would not have been my personal first choice, but maybe with hindsight, it was a good thing, because it does eliminate this potential misunderstanding of what we intend. I've heard some people make the comment that if there is no ready active market, then the financial instrument has no market value, whereas the Board was requiring estimates to be made.

Our definition of a market value, of course, is in Statement 107 (also in Statement 115) which is really talking about a situation where you have an exchange. It's a current transaction between ready buyers. The notion is that this is not a forced sale, it's not a liquidation sale at all. We have subsequently addressed in our standards the impairment of fixed assets. We have a very comparable definition that again has the same underlying notions behind it. That definition also emphasizes the fact that you need to make estimates on occasion. Yes, if there is a ready active market, you should use that, and that is probably the best number to use, but that if there is none, then you should use estimation techniques. The notion of fair value now is incorporated into a number of our documents obviously, and we're trying to emphasize the fact that various techniques can be used. We're restricted to one or the other, but we're pointing out that the notion of fair value does involve an estimation process.

We issued Statement 115 without including liabilities. Within a couple of months, however, we received a request from a number of life insurance companies, asking us to undertake a separate project to address the valuation of liabilities. In their letter, they talked about the problem of unrepresentative volatility in shareholders' equity. They talked about valuation of the corresponding liabilities or related liabilities. So clearly, it implied a notion that not all liabilities would necessarily be marked to market. We were going to take that back to the Board – whenever we get a request for an item like that, a new project, we do have to take that request to the Board for public discussion. By the way, all the Board meetings are conducted in public. They are open to public observation by anyone who wishes to come up to Norwalk, Connecticut to observe the process.

We did not immediately move forward on this particular request, however, because we were told that insurance company representatives wanted to provide us with some additional information that would help us. I pointed out that this was an issue that the Board talked about on two different occasions. I don't mean individual dates. We spent three months, four months in 1991 and another four months in 1992. I wasn't sure that the Board members would necessarily be compelled, on the basis of a letter alone, to add a separate project simply on the valuation of liabilities. And so, insurance company representatives volunteered to put together some information for us that was eventually done under the shield of ACLI. We then agreed to talk, and they met with the Board members and staff on December 1, 1993. Most of their conversations related to how you determine the fair value of liabilities and we pointed out that the question of which liabilities is also one that we felt needed to be addressed (if we were only doing this in the context of trying to solve the problem that some people felt 115 created).

We have not heard an official response from them yet. They had planned to make earlier deadlines and those kept getting extended. I am not finding fault, because I understand how deadlines slip. I work at the FASB and we have similar problems. We have established certain planned objectives and sometimes the issues just don't get resolved in time to meet those objectives, those timetables. We have slippage ourselves. In any case, I have been informally told that they will be telling us very shortly that they were unable to come up with a solution or guidance to suggest to us. In that event, we will not be getting anything directly from this ACLI working group. In a sense, I hope that this conference might also give us some additional information that will be useful to us in addressing that agenda request to have a separate project on the valuation of liabilities. As I said, we do not have a separate project on the valuation of liabilities yet.

Now, what is interesting is, because we've been holding up that particular request for a new project, events have caught up and gone around or circumvented that request. Another one of our projects – the project on accounting for derivatives and hedging – now has brought the same issue right to the Board's attention. The Board, in deliberating this project on derivatives and hedging, has come up with an approach that involves two alternatives. The one would be to report all the derivatives at fair value. The second approach would be to permit companies to choose to report all financial instruments at fair value: assets as well as liabilities. In its preliminary discussions, the Board has decided that it would, for the most part, follow the valuation guidance that we find in Statement 107 on disclosure of fair values. But 107 did exclude from its scope the valuation of insurance contracts. It also obviously excluded the valuation of core deposit intangibles. It simply said that the fair value of deposit liabilities needs to be the amount payable on demand. If there's a core deposit intangible, that's an intangible asset; that's not part of the liability.

We are soon going to be bringing to the Board a discussion of the valuation of insurance liabilities as part of the hedging derivatives and hedging project. While this one request for separate project was held in abeyance until we received information from the ACLI working group, which will now likely not be forthcoming after all, the issue is before us anyway. This is why I do look forward to say that the particular content of this conference should at least be additional information that we can all process at the FASB in reaching our decisions. I don't have a position on what the Board will do; we have not deliberated it, but I just wanted to point out to you that this is a very timely topic now, since our derivatives project has brought it to the floor.

ARNOLD A. DICKE
*USLIFE Corporation*

## 2. Comparison of methods for fair-value life insurance liabilities

*This paper gives a useful introduction to the whole subject. His biography (see p. 364) provides evidence of his expertise.* – Ed.

Let me comment on some of the terms in the title of this chapter. First of all, the term 'fair value' should lead one to conclude that this is a discussion of formal methods for determining accounting values under generally accepted accounting principles (GAAP) in the USA. The term 'fair value' is used rather than 'market value', because it is (correctly, I believe) held by the Financial Accounting Standards Board (FASB) that a market value can only mean a value determined as the price at which a willing buyer and a willing seller engage in a transaction. Any analytical estimate of the market value has to be something other than the market value itself. For such analytic estimates, FASB has come up with the term 'fair value'.

The type of liability for which we seek a fair value is a life insurance liability. Such liabilities have a number of characteristics which make them rather more difficult to value than some other forms of liabilities. First of all, and most obviously, life insurance liabilities represent an uncertain obligation, and thus require statistical calculation. There is often more than one contingency which must be taken into account when life insurance is valued. In addition to mortality risk, there may be morbidity risk (as, for instance, in the waiver of premium provision) and withdrawal risk. Another unusual aspect of life insurance liabilities is that it is traditional to include with the insurance company's liabilities the insurance company's right to receive future premiums or considerations from the other party to the contract. Thus, the life insurance liability is the net of cash outflows required and cash inflows expected. Finally, life insurance liabilities have virtually no secondary market. This means that the very concept of a market value for life insurance liabilities is somewhat ungrounded. There is a reinsurance market for blocks of life insurance business, but these always involve the assets as well as the liabilities, making the market value of liabilities a derivative concept at best. About five years ago, several securitizations of life insurance cash flows were put together, but no market has developed. Recently, there have developed certain 'viatical' companies which attempt to make a profit by purchasing life insurance contracts from persons in bad health. This relatively new development provides a market value for at most a small collection of life insurance policies.

Another unusual aspect of life insurance is that it is subject to at least four different accounting systems. Life insurance companies remain solvent as long as they have surplus under statutory accounting rules, which are set up by the states who have the power in the USA to regulate the insurance industry. Statutory accounting is intentionally very conservative and aimed at protecting policyholders, not at reflecting management performance. Because statutory accounting is not useful for investors and shareholders, there was developed a separate set of rules that were adopted as GAAP for life insurance. These are the rules with which we will be most concerned today. I will give a brief synopsis of the most pertinent of these rules later.

Life insurers are also subject to special rules for tax accounting, which means that in all the other accounting systems tax must be explicitly calculated and not assumed to be a percentage of accounting profit. Finally, many companies have adopted management-basis accounting because all three of the required systems fail to properly represent the performance of lines of business in a way that is optimal for management decisions.

In considering an accounting system as it applies to life insurance, it is important to start by remembering the functions of life insurance. These can be conveniently grouped into two categories: protection and savings. For each of these functions, it is desirable to have earnings emerge in a particular manner. Insofar as a life insurance contract focuses on protection, it is customary to arrange for earnings to emerge over time as the insurance company is released from the risk which it is insuring. On the other hand, insofar as the insurance contract is primarily a savings vehicle, it is logical to have earnings emerge as a net spread on the assets under management.

This indeterminateness regarding the proper emergence of profits may possibly be another reflection of the lack of a robust market for insurance liabilities. Some of the research currently being carried on regarding insurance pricing may be relevant in this regard. Harry Panjer reports that research at Waterloo is attempting to show that the price of protection-oriented insurance products can be represented as the mean of a distribution, but not the best estimate loss distribution. In effect, the new distribution always produces a larger mean, representing the addition to the best estimate mean that is necessary to account for the risk inherent in the insurance product. The new distribution may, in some cases, involve a multiple of the force of mortality. In other words, the new distribution may signify the addition of margins in the mortality assumption, a practice which has been common in actuarial circles for centuries and which is the basis for the release from risk earnings model.

In any case, the two extremes of earnings emergence will give us points of comparison for the models utilized in current GAAP accounting. Current GAAP accounting is based on three liability-side standards, each relating to insurance contracts in which it is perceived that a different balance between protection and savings elements was present.

Let me quickly review the treatment of liabilities under these three standards. First of all, there is Statement of Financial Accounting Standards No. 60

(SFAS 60), the oldest of the three standards. SFAS 60 sets up a benefit reserve, which is based on conservative assumptions – assumptions which have provisions for adverse deviations, or margins, in them. This is one of the few places in GAAP accounting where explicit margins are permitted. The cash flows are discounted at the average asset earnings rate. This is an old way of doing things that does not take account of the new financial technology. However, it is the way GAAP is applied to most of the traditional forms of insurance, including term and whole life insurance and immediate annuities (annuities already in payment status). SFAS 60 also defers policy acquisition costs by setting up a deferred policy acquisition cost (DPAC) asset and releasing it into earnings as a percent of premium received.

When sale of universal life and deferred annuities became common, SFAS 60 was supplemented by a new standard, SFAS 97. Under SFAS 97, there is no benefit reserve. In fact, there are no premiums; the money that the insurer holds is considered to be the policyholder's money held on deposit, not a benefit reserve.

SFAS 97 does, however, provide for a deferred policy acquisition cost asset. The deferred policy acquisition cost is amortized as a constant percent of 'estimated gross profits'. These 'gross profits' are gains and losses expected to be earned by the various aspects of the insurer's business: risk coverage, investment services, administrative services, etc. For each, the insurer makes an explicit charge. Thus, expected gross profits equal the excess of the cost of insurance rates that are charged over the benefit claims that are expected to be paid, plus the excess of contract administration charges over the expected cost of administration, plus the excess of investment earnings over interest credited, and so forth. Over time, SFAS 97 provides for the adjustment of the expected costs and earnings to an actual basis. This process is called 'unlocking'.

Finally, we now also have SFAS 120, which determines GAAP for certain participating, or dividend-paying, contracts. This standard actually just points to AICPA Standard of Practice 95-1, which contains the formulas. This standard sets up a benefit reserve, as was the case for SFAS 60. However, the SFAS 120 benefit reserve is more like a statutory reserve than an SFAS 60 benefit reserve. It is based on highly conservative assumptions, and the assumptions are never unlocked. The deferred policy acquisition cost is amortized as a percentage of 'estimated gross margins'. Gross margins are defined as the sum of premium and investment earnings, less benefits, expenses, other expected expenditures, and reserve increases; in other words, 'gross margins' are very like what actuaries usually call 'book profits', except that acquisition costs are deferred.

Assets are now accounted for under SFAS 115. SFAS 115 is relatively new: it was first applied in 1994. It requires that securities be held in one of three categories: *trading securities*, for which the securities are held at market or 'fair' value and unrealized capital gains and losses go through earnings; *hold-to-maturity securities*, which are held at book, meaning unrealized capital gains and losses are not reflected at all; and *available-for-sale securities*, which are held at fair value, but for which unrealized capital gains and losses go through equity rather than earnings.

SFAS 115 caused consternation among actuaries and others involved in the life insurance industry because the 'fair value' concept was applied only to the asset side. This caused an asymmetry in the reaction of assets and liabilities to changes in interest rates.

How do the accounting standards applicable to insurance liabilities react to interest rate changes and the realized and unrealized capital gains or losses that may result? Under SFAS 60, benefit reserves and DPAC are unaffected by such changes. Under SFAS 97 and SFAS 120, both realized and unrealized capital gains or losses affect the amortization of the deferred policy acquisition cost. A realized capital gain under SFAS 97, for example, is investment income and, therefore, increases the current period gross profit. With a larger gross profit, more deferred policy acquisition cost can be amortized in the current period. The net result is almost like spreading the capital gain, because if more of the deferred policy acquisition cost is amortized in the current period, there is less deferred policy acquisition cost to be absorbed in later periods (so long as recoverability does not come into play). It is noteworthy, and odd, that the impact depends on the fraction of the gross profits used to amortize the deferred policy acquisition cost. In other words, the extent to which capital gains and losses impact the DPAC amortization depends on the profitability of the product. If 99% of the gross profits are needed to amortize the deferred policy acquisition cost, then almost all the capital gains and losses will be 'spread.' However, if only 50% of the gross profits are needed to amortize the DPAC, only 50% of the gains and losses will receive this treatment.

What about unrealized capital gains and losses? The SEC has published a position that holds that unrealized gains and losses are to be treated the same as realized gains and losses. The impact on the amortization of the DPAC asset is to be reported in equity or through earnings, depending on whether the assets are available-for-sale or trading securities. In addition to the DPAC, other items, such as policyholder balances and deferred taxes, may also be impacted. All these effects tend to mitigate the impact of SFAS 115 on the balance sheet. However, a significant impact remains, as was seen in the financial reports issued for 1994.

Fluctuations in the GAAP equity during the period since the beginning of 1994 in which SFAS 115 has been applied to insurance company financials were as much as 30% for many well established companies. At least one relatively new company, which was very healthy on a statutory basis, showed negative GAAP equity at the end of 1994. You will recall that negative GAAP equity has nothing to do with insolvency; solvency is determined only by statutory surplus.

It is no surprise that the one-sided marking to market of assets and not liabilities leads to spurious volatility in insurance company balance sheets. It is possible to study this effect and the possible mitigation of this effect by adjustments to liability accounting by using certain relatively simple models.

Models of this sort were developed by a group headed up by Don Sanning of Principal Mutual and including Kevin Palmer of IDS, George Silos of New York Life and Alan Goldberg of Providian.

Let me explain how this group's models and graphs work. Figure 1 shows GAAP equity plotted against policy year for a block of immediate annuities backed by long-term bonds whose cash flows match those of the liabilities exactly. The graph slopes downward to the right, because each year the earnings are assumed to be distributed. Thus, the graph represents the equity that continues to be associated with the product. Whether the graph shows book value accounting prior to SFAS 115 or fair value accounting after, the graph is a downward sloping straight line, as long as it is assumed that interest rates remain unchanged.

What does it look like under pre- and post-SFAS 115 accounting if interest rates change? Assume a 2% level change in interest rates in year three and assume exact cash flow matching was practiced. Figure 2 shows that the interest rate change has no impact on pre-SFAS 115 equity. But under SFAS 115 the fair value of the assets decreases and so does shareholders' equity. This reduction in equity is spurious from an economic point of view and thus represents a problem.

While the SEC-mandated treatment of the DPAC partly mitigates such spurious changes in equity, it would be preferable to find a more comprehensive and complete method for this purpose. Such a method can be found – in fact,

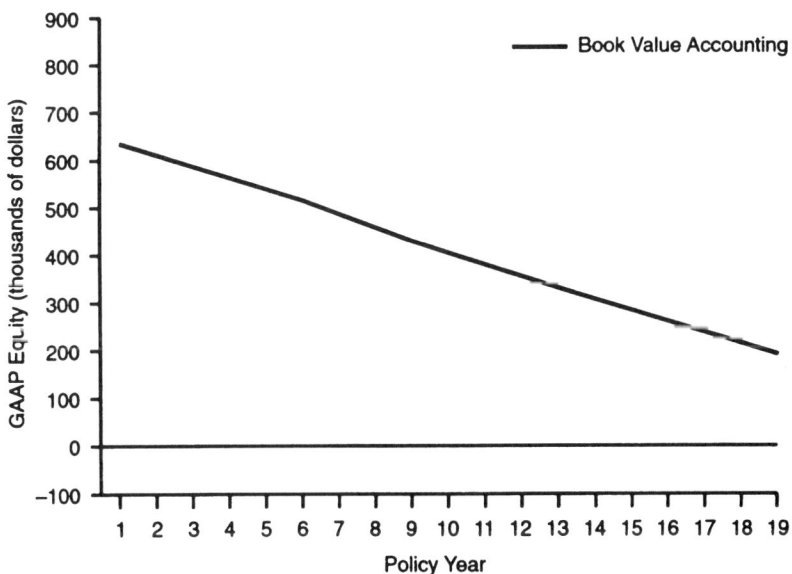

*Figure 1.* Immediate annuities – no change in interest rates.

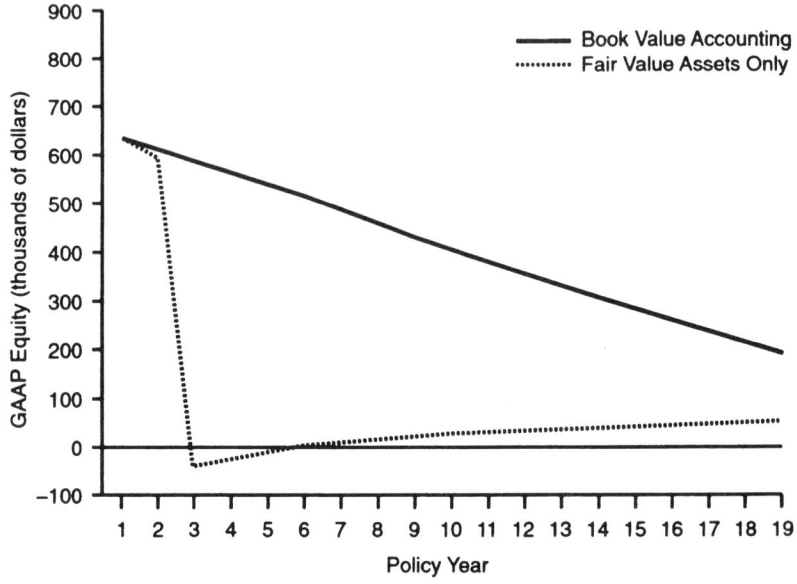

*Figure 2.* Immediate annuities – exactly cash flow matched, 2% increase in interest rates in year 3.

this presentation includes a catalogue of methods that can be used to mitigate the effect of SFAS 115.

In discussing the catalogued methods, I will take the point of view of the users of financial statements. The issuers of financial statements obviously have a strong interest in these methods, but my concern will be for the users. GAAP financials are intended for current and prospective shareholders, primarily, as well as people who work for shareholders, such as analysts, and people otherwise involved in investing in the company. GAAP financials are not, it should be noted, designed for policyholders and regulators – statutory accounting is designed for these users.

These methods fall naturally into three categories (see Table 1). The first category, 'Type A' methods, are what may be called 'discounted cash flow surrogates for market value'. These are the methods most people envision when they begin thinking about marking liabilities to market – the methods that people have in mind when they say, "Even if there is no direct market for insurance liabilities, isn't there some analytic way to approximate market value?" My catalogue has two Type A methods. The 'Type B' methods are completely different. These arise from the observation that life insurers manage interest-rate risk daily. The industry has been dealing with the problem of interest rate sensitivity for a long time, and it has developed a number of management techniques. Perhaps one or another of these techniques could be used to mitigate the spurious effects of SFAS 115. The catalogue lists four Type B methods. Finally, 'Type C' methods involve adaptations of the existing

*Table 1.* Catalogue of methods

| | |
|---|---|
| Type A | Discounted cash flow surrogates for market value |
| | (1) Liability-spread discounted policy cash flow method |
| | (2) Discounted book profit (actuarial appraisal) method |
| | (*Variation 1:* IRR at issue for discount rate) |
| Type B | Interest-rate-risk management techniques |
| | (1) Interest maintenance adjustment |
| | (2) Cash flow valuation method |
| | (3) Cash flow ratio method |
| | (4) Discounted policy cash flow method with cash flow testing |
| Type C | Adaptation of existing accounting framework |
| | (1) Unlocking of the interest rate assumption |
| | (*Variation 1:* constrained unlocking of interest rates) |
| | (2) Extension of participating contracts method |
| | (3) Combination of liability spread DCF method and current GAAP methods |
| | (4) SFAS 115 for liabilities |

accounting framework to deal with situations in which interest rates are not static. There are several ways to do this as well. My catalogue describes four specific proposals.

Next, let me go through the catalogue of methods category by category. To begin with, Type A methods are surrogates for market value. The catalogue lists Method A(1) as the 'liability-spread discounted cash flow method'. Another name for it could be the 'bond valuation method'. One of the methods used for valuing bonds is to compare the internal rate of return on the bond at issue to Treasuries, either a single Treasury for the same duration or a yield curve of Treasuries at the time of issue, and to determine a spread or spreads over Treasuries at issue; then, lock in these spreads. At each future duration, the value of the liability is the value of the expected cash flows discounted at a rate equal to the current Treasury rate, plus the fixed spread or spreads.

This method is well suited to financial products like GICs and single premium deferred annuities. It is not as well suited to protection-oriented products, particularly those with long streams of recurring premiums, because the cash flows may be alternately positive and negative, making it hard to solve for internal rates of return.

In addition, Method A(1) can be criticized with respect to the pattern in which earnings are released. This may seem to be more of a problem for issuers than users of the financial statement. However, it can be a problem for the users as well. Users have become accustomed to a certain pattern of release of earnings in GAAP – for example, as a percent of premium. But, under Method A(1), the earnings are released as a difference between spreads. As an example, suppose a product is backed by bonds. Each bond has a yield that could be expressed as a spread over Treasuries. Either the spread is known directly or Method A(1) can be used to determine one. The same thing can be done for the liabilities. Then, what are the earnings? They are the difference between these two spreads: the asset-side spread and the liability-side spread. Earnings therefore emerge as a percentage of assets or, approximately, reserves. This pattern of emergence is very different from that which develops under current GAAP standards, especially for protection-oriented products such as whole life.

Another Type A method is the actuarial appraisal method, which is, in fact, a version of value-added or embedded-value accounting. Under this method, the value of liabilities is based on discounted net book profits, rather than on discounted liability cash flows. If the actuarial appraisal value of a company and the market value of the assets are known, the balancing item is the value of the liability. This method was presented to FASB, but received a cool reception. The Board appears to object to the assets coming into the calculation of liabilities in any way, shape or form. But actuaries are familiar with this method, so it has been added to the catalogue.

The actuarial appraisal method requires a discount rate. But how do you select a discount rate? It would be best to base this rate on actual assumption reinsurance transactions in the market. This is not completely infeasible – there *are* such transactions. Consultants have a pretty good idea of what discount rate is implicit in each transaction. Of course, while the rate determined from reinsurance transactions is appropriate as a discount rate for the net book profits, it is not appropriate as a discount rate for the liabilities alone. There is no market for stand-alone liabilities. No one buys life insurance liabilities independent of assets, so no prices are available. Consequently, it is impossible to observe a liabilities-only discount rate in the market. The appraisal method thus has one advantage over the discounted cash flow method: there actually is a market, but this market is very thin. There are few transactions, and of these, few involve liabilities similar to those of a given company. This sparseness is a problem for the actuarial appraisal method. One alternative would be to use a spread-at-issue method to get a discount rate.

One of the really nice things about Method A(2) is that it incorporates statutory restrictions: statutory reserves and even, if you like, risk-based capital restrictions. It is implicitly assumed in discounted cash flow methods that the cash flows are 'free', in the sense that they are available for immediate reinvestment. This is not true for all insurance cash flows, since statutory constraints must be satisfied. The appraisal method takes account of these constraints; Method A(1) does not.

The actuarial appraisal methodology is understood by the industry, but as I said, it is not accepted by FASB. Thus, it probably will not see the light of day, but it is a valid method, so it is in the catalogue.

Now, let us turn to Type B methods. These are methods that make use of interest rate risk management techniques that companies have developed. The first one, Method B(1), is called the interest maintenance adjustment (IMA). It is similar, but not identical, to the interest maintenance reserve (IMR) used in statutory accounting. Unlike the IMR, the IMA is two-sided: it can be an asset or a liability, depending on whether more capital gains or capital losses have been deferred. Other than that, it works just like the IMR, except that the adjustment is run partly through equity to take account of the fact that you have some available-for-sale assets.

Variations of this method were proposed to FASB by many respondents commenting on SFAS 115 in its proposal stage. The IMA solves the gains trading problem, which seemed to be the most serious problem SFAS 115 was developed to solve. Gains trading is the buying or selling of certain assets on a particular date in order to affect reported earnings. An example of the mischief caused by gains trading is the sale of what amounts to half of a hedge. If a GIC is backed by assets which are exactly matched to the liability, and if interest rates fall, a company can record capital gains on those assets by selling them and replacing them with assets with a lower coupon rate. While the company books a gain, it leaves an unhedged position on its balance sheet. That is what FASB was trying to avoid. Since the IMA is in some ways analogous to hedging, and since FASB requires a test to be done before hedge accounting is permitted, it is proposed that use of the IMA be restricted to situations in which a test is passed demonstrating that assets are correlated to liabilities.

The other Type B methods are all based on cash flow testing, which is the other commonly used technique for interest rate risk management. Method B(2) uses cash flow testing techniques to produce a liability value. Cash flow testing is used to determine a set of assets whose future cash flows are adequate to support the liabilities. The carrying value of the assets, whether it be market value or book value or some combination, is called the fair value of the liabilities. Variations of this method apparently are used in most of the other English speaking countries of the world. This may be a factor in its favor when FASB considers it, because the Board has on occasion asked about models that have been used in other countries.

It should be recognized that the cash flow valuation method (CFVM) goes beyond what actuaries normally do in the USA for statutory adequacy testing. Rather than just testing a pre-set statutory reserve, the CFVM involves using cash flow testing to set a reserve. This has been done; for instance, see the Proceedings of the 1987 Valuation Actuary Symposium, where an example is worked out.

A simplified version of this approach that can be applied on an individual policy basis is Method B(3), the 'cash flow ratio method'. To apply this method, one determines an adequate set of assets, as for the CFVM, but then take the ratio of the carrying value to the book value of these assets and apply that ratio to all the calculated GAAP numbers, such as the benefit reserve and the deferred policy acquisition cost. The change so determined is allocated to earnings or equity, depending on whether the assets are trading securities or available-for-sale. Again, this requires setting the reserve through cash flow testing, not just testing a pre-set reserve. But it is an approach that provides individual policy values, which should please FASB. Board members have stated that they believe liabilities should be valued policy-by-policy, not as a group or on a block of business basis.

The final Type B method is a synthesis of two methods. Method B(4) resulted from the attempt by one company to use discounted cash flow methods for SFAS 107 disclosures. The company discovered that its portfolio did not track Treasuries very well. That is, the spread of its portfolio relative to Treasuries was volatile because the spreads relative to Treasuries of the corporate bonds in which it had invested changed from time to time. The problem may be called 'index disconnect'. One solution would be to find an appropriate corporate bond index. Rather than use an index, the company decided it would like to use the market yield on its own asset portfolio as a discount rate. Using the portfolio yield can cause a problem, however: the choice of assets can affect the value of the liabilities. To see this, suppose a company holds a high percentage of junk bonds or 'high yield' assets. These assets have a higher yield than higher quality bonds; consequently, the discounted cash flow value for the company's liabilities is lower. This effect goes in the wrong direction, even if it is agreed to allow the liability value to be connected to the asset yield. To correct this problem, the 'asset-choice problem', the company decided to make use of cash flow testing to ensure that the discounted cash flow liability was adequate. This allowed the company to use a relatively familiar technique to calculate liability values on an individual policy basis and still to be comfortable that it was not deluding itself by choosing assets whose high yield produces a too low liability value.

Finally, let us turn to Type C Methods. Type C Methods modify or expand current GAAP methods. Their advantage is that they start with a current GAAP method, so the change is limited to the insurance industry. In fact, apart from SFAS 60, the effect is limited to the life insurance industry.

First, let us discuss Method C(1). Method C(1) calls for unlocking the interest rate in SFAS 60. The idea is to take the average asset portfolio rate to be the 'market yield' instead of the 'book yield'; i.e. the ratio of coupons to fair value rather than to book value. This method is obviously easy to implement, since current systems need no change. But Method C(1) suffers from the asset-choice problem just described. One variation of Method C(1) uses fancy mathematical techniques to fix this problem. The asset-choice problem is a major barrier to this straightforward technique. Also, extending the method to products governed by SFAS 97 or SFAS 120 would be very problematic.

Method C(2) is an interesting possibility. The idea is to extend the new participating contract standard, SFAS 120, to all contracts now covered by SFAS 60. Recall that under SFAS 120, the deferred policy acquisition cost is amortized as a percentage of gross margins. This could also be done for SFAS 60 products. This would allow the application of the deferred policy acquisition cost adjustment to realized and unrealized capital gains and losses connected with SFAS 60 liabilities.

Method C(3) is a variation of Method A(1) that was devised by Kin Tam, Kevin Palmer, Alan Goldberg and myself. The method is a combination of

Method A(1), the liability-spread discount cash flow method, and the current SFAS 60 method. The intent is to solve the recurring premium problem that plagued Method A(1) while retaining the financial instrument treatment of Method A(1) for single-premium products. Method C(3) bases the discount rate on the spread at issue over Treasuries, just like Method A(1). This means the method works well for financial products or products with only one premium. But if there are more than one premium, the method incorporates a separate deferred policy acquisition cost which is amortized over gross margins. Thus, the earnings are assumed to be initially released as a difference between the asset and liability spreads as was the case for Method A(1). However, if that difference becomes negative, the method begins to release some of the earnings as a percentage of premium. The method thus manages to slide smoothly from a method that releases earnings as a difference in spreads over to a method that releases earnings as a percentage of premium as the product changes from a financial to a protection product.

Method C(3) operates much the way that would be expected if valuation were performed using the adjusted distribution model described previously. In effect, the multiplicative factor applied to the force of mortality would be irrelevant in the case of contracts with certain payment, such as GICs. As mortality risk becomes more important, so would the impact of the multiplicative factor. Since this factor essentially represents margins added to the mortality assumption, a relationship of this model to Model C(3) may be presumed.

Finally, one more model was added recently to the catalogue. Method C(4) mimics SFAS 115 on the liability side. Three categories of liabilities are set up, with hold-to-maturity liabilities accounted for on the current basis without adjustment. Available-for-sale and trading liabilities are to be accounted for on a fair-value basis. This method was proposed mainly to exploit its parallel structure with SFAS 115 asset accounting. However, if true markets for insurance liabilities do emerge, these three categories will have more meaning than they appear to have at present.

How do we judge these methods? What do we want these methods to do? To begin with, they should mitigate balance sheet volatility and respond appropriately to changes in interest rates. They should disclose any real economic volatility, but avoid spurious indications of volatility. Is it important that the method come close to current accounting? At least for protection products, it may be preferable to continue to release earnings over the premium paying period. For financial products, a change may be indicated. Figure 3 represents the cash-flow matched immediate annuity again, showing the effect of an interest rate jump under pre- and post-SFAS 115 accounting. The graph now has a third line, showing Method A(1) (or Method C(3)). Method A(1) is seen to counteract the spurious volatility introduced by SFAS 115. Almost all of the proposed methods have the same result for cash-flow matched immediate annuities. If the annuity is not cash-flow matched, the result is even more remarkable. Figure 4 shows the same product, but backed with five-year bonds. The pre-SFAS 115 line still slopes down to the right. Current accounting with

18    A.A. Dicke

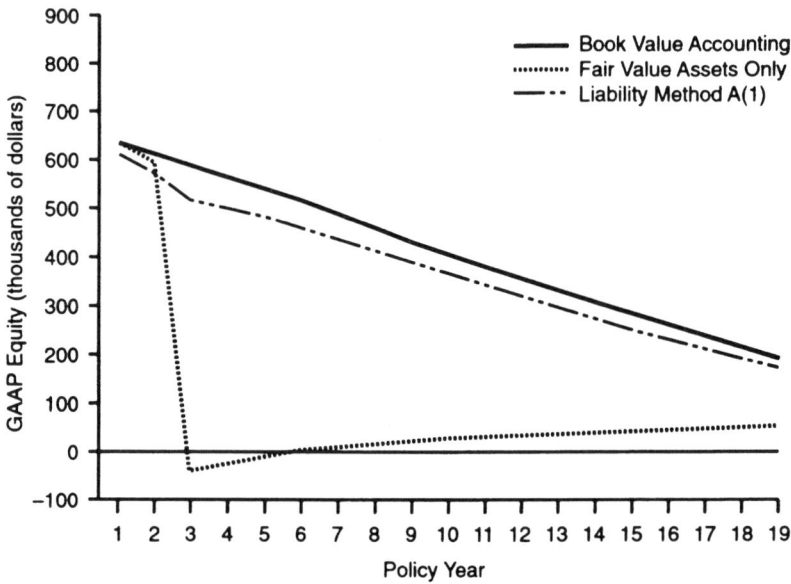

*Figure 3.* Immediate annuities – exactly cash flow matched, 2% increase in interest rate in year 3.

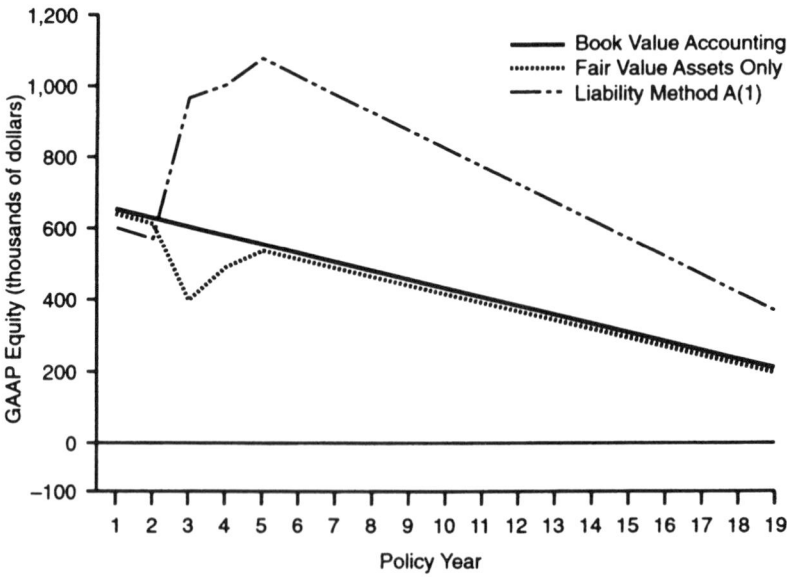

*Figure 4.* Immediate annuities – mismatch with 5-year bonds, 2% increase in interest rates in year 3.

SFAS 115 now shows a dip in year three. Why? Because the fair value of the assets falls when interest rates rise. Method A(1) shows a large increase in equity, as would be expected economically. The liability is much longer than the asset, so the fall in liability value exceeds the drop in asset value. In sum, the current GAAP accounting method literally goes the wrong way in some circumstances.

Figure 5 shows earnings emergence for a non-par whole life protection contract. Instead of plotting equity on the $Y$ axis, this graph plots earnings or changes in equity. Under book value accounting with or without SFAS 115, when there is no change in interest rates, earnings are seen to decline over the years. This is a reasonable result. But under Method A(1), the discounted cash flow method, earnings have a completely different pattern. Recall that under Method A(1) earnings are released as the difference in spreads, and are thus proportional to assets. So, as a reserve builds up, earnings gradually increase. This means the actuary has to give his or her CEO the following message: "I would like to change the accounting method. There's just one little problem. Instead of any earnings coming in during your tenure as CEO, they'll come in when your successor comes along, or maybe his successor. You can make me that successor, if you like what I've done for you."

This position would probably be a little hard to sell, so let us turn to Figure 6 to see how Method C(3) handles these protection products. As suggested previously, Method C(3) is close to current accounting when there is no change in interest rates. Thus, earnings emerge primarily as a percentage of premium, as would be the case under current accounting.

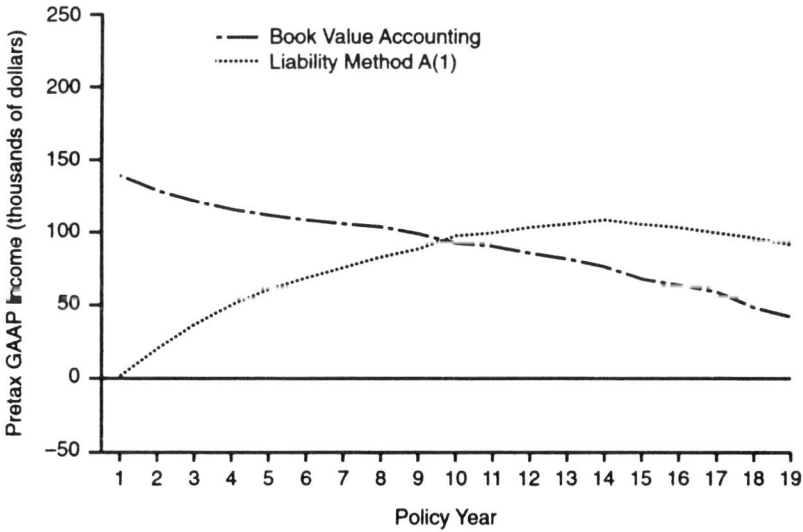

*Figure 5.* Non-par whole life – no change in interest rates.

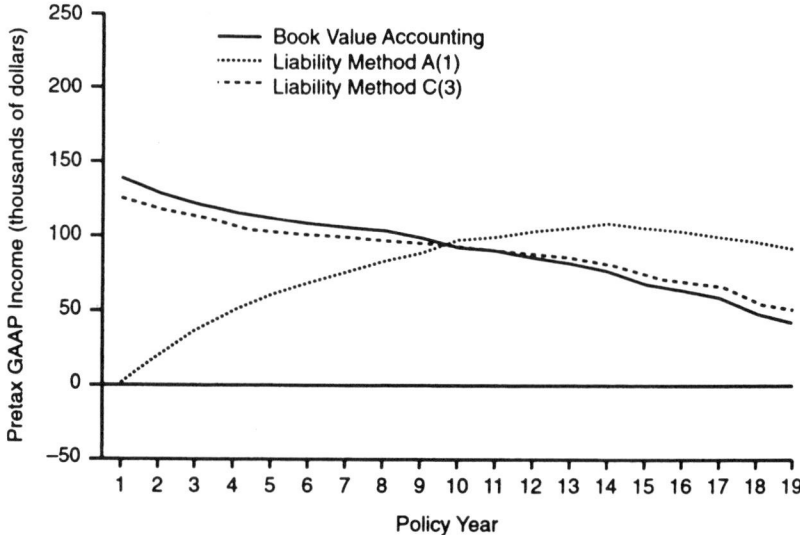

*Figure 6.* Non-par whole life – no change in interest rates.

Assuming that there are academics in the audience, or at least persons inclined to approach a problem with an eye towards theoretical structure, I believe the question of an appropriate GAAP standard for the valuation of liabilities is very interesting. Some of the preconditions for the usual financial analysis are missing. For example, as I have said, there is no functioning market for insurance liabilities. Second, there are constraints represented by the statutory accounting system which cannot be ignored if a theoretically correct result is desired. But perhaps the most intriguing difficulty is the lack of clear definition of the purpose of GAAP financials. What is it exactly that the users of GAAP financials expect to find out? Obviously, they are interested in the stability and profitability of the business. For some insurance products, these aspects of the business only unfold over time, while for other products the impact is immediate. Striking a balance between these different requirements requires art as well as science, and it makes life insurance accounting a uniquely interesting theoretical problem.

DOUGLAS C. DOLL, C. PHIL ELAM,
JAMES E. HOHMANN (Chairperson), JACQUELINE M. KEATING,
DOUGLAS S. KOLSRUD, KAREN OLSEN MacDONALD,
S. MICHAEL McLAUGHLIN, THOMAS J. MERFELD,
STEPHEN D. REDDY, ROBERT R. REITANO,
RICHARD S. ROBERTSON, EDWARD L. ROBBINS,
DAVID Y. ROGERS and HENRY W. SIEGEL
*John Hancock Life Insurance Co.*

## 3. Fair valuation of life insurance company liabilities*

*Comment: If one had to pick out the most comprehensive paper in the selection, one might well chose this report of the Task Force of the American Academy of Actuaries. While all of the members of the Task Force made significant contributions, the presenters deserve special commendation. From the point of view of the exciting exchange, this paper seems a clear winner. – Ed.*

### INTRODUCTION

Historically, accounting authorities have prescribed a high degree of consistency between the asset and liability sides of balance sheets. However, a significant departure from that premise occurred in May, 1993 with the issuance of Statement of Financial Accounting Standards (SFAS) No. 115. According to SFAS 115, certain classes of assets are to be carried at 'fair value', while other assets and all liabilities remain at book value. The scope of SFAS 115 includes financial institutions and consequently, insurance companies are also required to abide by the standard.

Prior to issuing SFAS 115, the Financial Accounting Standards Board (FASB) developed an Exposure Draft No. 119-A (ED 119-A). The American Academy of Actuaries Committees on Life Insurance Financial Reporting (COLIFR) and Property and Liability Financial Reporting (COPLFR) submitted comments on ED 119-A, and ultimately testified before the FASB. A major theme of communication with the FASB was that accounting principles should be applied consistently to both sides of the balance sheet. At one point, it was noted that if fair values of liabilities were required, the actuarial profession had the training and tools available to make the computations.

---

*This paper was prepared by members of the American Academy of Actuaries Fair Valuation of Liabilities Task Force (with the exception of Thomas J. Merfeld, who contributed to the paper but is not a member of the Academy).

Ultimately, the FASB adopted ED 119-A as SFAS 115. With respect to the Academy's concerns, SFAS 115 was largely unchanged from the Exposure Draft.

The American Academy of Actuaries appointed a Fair Valuation of Liabilities Task Force (Task Force) in January, 1994 to address the issue. The charge of the Task Force was to study the question of fair valuation of liabilities from a largely academic perspective. Specifically, it was to ignore current Generally Accepted Accounting Principles (GAAP), and instead, analyze, and catalog direct methodologies that captured the economics of the liabilities themselves. Of the methodologies studied, option pricing is probably the least familiar to the actuarial profession. Accordingly, efforts were made to describe the theoretical foundation of this approach.

The Task Force has assembled this 'white paper' of its findings. Beginning with an executive summary, the white paper describes the methods considered. Furthermore, the white paper highlights strengths and weaknesses attributed to the various methods. Notwithstanding the Task Force's directive to ignore GAAP, various methods of addressing fair valuation within the GAAP reporting framework surfaced during our investigation. While they do not respond directly to our charge, we suspect they will be of general interest to our readers. Consequently, we have described some of these methods (though we have purposely distinguished them from direct approaches and classified them as mitigation methods). We have also placed them in later sections of the paper. These approaches are generally seen as tempering the one-sided nature of SFAS 115, rather than fair valuing liabilities directly.

## Executive summary

While this paper is entitled *Fair Value of Life Insurance Company Liabilities* (FVL), it is clear that what we seek is a Market Value of Liabilities (MVL) as it might be defined if a sufficiently deep market existed. Although this market does not exist in reality, or at least related trades are rare enough that the market is very thin and prices sparse, this in no way precludes the theoretical exploration of market value pricing in a hypothetical market. After all, the financial markets repeatedly introduce new products, and both buyers and sellers are able to develop sensible approaches to their 'fair' prices, which in turn tend to form the foundation for trading activities and ultimately, market prices.

The market is able to accommodate new products in a rational manner by the so-called 'law of one price' and its corollary, the 'similarity principle'. This law is the basis of analysis for new financial instruments. More specifically, this law applies to financial instruments which behave identically, and states that they must be priced identically. Otherwise, market participants will 'arbitrage' the situation, buying the cheap and selling the dear, and realize immediate profits with no future risk. Consequently, while counter-examples to this law may be found, the market activities of arbitragers will put upside pressure on the price of the cheap contracts through buying, and downside pressure on the dear contracts by selling, until the prices stabilize to what would be called the market equilibrium prices. These prices need not agree exactly, but only to within a margin reflective of trading costs. While formally relating to identical contracts, this law can easily be seen to extend to similar contracts, with the notion that the more similar the provisions, the more similar are the prices. Again, market participants would otherwise put pressures on the unacceptably disparate prices until a market equilibrium resulted. For example, an option on a stock can be priced in theory using this law. As it turns out (see Appendix A, p. 75), a stock option can be replicated by a portfolio of stock and risk-free bonds, whereby 'replicated' means that the portfolio and option behave identically in theory. Consequently, the price of the stock option is in theory equal to the price of the replicating portfolio, which is of course known. As another example, using the similarity principle rather than replication, consider private placements. In general, private placement pricing follows public bond pricing in a way that reflects their similarities (maturity, quality and embedded options), and their differences (the most significant being liquidity). While private placements are relatively easy to sell, the comparative thinness of the market makes such sales subject to higher bid/ask spreads in order to compensate the investment banker for either inventorying the bonds, or to aid in its sale to a third party. This extra cost is built into the initial price. Further, public bonds with thinner markets tend to trade at spreads nearer to those of private placements, while private placements issued under Section 144A of the SEC regulations, correspondingly more liquid than traditional privates, trade at spreads closer to public bond spreads.

In summary, everywhere one observes market activity, one finds applications of the law of one price and the similarity principle. It is the basis by which the market evaluates new products, perhaps by first decomposing them into simpler, more identifiable parts, and it is also the basis by which the market keeps a discipline on the relative valuation of old products. Consequently, while there is currently no active market for the trading of insurance company liabilities, this does not preclude the estimation of fair values, as the market has already developed the necessary tools and discipline to accommodate similar situations on numerous occasions.

### *Two pricing paradigms*

When applying the approach articulated above to an insurance company liability at least two pricing paradigms emerge. In both cases the paradigm actually reflects a sequence of pricing methodologies which differ in their implementation from the simplest yet most judgmental, to the more complicated yet more objective. While detailed below, the transition in the sequence occurs by eliminating, one by one, judgmental risk spreads in the discount rate as applied to relatively simplified cash flows, and instead modeling the risk more explicitly through scenarios of more complicated cash flows.

The two pricing paradigms differ in a number of ways. First, one is constructive, evaluating liabilities directly, as one values assets, while the other is deductive, first evaluating the insurance enterprise, then deducing the value of liabilities from this and the known value of assets. Second, the constructive approach values payments as defined in terms of actual cash flows, as is typically the case for assets, while the deductive approach values payments not in terms of the firm's cash flows, but in terms of the firm's distributable earnings, as these reflect the values actually purchased by a given buyer. A third difference is really a corollary of the second, and that is that the values produced in the constructive methods do not explicitly recognize accounting standards, while the deductive method is fundamentally driven by the notion of earnings. Throughout this paper, the constructive method may also be referred to as the option pricing method, whereas the deductive method may also be referred to as the appraisal method.

While both methods are theoretically defensible and appealing, they can produce different answers and do not yield identical answers except in the simplest, most contrived hypothetical case. But then why should they be consistent? In the financial markets, order is kept by arbitragers and their ability to buy the cheap and sell the dear. If the market does not allow active trading, actual pricing can easily diverge from theoretical pricings, and moreover, theoretical pricings can be internally inconsistent.

There is currently a relatively thin market for buying and selling insurance enterprises, and the pricings reflect valuations of distributable earnings, but there is no market for the third party purchase or sale of individual liability contracts (absent special cases such as the viatical market or secondary GIC market). Imagine that we had two choices when buying a firm. First, we could buy the enterprise in total based on distributable earnings. Secondly, we could replicate the enterprise by buying the individual assets and liabilities which make up the firm. Ignoring distribution capabilities, could the net prices disagree by more than the transaction costs of one approach versus the other? We believe not; arbitragers would trade to reduce the gap and establish a market equilibrium.

In summary, we believe that the constructive methodology below provides a valuation of liabilities which is more consistent with asset valuation and reflective of valuations in the thin secondary GIC market. The distributable earnings approach, on the other hand, is more reflective of valuations in the thin company or block acquisition market. We currently have no consensus on which method is more appropriate.

*Fair value of liabilities – constructive methodologies*

The constructive methodologies for the fair value of liabilities (FVL) are based on the similarity principle corollary of the law of one price. That is, we seek to find similar instruments currently in the financial markets, and value liabilities in a way reflective of the valuation of those contracts. Viewed from the perspective of the contract holder, a life insurance company contract is simply an investment whereby for a given price (single or periodic payments), the insurance company agrees to pay given amounts based on the realization of a certain contingency or contingencies. In addition to this basic structure the insurer and/or insured have certain financial options which can be elected, and at least modify the basic structure, if not cancel it altogether. From the asset market's perspective, then, one is fundamentally valuing the series of payments contractually defined, as well as the embedded options of both parties. For all such features, comparable features exist in actively traded securities which trade at prices consistent with those provided by the theoretical models. Consequently, we merely aim to apply these well understood techniques in this new setting of liabilities.

The simplest methodology under this paradigm is the risk-adjusted present value approach. Here, one simply defines a series of cash flows which are feasible under the contract, then discounts these flows at an interest rate reflecting both the riskless time value of money (treasury rates, say) and a risk spread adequate to compensate the investor for the risk that the actual cash flows may be different and specifically, less favorable, than those initially defined. Actual cash flows may vary, for example, due to a prepayment or extension (embedded options), default (credit risk), or loss on sale relative to a 'fair' value prior to maturity (liquidity risk). This method involves significant judgment, but this approach can operate efficiently in an actively traded market even if no theoretical model exists to substantiate the pricing. For example, callable bonds have existed longer than fixed income option pricing models have. A 10-year bond, callable from years 5-10, might be sold at par (i.e. 100) with a coupon of 9.50%, where the net spread to treasuries of 1.50%, say, would reflect call risk, default risk and liquidity risk. In this example, the market defines the 'feasible' cash flows to be those realizable if the bond is not sold at a loss, and neither calls nor defaults. The spread of 1.50% is then a measure of the risk that one or the other event may occur. While it is entirely logical and conventional in the bond markets to define cash flows on the basis of 'no call, no default, no sale', one could have as easily assumed that the cash flows would end in a call in year 5, with a principal repayment of 104.75. Based on these feasible cash flows, one would infer that the bond was selling at a discount, and that the actual yield was higher than 9.50% (i.e. 10.25%), and that the risk spread to the five-year treasury of 7.25% was larger than 1.50% (i.e. 3.00%). The purpose of this illustration is to show that in theory, any set of feasible cash flows can be used initially, as long as the risk spread adequately reflects the risks that cash flows differ from those assumed. When 'worst case scenario' flows are assumed, risk spread can even be negative.

The weakness of this method is the difficulty in judgmentally determining the necessary risk spread or more generally, the relationship between the risk spread and the feasible cash flow stream assumed. The solution to this weakness

is to model the various risks, one by one, so that these risks are reflected in the variable nature of the cash flows rather than in the discount rate applied to one fixed set of cash flows. In general, one stochastically generates the various cash flows possible under the contract, which then reflect the possible losses and gains, and then discounts these flows with a rate reflecting:
- Risk-free time value of money (Treasury rates);
- Risk aversion to the risk modeled; and
- Risk spread for risks not modeled.

In this analysis, we explicitly recognize that in general, a given risk has two effects on the necessary risk spread. First, one must be compensated for actual losses expected (i.e. the average loss), and second, one must be compensated to take the risk that actual losses may differ from the average. This second component reflects the buyer's utility function, in theory, while in practice one can identify this risk as a capital risk, for which one must be paid an appropriate return for holding the necessary risk capital.

Evaluating embedded option risk comprises a significant part of this report. One reason for this is that option pricing plays a critical role in both the constructive and deductive pricing paradigms. Secondly, option pricing is fundamentally more complex than is the pricing of any other risk found in financial instruments. On the other hand, the added complexity of the modeling has a great pay-off, which is that the valuation of the variable cash flows automatically reflects both the expected loss and the necessary spread required by the market to assume this risk. That is, for option-adjusted valuations, one only needs to discount for:
- Risk-free time value of money (Treasury rates); and
- Risk spread for risks not modeled.

For the above bond example, an option pricing model, which projects the various payoffs obtainable from the bond would identify that the option was worth 50 basis points say, so that 100 basis points of the risk spread was compensation for credit risk and liquidity risk. That is, if one used 9.00% to discount the option-adjusted cash flows in the model, a price of 100 would result, which is the same as applying 9.50% to the noncallable cash flows.

To apply this idea to life insurance company liabilities, one must draw upon a substantial body of knowledge. Appendix A reviews option basics, overviews option pricing from stock options to bond options, and completes the transition to pricing liability options. Appendix B briefly describes the Heath *et al.* model for interest rate movements which is used for some of the calculations, while Appendix C discusses various approaches to establishing the risk spread on liabilities for use in an option pricing model. In effect, these spreads reflect insurance company credit risk to the contract holder, variously defined. Finally, Appendix D reviews various types of contract holder behavior models one must use in the option pricing models.

Several definitions are explored in Appendix C because there is no efficient market for life insurance company liabilities which would force these definitions to collapse into one notion. For example, credit risk could be defined in terms of what regulators, management and contract holders would prefer, and in many cases expect (i.e. Treasury or AAA risk), or it could be defined as the actual general credit of the industry, due to the guaranty fund mechanism, or the actual company-specific credit rating as implied by its claims paying rating. In general, this last definition is more comparable to what is used in the asset markets. However, even here, lack of market efficiency can create a gap between the hypothetical spread implied by this rating, and the real spread or implied cost of funds reflected in pricing. In an efficient market, this gap cannot occur and A-rated companies, say, always borrow at spreads appropriate for their rating. For insurance companies, we generally favor either hypothetical spreads appropriate for the claims paying rating, appropriately adjusted for liquidity, or the actual spreads in the company's cost of funds, which automatically reflect liquidity risk.

In the bond example, as well as for insurance company liabilities generally, the spread for credit risk has two components, one reflecting average losses, the other being compensation for taking risk. In the bond example above, one might expect 35 basis points of losses on average, based on historical experience for the quality, while much of the remaining 65 basis points can be thought of as reflecting compensation for taking the risk that losses are variable, and may well be different from this average. Such spreads can be viewed within a return on capital model as noted earlier. Of course, some of the remaining 65 basis points reflects liquidity risk, relative to Treasuries, as even the deepest bond markets have wider bid/ask spreads than the Treasury market.

As noted previously, credit risk can also be modeled explicitly, so that the corresponding charge may be removed from the discount rate. For example, from each path in the option pricing model for the bond one can construct 100 paths, say, each reflecting randomly generated occurrences of default and loss. On average, if modeled correctly, these losses would average 35 basis points, so a discount rate of about 8.65% (9.00–0.35) would be used in the model. Further, by explicitly developing an annual charge in every scenario of say 55 basis points, reflecting the cost of the risk capital assumed to be held to allow the assumption of credit risk, the discount rate needed in the model would reduce to about 8.10%.

Finally, in theory one could also explicitly model liquidity risk as the loss incurred on sale, relative to the theoretically fair price, due to the bid/ask spread. When all risks are modeled, including the necessary costs of capital, treasury rate discounting will suffice in theory. Logically, this same process and theory can be followed for life insurance company liabilities. However, it seems prudent not to model all risks, but only those which are sufficiently complex or variable as to preclude the judgmental development of the necessary component of the risk spread. For example, embedded options are routinely modeled in the asset markets because their values are so variable, and no simple rules of thumb for the equivalent spread will suffice. On the other hand, credit risk is effectively never modeled, as spreads appropriate to financial ratings and reflective of historical experience seem to suffice for most applications. Finally, liquidity spreads are again virtually never modeled explicitly, but generally judgmentally established based on the similarity principle, as limited by prices which the market can bear. The constructive method takes this same approach for liability valuation; explicitly model embedded options on option rich contracts, and then use discount rates reflective of insurance company credit-risk (real risk based on a claims paying ratings or implied by costs of funds), modified in the former case by the inherent illiquidity of these contracts. By definition, the cost of funds approach reflects the total risk spread, so no separate adjustment for liquidity is necessary.

*Fair value of liabilities – deductive methodologies*

The deductive, or appraisal methodologies for the FVL are based on appraisal value (AV) in the relatively thin market of insurance company or insurance block transactions. In this setting, one is typically 'buying' a block of liabilities together with a block of supporting assets. The price may be either positive or negative. In this latter case, the buyer receives additional funds from the seller, equal to the negative price.

Given such a price, and knowledge about the fair or market value of assets (FVA), it is easy to derive the implied fair value of liabilities. That is,

$$FVL = FVA - AV,$$

or, the fair value of liabilities must equal the fair value of assets, less the appraisal value of the enterprise (i.e. the price). This value of liabilities is self-evident, since theoretically, it can be realized through a market trade. Specifically, one can purchase an insurance block or enterprise, sell the assets, and for the above net proceeds, have indirectly purchased the block of liabilities.

The above equation may at first seem illogical, because in theory the fair value of the enterprise not only reflects the fair value of assets, but also the actual assets reflected in the FVA calculation. Theoretically, one can have two AV values corresponding to one FVA value, and correspondingly, the above formula produces two FVL values.

For example, a buyer would instinctively pay less for a life insurance block if assets equaled S&P call options, than if assets equaled a well diversified bond portfolio, assuming that the buyer had to hold the given assets. However, here again we see market arbitrage at work. Experienced buyers know that they do not have to hold the given assets, but can instead sell them at the market price, and replace them with a more appropriate asset portfolio. In doing so, one reduces the original FVA somewhat for transaction costs, but will increase the theoretically fair AV value substantially by virtue of the fact that the insurance block is now hedged by a more appropriate asset portfolio. In a competitive market of knowledgeable investors, therefore, AV will not necessarily explicitly reflect the actual assets in the block if an asset arbitrage, defined in terms of the effect on AV relative to the effect on FVA, is possible. That is, in theory

AV will be calculated in a competitive market for a block sale nearer to the maximum of all values produced by asset portfolios which can be purchased with proceeds from the sale of the original assets.

In this hypothetical model of an efficient market, the implied value of FVL is therefore unique, and effectively minimized. In practice, however, we concede that blocks do not necessarily trade at this maximum AV price, and consequently, the implied FVL on purchase may well be larger than that achievable after an asset portfolio restructuring. However, the notion that an insurance block buyer can restructure the asset portfolio and resell the block at a theoretical profit is no more counter-intuitive than an investment banker buying a GNMA portfolio and profitably reselling it as tranches of a CMO. In both cases, the potential profit is a reflection of a value-added of the buyer, and not necessarily an initial mispricing in the market.

For the application of this technique for the purpose of fair valuing liabilities, we advocate the use of the actual given asset portfolios backing these liabilities. If the above arbitrage is feasible, the insurer can implement the corresponding asset portfolio restructuring, and then reap the rewards of a smaller FVL value. As with the constructive methodologies for FVL, these indirect methodologies again form a sequence of approaches from the simplest yet most judgmental to the most complicated and objective. As noted before, in contrast to the asset markets where cash flows are the basis of value, insurance block evaluations are based upon distributable earnings. These earnings, defined as after-tax statutory income adjusted for capital gains/losses and changes in required risk capital, form the basis of value because it is precisely these values which can be removed from the block annually and distributed to the buyer as returns on the initial investment.

Below, we describe in some detail the appraisal method for calculating AV, which is analogous to the risk-adjusted present value (RAPV) approach of liability valuation. A feasible and likely set of distributable earnings are projected, then discounted by rates which reflect both the risk-free time value of money and an appropriate risk spread to compensate the buyer for the host of risks and contingencies which may significantly alter the original projection. In contrast to the RAPV method for liability valuations, however, it is common to supplement this initial valuation with some sensitivity tests by which one explicitly models, albeit on a deterministic basis, other sets of feasible distributable earnings in which one or another of the risks of the block are reflected in a conservative way.

From this initial valuation, whereby all risks are represented in the assumed risk spread, one can again proceed along the sequence of explicitly modeling individual risks and capital costs, one by one, and correspondingly eliminating from the discount rate charges for these risks. For example, one can option-adjust this initial valuation to produce the option-adjusted value of distributable earnings (OAVDE).[1] The modeling here largely proceeds as in section 1,

---

[1] See Becker, David N., 'Use of cash flow testing in product development', RSA 19 (4B).

only rather than focus on cash flows of liabilities (and assets), one instead models the effects of embedded options on distributable earnings. As for the direct methodology, once explicitly modeled, option risk may be eliminated from the risk spread, which would then reflect other risks such as mortality, morbidity, and other life and casualty insurance contingencies, asset credit risk, as well as expense risk. As in the case for constructive valuation methods, judgment is required as to the choice of which risks must be explicitly modeled, as opposed to which risks may be valued based on the simpler method of defining the corresponding risk spread to equal expected losses plus a return of required risk capital. We again recommend that as the most complex risk, option risk be valued in option rich insurance company liabilities. For term life and health insurance and casualty products, option risk is very limited. For these products the contingency risk (which is not the focus of this paper) is most important for explicit modeling.

As a final point, it should be noted that the required risk capital assumption is explicitly incorporated into these deductive methodologies, as the adjustments to statutory earnings include an adjustment for changes in this risk capital. Consequently, once defined, returns on risk capital initially loaned to the block are easily modeled by correspondingly adjusting statutory earnings for these capital costs. In this way, only expected losses due to risks need be modeled, while the corresponding risk premiums will be captured through this required risk capital assumptions.

## Option pricing method

### Definition of method

This approach (which was referred to earlier as the 'constructive approach') to calculating the fair value of liabilities is adapted from the fixed income capital markets. Specifically, option pricing is used extensively to price securities with embedded options. If one views an insurance policy or contract from the perspective of its owner, it becomes obvious that insurance company liabilities are the assets of their customers, and therefore, can be evaluated in the context of asset pricing techniques.

While the theory behind option pricing is very complex and discussed extensively in Appendix A, application of the methodology is more straightforward. Typically, option pricing computations are performed using a lattice approach or an interest rate path generator ('scenario') approach. Both of these are viable; however, because prospective cash flows on insurance liabilities are usually affected by historical treatment effects, scenario based models are preferable (this is discussed further in Appendix A). Basically, scenario based option pricing involves the generation of multiple interest rate scenarios or paths, followed by the explicit projection (for each scenario) of the corresponding liability cash flows. Once the cash flows have been projected, they are discounted for each scenario using interest rates that are a function of those comprising the scenario. Finally, the present values are averaged over all of the scenarios to arrive at a 'price' or fair value of the liabilities.

*Discussion of method*

In order to perform the projections referred to above, various assumptions are required including the following.
- Theory of interest rate behavior: Given that multiple interest rate paths are central to this methodology, assumptions must be made regarding their behavior. These usually involve some probability distributions and parameterization. A key issue is the existence of arbitrage opportunities in the interest rate structure. For option pricing purposes, scenarios are modeled to be arbitrage free. This is discussed further in Appendix A, and a specific interest scenario generator is discussed in Appendix B.
- Policyholder behavior functions: These are discussed in Appendix D, and address issues such as excess lapsation, policyholder loan utilization, dynamic premium payments, and dynamic fund transfers.
- Competitive environment: This issue is addressed as a subset of excess lapsation, but is intended to capture the market substitutes for the insured's contract.
- Company attribute and behavior functions: Attributes include the effects of infrastructure such as acquisition and maintenance expense levels. Behavior functions address issues such as interest crediting or policyholder dividend strategies. While essential for appraisal methods (discussed in the next section), investment strategies may or may not be reflected in projections for option pricing. One approach is to assume that companies establish crediting and dividend policy entirely from competitive considerations and customer price elasticity, another, is to assume that spreads from actual investment earnings also influence the decisions.
- Option adjusted spread: In order to determine prices or fair values in today's terms, projected cash flows must be discounted. Under option pricing, forward rates are usually adjusted for option spreads and used for the discounting. An advantage of option pricing applications in the capital markets is that they are used to price and reprice portfolios in relatively 'thick' secondary markets. Therefore, option adjusted spreads can be derived from actual price information. Option adjusted spreads for insurance liabilities cannot be similarly calibrated because a corresponding thick secondary market does not exist. Therefore, except for new business, where an option spread can be derived from prices in the retail market, a number of different approaches to option adjusted spread determination can be used and are discussed in Appendix C.

Given that most actuaries are less familiar with option pricing than other potential approaches to fair valuation of liabilities, a substantial amount of text and illustrative computations are developed in the balance of this section using an interest rate path generator approach. This should not be interpreted as a bias by the task force in favor of option pricing methodology, but is merely intended to provide users of this paper with enough background to evaluate option pricing on equal footing with the other methods where users are likely to assimilate more easily because of their actuarial or accounting knowledge.

A class of interest rate models that may be necessary or desirable for valuing a block of liabilities is that of interest rate path generator models. Such models will produce a series of interest rate paths, each generally given an equal probability of occurring, which emanate from a designated starting yield curve. Each path represents the transition through time from one yield curve to another in intervals such as 3 months, beginning with the designated yield curve. This class of models can be distinguished from interest rate lattice models in that, for the lattice model, one cannot determine a unique path that interest rates took to get to any future state of rates within the model, whereas for a path generator model, an interest rate history or path can be traced backward to the designated starting yield curve.

This property of the path generator model class lends it to valuing blocks of liabilities whose current values or associated behaviors are somehow dependent upon the path that rates took to get to the current point in time. There are, in fact, some insurance liabilities, such as single premium deferred annuities (SPDAs) and Universal Life (UL) contracts, which have these properties, with regard to interest credited rates and policyholder behavior. For any given path produced by an interest rate model, the insurance liability cash flows can be projected. These cash flows can then be discounted by the short term (one period) interest rates for each period along that path to obtain a present value of the cash flows for that path as of the start date. The average of the discounted present values of liability flows for all the paths produced by the model would represent the option adjusted value of that particular block of liabilities.

There are many kinds of path generator models. Even for the same model, there are many input parameters that will influence the dynamics of the yield curves produced by the model, such as the volatility of interest rate movements, the disposition to yield curve inversions, how low or high rates are allowed to get, and whether or not the collective set of interest rate paths will be arbitrage-free. The range of possible model implications is too broad to fully examine here. Rather, in the examples in this section, we shall examine the application of two families of path generator models. One, known as Heath, Jarrow, Morton, is discussed briefly in Appendix B, while the other is generally available as part of a vendor software package.

Sample calculations are displayed below for both a hypothetical SPDA block and a UL block of liabilities. Both blocks contain interest sensitive elements in the credited rates and policyholder surrender behavior. The blocks differ in that the UL block has an expected ongoing, although uncertain premium stream, a significant mortality component, and a policy loan component, while the SPDA typically has none of these.

As mentioned above, different interest rate scenario generators have been utilized in the computations. Furthermore, different projection systems have also been used and correspond exactly with the Scenario Generator 1 versus Scenario Generator 2 values. Given these platform and generator differences, the broad consistency of results argues in favor of the portability of the methodology. Finally, for simplicity of discussion, we will generally refer only to figures produced on the first projection system using the first scenario generator.

*Valuation approach*

One of the open issues in valuing a block of insurance liabilities is the rate to use when discounting projected cash flows. One point of view argues for discounting at Treasury rates only. Another says to discount at a spread over Treasury to reflect either the entity's own credit risk or the expected earnings rate on assets backing the block. A more complete discussion of discounting spreads can be found in Appendix C of this report. In the analysis that follows, the present values of the liabilities have been calculated at three different spreads over Treasury: 0, 50, and 100 basis points. In addition, the discount rate that would equate the present value of liabilities to the single premium less acquisition costs is also shown. This spread will represent the spread to Treasuries that the net premium received would need to earn to fund the projected liability cash flows. This spread is also called the 'cost of funds' spread. A building block approach is used, by valuing a simplified core version of the SPDA or UL first, and then adding one feature or modifying one parameter at a time until the ultimate target product has been valued. The advantage to such an approach is that intuition for the value of various components of the product can be gained in this process, which may help in determining what discount rate and other valuation assumptions ought to be. In addition to varying product features, certain key interest rate model parameters are also examined to determine their level of correlation to the valuation results. Specifically, the number of paths generated and the interest rate volatility assumption will be tested.

Another important valuation issue is the testing horizon. In most of the valuations done here, a 20-year horizon has been assumed. At the end of the testing horizon, some value must be assigned to the block of business. The policyholder account value has been assumed for this purpose. This will be incorporated into the valuation of the block by assuming a 100% surrender rate at the end of the testing horizon. The significance of both the 20-year horizon and the terminal value can be tested using periods shorter and longer than 20 years. The results of such a test are shown later in the course of this analysis. In a similar vein, the periodicity of SPDA and UL cash flows and interest rate paths could also be tested (not done here) to balance refinement of results with calculation speed. Quarterly time intervals have been used here throughout.

## Hypothetical SPDA product

*SPDA product specifications*

Total single premium: $100 000 000
Total average $20 000
  single premium:
Credited rate (CR): Initial rate = Initial 5 yr CMT = 0.052
                                    (bond equivalent yield)
                    Target rate = Current 5 yr CMT − 0.0075
                    Renewal rate = max (0.04, (0.5 × target rate)
                                    + (0.5 × prior credited rate)))
                    Reset      = Annually
                    frequency

Surrender-charges (SC): SC% × account value, where SC% is determined as shown below:

| Year | SC% |
|------|-----|
| 1    | 7   |
| 2    | 6   |
| 3    | 5   |
| 4    | 4   |
| 5    | 3   |
| 6    | 2   |
| 7    | 1   |
| 8+   | 0   |

10% of account value may be withdrawn each year without charge.

*Policyholder surrender behavior*

$$a + 0.0575 \times \arctan[(220 \times (\text{current 5 yr CMT} - \text{current credited rate} - \text{current SC}/3)) - 3.3]$$

where, $a = 0.12$ if SC > 0; $a = 0.17$ if SC = 0.

Ten percent of the values paid out at surrender are assumed to be free of surrender charges.

*Mortality* All the contracts are assumed to pay death benefits equal to the account value. The assumed mortality rates, by contract year, are set out below.

| Policy year | Mortality rate | Policy year | Mortality rate | Policy year | Mortality rate |
|---|---|---|---|---|---|
| 1  | 0.010 | 11 | 0.035 | 21 | 0.095 |
| 2  | 0.012 | 12 | 0.039 | 22 | 0.105 |
| 3  | 0.014 | 13 | 0.043 | 23 | 0.115 |
| 4  | 0.016 | 14 | 0.047 | 24 | 0.125 |
| 5  | 0.018 | 15 | 0.051 | 25 | 0.135 |
| 6  | 0.020 | 16 | 0.055 | 26 | 0.145 |
| 7  | 0.023 | 17 | 0.063 | 27 | 0.155 |
| 8  | 0.026 | 18 | 0.071 | 28 | 0.170 |
| 9  | 0.029 | 19 | 0.079 | 29 | 0.185 |
| 10 | 0.032 | 20 | 0.087 | 30 | 0.200 |

*Expenses/Taxes*

| | |
|---|---|
| Per policy annual maintenance expense ($) | 40 |
| Per death expense ($) | 40 |
| Per surrender expense ($) | 40 |
| Acquisition cost (per premium) (%) | 6 |

Note: Taxes are ignored in these illustrations.

*Valuation of SPDA cash flows – base product-stripped*
A good starting place is to value an SPDA that has no expected lapses, deaths, or expenses, and credits the current 3 month Treasury rate every 3 months. The only cash flows in this valuation will be the payout of the accumulation value at the end of the testing horizon for each path. These flows should discount to the single premium using the short term Treasury rates as the discount rates along each path. Verifying this will provide a simple check on the integrity of the interest rate model. These results are shown below.

*SCENARIO GENERATOR 1 VALUES*

| Discount rate | Present value of liabilities (000s) |
|---|---|
| TSY + 0   | 100 000 |
| TSY + 50  | 90 789 |
| TSY + 100 | 82 445 |

| SCENARIO GENERATOR 2 VALUES | |
|---|---|
| Discount rate | Present value of liabilities (000s) |
| TSY + 0 | 100 000 |
| TSY + 50 | 91 158 |
| TSY + 100 | 83 134 |

*Crediting 5-year treasury rate with 5 year reset* A slight variation of the first example helps check the arbitrage-free properties of the interest rate paths. In this variation, the product credits the 5 year Treasury rate and resets this rate at the end of every five years. If the model is truly arbitrage-free, the end of horizon cash flows still ought to discount back to the single premium at the short term Treasury rates with very little slippage. The results below appear to confirm this:

| SCENARIO GENERATOR 1 VALUES | |
|---|---|
| Discount rate | Present value of liabilities (000s) |
| TSY + 0 | 99 181 |
| TSY + 50 | 90 033 |
| TSY + 100 | 81 748 |
| TSY − 4 | 100 000 |

| SCENARIO GENERATOR 2 VALUES | |
|---|---|
| Discount rate | Present value of liabilities (000s) |
| TSY + 0 | 100 128 |
| TSY + 50 | 91 192 |
| TSY + 100 | 83 090 |
| TSY − 1 | 100 000 |

The 4 basis point slippage for generator 1 is attributable to the fact that the SPDA credited rate mechanism automatically reinvests or compounds the credited interest each quarter at the same effective annual rate, as opposed to the short-term rates for the balance of each 5-year period. Had the SPDA compounded its credited interest at the short term rates for the balance of each 5-year period, then a discount rate of Treasury flat would have produced present value of exactly $100 million. In an arbitrage free model, reinvestment at the short term rates would result in slightly higher credited rates, offsetting the 4 basis point advantage indicated above.

*Acquisition costs* The inclusion of a 6% acquisition cost increases the break-even spread, but does not alter the present value of future liability flows at a given discount rate, as shown below.

*SCENARIO GENERATOR 1 VALUES*

| Discount rate | Present value of liabilities (000s) |
|---|---|
| TSY + 0 | 99 181 |
| TSY + 50 | 90 033 |
| TSY + 100 | 81 748 |
| TSY + 28 | 94 000 |

*SCENARIO GENERATOR 2 VALUES*

| Discount rate | Present value of liabilities (000s) |
|---|---|
| TSY + 0 | 100 128 |
| TSY + 50 | 91 192 |
| TSY + 100 | 83 090 |
| TSY + 39 | 94 000 |

The inclusion of acquisition costs creates a dilemma because the incurral of these costs coincides with the time of valuation (i.e. at the policy issue date). One could either include or exclude such expenses from other future liability flows. In the tables presented here, all acquisition costs are cast as expenses already incurred, and therefore have no impact on the present value of liabilities at some fixed rate. However, the acquisition costs will impact the required spread over Treasuries that the net premium received will need to earn to fund all other liability flows.

*Mortality* The mortality decrement shortens the life of the contract and has the effect of slightly increasing the present value of liabilities. The shorter amortization period also increases the break-even spread needed to cover up-front costs.

*SCENARIO GENERATOR 1 VALUES*

| Discount rate | Present value of liabilities (000s) |
|---|---|
| TSY + 0 | 100 585 |
| TSY + 50 | 93 187 |
| TSY + 100 | 86 411 |
| TSY + 43 | 94 000 |

SCENARIO GENERATOR 2 VALUES

| Discount rate | Present value of liabilities (000s) |
|---|---|
| TSY + 0 | 100 216 |
| TSY + 50 | 93 131 |
| TSY + 100 | 86 637 |
| TSY + 48 | 94 000 |

*Policyholder surrenders*  Policyholder surrenders, including interest-sensitive surrenders, both shorten the liability and increase its value. The increase in value is attributable to both the shorter amortization period for expenses, and the option antiselection against the company by policyholders surrendering their contracts.

SCENARIO GENERATOR 1 VALUES

| Discount rate | Present value of liabilities (000s) |
|---|---|
| TSY + 0 | 101 893 |
| TSY + 50 | 98 727 |
| TSY + 100 | 95 731 |
| TSY + 130 | 94 000 |

SCENARIO GENERATOR 2 VALUES

| Discount rate | Present value of liabilities (000s) |
|---|---|
| TSY + 0 | 102 726 |
| TSY + 50 | 99 825 |
| TSY + 100 | 97 074 |
| TSY + 159 | 94 000 |

*Surrender charges*  The inclusion of surrender charges offsets some of the extra cost generated by surrender activity. The surrender charges were assumed to apply to 90% of the surrendered account values (10% were assumed to be free of surrender charge), but not to the account values paid out at death.

*Fair valuation of life insurance company liabilities* 39

SCENARIO GENERATOR 1 VALUES

| Discount rate | Present value of liabilities (000s) |
|---|---|
| TSY + 0 | 100 652 |
| TSY + 50 | 96 275 |
| TSY + 100 | 92 164 |
| TSY + 77 | 94 000 |

SCENARIO GENERATOR 2 VALUES

| Discount rate | Present value of liabilities (000s) |
|---|---|
| TSY + 0 | 101 702 |
| TSY + 50 | 97 700 |
| TSY + 100 | 93 932 |
| TSY + 92 | 94 000 |

*Credited rates – annual reset* Resetting crediting rates annually, which is a common practice, without changing the credited rate basis from the 5-year Treasury rate, has a significant cost associated with it in this yield curve environment, as shown below:

SCENARIO GENERATOR 1 VALUES

| Discount rate | Present value of liabilities (000s) |
|---|---|
| TSY + 0 | 104 273 |
| TSY + 50 | 99 321 |
| TSY + 100 | 94 689 |
| TSY + 108 | 94 000 |

SCENARIO GENERATOR 2 VALUES

| Discount rate | Present value of liabilities (000s) |
|---|---|
| TSY + 0 | 104 578 |
| TSY + 50 | 100 035 |
| TSY + 100 | 95 773 |
| TSY + 126 | 94 000 |

*Credited rates – renewal target* Resetting credited rates to a renewal target can have a substantial effect. In our example, the renewal rate was reset to the current 5-year Treasury less 75 basis points.

SCENARIO GENERATOR 1 VALUES

| Discount rate | Present value of liabilities (000s) |
|---|---|
| TSY + 0 | 98 060 |
| TSY + 50 | 93 759 |
| TSY + 100 | 89 717 |
| TSY + 47 | 94 000 |

SCENARIO GENERATOR 2 VALUES

| Discount rate | Present value of liabilities (000s) |
|---|---|
| TSY + 0 | 98 187 |
| TSY + 50 | 94 238 |
| TSY + 100 | 90 520 |
| TSY + 53 | 94 000 |

*Credited rates – lagging new money rates*   The next refinement to our SPDA product is the introduction of a lag factor in the credited rate formula. Specifically, the reset rate is assumed to recognize 50% of the new money benchmark. While lag statistics are utilized in the industry, they have yet to be truly tested in a rising rate environment. These results show a slight savings as credited rates are pushed slightly lower with this strategy.

SCENARIO GENERATOR 1 VALUES

| Discount rate | Present value of liabilities (000s) |
|---|---|
| TSY + 0 | 97 621 |
| TSY + 50 | 93 452 |
| TSY + 100 | 89 528 |
| TSY + 43 | 94 000 |

SCENARIO GENERATOR 2 VALUES

| Discount rate | Present value of liabilities (000s) |
|---|---|
| TSY + 0 | 97 467 |
| TSY + 50 | 93 726 |
| TSY + 100 | 90 196 |
| TSY + 46 | 94 000 |

*Credited rates – minimum guaranteed rate* The introduction of a minimum guaranteed rate (4% in this case) has a slight cost as one might expect. A somewhat higher guarantee could have a significantly higher expected value.

SCENARIO GENERATOR 1 VALUES

| Discount rate | Present value of liabilities (000s) |
|---|---|
| TSY + 0 | 98 042 |
| TSY + 50 | 93 824 |
| TSY + 100 | 89 856 |
| TSY + 48 | 94 000 |

SCENARIO GENERATOR 2 VALUES

| Discount rate | Present value of liabilities (000s) |
|---|---|
| TSY + 0 | 97 948 |
| TSY + 50 | 94 161 |
| TSY + 100 | 90 591 |
| TSY + 52 | 94 000 |

*Renewal expenses* Renewal expenses can have a surprising impact on the present value of the liability flows, and in our example amounted to about 18 basis points annually.

SCENARIO GENERATOR 1 VALUES

| Discount rate | Present value of liabilities (000s) |
|---|---|
| TSY + 0 | 99 535 |
| TSY + 50 | 95 279 |
| TSY + 100 | 91 276 |
| TSY + 66 | 94 000 |

SCENARIO GENERATOR 2 VALUES

| Discount rate | Present value of liabilities (000s) |
|---|---|
| TSY + 0 | 99 449 |
| TSY + 50 | 95 630 |
| TSY + 100 | 92 029 |
| TSY + 73 | 94 000 |

Renewal expenses represent the final adjustment to our original stripped SPDA.

We see that the present value of our refined SPDA (assuming a discount rate of Treasury flat) is slightly lower than our stripped version, but almost $6 million greater than the assets on hand after paying acquisition costs. Therefore, if our methodology and assumptions are appropriate, the issuer loses nearly $6 million at issue on a present value basis. This is consistent with the statement that the issuer would have to earn 66 basis points over the Treasury curve to fund all the expected liability flows. While the insurer may fully expect to achieve this, it can only book the incremental earnings as they are earned and not up front. In other words, if an insurer invests $94 000 000 in bonds with a nominal yield of 66 basis points over Treasury, it would not book $100 000 000 because its market value would only be $94 000 000. Over time, however, the assets may provide the necessary income to fund the liabilities that carry a $100 000 000 book value (but which were discounted at Treasury flat). This highlights a key question of the proper discount rate to use in valuing projected liability flows. Clearly, an asset cannot be written up now in anticipation of being paid yields above Treasury, unless those expectations have changed since the asset was purchased (as they would if Treasury rates have fallen or default risk has lessened in the market's view). Given this, should an insurer be allowed to mark down a stream of liability flows versus Treasury rates because of its own credit rating or realized cost of funds?

It seems that relief could also come from another source by virtue of the fact that the insurance company has some control over the credited rates. While the dynamic surrender behavior tends to keep insurer credited rates from getting too far out of line, an insurer could alter its strategy if it felt that doing so has a net economic benefit. Our current methodology could be used to evaluate such alternative strategies, taking directly into account the assumed dynamic surrender behavior. It is quite possible that an alternative strategy may imply a lower present value of the liability block, but that such a strategy might be inconsistent with attracting new business or maintaining a desired market share. Still, the ability of the insurer to lower its ultimate payout on business already written perhaps should be given credit and be taken into account in the valuation process. To explore this point, a few crediting strategy alternatives were tested against each other. Specifically, target renewal spreads of greater than 75 basis points were examined.

*SCENARIO GENERATOR 1 VALUES*
*Present value of liabilities (000s) (as a function of renewal target spread)*

| Target spread | 0.0075 | 0.0100 | 0.0150 | 0.0200 | 0.0250 |
|---|---|---|---|---|---|
| TSY + 0 | 99 535 | 98 199 | 96 042 | 94 612 | 93 678 |
| TSY + 50 | 95 279 | 94 126 | 92 311 | 91 145 | 90 386 |
| TSY + 100 | 91 276 | 90 289 | 88 784 | 87 859 | 87 261 |
| Break-even spread | 66 | 52 | 27 | 9 | (5) |

SCENARIO GENERATOR 2 VALUES
Present value of liabilities (000s) (as a function of renewal target spread)

| Target spread | 0.0075 | 0.0100 | 0.0150 | 0.0200 | 0.0250 |
|---|---|---|---|---|---|
| TSY + 0 | 99 449 | 97 980 | 95 866 | 94 649 | 93 874 |
| TSY + 50 | 95 630 | 94 353 | 92 553 | 91 544 | 90 905 |
| TSY + 100 | 92 029 | 90 927 | 89 413 | 88 594 | 88 082 |
| Break-even spread | 73 | 55 | 28 | 11 | (4) |

These numbers suggest that at least for the given surrender function, the insurer has the ability to significantly lower the present value of the net liability flows by cutting renewal rates. Whether or not these credited rates could co-exist with ongoing new business is a separate issue.

A similar exercise regarding the policyholder surrender function is also helpful. However, in this case, the surrender behavior is not directly under the insurer's control. The company can only set one of the parameters that affects it (i.e. the credited rate). The sensitivity of the present value of liabilities to lower or higher surrenders, including immediate full surrender, is information that potentially could be factored into a fair valuation of a block. Several multiples of the base lapse rate were tested, the results of which are shown below.

SCENARIO GENERATOR 1 VALUES
Present value of liabilities (000s) (as a function of surrender rate)

| Surrenders | 0 × base | 0.5 × base | 1 × base | 2 × base | 3 × base | 5 × base | Immediate full surrenders |
|---|---|---|---|---|---|---|---|
| TSY + 0 | 97 771 | 99 054 | 99 535 | 99 630 | 99 381 | 98 757 | 94 690 |
| TSY + 50 | 90 720 | 93 748 | 95 279 | 96 530 | 96 900 | 96 948 | 94 574 |
| TSY + 100 | 84 258 | 88 813 | 91 276 | 93 573 | 94 514 | 95 193 | 94 458 |
| Break-even spread | 26 | 48 | 66 | 93 | 111 | 135 | 300 |

SCENARIO GENERATOR 2 VALUES
Present value of liabilities (000s) (as a function of surrender rate)

| Surrenders | 0 × base | 0.5 × base | 1 × base | 2 × base | 3 × base | 5 × base | Immediate full surrenders |
|---|---|---|---|---|---|---|---|
| TSY + 0 | 95 483 | 98 292 | 99 449 | 99 832 | 99 429 | 98 868 | 94 227 |
| TSY + 50 | 88 898 | 93 433 | 95 630 | 97 142 | 97 335 | 97 423 | 94 189 |
| TSY + 100 | 82 855 | 88 904 | 92 029 | 94 567 | 95 314 | 96 017 | 94 152 |
| Break-even spread | 11 | 44 | 73 | 111 | 134 | 177 | 300 |

44  D.C. Doll et al.

The figures illustrate that the effect of higher or lower lapses is far from linear. Different surrender formulas could also be explored to determine a worst case surrender scenario in terms of maximizing the present value of all liability flows. To pursue this further, several step functions were tested. Of those tested, the lapse formula that produced the highest present value of liabilities was the following:

$$\text{Lapse rate} = 0 \quad \text{if } [5 \text{ year CMT} - (CR + DC)] \leq 0.015$$
$$= 1 \quad \text{otherwise}$$

### SCENARIO GENERATOR 1 VALUES

| Discount rate | Present value of liabilities (000s) |
|---|---|
| TSY + 0 | 102 068 |
| TSY + 50 | 97 172 |
| TSY + 100 | 92 565 |
| TSY + 84 | 94 000 |

### SCENARIO GENERATOR 2 VALUES

| Discount rate | Present value of liabilities (000s) |
|---|---|
| TSY + 0 | 102 762 |
| TSY + 50 | 99 113 |
| TSY + 100 | 95 630 |
| TSY + 124 | 94 000 |

While the above formula does not necessarily represent optimal efficiency of surrender option exercise from the policyholder's perspective, it does represent optimal efficiency in terms of the cost of that option from the company's perspective. The difference in the present value of liabilities under a 'best estimate' assumption versus a 'worst case' assumption (99 535 vs. 102 068 in our example for generator 1) is potentially significant because the surrender behavior of policyholders may be largely beyond the company's control.

*Testing horizon*  As mentioned earlier, the time horizon potentially can have an impact on the valuations. Below is a summary of the impact of varying the horizon from 10 to 30 years. Ten years appears to be an insufficient horizon, while projecting beyond 20 years appears to make little difference in this case.

## SCENARIO GENERATOR 1 VALUES
Present value of liabilities (000s) (as a function of testing horizon)

| Horizon | 10 years | 15 years | 20 years | 25 years | 30 years |
|---|---|---|---|---|---|
| TSY + 0 | 99 750 | 99 616 | 99 535 | 99 508 | 99 469 |
| TSY + 50 | 96 304 | 95 581 | 95 279 | 95 185 | 95 134 |
| TSY + 100 | 93 005 | 91 763 | 91 276 | 91 129 | 91 069 |
| Break-even spread | 85 | 70 | 66 | 64 | 64 |

## SCENARIO GENERATOR 2 VALUES
Present value of liabilities (000s) (as a function of testing horizon)

| Horizon | 10 years | 15 years | 20 years | 25 years | 30 years |
|---|---|---|---|---|---|
| TSY + 0 | 100 028 | 99 666 | 99 449 | 99 426 | 99 430 |
| TSY + 50 | 96 810 | 95 999 | 95 630 | 95 557 | 95 547 |
| TSY + 100 | 93 731 | 92 523 | 92 029 | 91 915 | 91 895 |
| Break-even spread | 96 | 79 | 73 | 70 | 70 |

*Number of paths* The number of paths used to project cash flows is an important input parameter. Fifty paths were used in all the above tests. One concern is how volatile the valuations might be from one set of randomly generated paths to another. Another question is how many interest rate paths must be run to reasonably measure the option costs embedded in the liability block. Each of these concerns is addressed briefly in the series of numbers below.

## SCENARIO GENERATOR 1 VALUES
Present value of liabilities (000s) using 20 paths

| | Trial 1 | Trial 2 | Trial 3 | Trial 4 | Trial 5 |
|---|---|---|---|---|---|
| TSY + 0 | 99 459 | 99 295 | 99 693 | 99 900 | 99 562 |
| TSY + 50 | 95 202 | 95 032 | 95 436 | 95 629 | 95 302 |
| TSY + 100 | 91 197 | 91 022 | 91 432 | 91 612 | 91 295 |
| Break-even spread | 65 | 63 | 68 | 70 | 66 |

### SCENARIO GENERATOR 1 VALUES
Present value of liabilities (000s) using 50 paths

|  | Trial 1 | Trial 2 | Trial 3 | Trial 4 | Trial 5 |
|---|---|---|---|---|---|
| TSY + 0 | 99 535 | 99 852 | 99 827 | 99 676 | 99 459 |
| TSY + 50 | 95 279 | 95 587 | 95 555 | 95 432 | 95 205 |
| TSY + 100 | 91 276 | 91 575 | 91 539 | 91 421 | 91 204 |
| Break-even spread | 66 | 69 | 69 | 67 | 65 |

### SCENARIO GENERATOR 1 VALUES
Present value of liabilities (000s) using 100 paths

|  | Trial 1 | Trial 2 | Trial 3 | Trial 4 | Trial 5 |
|---|---|---|---|---|---|
| TSY + 0 | 99 603 | 99 566 | 99 619 | 99 508 | 99 732 |
| TSY + 50 | 95 348 | 95 302 | 95 363 | 95 259 | 95 463 |
| TSY + 100 | 91 346 | 91 291 | 91 359 | 91 262 | 91 448 |
| Break-even spread | 67 | 66 | 67 | 65 | 68 |

### SCENARIO GENERATOR 2 VALUES
Present value of liabilities (000s) using 20 paths

|  | Trial 1 | Trial 2 | Trial 3 | Trial 4 | Trial 5 |
|---|---|---|---|---|---|
| TSY + 0 | 99 111 | 99 870 | 99 179 | 99 691 | 99 097 |
| TSY + 50 | 95 275 | 96 032 | 95 371 | 95 827 | 95 253 |
| TSY + 100 | 91 658 | 92 413 | 91 780 | 92 183 | 91 629 |
| Break-even spread | 68 | 69 | 69 | 75 | 67 |

### SCENARIO GENERATOR 2 VALUES
Present value of liabilities (000s) using 50 paths

|  | Trial 1 | Trial 2 | Trial 3 | Trial 4 | Trial 5 |
|---|---|---|---|---|---|
| TSY + 0 | 99 449 | 99 686 | 99 176 | 99 452 | 99 538 |
| TSY + 50 | 95 630 | 95 834 | 95 347 | 95 626 | 95 683 |
| TSY + 100 | 92 029 | 92 201 | 91 735 | 92 017 | 92 047 |
| Break-even spread | 71 | 75 | 69 | 73 | 73 |

SCENARIO GENERATOR 2 VALUES
Present value of liabilities (000s) using 100 paths

|  | Trial 1 | Trial 2 | Trial 3 | Trial 4 | Trial 5 |
|---|---|---|---|---|---|
| TSY + 0 | 99 466 | 99 536 | 99 221 | 99 663 | 99 485 |
| TSY + 50 | 95 648 | 95 698 | 95 383 | 95 806 | 93 630 |
| TSY + 100 | 92 047 | 92 079 | 91 765 | 92 168 | 91 995 |
| Break-even spread | 73 | 73 | 69 | 75 | 72 |

This brief analysis is not conclusive. For generator 1, it would appear that 50 paths provide more stability of results than 20 paths, and 100 more than 50, although the differences are not dramatic. More testing is probably warranted on this issue.

*Volatility of interest rates* The cost of policyholder options will be a function of the level of interest rate volatility assumed. To illustrate this sensitivity, we tested lower and higher levels of volatility and noted the results as follows.

SCENARIO GENERATOR 1 VALUES
Present value of liabilities (000s) (as a function of volatility)

|  | 0 × base volatility | 0.5 × base volatility | 1.0 × base volatility | 1.5 × base volatility | 2.0 × base volatility* |
|---|---|---|---|---|---|
| TSY + 0 | 98 413 | 98 612 | 99 535 | 101 017 | 102 550 |
| TSY + 50 | 94 025 | 94 288 | 95 279 | 96 764 | 98 253 |
| TSY + 100 | 89 907 | 90 226 | 91 276 | 92 762 | 94 210 |
| Break-even spread | 50 | 53 | 66 | 84 | 103 |

*Capped at 30%.

GENERATOR 2 VALUES
Present value of liabilities (000s) (as a function of volatility)

|  | 0 × base volatility | 0.5 × base volatility | 1.0 × base volatility | 1.5 × base volatility | 2.0 × base volatility* |
|---|---|---|---|---|---|
| TSY + 0 | 97 603 | 98 061 | 99 449 | 101 305 | 103 196 |
| TSY + 50 | 93 561 | 94 139 | 95 630 | 97 477 | 99 293 |
| TSY + 100 | 89 781 | 90 445 | 92 029 | 93 865 | 95 613 |
| Break-even spread | 45 | 52 | 71 | 98 | 122 |

*Capped at 30%.

As with the surrender assumptions, the effect of the volatility assumption is seen to be non-linear. This reflects the fact that the cost of the policyholder option to surrender in rising rate scenarios, coupled with the company's assumed credited rate strategy, increases significantly if interest rates are assumed to be more volatile.

## Hypothetical universal life product

### UL product specifications

Gross premiums: Discussed under flexible premiums
Credited rate: Same as SPDA product.
Surrender charges: SC × specified face amount (in units), where SC is determined below:

| Year | SC | Year | SC |
|------|----|------|-----|
| 1 | 45 | 9 | 21 |
| 2 | 42 | 10 | 18 |
| 3 | 39 | 11 | 15 |
| 4 | 36 | 12 | 12 |
| 5 | 33 | 13 | 9 |
| 6 | 30 | 14 | 6 |
| 7 | 27 | 15 | 3 |
| 8 | 24 | 16+ | 0 |

Policyholder surrender behavior: Same as SPDA product.
Mortality: Same as SPDA product.
Specified face amount: $400 000 000
Death benefits: Specified face amount + account value

*Expenses* All expenses are assumed to be the same as for the SPDA, except that acquisition costs are assumed to average 16% of first year premium, and all other renewal per premium expenses are assumed to average 6%.

*Policy loan utilization* The policy loan utilization, expressed as a percentage, is assumed to be:

$$\text{LOANPCT}_t = 100 \times \max(0.15, \min(0.50, 0.15 + A \times (5\text{ Yr CMT}_t - CR)))$$

where $A = 5$ or $10$.

### Valuation of UL cash flows

Estimating the present value of liability flows for a UL product would appear to be a more difficult task than for an SPDA. There are at least three reasons that this would be the case. First, there exists the possibility, indeed the probability, of future premium income, albeit in unknown quantities. Second, there exists a significant mortality component that is absent in SPDA contracts. Given that mortality is at least partially funded by explicit contract charges and largely independent of interest rates or spreads, it may be instructive to perform further analysis where attempts are made to factor out its impact. For this illustration, however, no such attempts are made. Finally, there are policy loan provisions that can have a meaningful impact on policy credited rates.

Except for these clear distinctions, these two product forms are otherwise very similar. Because of this, we will start with our hypothetical SPDA from the prior example and layer on the three distinct UL attributes mentioned above. In addition, certain other assumptions specific to our UL product will be reflected, such as acquisition costs and surrender charges, as described previously.

*Flexible premiums* Future UL premiums are largely unrestricted as to timing and amount. While over a decade of experience gives some indication as to what premium flows an insurer might expect, there is still a wide range of possible outcomes. The contract year and interest rate scenarios can have a significant bearing, in addition to other external factors that may be difficult to estimate. For the immediate purpose here, a few possible premium scenarios will be tested to get a feel for the possible range of outcomes. The last of these premium scenarios, which contains a dynamic element, represents our best guess as to the premium flow for our UL policy under any interest rate scenario.

Four UL premium scenarios were tested in addition to our starting single premium scenario 1. The premium scenarios tested are described below:

*PREMIUM SCENARIOS (in $ millions)*

| Policy year | Scenario 1 | Scenario 2 | Scenario 3 | Scenario 4 | Scenario 5* |
|---|---|---|---|---|---|
| 1 | 100 | 100 | 100 | 100 | 100 |
| 2 | 0 | 100 | 100 | 50 | 50 |
| 3 | 0 | 0 | 100 | 45 | 45 |
| 4 | 0 | 0 | 100 | 40 | 40 |
| 5 | 0 | 0 | 100 | 35 | 35 |
| 6 | 0 | 0 | 0 | 30 | 30 |
| 7 | 0 | 0 | 0 | 25 | 25 |
| 8 | 0 | 0 | 0 | 20 | 20 |
| 9 | 0 | 0 | 0 | 15 | 15 |
| 10+ | 0 | 0 | 0 | 15 | 15 |

*Scenario 5 premiums are subject to the following dynamic adjustment:

Dynamic premium = base premium * max(0.50, (1.20 − 25 × (5 year CMT − CR))).

The results for these five premium scenarios are summarized below.

*SCENARIO GENERATOR 1 VALUES*
*Present value of liabilities (000s) (as a function of premium)*

|  | Scenario 1 | Scenario 2 | Scenario 3 | Scenario 4 | Scenario 5 |
|---|---|---|---|---|---|
| TSY + 0 | 99 535 | 101 926 | 107 508 | 104 682 | 105 006 |
| TSY + 50 | 95 279 | 94 099 | 92 113 | 94 368 | 94 696 |
| TSY + 100 | 91 276 | 86 760 | 77 796 | 84 780 | 85 110 |
| Break-even spread | 66 | 51 | 44 | 52 | 54 |

*SCENARIO GENERATOR 2 VALUES*
*Present value of liabilities (000s) (as a function of premium)*

|  | Scenario 1 | Scenario 2 | Scenario 3 | Scenario 4 | Scenario 5 |
|---|---|---|---|---|---|
| TSY + 0 | 99 449 | 102 243 | 109 198 | 106 123 | 107 167 |
| TSY + 50 | 95 630 | 95 232 | 95 536 | 96 704 | 97 831 |
| TSY + 100 | 92 028 | 88 640 | 82 793 | 87 934 | 89 140 |
| Break-even spread | 73 | 59 | 56 | 65 | 72 |

Most of the scenario results indicate a lower liability value relative to the single premium scenario. To understand why this is so, one must look at how the liability model is accounting for the future premium. The premium income itself is considered a negative liability flow, off-setting policyholder benefits and expenses. Then there is the impact of future premiums on future expenses and benefits resulting from an increase in account values. The incremental premium income in the above example does not offset the additional future benefits and expenses when discounted at Treasury flat. However, it does when discounted at somewhat higher rates, resulting in lower liability estimates.

*Expenses and surrender charges* The next step taken was to reflect UL per premium expenses and surrender charges in our valuation. Policyholder surrender behavior is assumed to follow the same SPDA formula; therefore, UL surrender charges were converted to a percentage of account value charge.

The resulting valuations are summarized below.

*SCENARIO GENERATOR 1 VALUES*
*Present value of liabilities (000s) (as a function of premium)*

|  | Scenario 1 | Scenario 2 | Scenario 3 | Scenario 4 | Scenario 5 |
|---|---|---|---|---|---|
| TSY + 0 | 96 333 | 98 708 | 104 762 | 101 237 | 101 588 |
| TSY + 50 | 91 312 | 89 723 | 87 615 | 89 292 | 89 639 |
| TSY + 100 | 86 641 | 81 374 | 71 779 | 78 278 | 78 622 |
| Break-even spread | 129 | 84 | 61 | 74 | 75 |

*SCENARIO GENERATOR 2 VALUES*
*Present value of liabilities (000s) (as a function of premium)*

|  | Scenario 1 | Scenario 2 | Scenario 3 | Scenario 4 | Scenario 5 |
|---|---|---|---|---|---|
| TSY + 0 | 95 378 | 98 136 | 105 543 | 101 830 | 102 860 |
| TSY + 50 | 90 737 | 89 944 | 90 139 | 90 584 | 91 695 |
| TSY + 100 | 86 409 | 82 313 | 75 870 | 80 211 | 81 397 |
| Break-even spread | 119 | 89 | 72 | 82 | 87 |

While the present values have changed modestly, the break-even spreads are quite high, suggesting that UL mortality profits are necessary to cover the higher acquisition costs.

*Mortality* Our SPDA product had a minor mortality component (i.e. the forgone surrender charge in the event of death). A UL product, on the other hand, must have a significant mortality component (in relation to the account value) to be considered life insurance for tax purposes. For our hypothetical product, we assumed a specified face amount of $400 million, and an option 'B' type death benefit. For these policies, the death benefit equals the face amount plus the account value, so that the net amount at risk always equals the face amount.

Charges to cover the expected cost of mortality are deducted each month from the account value. If the charges cover only the expected costs and no profit margin, then we might expect little or no change in the present value of liability flows. However, the numbers below suggest that the incidence of mortality charges, with larger charges in later periods, can impact the overall value.

*SCENARIO GENERATOR 1 VALUES*
*Present value of liabilities (000s) (as a function of premium)*

|  | Scenario 1 | Scenario 2 | Scenario 3 | Scenario 4 | Scenario 5 |
|---|---|---|---|---|---|
| TSY + 0 | 96 642 | 98 767 | 104 698 | 101 239 | 101 600 |
| TSY + 50 | 93 718 | 91 692 | 89 300 | 91 127 | 91 486 |
| TSY + 100 | 90 913 | 85 046 | 75 027 | 81 748 | 82 106 |
| Break-even spread | 233 | 108 | 68 | 88 | 90 |

## 52   D.C. Doll et al.

*SCENARIO GENERATOR 2 VALUES*
*Present value of liabilities (000s) (as a function of premium)*

|  | Scenario 1 | Scenario 2 | Scenario 3 | Scenario 4 | Scenario 5 |
|---|---|---|---|---|---|
| TSY + 0 | 95 510 | 97 823 | 105 901 | 101 742 | 102 070 |
| TSY + 50 | 92 640 | 91 390 | 92 665 | 92 425 | 92 333 |
| TSY + 100 | 89 902 | 85 334 | 80 336 | 83 776 | 83 320 |
| Break-even spread | 217 | 107 | 85 | 99 | 96 |

As a further illustration, a 15% profit margin was added into the mortality charges. While admittedly simple, the computations are enlightening. In reality, mortality margins can be quite complex. This margin lowers the liabilities across the board because account values, and thus surrender and death benefits, are reduced in the process with no corresponding reduction in income. (Excess mortality charges could affect surrender behavior, but we have assumed no change here.) Any expected profit from mortality will result in a lower break-even spread for the assets on hand.

*SCENARIO GENERATOR 1 VALUES*
*Present value of liabilities (000s) (as a function of premium)*

|  | Scenario 1 | Scenario 2 | Scenario 3 | Scenario 4 | Scenario 5 |
|---|---|---|---|---|---|
| TSY + 0 | 85 811 | 88 215 | 94 875 | 91 003 | 91 355 |
| TSY + 50 | 83 629 | 81 864 | 80 128 | 81 579 | 81 930 |
| TSY + 100 | 81 508 | 75 884 | 66 456 | 72 836 | 73 187 |
| Break-even spread | 41 | 33 | 37 | 37 | 39 |

*SCENARIO GENERATOR 2 VALUES*
*Present value of liabilities (000s) (as a function of premium)*

|  | Scenario 1 | Scenario 2 | Scenario 3 | Scenario 4 | Scenario 5 |
|---|---|---|---|---|---|
| TSY + 0 | 87 958 | 89 790 | 97 843 | 93 646 | 93 701 |
| TSY + 50 | 85 505 | 83 500 | 83 165 | 83 765 | 83 319 |
| TSY + 100 | 83 156 | 77 586 | 69 562 | 74 636 | 73 748 |
| Break-even spread | 82 | 46 | 47 | 49 | 46 |

*Policy loans* Policy loans are an asset of the insurance company that can also have a direct bearing on some of the insurance contracts they support. In our hypothetical UL product, we assume a policy loan rate of 8% (the rate charged to the policyholder). On any portion of the account values that have been loaned out to policyholders, a credited rate of either 6% or 7% has been assumed, implying either a 200 or 100 basis point margin on the loaned values. Finally, we need a loan utilization algorithm to predict the amount of loans that will be taken out by policyholders. The algorithm chosen was as follows:

$$\text{LOANPCT}_t = 100 \times \max(0.15, \min(0.50, 0.15 + A \times (5 \text{ Yr CMT}_t - CR))),$$

where LOANPCT is the percentage of account values expected to be loaned out at time $t$, and $A$ is either 5 or 10. The algorithm takes into account the fixed loan rate and likelihood of increased borrowing as interest rates rise. The impact of loans on the liability flows is shown below, for premium scenario 5, assuming a mortality profit margin of 15%.

*SCENARIO GENERATOR 1 VALUES*
Present value of liabilities (000s) (as a function of policy loans)

|  | No loans | $CR = 6\%$; $A = 5$ | $CR = 7\%$; $A = 5$ | $CR = 6\%$; $A = 10$ | $CR = 7\%$; $A = 10$ |
|---|---|---|---|---|---|
| TSY + 0 | 91 355 | 91 578 | 94 726 | 91 202 | 94 512 |
| TSY + 50 | 81 930 | 82 184 | 84 718 | 81 917 | 84 569 |
| TSY + 100 | 73 187 | 73 465 | 75 438 | 73 296 | 75 347 |
| Break-even spread | 38.7 | 40.0 | 53.7 | 38.5 | 53.0 |

*SCENARIO GENERATOR 2 VALUES*
Present value of liabilities (000s) (as a function of policy loans)

|  | No loans | $CR = 6\%$; $A = 5$ | $CR = 7\%$; $A = 5$ | $CR = 6\%$; $A = 10$ | $CR = 7\%$; $A = 10$ |
|---|---|---|---|---|---|
| TSY + 0 | 93 701 | 89 410 | 94 065 | 88 577 | 94 055 |
| TSY + 50 | 83 319 | 81 588 | 85 741 | 81 218 | 86 423 |
| TSY + 100 | 73 748 | 74 361 | 78 052 | 74 415 | 78 999 |
| Break-even spread | 46 | 35 | 61 | 31 | 66 |

The results indicate that the loan credited rate is material, but for the range of parameters considered, the dynamic utilization function did not appear to be. Results for other premium scenarios showed similar patterns.

*Sensitivity of policyholder surrenders* The importance of the assumed premium level and mortality charges suggests that the policyholder surrender assumption will be quite important. This is confirmed in the table below, in which a wide range of multiples of the base surrender function were tested. All of these cases assumed premium scenario 5, a loaned credited rate of 6%, and a policy loan utilization factor of 5 (i.e. $A = 5$).

SCENARIO GENERATOR 1 VALUES
Present value of liabilities (000s) (as a function of surrender rate)

| Surrenders | 0 × base | 0.5 × base | 1 × base | 2 × base | 3 × base | 5 × base | Immediate full surrenders |
|---|---|---|---|---|---|---|---|
| TSY + 0 | 79 828 | 87 653 | 91 578 | 94 569 | 95 116 | 94 321 | 82 993 |
| TSY + 50 | 66 433 | 76 535 | 82 184 | 87 564 | 89 651 | 90 669 | 82 892 |
| TSY + 100 | 54 195 | 66 288 | 73 465 | 80 990 | 84 483 | 87 176 | 82 790 |
| Break-even spread | 15 | 16 | 40 | 77 | 105 | 148 | 484 |

SCENARIO GENERATOR 2 VALUES
Present value of liabilities (000s) (as a function of surrender rate)

| Surrenders | 0 × base | 0.5 × base | 1 × base | 2 × base | 3 × base | 5 × base | Immediate full surrenders |
|---|---|---|---|---|---|---|---|
| TSY + 0 | 85 072 | 87 723 | 89 410 | 90 936 | 91 091 | 89 909 | 78 318 |
| TSY + 50 | 73 963 | 78 461 | 81 588 | 85 165 | 86 673 | 87 098 | 78 286 |
| TSY + 100 | 63 841 | 69 960 | 74 361 | 79 774 | 82 509 | 84 413 | 78 255 |
| Break-even spread | 5 | 20 | 35 | 61 | 82 | 108 | N/A |

*Summary*

The series of tests in this section illustrates the potential ranges of values that could be placed on a block of SPDA or UL liabilities. The discount spread to Treasuries is clearly a key parameter in this valuation process. Additionally, the ability to drop the credited rate to the guaranteed rate would appear to lower the liability value considerably; yet taking credit for such action before it actually occurs would not seem to be representative of the fair value of future liability flows, given current expectations and the going concern nature of the enterprise.

The uncertainty of policyholder surrenders also is a concern, because the worst case scenario does result in considerably higher liability value than the expected case. UL offers additional challenges due to uncertain future premiums and expected mortality profits. Using best guess assumptions would appear to be justifiable in each case, although the premium flows are probably subject to large fluctuations.

Except for the discount spread, any attempt to standardize these assumptions would probably defeat the objective of establishing a 'fair value'. Assumptions regarding premiums, mortality profits, credited rates, and surrender behaviors would have to take into account product and company specifics in order to capture fair value. The range of results included herein suggests that to do otherwise would result in values better characterized as 'arbitrary' rather than 'fair'.

Selecting the discount spread is pivotal; other than the well defined cost of funds spread, the tests above shed little light on what spread might be appropriate (see Appendix C for more discussion). Making and justifying that selection will require considerations beyond the analysis and results presented immediately above.

## Strengths and weaknesses

This method for determining the fair value of liabilities has both strengths and weaknesses, a few of which are listed below.

*Strengths*
1. The method is theoretically sound. It explicitly addresses insurance cash flows including the dynamics associated with embedded options.
2. The method is comprehensive. Given its focus upon cash flow, it is more readily portable among differing liabilities than one that would need to address the intricacies of various reserving methodologies from one line of business to another.
3. Fair valuation of liabilities can be developed independently of the underlying asset portfolio. This is also a controversial attribute of the methodology.
4. Fair valuation is directly linked to market conditions and therefore is potentially volatile. This can be viewed as either a strength or weakness depending upon one's perspective. To the extent that fair valuation of liabilities is intended to more accurately depict the financial position of a company, it is probably a strength. To the extent that one's objective is to observe a smooth progression of value (eliminating the 'noise'), it is probably a weakness.
5. The method is consistent with that used in the capital markets for other financial instruments and for insurance company GICs traded in the secondary market.

*Weaknesses*
1. The method is complex and somewhat unfamiliar to many industry practitioners. It requires strong technical knowledge and substantial computational effort. It may be impractical for smaller companies to implement.
2. The method is heavily dependent upon option adjusted spread. Given that there is no 'single' right answer for secondary market liabilities, a variety of results could be produced.

3. Fair valuation of liabilities can be developed independently of the underlying asset portfolio. This is a controversial attribute of the methodology.
4. Fair valuation is directly linked to market conditions and therefore is potentially volatile. This can be viewed as either a strength or weakness depending upon one's perspective. To the extent that fair valuation of liabilities is intended to more accurately depict the financial position of a company, it is probably a strength. To the extent that one's objective is to observe a smooth progression of value (eliminating the 'noise"), it is probably a weakness.
5. The method ignores statutory reserves and required surplus.

APPRAISAL METHOD

*Definition of method*

This approach to calculating the fair value of liabilities was referred to earlier as the 'deductive approach' and is based on the practice typically used by actuaries in placing an economic value on a segment of business. This practice will be referred throughout this section as actuarial appraisal with the resulting value referred to as appraisal value. The appraisal value often provides the basic component of market value; the value for which a business can be bought or sold in an active marketplace between willing buyers and sellers. The actual ultimate sales/purchase price differs from the appraisal value by a number of factors including differences in the buyer's and seller's desired rates of return, expense levels, and tax situations.

Actuarial appraisal is defined in Actuarial Standard of Practice No. 19[2] as: "An assessment of value based on projections of expected future earnings, discounted to present value at appropriate risk-adjusted rates of return." Expected future earnings are determined by projecting asset and liability cash flows. Asset cash flow assumptions include interest and scheduled maturities payments, unscheduled prepayments such as bond calls and mortgage prepayments, expected default levels and reinvestment assumptions. Liability cash flow assumptions are made for premium and deposit collections, benefit claim costs, policyholder persistency and expenses. In addition, actuarial appraisals also include assumptions for statutory capital requirements, federal income taxes, and other expected cash flows. A basic feature of this method is that the appraisal value treats the assets and liabilities as a 'bundled' package. Buyers of insurance companies and blocks of business are not only assuming the liabilities of the seller but normally assume a group of assets associated with

---
[2] The Actuarial Standards Board (ASB) has promulgated a set of professional standards designated as Actuarial Standards of Practice. These standards provide guidance on how to apply fundamental concepts and methodological principles in actuarial practice. According to the American Academy of Actuaries Code of Professional Conduct Precept 4; "An actuary shall ensure that professional services performed by or under the direction of the actuary meet applicable practice standards."

those liabilities. Whereas other methodologies for calculating the fair value of liabilities, discussed in other sections of this document, may treat insurance company assets and liabilities as separate and independent financial instruments, this methodology recognizes the interdependence of asset and liability cash flows. Thus, the actuarial appraisal method of calculating the fair value of liabilities focuses on the appraisal value and treats the fair value of liabilities as a residual amount. The fair value of liabilities is calculated by subtracting appraisal value from the fair value of assets for the segment of business being evaluated.

*Discussion of method*

We will begin with an illustration of the method. This will be based on the hypothetical SPDA product described in section 1. The first illustration employs some simplified assumptions (e.g. level interest rate scenario, and no capital requirements in excess of statutory capital needs). From there we will add variables to demonstrate sensitivity to assumptions.

*Definitions*
Define

$$FVL = FVA - AV$$

where:

$AV$ = appraisal value

$FVA$ = fair value of assets

$FVL$ = fair value of liabilities

FVA can be determined by either accessing widely-available secondary market data or, for assets which are not actively traded in a secondary market, discounted cash flow or other established techniques can be used. As discussed below, the expected cash flows used in determining market yields will be used in calculating AV.[3]

Generally speaking, AV is defined as the discounted value at a risk rate of return of the following broad classes of financial statement line items:
- The sum of
  premiums;
  investment income; and
  other miscellaneous income;
- Less the sum of:
  benefits;
  commissions and expenses;

---

[3] Actuarial appraisals of entire companies usually use statutory book values and book yields in lieu of market values and market yields.

increases in statutory reserves;
increases in other capital requirements;
federal income taxes; and
other miscellaneous expenses.

It is important to note that since future investment income is often a significant element of AV market values and market yields on assets may significantly affect AV.

In developing appraisal values, multiple interest scenarios and dynamic behavioral functions (discussed in section 1 and appendices B and D) are typically employed to ensure proper valuation of embedded options. In the examples that follow, however, we have taken a simplified approach and performed illustrative calculations under only a few deterministic scenarios. Furthermore, we have also ignored taxes.

*Base case*

An important factor in determining AV is the risk rate of return, commonly referred to as the discount rate. The discount rate used for actuarial appraisals incorporates a margin over the risk-free rate to compensate the insurer for the risk inherent in the block of business being valued. Most often the discount rate takes the form of a single interest rate and will recognize the cost of capital of the buyer or seller since the discount rate must exceed the insurer's cost of capital in order to increase the economic value of the company. The discount rate can vary for different blocks of business since the level of risk will vary by type of product or coverage.

For the base case, a discount rate of 10% will be assumed. We will begin with $100 000 000 of newly issued SPDA premium and $93 700 000 of assets backing statutory liabilities. The product is the same one illustrated in the previous section. The computations are shown below.

| *Present values ($000) (discount rate 10%)* | |
|---|---|
| FVA | 100 000 |
| AV | 3 911 |
| FVL | 96 089 |

Initially, one might be alarmed that the FVL exceeds the statutory liabilities. It is important to realize, however, that commission and other policy expenses are provided for in the FVL (and not in the statutory liabilities). If we were to view the figures immediately after the payment of commission, both the FVA and the FVL would reduce by $6 million.

*Impact on AV of changes in discount rate*

It is informative to look at the impact of the discount rate on this newly issued block of liabilities. To the extent that the discount rate used in calculating the actuarial AV is the same as that used in pricing the business segment, no additional value will be created at issuance of the contract. However, if the discount rate is less/greater than the implied pricing interest rate, a gain/loss of value at issue will result.

The following table shows the effect of increasing the discount rate to 14%.

|  | *Present values ($000)* | |
|---|---|---|
|  | *Discount rate* | |
|  | 10% | 14% |
| FVA | 100 000 | 100 000 |
| AV | 3911 | 2877 |
| FVL | 96 089 | 97 123 |

The hypothetical SPDA is priced to return in excess of 14% ignoring the cost of required surplus and multiple scenario valuation of embedded options. Thus, increasing the discount rate from 10% to 14% reduces appraisal value, but keeps the FVL below the single premium.

*Impact on AV of changes in market interest rates*
The AV of an insurance company will normally be affected by changes in interest rates. As interest rates rise, both the fair value of assets and liabilities fall. Likewise, as interest rates fall, the fair value of assets and liabilities rise. The relative degree to which a rise or fall in interest rates impacts appraisal value depends on the durations or relative timings of the expected asset and liability cash flows.

Suppose that in an environment where liabilities are held at fair value, expected asset cash flows are invested to have exactly the same timing as expected liability cash flows; i.e. assets and liabilities are precisely matched. Then as interest rates rise or fall, the appraisal value will change with the change in fair value of assets; i.e., each will change proportionately by an equal amount. However, a precise matching of assets and liabilities is rarely achieved and a change in interest rates will normally affect AV.

Assume that expected asset cash flows are invested longer than expected liability cash flows. A fall in interest rates will result in an increase in AV since the resulting increase in the fair value of assets will only be partially offset by a rise in the fair value of liabilities. Likewise, a rise in interest rates will result in a greater fall in the fair value of assets than in the fair value of liabilities and the result will be a net reduction in AV. When expected asset cash flows are invested shorter than expected liability cash flows, the effects on appraisal value are reversed.

The following table illustrates the impact on the fair value of liabilities under three deterministic scenarios. The base case assumes a level interest rate environment. The rising interest rate scenario approximates interest rates instantaneously rising 1.00% whereas the falling interest scenario approximates rates instantaneously falling 1.00%.

|  | Present values ($000) | | |
|---|---|---|---|
|  | | Discount Rate 10% | |
|  | Level | Rising | Falling |
| FVA | 100 000 | 95 476 | 104 794 |
| AV | 3911 | 1654 | 4343 |
| FVL | 96 089 | 93 822 | 100 451 |

As can be seen, a rising interest rate scenario results in a decrease in FVL of $2 267 000 whereas falling interest rates increase FVL by $4 362 000. This implies that asset cash flows are invested longer than liability cash flows.

*Statutory capital requirements included in actuarial appraisals*
Statutory reserve requirements are normally included in the calculation of the actuarial appraisal of insurance companies since statutory earnings affect the availability of dividends to owners. Statutory reserves are required by law to equal or exceed the cash value available to the policyholder and, in many cases, the statutory reserve is equal to or slightly exceeds the policyholder cash value. In addition to statutory reserve requirements, minimum capital and surplus requirements are often included in the determination of actuarial appraisal value. These capital requirements represent the minimum level of additional surplus which is required to support the business in force recognizing factors such as asset default risk, asset/liability mismatch risk and liability mispricing risk. Beyond regulatory requirements, an insurer may choose to hold additional capital to meet its own assessment of the risks of its business or that of rating agencies.

The example below uses a 10% discount rate and compares the base case of no required surplus to the cases with required surplus (RS) equal to 4% and 5% of statutory reserves.

|  | Present values ($000) | | |
|---|---|---|---|
|  | NO RS | 4% RS | 5% RS |
| FVA | 100 000 | 100 000 | 100 000 |
| AV | 3911 | 2734 | 2438 |
| FVL | 96 089 | 97 266 | 97 562 |

As shown above, for new issues, AV decreases as the required surplus level is increased. Accordingly, FVL increases to reflect the cost of additional capital. In reality, trade offs would occur in credited rate and discount rate to reflect the additional capital. Therefore, this area should undergo further study.

*Reasons for interlocking asset and liability assumptions*

Actuarial appraisals normally recognize the relationship between assumptions for assets and liabilities. Among other things, the amount of interest credited to the interest sensitive liabilities should depend upon the earnings rates of the corresponding assets purchased (at least in the long run). The earnings on underlying assets will depend upon the economic environment when they were purchased, options embedded in the securities, and the future economic environment. The level of policyholder crediting rate, relative to new money rates, will in turn affect the amount of policy lapsation which will occur (which affects earnings discounted in an appraisal). Accordingly, the fair value of liabilities will not only be affected by the future outlook of interest rates but also by where interest rates have been.

*Strengths and weaknesses*

This method for determining the fair value of liabilities has both strengths and weaknesses, a few of which are listed below.

*Strengths*
1. Actuarial appraisals are based upon well-established actuarial techniques.
2. The appraisal method provides a linkage to actuarial pricing methodology and profit measures.
3. The method can recognize the cost of capital.
4. It is theoretically consistent with the perspective that the insurance company is an asset and that the GAAP financial statement value of equity should approximate the fair value of that asset.
5. Under current literature, this method would be expected to produce only a minimal adjustment to GAAP financial statements in a purchase situation in order to true-up appraisal value to actual purchase price.
6. It creates a linking between the left and right sides of the balance sheet and thereby ensures consistency in fair value adjustments.

*Weaknesses*
1. There is not a definitive method to choose discount rate.
2. The sensitivity of the relationship between discount rate and assumed pricing return may create inconsistencies between companies.
3. There is a dependency of FVL on fair value of supporting assets.
4. Resulting values depend on statutorily determined values (reserves, required surplus, etc.) which are subject to difference by jurisdiction and in application (for example, permitted practices or a lack of a comprehensive accounting basis).

## Interest Maintenance Reserve Method

### Definition of method

Identify those investments which support long-term liabilities. For those assets, establish the difference between the statement value of the assets and the amortized cost as an offsetting liability or asset. Thus, for these investments, any unrealized gain or loss would not be recognized in equity. For realized gains and losses on investments supporting long-term liabilities, establish a liability or asset for the amount of gain or loss and amortize it over the life of the investment sold. Realized and unrealized gains and losses attributable to credit changes rather than interest rate changes would be recognized immediately. No offsetting liabilities or assets would be established.

### Discussion of method

This methodology applies to fixed income invested assets that support long-term liabilities in an insurance company. If the market value of such an investment increases as a result of decreases in interest rates, and if the investment is sold, a gain would be realized. Because of the long-term liabilities, it is necessary that proceeds from the sale must be reinvested to produce income to continue to support the liabilities. Because market interest rates are lower than the coupon on the investment sold, the investment income on the new investment will be less than on the old, assuming comparable credit and maturity for the new investment. In fact, the present value of the reduced future income will equal the gain on the sale of the investment, after adjustment for the differences in terms of the old and new investments. Thus, the investment transaction has little, if any, effect on the economic value of the entity.

Under existing accounting, the sale would produce a gain which would be currently recognized in net income. Future net income would be reduced by amounts which have a present value equal to the gain on the investment sold. In order to bring the accounting into accord with the economic substance of the transaction and to avoid 'front-ending' future net income, this proposal would establish a liability equal to the amount of the gain on sale. This liability would be amortized into future income over the life of the investment sold.

If interest rates increase, the value of an investment decreases, and if the investment is sold at a loss, the inverse applies. An asset is established equal to the amount of the loss, and the asset is charged to income over the life of the investment sold. Similar considerations apply if investments are not sold but are carried in financial statements at market values. If the investments appreciate in value, that additional value would be offset by future reductions in value. If the investment is held to maturity, the unrealized gain on the investment would ultimately be charged back against equity as the security is ultimately matured for its face value. If the investment is sold, the unrealized gain would become a realized gain and an offsetting liability would be established as described earlier. Accordingly, when investments which support long-term liabilities are valued at market, the unrealized gain or loss on such investments should be offset by a liability or asset equal to the amount of such unrealized gain or loss.

It may seem strange to some to allow the terms of an investment which the company no longer owns to determine the amortization of the liability or asset used to defer the gain or loss. A strong theoretical argument can be made that the appropriate amortization period is the duration of the liability. Alternatively, the duration of the new investment might be used. The problem with use of the duration of the liability is that such duration is often not objectively determinable, or can vary with market conditions. If asset and liability durations are appropriately matched, the two durations would be equal or approximately so. Use of the life of the investment sold rather than the duration of the liability essentially affects the timing of the gain or loss resulting from the mismatching of asset and liability durations. The problem with use of the duration of the new investment is that proceeds from investment sales are normally not directly placed in specific new investments. Rather, they may be held in cash or short term investments for a period of time, commingled with other new cash flows, and ultimately reinvested. Identification of the new investment would be difficult and arbitrary. Unless the company is changing its asset/liability management strategy, the duration of the new investment would be comparable to that of the investment sold, so the duration of the former would be a reasonable proxy for the duration of the new investment.

The method requires identification of those investments supporting 'long-term liabilities', thereby requiring a definition of 'long-term'. The logic underlying the method suggests that the key distinction would be whether the proceeds from a sale of investment would need to be reinvested to support the obligations represented by the liabilities. This suggests that liabilities longer than one or two years should be considered 'long'. For practical reasons, determination of whether liabilities are 'long' should be made based on the average life of categories of liabilities rather than a detailed separation of those parts of the liabilities which are 'long' or 'short'. Perhaps it would be sensible to have a rule such as one stipulating that a category of similar liabilities would be considered 'long' if the average life of the category exceeds 3 years. Such a rule suffers from arbitrariness. However, arbitrary classification of items as 'long' or 'short' term are not unknown in accounting theory. Identification of those investments which support long-term liabilities would be facilitated by appropriate segmentation of investments. Where that is not done, or where asset segmentation classes support both long term liabilities and other liabilities or surplus, proration of investments would be satisfactory. When market values of investments are below cost, and assets are established to offset the difference between the carrying value and cost, future income should be tested to assure that the asset is recoverable.

## Strengths and weaknesses

This method for determining the fair value of liabilities has both strengths and weaknesses, a few of which are listed below:

*Strengths*
1. The method does not require that investments be carried at market, but rather prescribes appropriate accounting when investments are carried at market. Thus it applies equally to companies with different approaches to classification of investments as 'held to maturity' or otherwise.
2. The methods can be applied to all financial institutions, with significant effect only for those with substantial long-term liabilities.
3. For assets supporting long-term liabilities, the proposed method eliminates the problem of 'gains trading'.
4. The method eliminates the need to make distinctions among investments based on 'management intent'. Such distinctions are arbitrary, somewhat illogical, and lead to problems of comparability.
5. The method eliminates the need to avoid including unrealized gains and losses in net income.
6. The method is consistent with the manner in which many companies manage this business. Financial statements should reflect management practices.

*Weaknesses*
1. The method does not affect the valuation of liabilities but rather the valuation of assets.
2. The method does not move in the direction of a market valued balance sheet.
3. Fails to address the true economics of the liabilities.

## MARKET YIELD ADJUSTMENT METHOD

### Definition of method

Fair value of liabilities is defined as current GAAP reserves adjusted to reflect differences among the market and book yields of underlying assets and the historic GAAP valuation interest rate. The approach begins with the current GAAP reserves and deferred acquisition costs. The fair value of the liabilities is defined as the current GAAP liabilities adjusted to reflect the difference between book yield rates and market yield rates on the portfolio of assets backing the liabilities. One of the tenets of this method is that the fair value of the liabilities is equal to the present value of a future stream of cash flows discounted at the market yield rate underlying the portfolio of assets backing the liabilities.

Using the following notation:

$L(t)$ = Fair value of the liabilities

$R(t)$ = Current GAAP liabilities

$i$   = Book yield rate on assets backing the liabilities

$i'$  = Market yield rate on assets backing the liabilities

$v$  = Valuation rate used in determining current GAAP liabilities

If the current liability $R(t)$ is equal to the present value, discounted at the valuation rate $v$, of future benefits less future net premiums, this method results in the following formula for the fair value of the liabilities:

$$L(t) = R(t) + \{(i' - i)/(i' - v)\} \times [R'(t) - R(t)]$$

where $R'(t)$ is calculated by discounting at $i'$ rather than $v$ in the formula for $R(t)$.

### Discussion of method

This method assumes that reserves calculated under current GAAP produce the accurate reserve when the assets backing the liabilities are earning the book yield rates. While this method may be simpler to implement than other methods, it maintains any shortcomings of the current GAAP liability systems.

The change in the fair value of assets backing the policy liabilities is somewhat offset by the change in the value of the policy liabilities. Generally, the offset will not be exact unless the portfolio is constructed so that the asset cash flows in each year $t$ are equal to $(i - v) \times R(t) + c(t)$, where $c(t)$ is the projected benefit payments less net premiums under the current GAAP reserves.

Another issue to consider is how the changes in value flow through the GAAP statement. Under SFAS 115, some of the changes in asset market values flow through income and others flow through equity. Distortions will occur if the changes in liability values do not flow through the statement in the same way as the changes in the asset values. The method requires an allocation of assets to liability groups. The allocation could be a segmentation of the asset portfolio or a prorata share of a larger portfolio. This issue may have been addressed already for cash flow testing or other statutory or GAAP purposes.

Under this methodology, the value of a block of liabilities is dependent on the portfolio of assets backing those liabilities and is affected by the duration and quality of the asset portfolio. As such, the value of two comparable blocks of liabilities could differ because of differences in the asset portfolios backing those liabilities. For certain SFAS 97 liabilities, such as universal life, where the current GAAP reserve is equal to the account value, the application of the formula given above will require that the account value be restated as the present value of future benefits less net premiums.

### Strengths and weaknesses

This method for determining the fair value of liabilities has both strengths and weaknesses, a few of which are listed below.

66   D.C. Doll et al.

*Strengths*
1. Relatively simple to implement.
2. Implementation of methods may result in little net effect on GAAP earnings and equity, if assets and liabilities are fairly well matched.
3. Strong analogies exist with other non-insurance liabilities.

*Weaknesses*
1. Dependency on a specific asset portfolio.
2. Fails to address the true economics of the liabilities.

### MARKET TO BOOK ADJUSTMENT METHOD

#### Definition of method

Fair value of liabilities is defined as current GAAP reserves times the ratio of the market value to book value of the asset portfolio backing the liabilities. The approach begins with the current GAAP reserves and deferred acquisition costs. The fair value of the liabilities is defined as the current GAAP liabilities adjusted to reflect the market value of the portfolio of assets backing the liabilities. This method is based on the assertion that current GAAP liabilities have been deemed to be adequate as a result of cash flow testing or other analysis. Therefore, if the cash flows from a block of assets are adequate to fund the liability cash flows, the same block of assets are adequate when the reporting basis is changed from book value to market value.
Using the following notation:

$L(t)$ = Fair value of the liabilities

$R(t)$ = Current GAAP liabilities

$BV(t)$ = Book value of the assets backing the liabilities

$MV(t)$ = Market value of the assets backing the liabilities

The fair value of the liabilities is:

$$L(t) = R(t) \times [MV(t)/BV(t)]$$

This method assumes that reserves calculated under current GAAP produce the accurate reserve when the assets backing the liabilities are earning the book yield rates. While this method may be simpler to implement than other methods, it maintains any shortcomings of the current GAAP liability systems. The change in the fair value of assets backing the policy liabilities is offset by the change in the value of the policy liabilities. Under this method, the offset is exact and the only change in equity is the change in the value of the assets that are not backing policy liabilities.

Another issue to consider is how the changes in value flow through the GAAP statement. Under SFAS 115, some of the changes in asset market values flow through income and others flow through equity. Distortions will occur if the changes in liability values do not flow through the statement in the same way as the changes in the asset values.

The method requires an allocation of assets to liability groups. The allocation could be a segmentation of the asset portfolio or a prorata share of a larger portfolio. This issue may have been addressed already for cash flow testing or other statutory or GAAP purposes. Under this method, the value of a block of liabilities is dependent on the portfolio of assets backing those liabilities and affected by the duration and quality of the asset portfolios backing those liabilities.

### Strengths and weaknesses

This method for determining the fair value of liabilities has both strengths and weaknesses, a few of which are listed below.

*Strengths*
1. Simple to implement.
2. Implementation of methods may result in little or no net effect on GAAP earnings and equity.

*Weaknesses*
1. Dependency on specific asset portfolio.
2. May be viewed as unduly simplistic.
3. Not accurate if assets and liabilities are mismatched.
4. Fails to address the true economics of the liabilities.

## DAC OFFSET METHOD

### Definition of method

Under this methodology, any and all unrealized gains and losses countable in the GAAP balance sheet are taken into account in determining expected gross profits (EGP) or expected gross margins (EGM) to the extent that such invested assets are in support of SFAS 97 or SFAS 120 net GAAP liabilities (NGL). This has the effect of causing greater amortization of the deferred acquisition cost asset (DAC) in periods of large unrealized gains, and lesser amortization in periods of large unrealized losses, on lines of business where DAC amortizes in relation to such EGPs or EGMs.

### Discussion of method

Let us assume for purposes of this discussion that all unrealized gains and losses are interest-related, rather than credit-related, and that unearned revenues generated from excess initial front end loads are considered as negative DAC values from a mathematical perspective. The DAC offset method tends to value a bundle of both assets and liabilities. Additionally, and more importantly, it generally tends to cause net GAAP liabilities to move directionally in the same manner as they would under changes in the interest rate environment. The method has the desirable properties of being of no effect on current GAAP accounting results when the yield curve has not changed, causing a lower NGL in a time of unrealized losses, and a higher NGL in time of unrealized gains. While it generally is directionally consistent with market value movements of liabilities, it does not generally reflect an accurate adjustment of the liability to market value itself. This is easily shown by the fact that the DAC itself can range from zero to the full amount recoverable from the EGP or EGM stream. Even so, it is possible to define a scenario where a fair value of the NGL can arguably be said to be reflected under the DAC offset method. The following reflects such a scenario.

Let us assume, under a yield curve that is consistent over time, that the investment earnings rate equals the DAC amortization rate. Further assume that all unrealized gains and losses are interest-related, and will reverse by the end of the DAC amortization period. If all other assumptions emerge as expected, the DAC at any point of time will be exactly equal to the present value of future EGP values less future deferrable expenses. Thus the benefit reserve held at book value, less the DAC, so adjusted, reflects a gross premium valuation, which is certainly one arguable candidate for a fair value of the net GAAP liability. Following this line of reasoning, to the extent that positive future net profits are expected to emerge (i.e. to the extent that DAC is currently below the recoverable maximum), the NGL is greater than the gross premium valuation and the closeness of this approach to fair market value begins to break down.

The constraints normally employed on such a methodology when applied in GAAP accounting include recoverability testing and forcing of negative gross profits to zero. The appropriateness of such constraints is questionable.

*Strengths and weaknesses*

This method for determining the fair value of liabilities has both strengths and weaknesses, a few of which are listed below.

*Strengths*
1. Such a secondary DAC is reasonably straightforward to calculate. It can be calculated in a parallel manner to the existing 'primary DAC' used for GAAP earnings, and methods of approximation appear to be workable. It can be shown, for example, that under certain assumptions the difference between those two amounts is equal to the accumulated unrealized gains and losses, multiplied by the weighted average DAC amortization%age.
2. It does not require explicit recalculation of current liabilities.

*Weaknesses*
1. The assumptions required to make it reflect an arguable market value are quite restrictive. Note in the above discussion section the effects that deviations from the 'perfect' assumptions have on such approximation. Such arguable market value, moreover, is just that. Possibly the strongest argument against the above gross premium valuation approach is the fact that it does not discount future profits at a risk rate of return.
2. It may not be appropriate under GAAP accounting to view the NGL as the element on which to make the 'fair value of liability' determination, as is being done under this approach. The gross benefit reserve may be the more appropriate candidate for adjustment to market value.
3. This approach would currently apply narrowly to only a portion of the liabilities which life insurance companies issue or have in force.
4. Fails to address the true economics of the liabilities.

INDEXED VALUATION OF INSURANCE LIABILITIES METHOD

*Definition of method*

This method is similar to a net premium valuation (NPV), i.e. present value of future benefits and expenses less present value of future net premiums, under best estimate assumptions, which is similar in concept to traditional GAAP for long-duration life insurance products but dynamically unlocked. One additional departure from the NPV approach is that the interest rate used for discounting would be related to an external index.

*Discussion of method*

Actuarial valuation methods are commonly used to determine the value of long term life insurance and annuity liabilities for various purposes. It is suggested that, with minor modification, actuarial valuation methods may be used to determine fair value of long term life insurance and annuity liabilities.

The approach described herein could be broadly grouped with appraisal methods. It bears some resemblance to appraisal methods in that they both involve projection of liability cash flows using assumptions as to future behavior of a book of insurance contracts. Typically, appraisal methods call for a range of realistic projection assumptions and a risk rate of interest is used in determining the present value of future profits. However, appraisal methods differ from liability valuation methods in two ways. First, appraisals include projections of not only liability cash flows but also asset cash flows. Second, appraisals attempt to measure future profits that will emerge from the book of contracts, given the specific assets and liabilities supporting the business. Thus appraisals are a measure of equity. Pure appraisal methods therefore require the conversion of the value of equity into separate components for assets and liabilities.

In this regard the value of liabilities is dependent on the value of assets, either directly, or indirectly due to the use of assumed investment income that will arise from the portfolio of assets supporting the liability. In contrast, the indexed valuation method determines the value of liabilities directly, and independent of supporting assets. The value of the liability is defined as the excess of the present value of future costs over the present value of future premiums. The definitions of costs and premiums, as well as the interest rate used for discounting, vary with the purpose of the valuation. For example, the liability, or reserve used in reporting to statutory authorities defines costs as death and endowment benefits. Premiums are defined as the net premium for such benefits, determined at issue. The rate of interest to be used for discounting is prescribed by law. Other assumptions used in the projection are essentially limited to mortality and morbidity rates, which are also prescribed by law.

As a second example, the liability currently determined for GAAP financial reporting purposes for traditional long duration life product follows similar principles. The definition of costs includes surrender benefits and maintenance expenses in addition to death and endowment benefits. Premiums are defined as the net premium for such costs, determined at issue. Assumptions to be used for projection and discounting are based on realistic expectations and the experience of the company. The interest rate used for discounting is typically based on company experience.

It is suggested that the fair value of liabilities under this approach be determined using indexed liability valuation methods based on definitions that follow.

- Costs are defined as death, endowment and surrender benefits plus future administrative expenses. For long duration accident and health contracts, realistic morbidity assumptions are also used.
- Premiums are defined as the net premiums expected to be received to cover such costs as determined at issue.
- Except for the interest rate, best estimate assumptions at the valuation date should be used in making the projections.
- The interest rate to be used for discounting future costs and future net premiums is defined by an external index at date of valuation. For example, the 5-year Treasury bond rate might be used for such an index.

The fair value of liabilities equals the excess of the present value of costs over the present value of net premiums based on costs, premiums and assumptions as defined above.

The approach is similar to that currently used in GAAP financial statements prepared in accordance with SFAS 60, with the exception of the objective, external index-based interest rate and the dynamic unlocking described herein.

The choice of an external index or measure for the interest rate to be used in discounting eliminates any dependence on the portfolio of assets held in support of the liabilities. The specific choice of index may need to be the subject of additional discussion. The approach described above is not currently followed in determining the value of liabilities for universal life, annuity and other fund accumulation insurance type products. Instead retrospective approaches are used. The liability equals accumulated deposit funds gross of surrender amounts. One school of thought is that the accumulated funds are equivalent to a demand deposit held on behalf of the policyholder. However, the policyholder's account value represents equity in the contract, which is intended to fund future benefits. Thus the appropriate liability may be viewed consistently with the view for traditional products, namely as the excess of the present value of future costs over the present value of future gross premiums. Hence the method recommended herein may be applied to such products. Future death, endowment and surrender benefits are able to be estimated, as are future gross premiums. Assumptions as to future experience may be selected, as they currently are for amortization of deferred acquisition costs in accordance with SFAS 97. A similar external index for the interest rate to be used for discounting is appropriate. A floor on the fair value equal to the current surrender value of the contracts has certain appeal and should be considered.

This approach is general enough to apply to deferred acquisition costs. Similar assumptions as to future experience and a consistent interest rate should be applied in determining DAC, which is defined identically to reserve liabilities, that is, the excess of the present value of future costs over the present value of future net premiums to cover such costs, as determined at issue. If total net premiums for all costs exceed the gross premium, a premium deficiency has arisen. Provision for the deficiency is made by constraining total net premiums to not exceed the gross premium.

*Strengths and weaknesses*

This method for determining the fair value of liabilities has both strengths and weaknesses, a few of which are listed below.

*Strengths*
1. Liability is independent of the underlying assets.
2. There is consistency with traditional GAAP accounting methodology.
3. It accomplishes in a rigorous manner what some of the more simplistic approaches referred to below purport to approximate.
4. It serves to promote comparability and consistency of interest assumption between companies.

*Weaknesses*
1. Administrative complexity of dynamic unlocking of multiple cells of business, especially if factor approaches are used.
2. Need to dynamically unlock deferred policy acquisition cost as well as benefit reserve, to keep the two items consistent with each other.
3. Fails to address the true economics of the liabilities.

## References

Black, F. and M. Scholes (1973). The pricing of options and corporate liabilities. *Journal of Political Economy*, **81**, 637–659.

Cox, J.C., S.A. Ross and M. Rubenstein (1979). Option pricing: a simplified approach. *Journal of Financial Economics*, **7**, 229–263.

Duffie, D. (1992). *Dynamic Asset Pricing Theory*. Princeton, NJ: Princeton University Press.

Ho, T.S.Y. and S.-B. Lee (1986). Term structure movements and pricing interest rate contingent claims. *Journal of Finance*, **41**, 1011–1029.

Ho, T.S.Y. (1992). Managing illiquid bonds and the linear path space. *Journal of Fixed Income*, June, 80–93.

Hull, J.S. (1993). *Options, Futures, and Other Derivative Securities* (2nd edn). Engelwood Cliffs, NJ: Prentice Hall.

Smith, C.W. (1976). Option pricing: a review. *Journal of Financial Economics*. **3**, 3–51.

Smith, C.W. (1990). Applications of option pricing analysis. In C.W. Smith (ed.), *The Modern Theory of Corporate Finance* (2nd edn). New York: North-Holland Publishing Co.

Tilley, J.A. (1992). An actuarial layman's guide to building stochastic interest rate generators. *Transactions of the Society of Actuaries*, **XLIV**, 509–564.

Tilley, J.A. (1993). Valuing American options in a path simulation model. *Transactions of the Society of Actuaries*, **XLV**, 499–550.

### Appendix A: option pricing theory

#### Introduction

In this Appendix we present an introduction to options terminology and applications, develop the lattice-based methodology to their pricing based on the idea of a replicating portfolio, and bridge the gap between this methodology and scenario-based approaches. We begin with a fairly complete presentation of the lattice approach as it applies to a European stock option, as this example allows the clearest exposition of the methodology. This approach is then generalized to American stock options, then to options on some fixed income instruments, both assets and liabilities. Numerical illustrations of this methodology are provided in these latter cases. Finally, we discuss the applicability of the lattice approach to assets and liabilities generally, and note an important criterion for a security to satisfy to allow such valuations: path independence. While many liabilities and some assets do not satisfy this criterion, fortunately there is an alternative methodology. Specifically, this alternative approach is 'path-based' or 'scenario-based' option pricing, which is introduced here and fully developed and illustrated in an earlier section.

While formulas are provided for completeness, an attempt has been made to describe each formula's interpretation in the text.

#### Basic definitions

An option on a financial contract grants the holder the right, but not the obligation, to either buy ('call' option) or sell ('put' option) a security (the 'underlying' security) at a price either fixed in dollar terms (the 'strike' price), or less commonly, fixed in relationship to some external index. The term of the option is the period of time over which the option's 'exercise' is allowed. 'European' options allow only a single exercise, at the end of the term or 'expiration' date, while 'American' options allow exercise anytime from a predefined date to the expiration date.

An option on a stock or stock index is usually European, granting the holder (the 'long' position) the right to buy or sell the underlying on a fixed date for a fixed price. A callable bond, on the other hand, is a 'package' which from the investor's perspective, is a long bond position and a 'short' call position, allowing the borrower to 'call' (i.e. prepay) the loan over a period of time (i.e. American design) at a price that is fixed in advance, yet typically variable over the call term. This price is usually defined as par plus a 'call premium', where the premium is related to the coupon rate. A given bond can have an embedded put option, which gives the investor the option to sell the bond back to (i.e. demand prepayment from) the borrower. Bonds can have both embedded puts and calls. An investor can also buy a call option on a bond, often called a warrant, which grants the right to buy a given bond at a given price sometime in the future.

## Insurance company examples

Insurance company liabilities are also rich in their option structure, which for the most part put the insurer in the role of the short position. Universal life (UL) and single or flexible premium deferred annuity (SPDA/FPDA) contracts grant the contract holders both put and call options. For example, a partial or full withdrawal of funds from the contract at 'book' value is an exercise of a put option, whereby the policyholder 'sells' back to the company part or all of its contractual obligations at a price indexed by the book value method of fund valuations. Similarly, such policyholders also have call options, or rights to buy additional amounts of the insurer's contractual benefits by contributing additional premiums or considerations. Minimum interest rate guarantees are formally equivalent to an embedded 'interest rate floor' contract, which in turn is equivalent to a series of call options for the contract holder.

One example of a liability in which an insurer holds a long option position is a so-called 'callable' guaranteed investment contract (GIC). A callable GIC is largely identical to a callable bond in structure, only here the insurer is the borrower rather than investor. Because the borrower on a callable bond is long the option, so too is an insurer in this case. Subtle differences between callable GICs and bonds are that GICs can be coupon bearing (simple-interest GICs) or not (compound GICs), and often there is no call premium (i.e. callable at book).

## Option election efficiency

While an option is a right, but not an obligation, option pricing theory often treats options as obligations. That is, it is assumed that the long position will be 100% 'efficient' in exercising their right, which is to say that the long will always elect when it is most financially advantageous to do so, and will never elect when it is financially disadvantageous. Stock options and embedded call options in bonds are typically treated this way because in all such cases, the anticipated level of sophistication of the long position and experience demand this assumption. However, many counter-examples to the 100% efficiency rule exist, even for sophisticated investors/borrowers. For example, residential and commercial mortgage loans may be called, independent of the financial merits, simply because the property has been sold and the mortgage note is not assignable. Consequently, pools of such mortgages (mortgage-backed securities, commercial mortgage pools) are usually priced at far less than 100% efficiency. Similarly, though less frequently, a bond may be called even if somewhat 'out of the money' because the corporation is restructuring or consolidating its debt.

Conversely, many mortgages are far 'in the money' but not called because the borrower may be unsophisticated, or the value of the property and/or financial status of the borrower has deteriorated sufficiently to preclude refinancing. Finally, election of options on insurance company liabilities is also visibly less than 100% efficient. Again, contract holder sophistication can be a cause, as can change in insurability or even a strong agent/contract holder relationship.

*Considerations in option pricing*

Because options are 'contingent claims,' which is to say that their future value is currently unknown and contingent on future events, the problem of 'pricing' is a highly non-trivial one. In contrast, while the pricing of 'yearly renewable term' also involves contingencies, its pricing is simplified by the 'law of large numbers' which assures us that if properly underwritten, a large pool of similar risks should have fairly predictable contingency costs, even though any given individual's cost in the pool is entirely unpredictable.

In the financial markets, no such paradigm exists. While holding options on many stocks eliminates 'specific' or 'diversifiable' risk, one is ultimately left with an option on a market index, the future behavior of which is entirely unknown. Similarly, holding many callable bonds barely decreases the contingency risk of holding only one, because here 'contagion' risk is significant. That is, one logically expects that all calls will be elected in relatively similar conditions, and no spread of risk will occur. Even in pools, such as a MBS or a pool of UL contracts, only specific risk is eliminated, that is, the risk of one mortgage or one contract holder electing. However, the non-diversifiable risk in such pool is significant because unlike mortality, we don't really know to what 'average experience' the pool should converge. Why? Because such pools are typically priced at far less than 100% efficiency, so the major non-diversifiable risk is that the efficiency of the pool will increase.

One approach to contingent claim pricing is implied by the von Neumann–Morgenstern theorem, which says that subject to consistency assumptions on an investor's preferences, every investor will value a lottery (i.e. contingent claim) so as to maximize the expected utility of the potential net payouts. In theory then, we need a probability distribution of contingent benefits for the expectation, a discount rate for the present value, and a utility function to reflect the investor's level of risk aversion. Even in cases where the probability distribution of contingent claims and the discount rate is feasible to model (stock options), how do we estimate the market's utility function? Consequently, how do we determine even the theoretically fair market price for a simple European put on the S&P 500? The power of the von Neumann–Morgenstern theorem is in its generality and conceptual elegance, one weakness is in its application. The power of this next approach is in its stark simplicity. It is so simple, in fact, that its expected weakness is that it is too simple to be made to work.

### The replicating portfolio

The idea here is to price a complex instrument (an option, say) by decomposing it into a 'replicating portfolio' of simple instruments, the prices of which are known, where this replicating portfolio exactly reproduces (replicates) the behavior of the more complex instrument. If this decomposition can be accomplished (and there is no reason to believe that it can), the option pricing problem will be solved. Why? Because if two financial instruments behave identically in all circumstances, they must be priced identically. Why? Because if two such instruments had different prices initially, an investor could buy the cheap and sell the dear, creating an instantaneous profit with no future risk (recall, the two instruments behave identically), creating a 'risk-free arbitrage'. Such a situation could only exist temporarily since all investors would continue to 'arbitrage' this mispricing until the profit was gone, and hence the two prices would agreed to within trading costs. Hence, based on a simple model of market trading behavior, we derive the so-called 'law of one price', and conclude that the price of the option will equal the price of the replicating portfolio, which by assumption is known.

The magic of the replicating portfolio argument is that it can be made to work even in cases where the option is complex. Historically, the Black–Scholes model for pricing European puts and calls on a stock was the landmark paper that implemented this idea, but it was based on a stochastic calculus argument which was transparent to few for some time. A number of years later, Cox-Ross-Rubenstein developed a 'discretization' of the model, in which the replicating portfolio argument was made clear to all, and further proved that as the discrete time steps got finer and finer, their simple lattice-based formula converged to that of Black–Scholes.

### The Cox–Ross–Rubenstein-set up: European options

Following the Cox–Ross–Rubinstein approach, consider a one-period European call option on a stock currently worth 50, with a strike price of 60. We also assume that the stock price is 'binomial' so at the end of the period it will be in only one of two states, the up-state with value 75, and the down-state with value 25. This option can then be replicated with a portfolio of 'underlying' stock and a risk-free zero coupon bond as follows. If we invest $S in the stock, and $R in the bond, assumed to earn 4%, the following values are produced:

|            | Portfolio      | Option value |
|------------|----------------|--------------|
| Up-state   | $1.5S + 1.04R$ | 15           |
| Down-state | $0.5S + 1.04R$ | 0            |

As we have two equations in two unknowns, we can easily obtain:

$S = 15.00$

$R = (7.21)$,

which implies that we need to invest $15 in stock (buying 30% of one share), and borrow $7.21 at the risk-free rate. The value of this portfolio and the price of the call option is hence $7.79, which equals the out-of-pocket cost to build the replicating portfolio.

In the general binomial model we have:

|            | Portfolio  | Option value |
|------------|------------|--------------|
| Up-state   | $uS + rR$  | $O^u$        |
| Down-state | $dS + rR$  | $O^d$        |

and the value of the call-option becomes:

$$C = \frac{pO^u + (1-p)O^d}{r}, \qquad (1)$$

where $r$ is one plus the risk free rate, and $u(d)$ is one plus the up(down)-state stock return. That is, the call option in (1) is equal to an 'expected present value' (EPV) of its payoffs $O^u$ and $O^d$, where the up-state 'probability' $p$ is given by:

$$p = \frac{r-d}{u-d}. \qquad (2)$$

The value of $p$ is indeed a probability, i.e. $0 < p < 1$, because an arbitrage argument demands that $d < r < u$. That is, it must be the case that the risk free rate is between the up and down state returns of the risky investment.

It should be noted that the expected present value formula for $C$ in (1) is quite different from typical expected present value formulas in various actuarial applications because here, $p$ has nothing at all to do with the true probability of the 'up-state', since that probability has not even entered our argument. The probability $p$ does have an interpretation, however, as the 'risk-neutral' probability, or, the probability of an up-state in a risk-neutral world.

To see this, first note that $p$ is the unique implied probability of an up-state so that the current stock price equals the expected present value of its future prices:

$$S = [p(uS) + (1-p)(dS)]/r. \tag{3}$$

This is equivalent to noting that $p$ is the unique implied probability of an up-state so that the expected return on the stock equals the risk-free rate:

$$r = pu + (1-p)d. \tag{4}$$

Now in a risk-neutral world, all assets are priced by the EPV method to earn the same return, which must therefore equal the return on a risk-free bond or $r$. In particular, $S$ will be priced to earn $r$. Hence, $p$ is the implied probability of an up-state in a risk-neutral world.

In summary, while we clearly do not live in a risk-neutral world, the option pricing formula in (1), developed by the replicating portfolio argument, is exactly the same as what would have been derived assuming the world was risk neutral. Given that assumption, the parameter p would have been derived by the above argument to equal the implied probability so that the current stock price is the EPV of the next period price.

*The Cox–Ross–Rubenstein multi-step lattice: European options*

While the above argument works well in a simple binomial state world, where stock prices can take on only one of two values, what about the real world where the stock price probability distribution is more complex? As it turns out, many random variables of interest seem to follow a nearly normal or lognormal distribution. As is well known, such 'complex' distributions can be approximated to any given degree of accuracy with a binomial, not a one period binomial with two states, but with an n-period binomial with $n+1$ resultant states. We next pursue the extension of the above model to an n-period binomial state environment.

If each of the up and down states above was followed by additional up and down states, with similar relative return assumptions, the stock price 'lattice' would then look like:

$$\begin{array}{ccccccc}
 & & & & & & u^n S \\
 & & & u^2 S & < & & \\
 & & uS & < & & u^{n-1}dS & \\
 & S & < & & udS & < \ldots & \\
 & & dS & < & & \vdots & \\
 & & & d^2 S & < & & \\
 & & & & & & d^n S \\
\text{time:} & 0 & 1 & 2 & \ldots & n &
\end{array}$$

At each time point, there are a number of 'states' in which the stock price can be. Specifically, at time $k$, there are $k+1$ possible states. By starting at the $t=0$ stock value and moving from period to period, selecting either up or down states, one can generate all possible 'price paths' from time 0 to time $n$. In total, there are $2^n$ such paths. However, to price options we again begin at time $n$, when the European option value is well defined.

By starting at the $t=n$ stock values, the time of the assumed expiry of the European option, the call option's value in each state is well defined by the strike price as in the above one period example. That is, if $u^{n-k}d^k S > K$, where $K$ is the strike price, the option is worth $u^{n-k}d^k S - K$ in that state, otherwise the option value is equal to 0.

Using the 'backward substitution' formula (3), each of the time $n-1$ call option values can be calculated from the 'connecting' time $n$ 'state' values. The time $n-2$ call option values are next produced by the same procedure, and so forth. In the end, $C$ is again found to equal an EPV of the time $n$ option values, where the 'probabilities' of the time $n$ states are again given by $p$ in (2) and the $n$-period binomial formula:

$$C = r^{-n} \sum_{j=0}^{n} \binom{n}{j} p^j (1-p)^{n-j} O_n^E(u^j d^{n-j} S), \qquad (5)$$

where $O_n^E(\ )$ is the terminal (i.e. time $n$) value of the European call option in state $j$ when the stock price is as given in the parentheses.

In this $n$-step lattice, $p$ is again the risk-neutral probability in that over the $n$ periods, the EPV of terminal stock prices is $S$. That is, $p$ is the implied probability of an up-state in a risk neutral world so that the expected $n$-period stock return equals the risk-free rate.

European put options are modeled similarly, with the exception of the definition of $O_n^E(u^j d^{n-j} S)$. If $K$ is the strike price, we have:

$$\begin{aligned} \text{Call:} \quad & O_n^E E(u^j d^{n-j} S) = \max(u^j d^{n-j} S - K, 0) \\ \text{Put:} \quad & O_n^E(u^j d^{n-j} S) = \max(K - u^j d^{n-j} S, 0) \end{aligned} \qquad (6)$$

The put and call formulas in (6) can be inserted into (5) to obtain a formula more reminiscent of the Black–Scholes formula, which is developed below on page 91. Let $a$ denote the first $j$ value in (4) for which $O_n^E(\ )$ is non-zero as a call option. Then (4) can be rewritten:

$$C = S[1 - F(a-1; n, p')] - Kr^{-n}[1 - F(a-1; n, p)], \qquad (7)$$

where $F(;,)$ is the binomial distribution function with parameters $n, p$ or $n, p'$, evaluated at $a-1$, and $p' = up/r$.

Similarly, the put formula becomes:

$$P = Kr^{-n} F(a-1; n, p) - S F(a-1; n, p'). \qquad (8)$$

## Put–call parity: European options

From (7) and (8), one easily establishes the relationship between put and call prices known as 'put–call parity':

$$C - P = S - Kr^{-n} \tag{9}$$

Equation (9) says that a 'long European call' plus a 'short European put' exactly equals the value of the underlying security, less the present value of the strike price. The intuition behind (9) is simple. At expiry, the call is worth $S - K$ if $S \geq K$ and 0 otherwise, while the short put is worth $S - K$ if $S \leq K$ and 0 otherwise. Together, this options package pays $S - K$ at expiry in every time $n$ state. Hence, $C - P - S$ is a riskless investment which always pays $-K$ at time $n$, so its time 0 value must equal the risk-free present value of this payoff, as an arbitrage argument shows.

## Cox–Ross–Rubenstein: American options

American options can be equally well handled using lattice methods, except the resulting formulas cannot be simplified into the (7) and (8) structures, generally. To develop the approach, we return to the earlier discussion of the lattice method for an $n$-period binomial state environment. Consider any time $n - 1$ European option value, which is given by (1). Now consider that as an American option, we also have the ability to exercise at that time for the potential profit, say $E_{n-1}$, defined by the option. Simple arbitrage arguments show that the American call at time $n - 1$ cannot be worth less than $E_{n-1}$, nor can it be worth less than the associated European option (expiry at $t = n$), and finally, it cannot be worth more than the larger of these two values. Hence, the American option value at time $n - 1$ is given by:

$$O^A_{n-1} = \max[E_{n-1}, \text{EPV}(O^E_n(\ ), O^E_n(\ ))], \tag{10}$$

where the EPV is taken of the two time $n$ states connected to the time $n - 1$ state being valued.

The time $n - 2$ states are handled similarly, only:

$$O^A_{n-2} = \max[F_{n-2}, \text{EPV}(O^A_{n-1}(\ ), O^A_{n-1}(\ ))], \tag{11}$$

and so forth. In other words, the option value at each time-state is determined in two steps:
1. Calculate the EPV of the option values at the two future connecting time-states;
2. Replace the value in (1) with the actual value of the option at that time if exercised, when this value is larger.

While this methodology does not lend itself to simple closed form formulae, as in (7) or (8), it is custom designed for computer implementation.

## Fixed income preliminaries

When attempting to apply the above methodology to embedded options in fixed-income instruments, such as a callable bond, two issues arise:

1. *Complexity:* If $P_i^{(n)}$ represents the price of the bond at time $n$, state $i$, the assumed up and down state returns, $u^{(n)}$ and $d^{(n)}$ must vary with $n$ since as we approach maturity, $P_i^{(M)} \to$ for all $i$, so the $u^{(n)}$ and $d^{(n)}$ values must approach 1 as $n \to M$. In general, one expects that these values should reflect both the volatility of yields at the maturity on which the $P_i^{(n)}$ values are priced, as well as some measure of price sensitivity, such as duration, which translates yield volatility to price volatility.

2. *Consistency:* As a given bond moves from time 0 to its maturity at time $M$, it is clear that at minimum we need a model of $M$-period rates at time 0, $(M-1)$-period rates at time 1, and so forth. To consistently price all bonds on the same lattice, we really require a model of the entire yield curve at time 0, 1, ... up to 30 years, say, to handle short and long-dated options.

The difficulty in building such a 'yield curve lattice' is assuring internal consistency, by which is meant, an absence of riskless arbitrage. Since the option pricing methodology above is predicated on the assumption of no riskless arbitrage, it would not be sensible to apply this methodology within a lattice framework the yield curve dynamics of which allowed such an arbitrage. What needs to be verified in the lattice is that given any portfolio of bonds (long or short positions) for which the up and down state prices agree in the next period, i.e. the portfolio is riskless, it must earn exactly the risk-free rate during the period.

## Ho–Lee fixed income option pricing

While a number of models have been introduced which satisfy the no riskless arbitrage condition, the Ho–Lee model was the first to do so and allow an exact fit to the actual yield curve at time 0. Earlier models fit only one or a few points exactly, then interpolated the rest. In addition, the Ho–Lee lattice has a computational advantage of commutativity, which means that the time 2 state arrived at by an up and then a down shift from time 0, equals the time 2 state arrived at by a down and then an up shift.

While this model has shortcomings, such as the potential for negative interest rates, and a fairly limited model of yield curve dynamics, this computational advantage is valuable. At time $n$, there are $n+1$ states in the Ho–Lee lattice, while in noncommutative models with more powerful dynamics, there will be $2^n$ states, requiring significantly more computational effort. In some recent models commutativity is preserved, and certain Ho–Lee shortcomings avoided, but many have their own limitations or computational shortcomings.

In brief, while there are many equally good models, there is no perfect yield curve dynamics model yet, both theoretically and computationally, and so we illustrate only the Ho–Lee model for theoretical tractability and computational ease. (See Appendix B for another model.) If $P_i^{(n)}(T)$ denotes the price of a

T-period zero coupon bond in state $i$ of time $n$, $i = 0, \ldots, n$, the Ho–Lee approach is to model the two connected time $n + 1$ states, $P_{i+1}^{(n+1)}$, the up-state, and $P_i^{(n+1)}$, the down-state, based on 'perturbations' of the time $n + 1$ 'forward' yield curve price function implied by $P_i^{(n)}(T)$:

$$P_{i+1}^{(n+1)}(T) = F_i^{(n)}(T)h(T) \qquad P_i^{(n+1)}(T) = F_i^{(n)}(T)h^*(T), \tag{12}$$

where $F_i^{(n)}(T) = P_i^{(n)}(T+1)/P_i^{(n)}(1)$, denotes the one-period forward yield curve price function, and $h(T), h^*(T)$ are the up and down-state 'perturbation' functions derived to satisfy certain conditions discussed below.

The one-period forward yield curve price function defined above is exactly equal to the price function defined using the one-period forward yield curve. To see this, let $r_i^{(n)}(T)$ denote the continuous spot rates underlying the price function $P_i^{(n)}(T)$. Then the above formula for $F_i^{(n)}(T)$ can be rewritten:

$$\begin{aligned} F_i^{(n)}(T) &= \exp(-(T+1)r_i^{(n)}(T+1) + r_i^{(n)}(1)) \\ &= \exp(-Tf_i^{(n)}(T)) \end{aligned} \tag{13}$$

where:

$$f_i^{(n)}(T) = \frac{(T+1)r_i^{(n)}(T+1) - r_i^{(n)}(1)}{T} \tag{14}$$

denotes the implied $T$-period spot rate one period forward.

Alternatively, one can justify the implied forward yield curve price function by a simple trade. That is, it is possible to do a no-cost trade in state $i$ of time $n$ which guarantees that the price of a $T$-period zero coupon bond at time $n + 1$ is exactly $F_i^{(n)}(T)$. We simply borrow $P_i^{(n)}(T+1)$ dollars for one period at rate $r_i^{(n)}(1)$, and invest in the $(T+1)$ period zero coupon bond. This position costs nothing. At time $n + 1$, we repay the loan, which has now accrued to $P_i^{(n)}(T+1)/P_i^{(n)}(1)$ or $F_i^{(n)}(T)$ dollars, and for this cost we 'buy' the $T$-period bond remaining.

Returning to the Ho–Lee lattice 'perturbation' functions, to satisfy the no riskless arbitrage condition, it must be the case that for some constant $\pi$, the perturbation functions satisfy:

$$\pi h(T) + (1 - \pi)h^*(T) = 1, \tag{15}$$

independent of $T$.

This value, $\pi$, is reminiscent of $p$ in (2), because (15) can be rewritten to imply that today's price for a $T$-period zero equals the EPV of the next period prices (where we note that in the next period, the bond is a $(T-1)$-period zero):

$$P_i^{(n)}(T) = [\pi P_{i+1}^{(n+1)}(T-1) + (1-\pi)P_i^{(n+1)}(T-1)]P_i^{(n)}(1). \tag{16}$$

Formula (16) is identical to (3) in the stock price application. That is, $\pi$ is the implied probability of an up-state in a risk-neutral world, so that today's price for a $T$-period zero is the EPV of its possible prices in the next period.

Besides the no riskless arbitrage condition, Ho–Lee impose the computationally convenient condition that the resulting lattice be commutative, so that the two period combination, Up/Down, produces the same state as the Down/Up combination. This condition, along with criterion (15), produced a finite difference equation which Ho–Lee solved to produce the following perturbation functions:

$$h(T) = \frac{1}{\pi + (1-\pi)\delta^T}$$

$$h^*(T) = \frac{\delta^T}{\pi + (1-\pi)\delta^T} \quad (17)$$

where $\delta$ is a parameter we now discuss.

Because $h^*(T) = \delta^T h(T)$, it is obvious that for $h^*(T)$ to be a down (price) state, we must have $\delta < 1$. However, taking $\pi$ to be the implied binomial probability in the lattice, and letting $r_i^{(n)}(T)$ denote the $T$-period spot rates at time $n$ in the states $i = 0, 1, ..., n$, implied by the $P_i^{(n)}(T)$ prices, it is easy to show that at time $n$, the variance of these $n+1$ spot rates is:

$$\operatorname{var}[r_i^{(n)}(T)] = n\pi(1-\pi)(\ln \delta)^2, \quad (18)$$

so $\delta$ has the real-world interpretation as a parameter related to the assumed volatility of interest rates. By (18), this volatility assumption must be independent of the yield maturity (i.e. $T$). This means that at any time $n$, the yield curves in all possible $n+1$ states differ by 'parallel' shifts of a given yield curve.

To price options in the Ho–Lee framework, we again use the replicating portfolio argument of Cox–Ross–Rubenstein. However, most of the work is done by (1), we only require $p$, for which we need $u$, $d$, and $r$ in this context. From (12), we obtain that in state $i$ of time $n$:

$$u(T) = rh(T-1), \quad d(T) = rh^*(T-1), \quad r = 1/P_i^{(n)}(1),$$

from which it is easily derived from (15) that the Cox–Ross–Rubenstein $p$ equals the Ho–Lee $\pi$ as one might have anticipated.

The Ho–Lee iterative formula for the value of a bond with an embedded option is now an adaptation of (11) for stocks. The adaptation is required because bonds typically pay cash flows (coupons, sinking funds) over their life, which we ignored for stocks (i.e. dividends) for simplicity. Secondly, the formula below is slightly more complicated to simultaneously price puts or calls, American or European. Finally, we must recall that for bonds, an embedded call option is a short position to the investor, while an embedded put is a long position.

Following the stock model, we first calculate the counterpart to (1), denoted $C^*(n, i)$, the 'preliminary' value of the security in state $i$ of time $n$. This value equals the EPV of next period values plus next period payable cash flows:

$$C^*(n, i) = [\pi(C(n+1, i+1) + X(n+1, i+1))$$
$$+ (1-\pi)(C(n+1, i) + X(n+1, i))]P_i^{(n)}(1), \quad (19)$$

where $C(\,,\,)$ is the actual value of the security next period, and $X(\,,\,)$ is the fixed cash flow assumed to be omitted in the calculation of $C(\,,\,)$.

This is a preliminary value because as in the stock option case, an American call option would put a floor on the option's value and a ceiling on the callable security's value (i.e. a callable bond cannot be worth more than its exercised value), while an embedded American put would provide a floor on the security. Consequently, if $L(n, i)$ is the security's floor provided by the put option, and $U(n, i)$ the ceiling provided by the call, generalizing (11) we have:

$$C(n, i) = \max[L(n, i), \min(C^*(n, i), U(n, i))]. \tag{20}$$

In contrast to (11), the call option uses 'min' rather than 'max' since in (11), we are valuing the option itself, while in (20) we are valuing a security with an embedded call, which is formally a 'short' option position. Similar to (11), an embedded put option in a bond uses 'max' because here, the put is a 'long' position.

### Ho–Lee prices of callable bonds and GICs

As one example, consider a 20-year 8% coupon bond, callable from the end of year 16 at 104 (i.e. par plus a coupon), with call premiums linearly decreasing to 0 at time 20 (i.e. callable at par). We also assume 12% annual yield volatility which is used as follows. If the current yield on this bond is $r$, we define the annual standard derivation of $r$ to be $0.12r$, so by the usual assumption of independent time increments, quarterly volatility is $0.06r$, monthly volatility is $0.01\sqrt{12}r$, and in general, volatility for $100t\%$ of a year is $0.12\sqrt{t}r$.

Using the volatility appropriate for the time steps in the lattice, the parameter $\delta$ is obtained from (18) with $n = 1$ (i.e. the one-period volatility). While $\pi$ appears to be defined somewhat arbitrarily, it is known that as one refines the time steps in the lattice, the theoretically correct answer in the continuous framework requires $\pi = \frac{1}{2}$, so it is common to use this value in the discrete lattice as well.

To price the bond as a noncallable instrument, (19) is used directly, since the put/call modification in (20) is unnecessary. For (19), we begin at maturity, where $C(M, i) = 100$ for all $i$ states, and work 'backwards' to time 0, observing that $X(n, i) = 4$ at maturity and at 6 month intervals for coupon payments, and 0 otherwise. $C(0, 0)$ is then the noncallable bond price. For the callable bond we proceed as above, only now using modification (20) from time of maturity to 16 years to reflect the available American option. Here, we use $L(n, i) \equiv 0$ because the bond has no put, and $U(n, i)$ equal to the call premium plus par. For times below 16 years, (19) is used because the bond is noncallable in this range.

Below are listed prices of the callable and non-callable bond in different interest rate environments, plus the implied price of the embedded call option, using 12% volatility, monthly steps and $\pi = \frac{1}{2}$:

84   D.C. Doll et al.

| Yield | Non-callable | Callable | Option |
|---|---|---|---|
| 6.0 | 123.11 | 120.79 | 2.32 |
| 7.0 | 110.68 | 109.13 | 1.55 |
| 8.0 | 100.00 | 98.93 | 1.07 |
| 9.0 | 90.80 | 90.04 | 0.76 |
| 10.0 | 82.84 | 82.28 | 0.56 |

Similarly, below is the comparable table assuming 15% annual yield volatility, rather than 12%.

| Yield | Non-callable | Callable | Option |
|---|---|---|---|
| 6.0 | 123.11 | 120.38 | 2.73 |
| 7.0 | 110.68 | 108.72 | 1.96 |
| 8.0 | 100.00 | 98.56 | 1.44 |
| 9.0 | 90.80 | 89.70 | 1.10 |
| 10.0 | 82.84 | 81.99 | 0.85 |

Note that the value of the option increases with volatility. This is true for two reasons. First, higher volatility typically implies that there is a greater probability that the option will appear 'in the money' at some time in the future, and it will therefore have value in proportionately more time-states. Secondly, higher volatility typically implies that when 'in the money', the option will on average be worth more.

A callable GIC would be treated similarly. Assume that we have a 7%, 7-year compound GIC, callable from years four to seven at the guaranteed fund balance, which equals $100(1.07)^t$ at time $t$ (measured in years). The 'backward substitution' approach in (19) again begins at maturity, when $C(n, i) = 100(1.07)^7$ for all states $i$, and $n = 7f$, with $f$ equal to the number of steps per year in the lattice. Noncallable values for the GIC are obtained directly with (19), where $X(n, i) \equiv 0$ for all $n, i$. For the callable market value, the modification in (20) is made with $U(n, i) = 100(1.07)^{n/f}$ during the call period, $4f \le n \le 7f$, but is again unnecessary for $n < 4f$ when the GIC is noncallable. Because there is no put feature, $L(n, i) \equiv 0$.

Below are listed prices of the callable and noncallable GIC in several interest rate environments, at 12% volatility, plus the implied price of the embedded option.

| Yield | Non-callable | Callable | Option |
|---|---|---|---|
| 5.0 | 114.15 | 107.74 | 6.41 |
| 6.0 | 106.85 | 103.09 | 3.76 |
| 7.0 | 100.00 | 97.92 | 2.08 |
| 8.0 | 93.71 | 92.48 | 1.23 |
| 9.0 | 87.85 | 87.12 | 0.73 |

## Fair valuation of life insurance company liabilities

On a technical note, it should be pointed out that in the bond example, the 'yields' were 'bond yields', or the semiannual equivalent of the coupon rates on par bonds, while in the GIC example 'yields' were annual 'spot rates', or rates used to discount 'bullet' cash flows. Except for the semiannual vs. annual distinction, this difference in 'basis' was disguised by the simplicity of the examples which were based on flat yield curves. That is, we assumed the initial term structure underlying $P_0^{(0)}(T)$ has $r_0^{(0)}(T) \equiv r$, with $r$ chosen to equal the continuous equivalent of the rate given, so $r = 0.0688$ in the bond example, $r = 0.0677$ in the GIC example, when priced at 7%.

In general, one initializes $P_0^{(0)}(T)$ so that the implied term structure $(r_0^{(0)}(T))$ is equivalent to the spot yield curve assumed for pricing purposes. If this yield curve is given as a 'spot' curve, only the conversion to a continuous basis is necessary. If given as a bond yield curve, these yields must first be converted to the equivalent spot rate basis, then translated to continuous rates.

### Option election efficiency revisited

It was noted that many option pricing models assume 100% exercise efficiency on the part of the long position. In particular, this assumption is made in Black–Scholes/Cox–Ross–Rubenstein, as well as in the Ho–Lee model above. There are at least two simple ways to modify the lattice pricing models to reflect long position inefficiency, where by inefficiency is here meant that the long will not necessarily exercise when in the money. Exercising when out of the money will be discussed below.

First, one can hypothesize that the cause of this inefficiency is that the long position must incur hard costs plus expend significant effort to refinance the debt. We emphasize 'refinance' here as this is the logical expectation in the case of an interest-rate driven call, rather than simply a pay-off of the debt. This reluctance to call can be easily modeled by altering the pay-off functions in (20). For example, if the call payoff is par plus 4, or 104, and 2% refinancing costs are estimated, the bond could be priced as if the payoff were 106. To reflect 'effort', an extra 'point' or so could be added, resulting in an increase to the call premiums of 3%, say. Now instead of calling at 104, as (20) implies, the long will not act until rates fall further, to increase the price to 107, say, thereby reducing call exercises and the option value. That is, we simply define $U^*(n, i) = U(n, i) + 3$, when $U(n, i) \neq 0$, and $U^*(n, i) = 0$ otherwise.

For example, if the bond is repriced to reflect an increment of three to the non-zero call premiums, the following values are produced for the embedded option at 12% volatility:

| Yield | Original call schedule | Call schedule +3 | Change |
|---|---|---|---|
| 6.0 | 2.32 | 1.90 | (18.1)% |
| 7.0 | 1.55 | 1.27 | (18.0)% |
| 8.0 | 1.07 | 0.88 | (17.8)% |
| 9.0 | 0.76 | 0.63 | (17.1)% |
| 10.0 | 0.56 | 0.47 | (16.1)% |

Logically, the inefficiency assumption reduces the value (to the long) or cost (to the short) of the embedded option.

A second method to reflect 'in the money' inefficiency is to simply 'discount' the option values produced by 10–40%, say, thereby intuitively reducing 'efficiency' by 10–40%. However, the more explicit modeling method above may be preferred because one is forced to be explicit about the reason for inefficiency, and to model it. One then assumes the long is 100% efficient in exercising subject to this model's constraints. In the simple discount method, one has only the intuitive 'behavioral' model that say, 80% of the long positions will be 100% efficient, and 20% will not call at all. This behavioral model produces the same price as discounting the option value by 20% directly, because this model would suggest a price equal to a weighted average of the call and non-call prices, which is mathematically equivalent to the simple discounting of the embedded options. Of course, puts can be similarly handled, as can options on other underlying securities such as insurance company liabilities.

As noted, there is another type of 'inefficiency' whereby in addition to failing to exercise when 'in the money', one can often expect some level of exercise when the long is 'out of the money'. Both forms of inefficiency reduce the value of the option compared with the full efficiency model. However, while qualitatively similar, this second type of inefficiency must be modeled with extreme care. This is because rather than only reduce the value of the option to zero in the limit of such inefficiency, this second type can provide a real 'profit' to the short, which can ultimately create options with 'negative' value. That is, an option for which the 'short' both receives a premium for selling, plus obtains a contract with positive value. This situation, of course, defies the no-risk arbitrage condition in the most elementary way, and can not occur in actively traded markets. For example, while mortgage-backed securities are priced with both types of inefficiency, it is always the case that the 'option' on net retains positive value, for if the pricing assumptions implied otherwise, the market arbitragers would impose a 'reality check' to correct this mispricing.

When pricing contracts with embedded options which are not actively traded, such as UL or SPDA contracts, it is important to understand the effect of one's inefficiency assumptions, and to ascertain that on net, the option has real positive value. To do otherwise would be to risk future profitability on a very risky and counter-market assumption. For example, an assumption that a baseline level of lapsation occurs on an SPDA contract, independent of the level of credited vs. market rates, creates option election inefficiencies of both types. This is because one is positing that some longs (i.e. contract holders) will put (i.e. lapse) each year whether credited rates are above or below market rates. Assuming credited rates are based on asset portfolio earnings, the needed asset liquidations at market rates will then generate gains or losses to the short (i.e. insurer), the value of which are then adjusted by incremental gains or losses reflecting the relationship between surrender charges and unamortized acquisition expenses.

On the other hand, the typical 'adjustment formula' to the baseline withdrawal assumptions provides a partial 'efficiency adjustment' in that the propensity to surrender is posited as being negatively correlated to the attractiveness of the credited rate vis-à-vis the market rate. This adjustment formula does allow for contract holder inefficiency of the first type, however, in that in general, 100% surrender is not produced when the market rate prevails, even by a substantial amount.

Typically, this inefficiency is both explicitly modeled by recognizing the logical dampening effects of surrender charges, as well as indirectly adjusted by assuming that even when such charges are valued, less than 100% will surrender when 'in the money'.

*Applicability of lattice-based methodologies to complex contracts: the key criterion*

We next discuss in more detail the applicability of lattice option pricing methods to more complex contracts, such as mortgage-backed securities, UL and SPDA contracts. One immediate complication observed on liability contracts not found on assets is the presence of death claims as a contingency, in addition to option election. This is not a serious issue, however, for one could model these events very simply as cash flows, $X(n, i)$, related to the assumed mortality probabilities at time $n$ and the payable death benefits (face amount or fund balance). One could also model the $X(n, i)$ 'stochastically' as random variables with means reflecting the assumed mortality probabilities. Each lattice-based calculation would then provide a 'conditional fair market value' of the liability, conditional on the values of $X(n, i)$ generated by the model. The actual fair market value is then given by the 'law of total probability' as the average of the conditional values.

As for option election, a review of the lattice-based methodology confirms that to be used for more complicated securities, it is necessary that in the $(n, i)$ time state, the decision not to call, or call fully or partially, must be determinable based only on information available in that time state, or derivable from information available in the connected future time states:

$$(n + m, i + k) \quad \text{where } m \geq 0, \quad 0 \leq k \leq m.$$

More specifically, the decision to call cannot be based on information available only in earlier time-states. This was not a problem for a callable GIC or bond, since by the replicating portfolio argument, all that was needed to decide on option election was the one period spot rate in the $(n, i)$ time-state, and the values of the bond in the $(n + 1, i)$, $(n + 1, i + 1)$ time-states. These future values effectively summarized all pertinent information in all future connected time-states. For complicated securities, however, this decision paradigm is not possible in general.

For mortgage-backed securities, for example, underlying mortgage prepayment models are complex and reflect not only the current relationship of market yields to the given mortgage rate, but also what this relationship had been in the past. For example, if market rates are currently relatively low, the prepayment model will generate more prepayments if this is the first time this event has occurred, than if this event has also occurred earlier. Logically, this model posits 'hot money', or mortgagors who will prepay (i.e. refinance) as soon as it is profitable, 'warm money', or mortgagors who will not act quickly, but will be more prone to act as favorable conditions warrant, and 'cold money', or mortgagors who will probably not prepay under any circumstances. For example, after a long period of relatively low rates, a mortgage pool may be said to be 'burned out', in that virtually nothing but cold money is left. Options which exhibit this election behavior are often called 'path-dependent' options, in that their exercise reflects not only current circumstances, but past circumstances as well. That is, their exercise depends on the 'path' of interest rates from time 0 to the time-state of interest.

Surrender models for UL and similar contracts are currently not very complex, in that while a clear analogy exists to the behavior of mortgage pools, there has not been sufficient quantitative study of contract holder behaviors in different rate environments to support any but relatively simple models. In the MBS case, experience is tracked in every pool separately, and sophisticated econometric models applied to glean the underlying behavioral model for observed prepayments. In addition, these behavioral models are updated regularly. Because current insurance liability surrender models are fairly simple, and in particular do not reflect the 'path-dependency' feature above, it would appear that valuations of UL, SPDA, and whole life (WL) contracts are possible by lattice methods. However, this is generally not the case.

For example, it is logical to posit that policyholder behavior with respect to withdrawals (puts) and optional premium payments (calls) reflects the relationship between market rates and the credited rate. If both the market rate and credited rate reflect only the interest rate environment 'known' in time-state $(n, i)$; i.e. reflect 'new money' rates, a lattice-based valuation of the contract is possible. However, it is often the case that the credited rate reflects a 'portfolio' of assets either held, as in the 'portfolio-based' crediting strategy, or modeled, as in an 'average of past new money rates' crediting strategy. In either case, the time-state $(n, i)$ crediting rate depends on prior time states. Additionally, it is often assumed that the 'market rate' is that of a competitor, hypothetical or real, and so reflects the competitor's crediting rate strategy, which may again reflect experience in past time-states. Consequently, even when insurance company contract holder behavioral models are simple and not apparently path dependent, their dependence on credited and market rates effectively creates path dependence. In general then, such insurance liabilities, like complex assets, are often unsuitable for lattice-based option valuation methodologies.

*Yield curve models: lattice vs. scenario based*

The above discussion makes clear that in order to value complex assets or liabilities, a methodology is needed that begins at time zero, and models the behavior of interest rates up to each time-state. Within such a procedure, credited and market rates at each time-state can be developed from past experience, and option exercise behavior modeled from that. But what about the value of the option? How can we implement a 'replicating portfolio' argument in this new setting? Before addressing this, we first consider in more detail the relationship between the yield curve dynamics implied in lattice models, versus those implied in so-called 'scenario models'.

First, every lattice model, whether connected or not, implies a yield curve scenario model. For example, the Ho–Lee formulae in (12) give the prices in the time $n+1$ states of all zero-coupon bonds based on prices at time $n$ in the state to which they connect. A similar comment therefore follows for the underlying yield curves. So from time zero and the original yield curve, $r_0^{(0)}(T)$, two yield curves in the next period are well defined, $r_0^{(1)}(T)$ in the down (price) state, and $r_1^{(1)}(T)$ in the up (price) state. From either of these states, again two states are defined at time 3, and so forth. Hence, one easily generates yield curve scenarios by flipping a coin say, at each time-state, taking the up-state with heads, the down-state with tails. Each $n$ flips of the coin generates one $n$-period scenario or path, so the total number of paths implied by the Ho–Lee lattice is $2^n$. This is the same number of paths implied by a noncommutative lattice, where each time-state splits into two states in the next period, but generally, the yield curves on each path differ from those on every other path. The major implication of commutative vs noncommutative is the number of states implied at time $n$. Commutative lattice-based paths 'collapse' to only $n+1$ states at time $n$, while noncommutative lattices yield $2^n$ final states.

Consequently, virtually all scenario generators are 'binomial' in structure, in that from today's yield curve, two yield curves are modeled at time 1, while each of these in turn generates two yield curves at time 2, and so forth. Paths are again generated by synthetic coin flipping, each flip indicating whether the next step is up or down. Clearly, this structure is identical to the binomial path implied by the lattice models. It is also clear that given any such scenario generator, the one period rates in each time-state can be used in a backward substitution valuation of an option as in a lattice-based valuation.

## Option pricing on scenario-based models

The above two paragraphs make clear that the underlying yield curve models of lattice-based and scenario-based methods are identical, so it is natural to expect that option pricing on scenario models consistent with lattice models is possible, and indeed this is largely true. First, assume that in every time-state, defined either on a lattice or in the associated scenario model, a cash flow function is defined, $X(n, i)$. That is, in state $i$ of time $n$, a cash flow of $X(n, i)$ is payable. For commutative models we have $0 \leq i \leq n$, while for noncommutative models, $1 \leq i \leq 2^n$ by convention. While using the notation $X(n, i)$ may have a 'fixed' cash flow component, as a coupon payment or death claim, as well as a 'contingent' cash flow component such as call proceeds or a surrender value. That is, we assume that all option decisions are known. It is not difficult to then show that the value of these cash flows, and hence the embedded options, using lattice or scenario methods agree when calculated as follows. For the lattice method, we use the backward substitution implied by (19):

$$V(n, i) = \tfrac{1}{2}[V(n+1, i+1) + X(n+1, i+1) \\ + V(n+1, i) + V(n+1, i)]P_1^{(n)}(1). \tag{21}$$

For the scenario method, we define $V(0, 0)$ as the average present value of cash flows, where this average is taken over all possible paths from time zero to time $n$:

$$V(0, 0) = \frac{1}{N} \sum_i \sum_{j=1}^n PV[X(j, *)] \tag{22}$$

In formula (22), the summation over $i$ is intended to denote a summation over all possible paths, where each path represents an $n$-tuple of $i$ values, restricted so that the implied path is connected. As noted above, there are $N = 2^n$ possible paths in both commutative and noncommutative models.

The above result implies that either backward substitution on lattice-based models, or forward generation on scenario-based models can be used to value any security for which the cash flows are known or can be defined in any time-state. Consequently, European options are easy to handle because the option decision is straightforward. On the other hand, mortgage-backed securities, UL or SPDA contracts, etc. can be valued using scenario-based models, since cash flows can be predicted in every time-state using the option election 'model', and we can be confident that the same answer will result as if these cash flows were valued on a lattice. In general, American options with 100% election efficiency are problematic in a scenario based model, although Tilley has introduced a promising approach. Because of this theoretical equivalence, one can choose the model best suited to the problem. If option exercise can be determined based only on information at a time-state or later, lattice-based models work well. If information prior to the given time-state is needed, scenario-based models are preferred.

One exception to this rule is that lattice-based calculations on noncommutative lattices are rarely done unless the number of periods, $n$, is relatively small. This is due to the fact that in such a lattice, the number of steps implied by (21) is:

$$S = \sum_{j=0}^{n-1} (2^{n-j} - 1)$$
$$= 2(2^n - 1) - n \qquad (23)$$

In a commutative lattice, $S = n(n+1)/2$, a far more manageable number.

Because noncommutative lattices require enormous calculation time for even moderate values of $n$, it is common to choose the scenario based alternative for simplicity, as implemented below.

One advantage to scenario-based approaches not available to lattice-based methods is the ability to 'sample' paths. Formula (22) implies that an average of $2^n$ present values is needed for an exact answer, whether the yield curve dynamics are commutative or not. Each present value involves $2n - 1$ calculations for a total of $(2n-1)2^n$ additions or multiplications. On the surface, this is even worse than what (23) implies for a noncommutative lattice. However, one can view formula (22) as stating that the value at time 0, $V(0,0)$, is the mean of a distribution of $2^n$ values, each generated by one of $2^n$ possible paths. Viewed this way, it is natural to 'estimate' $V(0,0)$ by sampling from this distribution, rather than generating all possible paths. In general, the estimate can be improved by increased sampling, but more efficiently by judicious sampling methods. One such method involves creating two paths from each sampled point, the actual sampled point and its 'mirror' path, where downs and ups are interchanged. This method automatically generates paths symmetric about the hypothetical 'mean path,' and improves accuracy compared to straight random sampling. Another method involves 'partitioning' all paths into equivalence groups, sampling from each group separately, and combining results with appropriate weightings. This method avoids a problem of random sampling whereby many redundant paths near the 'mean path' are generated, and too few paths in the 'tails' which are more important.

See Tilley for a survey of methods and Ho for the 'linear path space' approach.

*Black Scholes and Cox Ross Rubenstein*

The Black–Scholes formulae for European puts and calls on a stock can be obtained from (7) and (8) by assuming that the stock's price follows a lognormal distribution over any time period, discretely approximating this distribution with the binomial, and carrying the resulting formulas to the limit.

By lognormally distributed is meant that if $S_t$ is the price at time $t$,

$$S_t = e^z S_0, \qquad (A.1)$$

where $z \sim N(t\mu, t\sigma^2)$, i.e. is normally distributed with mean $t\mu$, variance $t\sigma^2$.

The term 'lognormal' follows from the observation that $z = \ln(S_t/S_0)$ is normally distributed.

To approximate $z$ at time $t$ by an $n$-period binomial distribution, we first divide the time interval into $n$ parts, and let $u$ and $d$ denote (one plus) the up and down state returns over a period of length $t/n$. Also, let $q$ denote the up-state probability, and $S_t^*$ the binomial values of the stock price at time $t$:

$$S_t^* = S_0 u^j d^{n-j}, \quad j = 0, \ldots, n. \tag{A.2}$$

A simple calculation yields:

$$E[\ln(S_t^*/S_0)] = n \ln(d) + j \ln(u/d) \tag{A.3}$$

$$\text{var}[\ln(S_t^*/S_0)] = q(1-q)n[\ln(u/d)]^2. \tag{A.4}$$

Ideally, the parameters $u$, $d$ and $q$ would be chosen to match the first two moments of $z$ in (A.1), or, $t\mu$, $t\sigma^2$, respectively.

By a judicious choice for $u$ and $d$, equal to $\exp[\pm \sigma(t/n)^{1/2}]$ where $t$ is now the time of the option's expiry and $n$ the number in time steps, and utilizing probabilities for the up and down states (which converged to ½ as the step size decreased), Cox–Ross–Rubenstein were able to match first moments of the above lognormal with their binomial distributions, match second moments in the limit as $n \to \infty$, and prove that corresponding formulas in (A.6) and (A.7) converged to Black–Scholes European put/call formulas:

$$C = S\phi(A + \sigma\sqrt{t}/2) - Kr^{-t}\phi(A - \sigma\sqrt{t}/2), \tag{A.5}$$

$$P = Kr^{-t}\phi(-A + \sigma\sqrt{t}/2) - S\phi(-A - \sigma\sqrt{t}/2), \tag{A.6}$$

where $\phi$ is the normal distribution function, and

$$A = \frac{\ln(S/Kr^{-t})}{\sigma\sqrt{t}}.$$

While (A.5) and (A.6) appear structurally different from (A.6) and (A.7) respectively, recall that for the normal distribution:

$$\phi(-Z) = 1 - \phi(Z), \tag{A.7}$$

so the structures are the same.

One corollary of this observation is that put–call parity is evident:

$$C - P = S - Kr^{-t}. \tag{A.8}$$

APPENDIX B: HEATH, JARROW, MORTON INTEREST RATE MODEL

The Heath, Jarrow, and Morton (HJM) model starts with a Monte Carlo simulation of term structure movements. It assumes that term structure changes are due to several independent sources of noise. The changes are, in principle, continuous but in practice they are discrete. Time advances in discrete constant steps (e.g. quarters). The result of the model is a collection of random walks, called paths. Each path is a series of yield curves expressed as forward forces of interest. These are adjusted to make the set of paths arbitrage free, so pricing can be done on a risk-neutral basis.

This approach contrasts with binomial lattice models in several crucial ways. Simulation methods easily allow several sources of random fluctuation while binomial models are, in practice, limited to one. As a result, instantaneous interest rate movements in lattice models are perfectly correlated across maturities. While this is not too bad for longer maturities, it severely and unrealistically limits movements of shorter maturities. Second, simulation models offer independent sample paths while lattices essentially do not have paths. This is a serious problem when valuing a security whose cashflows depend on its history, such as a mortgage-backed bond. To handle this situation, the lattice is sometimes disconnected into a large number of paths from which a sample is selected. Despite the many paths available, the sample will be impaired because all the paths are strongly correlated. For example, half of the paths share the first period's 'up' move while the other half share the first period's 'down' move. Finally, simulation models have greater flexibility. Almost any asset or liability can be valued by one. This avoids the problems arising from using several inconsistent models to evaluate different components of a business.

Simulation models also have drawbacks. They are less intuitive than lattice models and require more sophisticated mathematics. Of course, the user does not have to worry about this. They are also less convenient for calculating optimal exercise strategies for American-style options. On a lattice this is done by examining all the possibilities, but that is more difficult using separate paths. Another difference is that a lattice model will produce the same answer each time it prices the same option, while a simulation model will not because of the random sampling process involved. Testing is necessary to determine the degree of pricing error that might be expected for a given option priced using a specific number of paths in the simulation model. Generally, a pricing error can be reduced by increasing the number of paths employed at the expense of increased computation or run time.

To use the model one would have to construct a cashflow module for each security to be valued. The cashflows can depend on the type of security, time, current interest rates and the history of interest rates. In general each path will have a different sequence of cashflows. The valuation procedure is, for each path, to discount each cashflow back to the present by applying the path's one period rates in succession. The total of the discounted cashflows is that path's price. The actual price is the average of the prices for all paths, since the paths are constructed to be equally probable. This simple valuation process is the benefit of making the arbitrage-free adjustment to the paths.

APPENDIX C: DISCOUNTING SPREAD

*Background*

Cash flows are discounted under any option pricing methodology. Cash flows are generated by a computer program based on product characteristics, policyholder demographics, policyholder behavior, company dividend and crediting policy, and, for certain products, a modeled pattern of future interest rates. Such cash flows often extend over a considerable time; as a consequence, they need to be discounted in order to represent fair value. The discounting process has a time value of money component and an adjustment spread component. The time value of money can be measured by risk-free rates of return. US Treasury debt is typically considered to be free from risk of default since the government has taxing authority in the economy. For this reason, US Treasury debt is considered to measure the pure time value of money. Insofar as risk-free rates are different at different terms to maturity, as they typically are, the discounting process should reflect this information. That is, cash flows scheduled at relatively distant times should be discounted at a higher rate than near term cash flows to the extent that long term rates exceed short term rates. An adjustment spread is then added to the schedule of risk-free rates to derive a schedule of discounting rates. In general, the adjustment spread is positive and can represent a risk premium necessary to entice creditors to supply funds to the financial intermediary. It can, however, be offset to the extent that the creditor receives a valuable service, such as investment diversification or mortality risk pooling, from the intermediary. The adjustment spread can also reflect the safety of the assets or capital project funded by the liabilities. In this context, the spread might be less for high quality corporate debt than for low quality debt or for a relatively safe project than for a relatively risky project. This issue is fundamental and will be discussed further below. At this point it is sufficient to note that the schedule of discount rates has two basic elements: a schedule of rates to reflect the pure time value of money and an additional adjustment spread.

The schedule of risk-free rates depends on whether product cash flows are themselves a function of the level of rates in the economy. If the cash flows are fixed, then the risk-free zero coupon rates constitute the appropriate measure of the time value of money. The adjustment spread is added to each zero coupon rate, and the cash flows are discounted to the present. If the cash flows themselves are sensitive to changing interest rates, then the family of arbitrage-free, one-period interest rate paths constitutes the appropriate measure of the time value of money. In this case cash flows are discounted backward from distant points in time to the present by a period-by-period method. The adjustment spread is added to each of the one-period rates. This process is repeated on a path-by-path basis, and the results averaged, until value convergence is achieved at a given level of precision. We will make no assumption about the magnitude or sign of the adjustment spread; that is, it can be great or small and positive or negative due to the myriad of product, company, industry and economic factors that affect it. Although the spread is customarily referred to as a discount spread, we will use the term 'adjustment spread' throughout our discussion of it to reflect this generality. Note that this spread is the same as that often referred to in the investment disciplines; that is, for example, a particular five-year AAA bond may trade in the market at an adjustment spread of 35 basis points.

In summary, under option pricing methodology: (1) projected cash flows are discounted, (2) the discounting process reflects the term structure of risk-free interest rates as a measure of the pure time value of money, (3) the schedule of discount rates is comprised of a further adjustment spread and (4) if cash flows are themselves affected by the level of rates, then cash flow projections and discounting are linked by a more complex simulation process.

Throughout our discussion, we will use the term 'reserves' to refer to fair value reserves unless otherwise noted. The core of our discussion is to explore elements of valuing insurance products under fair market value conventions. Reserving under fair market value has analogies to reserving under statutory conventions. Each methodology establishes a present value of a future obligation, but, whereas statutory reserves look to state mandates for the timing and amount of implicit cash flows and for the interest rate, fair value reserves look to best estimates for the timing and amount of explicit cash flows and to market rates of interest. This approach has clear analogies to securities valuation as employed in investment disciplines. Therefore, reserves in the discussion that follows refers to present values of insurance obligations as estimated under fair market methodologies.

We distinguish between the process of estimating fair value reserves and the way by which these reserves may ultimately be used in establishing financial reporting conventions under any particular system of accounting. We illustrate our reflections on approaches to the adjustment spread with some discussions about the level and dynamics of the fair value reserves that naturally flow from each approach. Our objective in doing so is to explore the actuarial structures of the respective approaches, rather than to recommend financial reporting standards. In establishing such standards, the appropriate body can act to supersede many aspects of our fair value approaches by ancillary reserves, deferred assets and other methods by which to adjust the level of reported reserves and the timing of earnings recognition. We will generally favor those methods under which earnings emerge smoothly over the life of the policies and that do not require artificial reserves to be established. We believe that the presence of such artificial characteristics casts doubt upon the underlying actuarial rigor of the approach.

The fair value of liabilities, like the fair market value of assets, can change dramatically from period to period as rates change. Under each approach, risk-free rates as of the financial statement date are used in the discounting process. To the extent that such rates change from one financial statement date to the next, the fair value of liabilities will change. In general, such value falls as rates rise and vice versa. The magnitude of the change depends heavily on product characteristics and can be substantial, especially for long-term, fixed cash flow obligations such as structured settlements. It is conceivable, however, that a particular product or company crediting policy could produce a change in the opposite direction. Although the inter-period change in liability fair value is explained primarily by the inter-period change in risk-free rates, the adjustment spread has important theoretical implications, such as how conservatively earnings are stated and over what schedule earnings are released. As a consequence, in the following discussion we assume that rates remain constant between periods in order to isolate these important elements.

We now consider more specific approaches to the adjustment spread. Under each approach we consider the underlying rationale of the approach – what it implies about the objective of fair value reserving – and we evaluate the approach. Consider the following grouping according to whether the approach takes the perspective of: (1) the issuing company or its product or (2) the public's expectations of the industry. The section on the public's perspective of the obligations employs a progressive discussion on the realism of the public's regard of the obligation from relatively naive to relatively sophisticated.

Following is a list of the approaches we address:
- *Company perspective*
    Average cost of debt
    Dedicated assets
    US Treasury
    Pricing cost of funds
- *Public perspective*
    US Treasury
    AAA corporate
    Industry average
    Claims paying rating

Let us now explore each of these approaches and discuss how they relate to one another.

*Company perspective*

*Average cost of debt*
This approach would set the adjustment spread at a level that the company believes represents its average debt cost of funds over a period of time. An assumption made under this approach is that a company's debt rating is a proxy for its claims paying ability. The rationale of this approach is that the fair value of reserves should relate to the creditworthiness of the insurance company as revealed in the public debt markets. A relatively risky debtor would experience a higher adjustment spread than a relatively safe debtor. As a result, the insurance reserves of a risky company would be stated lower than the reserves of a safe company; that is, such reserves would be discounted to

reflect the lower probability that the risky company is able to honor its future claims obligations.

With respect to the particular debt and the funds raised by it, company earnings in the issuing period would not be affected, provided that the company borrowed, during such period, at its average cost of funds. The borrower would experience gain or loss as a result of the debt over future periods depending on whether the funds were deployed in assets that earn a higher or lower rate than the effective cost of debt. If it borrowed, during a given period, at a marginal rate different than its average rate and restates the liability to its average cost of funds, then it would show a gain or loss immediately upon issuance. With respect to the insurance contracts of the company, earnings from them would flow smoothly over time in general. When the company determines that its average cost of funds has changed, however, the entire in-force reserves would presumably be restated up or down and would produce a potentially large gain or loss.

The approach can reflect realism insofar as the particular debt issued by the company is maintained on the company's books and on the creditor's books for the transaction amount. That is, the issuance would be fair valued according to a robust public securities market procedure at the clearing price. In general, however, the approach ignores the fundamental reality of the capital structure of a stock insurance company. Consider the following four levels in the capital structure: secured debt, insurance contracts, unsecured debt and common stock. If the company issues secured debt and the collateral retains its integrity, then the creditor has a senior claim on the assets specifically attached to the debt. This type of debt is senior to the insurance contracts and its cost does not relate in any way to the claims paying ability of the company. So it should not be used to value reserves as it would assume an unrealistically high probability of the company's ability to pay its future claims. If the company issues unsecured debt, then the creditor has a claim on such assets of the company as remain after resolution of the company's insurance contracts. Again, since this debt is junior to the insurance contracts in the company's capital structure, its cost does not relate well to the claims paying ability of the company. It should not be used to value reserves as it would assume an unrealistically low probability of the company's ability to pay its future claims. This method would appear, however, to provide useful information on the top and bottom bounds of the company's cost of raising funds through the issuance of insurance contracts.

In general, the fundamental problem with the approach is that the assumption that the company's average debt cost of funds reflects its claims paying ability is unsound. In addition, as a practical matter, many small and medium sized companies do not have good fair market information on their cost of funds since they either do not or cannot raise funds in such way.

*Dedicated assets*
This approach would set the adjustment spread to the weighted average spread on the assets dedicated to the insurance liabilities. The rationale of this classical

actuarial approach is that the liabilities are stated at such level as can be funded by the specific securities backing them. At issuance the company would establish a reserve consistent with the adjustment spread on securities it intended to acquire with premium proceeds. So in the period of issuance the company would reflect a gain provided that the product were profitable. To the extent that the company actually acquired assets at a spread in excess of the pricing spread, or did so during a subsequent accounting period, then the valuation adjustment spread would rise and the value of the liabilities would fall. As subsets to this approach, the adjustment spread can be set at the investment spread either gross or net of expected credit losses. An argument can be made for using the gross spread, on the basis that it is used for calculating investment income on the assets dedicated to the reserves. This argument looks to accounting conventions, however, and not to the actuarial reality of the approach. In fact, some bonds in most portfolios will experience credit losses. Use of the gross spread would cause the company to recognize a gain at policy issuance and subsequent losses. If the company uses the asset net spread, then it does not have the same earnings recognition problem. Although earnings would be recognized at issuance, at least the proper amount of earnings would be recognized, provided that credit losses emerge as expected.

Under this approach the company would recognize the entire gain in the product at issuance provided that it invested at its pricing spread. If the company's investment strategy were to produce higher yields than the pricing assumption by being more aggressive, then the adjustment spread would increase and the company would recognize a gain on the release of reserves, and vice versa. This same effect would be produced by securities market spread widening even if the investment strategy were unchanged. This approach would allow different companies (with different investment strategies) to establish different reserves for identical policies. On the one hand, this could be an advantage to the approach. To the extent that a particular company's investment spread is high due to its risky investment portfolio, then the fair value of its liabilities will be low to reflect the possibility that the company may not be able to honor its obligations. On the other hand, under certain assumptions about the meaning of fair value, the level of reserves held on a company's fair value balance sheet should reflect the price of a block of reserves in a secondary market transaction between two companies. Under this approach, fair value reserves would not have this characteristic. If a ceding company with, for example, a relatively conservative investment strategy, were to cede a block of policies in an indemnity transaction to a company with a relatively aggressive investment strategy, then the reinsurer would establish lower reserves on the policies than the ceding company had maintained. Reserves would be released from the system, although the same policies were insured and, due to the indemnity nature of the transaction, the same company is ultimately obligated to honor the contract. And the transaction price would not readily have reflected the level of reserves held.

The approach has the theoretical disadvantage of reflecting management actions, both of asset and liability natures, on the liability side of the balance sheet. For example, a decision to enter a completely new securities market would be reflected in policy reserves rather than in asset values or an asset reserve. The approach has the clear disadvantage of a company's capacity to manipulate reported earnings by restructuring the securities portfolio between high and low investment spread markets. In fact, it has the potentially alarming aberration of releasing reserves, producing earnings, and increasing surplus, as asset spreads increase during a securities market decline.

*US Treasury*
Under this approach liability cash flows would be discounted at the risk-free rates themselves, without any adjustment spread. The rationale of this approach recognizes that the company board and management typically do not write a policy with any reasonable belief that the company would become insolvent. As a consequence, according to this approach, the company effectively acts as though its policies were free from risk of default. This approach has a compelling nature to it because the issuing company makes decisions under the assumption that, under all conceivable circumstances, it will honor its policies. On the other hand, the approach does not reflect certain factors that are consistent with fair value methodologies. For example, it does not indicate the real (albeit not acted upon) possibility that the company would in fact default on its policies. Nor does it reflect the cost of raising funds that the market would demand or the smooth incidence of earnings recognition that an adjustment spread methodology ideally has.

*Pricing cost of funds*
This approach would set the adjustment spread, through a trial and error process, so that projected cash flows would discount to equal the policy's initial premium. The rationale of this approach presumes that the fair value of an insurance product is embedded in the premium structure of a successfully distributed policy; this fair value can be converted to a cost, to the company, of funds so attracted by the adjustment spread internal to the policy cash flows.

At issuance the company would establish an initial reserve equal to the initial premium less distribution costs. The company would not experience either gain or loss at issuance of the policy. The policy would generally have a reserve that is less than its cash surrender value for a significant period. The amount by which the cash surrender value exceeded the reserve would reflect management's belief that premium persistency would be adequate to recover distribution costs. Incidentally, note that this possibility is present under current GAAP conventions in cases where a contract's benefit reserve less the contract deferred acquisition cost asset is less than the contract's cash surrender value. Therefore, this characteristic of the pricing cost of funds methodology is consistent with current GAAP conventions.

The issuance adjustment spread may be adjusted for use in subsequent periods or may be locked in over the life of the contract. It is clear that, in subsequent periods, fair value reserves would be established according to the company's then-best estimates of future cash flows out of the policy. That is, as the company's experience with a particular block of insurance grew, it could achieve better estimates of emerging future cash flows out of the block. It is conceivable that the updated estimated cash flow pattern would reveal its own cost of funds – in such a case the company could discount future cash flows according to such new adjustment spread. It is also conceivable that the company would still be adding to the block of policies and could discount the seasoned products according to the adjustment spread used when pricing the company's products. Finally, if the block had been closed and the company's experience were in line with its pricing assumptions, then it could effectively lock in the adjustment spread established at issuance for use in subsequent periods.

Under this approach the company would recognize neither gain nor loss at issuance. Since the spread discounts the entire net policy cash flows to zero at issuance, there is no residual value at issuance to take through company earnings. Earnings are released smoothly over the life of the policy. The cost of funds approach establishes a liability that is independent of the assets backing the product. Instead, the cost generally reflects a myriad of factors, including the market's assessment of the riskiness of the company, any distribution franchise it may enjoy, and the efficiency of its administrative operations. This is consistent with the way industrial debtors measure borrowing costs. The market reflects its relative aversion to the company's prospects in the premium structure it agrees to pay. This approach is similar to the company's debt cost of funds except that a more integral link is made between the cost of funds and the claims paying capacity of the institution. In releasing earnings, the approach has the benefit of de-coupling assets and liabilities. On the asset side, to the extent that the company can earn a return in excess of the cost of funds spread implied by the premium structure, it will show asset-driven earnings. And on the liability side, to the extent that the company conserves the business or reduces expenses (in excess of its expectation at distribution), it will show liability-driven earnings.

*Public perspective*

*US Treasury*
Under this approach liability cash flows would be discounted at the risk-free rates themselves without any adjustment spread. Note that this approach also was included in the company perspective category with a different rationale. The primary rationale for this approach is that financial statements should be stated such that insureds bear no risk. Using no adjustment spread, the approach would establish fair value reserves at a level such that there is negligible risk that the company is not able to honor the terms of the contract.

State guaranty funds might imply to the insured public that funds accumulating for them with a US insurer are virtually free of credit risk. It is true that the guaranty funds do not have the backing of the full faith and credit of the US government's taxing authority behind them in the same way that the deposit insurance fund has for depository institutions. However, since the state insurance regulatory departments can, in the case of the failure of one of its companies, make assessments against all other insurers licensed in the state, the guaranty fund system has effectively mandated that all insurers support the solvency of each institution in a state. As a consequence, all insurance companies have letters of credit from each company in its state. The result could imply to the public that the funds are free of credit risk. This implication would be a mistake. State regulators commonly establish workout plans for insolvent companies that result in loss of money to policyholders. In addition, even when funds are made available, the resolution may take a substantial amount of time. So both credit and liquidity premiums ought to be assigned. Choosing an adjustment spread of zero is arbitrary with respect to the pricing cost of funds. Doing so will therefore produce either a gain or loss at issue, from an actuarial perspective, depending on whether the pricing cost of funds was below or above zero. In theory, a risk-adjusted guarantee fund premium could be paid that would have the effect of properly risk-adjusting reserves.

The approach has the benefit of comparability across companies. It is not likely to tend to track the price of secondary market reinsurance transactions, however. In general, it could understate fair value reserves on products that provide relatively greater risk intermediation services (such as term insurance) and overstate fair value reserves on products that are closer to investment products. In most cases, the incidence of earnings is not well matched. Instead, it would show unrealistic gains or losses early in the life of the policy and then turn around later in the life of the policy.

*AAA corporate*
This approach would set the adjustment spread to the spread on top quality corporate bonds.

The rationale of this approach is similar to the US Treasury approach except that it is somewhat less conservative. Under the AAA Corporate model, creditors of policy-related funds are considered to regard the insurance industry as they do the highest rated companies in the economy. That is, due to its generally conservative regulatory environment, the insurance industry is safe from the possibility of default. The approach is consistent with considering insurance products as commodities. That is, since all companies state their reserves using the same adjustment spread and since all reserve statements are considered to be at fair market, the implication is that no company is a better credit risk than any other company.

The approach has the same actuarial earnings release issues as the US Treasury approach. Again, since in general the choice of the AAA corporate

rate is arbitrary with respect to the pricing cost of funds, the emergence of earnings from the contracts will not occur naturally over the life of the contract. In general, it would be naive for the public to believe and act as though the industry has the overall creditworthiness of the strongest corporations in the economy.

*Industry*
This approach would set the adjustment spread at an industry average, probably by means of a formula and by product type. The spread would reset periodically and could be linked to, perhaps, the prevailing AA corporate bond spread to reflect the overall creditworthiness of the industry, which because of state guaranty funds, can be argued to be the actual creditworthiness of any insurer. The rationale of this approach is that reserves should be stated consistently across companies at levels that are close to market transaction values. It presumes that a robust industry average can be established.

At issuance and at subsequent financial statement dates, the company would establish a reserve equal to then-future projected cash flows discounted at the industry spread. Under this approach the company would recognize gain or loss immediately as a function of several idiosyncratic factors, such as distribution costs, administration expenses, product mix strategy (i.e. perhaps a given product is sold as a 'loss leader') and investment strategy. At subsequent financial statement dates, it would recognize further gain or loss depending on the change in the industry adjustment spread. So if the spread increased, the company's in force reserves would fall and earnings would be released. This would represent a measure, in a sense, of the extent to which the company issued policies at an advantageous time (i.e. prior to the spread increase). Assuming a constant spread over time and that the company issued the product at an implied cost of funds equal to the initial industry spread, earnings would be released smoothly over the life of the policy. Assuming that the industry spread is robust, an advantage of the approach is that it would set reserves at the same level for the entire industry. It would effectively unlock the cost of funds spread for financial statements subsequent to issuance for the average company.

In general, this approach is somewhat more sophisticated than either of the prior public perspective approaches, but still inadequate. It is more sophisticated than the former approaches in that it properly recognizes that providing funds to the insurance industry entails more risk than providing funds to the most creditworthy corporations in the economy. It does not recognize the heterogeneity of the industry, however. That is, providing funds to certain companies is more risky than providing funds to other companies. The adjustment spread should recognize this.

*Claims paying rating*
This approach would set the adjustment spread at a level that is consistent with the claims paying rating of the particular institution. The rationale of this

approach is similar to other public perspective approaches in that it is an attempt to reflect the risk to the policyholder of holding an insurance contract. This approach goes beyond approaches mentioned to this point in recognizing, not only the risk of the industry, but also of the particular company.

To the extent that the ratings, assigned by private ratings agencies, are robust, this approach generally has good reserve and earnings recognition characteristics. It tends toward the pricing cost of funds approach in that relatively low rated companies generally need a relatively low premium structure or high dividend payment structure to distribute their products. So this approach bears the added sophistication of reflecting company-specific risks. The approach has the disadvantage of relying on an external source to assess risk rather than on the market itself. That is, the real test of the public's perception of a given company is the effective cost of funds at which a policyholder is willing to provide funds to a company in a consummated transaction. Reliance on information from any source external to true market activity is generally artificial. In addition, the approach ignores differences in products issued by a company. A company that distributes second-to-die term insurance, for example, might be meeting such an intense market need that insureds are willing to earn a low effective return on funds to acquire it. On the other hand, insureds might require quite a high effective return to maintain dividends on deposit with the same insurer because such reserve provides almost no benefit that they could not obtain elsewhere. To the extent that claims paying ratings do not reflect the service-provided element of insurance contracts, they are ignoring important information.

*Conclusion*

We have presented several approaches to the adjustment spread associated with fair valuation of insurance liabilities. We have categorized these into those that take the perspective of the issuing company or its products and those that look to the public's expectations of the industry. In doing so we have focused on the actuarial structure of the contracts to describe the respective approaches and to evaluate them. As part of our description of various approaches, we have reflected on the actuarial characteristics of earnings release.

A focus on the creditworthiness and strategies of individual firms favors the company group of methods. Under each approach, fair value reserves are stated according to some function of company actions or capital adequacy level. The average cost of debt method argues that reserves should be held given the best measure of the company's borrowing costs in the market. The dedicated assets method sets reserves according to the return characteristics, and by extension, the riskiness of the assets backing the contracts and thereby provides some information about the probability of the direct writer's ability to honor the terms of the contract. The US Treasury method recognizes that company management typically acts as though it will honor all obligations without any contingencies. The pricing cost of funds method provides the clearest indication of the costs of the funds required to break even that are raised by an institution.

A focus on the public trust in the integrity of fair value reserves favors the public group of approaches. Under most approaches all companies would use the same adjustment spread and would hold the same fair value reserves. The US Treasury method assumes that the policyholder claims are satisfied completely. The AAA Corporate method treats insurance products as commodities that highly rated companies guarantee. The industry average method indicates a closer relation to actual industry cost of funds. The claims paying rating method is more sophisticated for recognizing company-specific risks.

## APPENDIX D: DYNAMIC BEHAVIORAL ASSUMPTIONS

### Background

A block of insurance liabilities can be viewed as a stream of future net cash flows. The net cash flows can be developed by projecting future premium payments and policy loan repayments to the company less future operating expenses, death claims, surrender/withdrawal payments, policy loan proceeds, and cash dividend payments from the company. Once the stream of net cash flows is isolated, the block of insurance liabilities can be valued much like other financial instruments. The resulting cash flow stream is often laden with options. The fair value of a cash flow stream includes the value of its embedded options, which can be highly sensitive to interest rate changes. For example, future surrender values vary with future crediting rates (or future dividend scales), and the degree of surrender activity depends on the relationship between future market interest rates and future crediting rates.

Option pricing and appraisal techniques provide a framework for assigning a fair value to a stream of contingent cash flows. But, one must first describe how the cash flows are expected to vary with future market interest rates.

### Policyholder behavior

To project future policyholder surrenders/withdrawals, policy loan utilization/ repayments, and discretionary premium payments, one must develop dynamic behavioral assumptions.

#### Surrenders/withdrawals
Traditional whole life policies provide policyholders with a cash value upon surrender. Non-traditional products, such as universal life (UL) and single premium deferred annuities (SPDA), typically allow policyholders to make full and partial withdrawals from their account value. To project future surrender/withdrawal activity, one must predict how policyholders will behave in different interest rate environments.

Policyholders often surrender their policies because they need cash for an upcoming expenditure. Similarly, they may elect to take systematic withdrawals from a deferred annuity to supplement their retirement income. These decisions usually have little to do with market interest rates (i.e. they occur even when a policy's crediting rate compares favorably with alternative investments). Policyholders also withdraw funds to transfer to new, more attractive policies. For example, when interest rates rise new policies generally provide higher crediting rates than old policies. By exercising the option to surrender their old contracts, policyholders can take advantage of higher yielding alternatives. The incentives to withdraw funds are tempered by (1) surrender charges, (2) tax consequences, and (3) changes in health.

If an efficient policyholder wishes to take advantage of a higher yielding alternative, the economic gain must compensate for any charges imposed upon surrender of the old policy. Non-traditional policies often deduct surrender charges from premature withdrawals. The surrender charges normally decrease to zero over a period of time, 5–10 years for deferred annuities and 10–15 for universal life products. Many non-traditional policies contain 'free partial withdrawal' provisions which waive surrender charges on partial withdrawals up to a stated amount. For example, many deferred annuity contracts waive surrender charges on the first 10% of the account value withdrawn in each year. Free partial withdrawal provisions effectively reduce the surrender charges. Surrender transactions may trigger policyholder taxation of the inside build-up. In some cases, an additional penalty tax also applies. The tax implications vary by type of policy (e.g. life insurance or annuity), tax qualified status, policyholder's age, and kind of transaction (e.g. simple surrender or IRA roll-over).

Life insurance policyholders must also consider the implications of any changes in their health. To replace an old life insurance policy with a new one, the insured must submit evidence of insurability. If the insured's health has deteriorated since purchase of the existing policy, new life insurance may be much more expensive. Serious health changes may even make the individual uninsurable. Even if there have been no health changes, the insured may be reluctant to go through the underwriting process again.

A model of policyholder surrender/withdrawal behavior should capture (1) the activity which is relatively independent of market interest rates, (2) the transfers to new, more attractive policies, (3) the dampening effect of surrender charges, (4) the tax consequences of the transaction, and (5) the implications of changing health conditions (for life insurance).

*Policy loans*
Virtually all permanent life insurance contracts include policy loan provisions. Recent tax law changes make policy loans undesirable in non-qualified deferred annuities. However, certain tax-qualified annuities and many old annuity contracts also provide policy loans. A loan provision permits a policyholder to access his or her cash value without surrendering the underlying insurance

contract. The contract treats the transaction as a loan instead of a withdrawal. The policy's cash value and death benefit provide the necessary collateral. The policyholder essentially borrows funds from his or her own policy. The loan may be repaid at any time. Otherwise, the outstanding loan and accumulated interest are deducted from the surrender value or death proceeds when the policy terminates.

A policy loan also affects the calculation of credited interest. The way in which loans affect credited interest varies by product type. Non-traditional products unbundle policy value calculations, providing explicit interest credits to policy account values. In contrast, traditional life products use dividends to reflect interest, mortality, and expense experience. Consequently, the marginal effect of policy loans on credited interest is less visible.

A UL policy provides a good example of the unbundled approach. Since a policy loan is not a withdrawal, the loan proceeds do not reduce the policy's account value. However, to determine credited interest, the account value is divided into two parts. The first part equals the portion of the account value backing the policy loan. This part is often called the impaired amount. The remaining portion of the account value constitutes the unimpaired amount. The basic crediting rate applies to the unimpaired amount. If there is no policy loan, this rate is credited to the entire account value. However, if a policy loan exists, a separate rate is credited to the impaired amount.

UL contracts typically link the crediting rate for the impaired amount with the policy loan interest rate. For instance, a contract may specify that the crediting rate for impaired amounts equals the policy loan interest rate less 2%. If the policy loan interest rate is 8%, the crediting rate for impaired amounts is 6%. Hence, policyholders realize a net cost on policy loans of 2%.

Some insurance contracts also contain 'preferred loan' provisions which either reduce or eliminate the net cost on policy loans up to a stated amount. For example, a policy loan for up to 10% of the account value may qualify for (1) a preferred loan interest rate of 6% and (2) an impaired amount crediting rate of 6%. Thus, policyholders realize a zero net cost on preferred policy loans. With traditional life insurance contracts, the effect of policy loans on credited interest is bundled up in policy dividends. The dividend calculation recognizes policy loan activity either directly or indirectly. Under the direct recognition method, the interest component of dividends is calculated separately for each policy. The calculation involves two steps. The first step determines the interest applicable to the unimpaired amount. The second step determines the interest applicable to the impaired amount. By calculating the interest component separately for each policy, the dividend passes the effects of policy loans directly to the policyholders who actually use the policy loan feature. The indirect recognition method essentially pools the effects of policy loans across all policies in a common dividend class. The calculation of the interest component of dividends still involves two steps. However, the calculation is made for an entire class of policies instead of policy by policy. The effects of policy loans are passed indirectly to all policyholders, including those who do not have policy loans.

Policy loans have important tax implications. If a life insurance policy avoids classification as a modified endowment contract, the policyholder can access the policy's value via a policy loan without triggering taxation of the inside build-up. For this reason, policy loans offer an attractive alternative to partial withdrawals. Policyholders often take out policy loans because they need cash for an expenditure. For example, the original reasons for purchasing the policy may include funding a child's college education with policy loans. In other cases, the need may be unexpected. Policyholders also use policy loans to remove funds from their insurance contracts and reinvest them in higher yielding alternatives. The crediting rates on old insurance contracts typically lag behind market interest rate changes. If market interest rates suddenly jump from 7% to 15%, the crediting rate on an old policy may rise to only 9%. But, a policyholder may be able to borrow from the insurance policy at a fixed 8% loan interest rate (and a fixed 2% net cost) and reinvest the proceeds at 15%.

Insurers experienced such disintermediation in the late 1970s and early 1980s. Prior to experiencing high levels of interest rate volatility, insurance policies contained fixed loan rate guarantees. The loan interest rates were set by the terms of the contract, ranging from 6–8%. When state regulators realized the potential for disintermediation, they adopted appropriate regulation to permit variable loan interest rates. Many new policies index policy loan interest rates to current market rates. This technique reduces the disintermediation risk by maintaining a reasonable relationship between the policy loan interest rate and market interest rates. However, some new policies and many older policies continue to provide fixed loan interest rates. The policy loan utilization model must recognize the potential for increased policy loan activity when market interest rates rise above policy loan interest rates. The model should also consider the degree to which marketing strategies and sales illustrations promote policy loan features.

*Flexible premiums*
Many non-traditional insurance policies provide flexibility in the amount and timing of premium payments. In some cases, policyholders have the right to deposit additional premiums under guaranteed crediting rates established at an earlier date. Policyholders can often defer regularly scheduled premiums to a later date. This premium flexibility enables policyholders to select against the insurance company when the crediting rates for new premiums lag behind market interest rate changes. For example, if market interest rates fall, policyholders have an incentive to pay additional premiums and lock into above-market rates. If market interest rates rise, policyholders may defer premium payments until crediting rates catch up with market rates.

The premium payment model should recognize the potential for antiselection when current crediting rate guarantees on new premiums lag market interest rate changes.

*Basis of assumptions*
Policyholder behavioral assumptions must be developed using sound professional judgement. Important factors to consider include:
- Distribution system;
- Policyholder's age;
- Size of contract; and
- Tax-qualified status.

Where possible, one should consider past experience for a given policy form or other similar policy forms sold by the same company or other companies, in that order of preference. In the absence of insurance company experience, one may draw upon experience with other financial products. One should also consider expected trends in experience. Policyholder behavior can change over time. For example, policyholders are likely to become more knowledgeable of their contractual options and alternative investments. Thus, one should expect policyholders to increasingly exercise their surrender/withdrawal, policy loan, and premium payment options when they can realize a financial gain.

Fair value calculations should reflect then-current behavioral assumptions for the entire block of business. One should periodically compare actual experience against assumptions. If actual experience deviates materially from expected experience, the underlying assumptions should be revised. Subsequent fair value calculations should incorporate the new assumptions.

One should also consider the impact of recent events on future experience. For example, a rating agency may downgrade the insurer. This event may lead to higher surrender activity. If a significant downgrade occurs, one should review policyholder behavioral assumptions and make appropriate changes. Subsequent fair value calculations should use the revised assumptions.

*SPDA example*
The SPDA product provides a simple example. Due to unfavorable tax treatment, the SPDA has no policy loan provision. The single premium feature precludes additional premiums. Policyholder behavioral assumptions consist only of surrender/withdrawal assumptions.

The surrender/withdrawal model should have the following characteristics:
- A minimum level of surrenders/withdrawals should occur even when a policy's crediting rate is well above rates on new, alternative investments.
- Surrenders/withdrawals should increase appropriately when a policy's crediting rate falls below the rates available on alternative investments.
- Surrenders/withdrawals should be tempered by the presence of a surrender charge.

One can achieve these characteristics with an arctangent function.

- For example, the surrender/withdrawal rate can be defined dynamically by:

$$SW_t = A_t + B \times \mathrm{ARCTAN}[M \times (AI_t - CR_t - AS_t) - N],$$

where:

$SW_t$ = annual surrender/withdrawal rate at time $t$;

$AI_t$ = interest rate on alternative investment at time $t$;

$CR_t$ = policy's crediting rate at time $t$;

$AS_t$ = amortized surrender charge at time $t$;

$A_t$, $B$, $M$, and $N$ are parameters chosen to produce (1) the desired minimum surrender/withdrawal rate, (2) the desired maximum surrender/withdrawal rate, and (3) an appropriately increasing surrender/withdrawal rate as the policy's crediting rate falls further and further below the rate on alternative investments.

The alternative investment rate ($AI_t$) is an important part of the surrender/withdrawal behavioral model. A proxy for the competitor's new SPDA rate can be defined by then-current Treasury rates. For example, one can use the then-current 5-year Treasury rate less 50 basis points for an alternative SPDA rate. Recent studies suggest that rates on new SPDAs fall more slowly than capital market rates. To reproduce this observed lag, one can use an appropriate moving average of the 5-year Treasury rate.

The amortized surrender charge ($AS_t$) equals the effective surrender charge at time $t$ (expressed as a %age of the account value) divided by an appropriate amortization period (such as three years). For the policyholder to gain by transferring to a new SPDA, the difference between the alternative SPDA rate and the policy's crediting rate must exceed the amortized surrender charge.

*UL example*

The UL product is more complicated than the SPDA product. Policyholder behavioral assumptions include surrender and withdrawal activity, policy loan utilization, and flexible premium payments. A UL surrender/withdrawal model should have the same characteristics listed for the SPDA model:

- A minimum level of surrenders/withdrawals should occur even when a policy's crediting rate is well above rates on new, alternative investments.
- Surrenders/withdrawals should increase appropriately when a policy's crediting rate falls below the rates available on alternative investments.
- Surrenders/withdrawals should be tempered by the presence of a surrender charge.

However, one should also consider several other factors:

- Surrenders should be higher in early months when some policyholders conclude that they can not afford the added expense of insurance premiums.
- The assumptions should recognize the secondary importance of crediting rates with life insurance. Although surrenders/withdrawals should increase when a policy's crediting rate falls below market rates, the degree of change should be less than for SPDA policies.

- Projected surrenders/transfers to new, more attractive policies should be tempered by the possibility of health changes and general discomfort with medical exams.

Note that the possibility of a change in the insured's health provides an opportunity for mortality antiselection. Policyholders who transfer to new policies tend to be those in good health. Consequently, those who stay with their old policies tend to be in poorer health. One can accommodate the additional considerations for life insurance within the ARCTAN surrender/withdrawal model described earlier for SPDAs.

In addition to a surrender/withdrawal model, one must develop explicit assumptions for policy loan behavior. The policy loan utilization model should have the following characteristics:

- A minimum level of policy loans should occur even when a policy's loan interest rate (or impaired crediting rate) is well above rates on new, alternative investments.
- Policy loan utilization should increase appropriately when the policy loan interest rate falls below the rates available on alternative investments.
- The use of policy loan illustrations and promotion of preferred loan features by sales representatives may lead to higher utilization rates.

For example, the policy loan utilization rate can be defined dynamically by:

$$LU_t = \max\{C_t, \min[D_t, C_t + E^*(AI_t - IA_t)]\},$$

where:

$LU_t =$ portion of the account values that are impaired by policy loans at time $t$;

$AI_t =$ interest rate on an alternative investment at time $t$;

$IA_t =$ interest rate credited on impaired amounts at time $t$;

$C_t$, $D_t$, and $E$ are parameters chosen to produce (1) the desired minimum utilization rate, (2) the desired maximum utilization rate, and (3) an appropriately increasing utilization rate as the policy's impaired amount crediting rate falls further and further below the rate on alternative investments.

The alternative investment rate $(AI_t)$ is an important part of the loan utilization behavioral model. When policyholders take out policy loans, they retain their underlying insurance policies. Thus, the alternative investment should probably be linked to the capital markets rather than the crediting rate available on new UL policies. For example, one can use the then-current 5-year Treasury note for an alternative investment.

Finally, one should develop explicit assumptions for premium payment behavior. The premium payment model should have the following characteristics:

- A base pattern of premium payments should be projected when the crediting rates for new premiums are in line with market interest rates. Early premium

levels may include many one-time transfers. Consequently, premium levels may decline over time.
- Premium payments should increase appropriately when market interest rates fall below the crediting rates on new premiums.
- Premium payments should decrease when market interest rates rise above the crediting rates on new premiums.

For example, the premium payments can be defined dynamically by:

$$P_t = BP_t \times \min\{F_t, [G_t + H \times (AI_t - NP_t)]\},$$

where:

$P_t$ = expected premium payment at time $t$;

$BP_t$ = base premium payment at time $t$;

$AI_t$ = interest rate on alternative investment at time $t$;

$NP_t$ = crediting rate for new premiums received at time $t$;

$F_t$, $G_t$, and $H$ are parameters chosen to produce the (1) desired minimum premium level, (2) the desired maximum premium level, and (3) an appropriate adjustment to the base premium payment when the crediting rate for new premiums is above or below alternative investment rates.

As with the policy loan utilization model, the alternative investment should probably be linked with the capital markets rather than the crediting rate on new UL policies. Thus, one can use the then-current 5-year Treasury note for the alternative investment.

*Insurance company behavior*

Insurers can influence policyholder behavior by resetting (1) the non-guaranteed elements of non-traditional products and (2) the dividend scales of traditional life insurance products. For example, insurers often have considerable discretion in resetting current insurance charges and crediting rates on universal life insurance policies. Policyholder surrenders are particularly sensitive to the difference in market interest rates and a policy's crediting rate.

*Resetting crediting rates*
Most insurers link crediting rates to the yield on the underlying investments. Product managers often identify stated investment and reinvestment strategies with each product line. The crediting rates are linked to the asset yields, less a required interest margin. The required interest margin is determined in product pricing. It typically provides for profit, expenses, and amortized acquisition costs.

When market interest rates rise, the asset portfolio's book yield gradually increases. The current yield on new assets reflects the higher market interest rates, while the yield on older investments reflects prior, lower market levels.

Similarly, when market interest rates fall, the asset portfolio's book yield gradually decreases. Consequently, the asset yields and therefore the renewal crediting rates lag market changes. For a simple noncallable bond strategy, the degree of lag varies with the maturity structure of the underlying investments. Short-term bonds mature quickly and thus allow crediting rates to follow market changes. But, short-term yields are often lower and may produce uncompetitive crediting rates for new business. Long-term bonds turn over slowly. The resulting crediting rates are less responsive to market changes. However, long-term yields generally produce higher crediting rates for new business.

*Important considerations*
The crediting strategy is an important element of the fair value calculation. Obviously, different crediting strategies produce different liability values. One can not identify the appropriate crediting strategy in a vacuum. Rather, one must consider how the product manager actually resets crediting rates.

Ideally, the product manager will have considered the crediting strategy in the product design and pricing processes. The crediting strategy has important pricing and profitability implications. Using option pricing models, one can compare the relative costs of alternative crediting strategies. The product manager should consider the expected investment returns and stated financial objective to determine what crediting strategies the insurer can afford.

*SPDA example*
Again, the SPDA product provides a simple example. Policyholder premiums accumulate with interest, and a declining scale of surrender charges applies to early withdrawals. Thus, company behavioral assumptions consist only of a crediting strategy. Future crediting rates can be projected by simulating the investment operations and backing into the crediting rates. However, it is useful to translate the resulting rates into an explicit crediting strategy. One can often achieve the desired characteristics by modeling future crediting rates as a function of the current crediting rate and future market rates.

For example, suppose that the desired crediting strategy has the following characteristics:
- The initial crediting rate is linked to the then-current 5-year Treasury rate.
- The crediting rate resets annually, moving partially towards the then-current initial crediting rate on new policies.
- The crediting rate is guaranteed by the terms of the contract to be at least 3%.

One can achieve these characteristics by defining future crediting rates with the following formula:

$$CR_t = \max\{3\%, CR_{t-1} + [RS \times (IR_t - CR_{t-1})]\},$$

where:

$CR_t$ = the crediting rate in effect at time $t$;

$CR_{t-1}$ = the crediting rate in effect at time $t-1$;

$RS$ = the crediting rate reset speed; and

$IR_t$ = the initial crediting rate on new policies at time $t$.

A reset speed of 20% means that crediting rates move one fifth of the difference between (1) the then-current initial rate on new policies and (2) the previous rate on the existing policy. One can define the initial rate on new policies by the then-current 5-year Treasury yield. For example, the initial crediting rate might equal the 5-year Treasury rate less 75 basis points.

*Additional consideration for UL*
As with the SPDA product, company behavioral assumptions typically consist only of a crediting strategy. Future crediting rates for a UL policy can be modeled using a similar formula. However, one may wish to complicate the crediting rate model slightly for new premiums. To maintain a reasonable relationship between the crediting rate for new premiums and the rate on then-current alternative investments, companies can provide separate rate guarantees for new premiums. The applicable rate guarantees typically run from the date of each premium payment. For example, the new money rates can be guaranteed for one year.

As the initial rate guarantees expire, the accumulated amounts begin to earn an old money rate. Old money rates can vary by product and/or year of issue. Since an old money rate applies to all premium payments (following expiration of the initial rate guarantee), the old money rate usually tracks a moving average of an appropriate market interest rate. For instance, one can define the old money crediting strategy by substituting the 36–month moving average of 5-year Treasury rates for the initial crediting rate on new policies ($IR_t$).

DAVID F. BABBEL

*The Wharton School, University of Pennsylvania*

# Comments on *'Fair valuation of life insurance company liabilities'*[1]

I have been asked to comment on the paper prepared by members of the American Academy of Actuaries Fair Valuation of Liabilities Task Force (hereafter Task Force). The Task Force has done a commendable job in presenting and making sense of the numerous approaches that have been applied toward the valuation of insurance liabilities. They compare and contrast the approaches, give critical appraisals of their strengths and limitations, and add their own views regarding the ultimate usefulness of the models. It was a gargantuan task to digest and assemble so much information and present it in a coherent, correlated framework. We all owe them a great debt of gratitude.

The stochastic interest rate valuation methodologies that are described in the Task Force paper, which I will focus on today, have been examined in the context of a paradigm imported from the corporate finance literature, which I do not think has served the insurance industry very well. It's ill-suited for financial institutions. If insurance assets and liabilities were freely traded, the problem would be transparent. The financial institutions' economic literature, particularly the work of Kim Staking [see chapter 7, this volume] deals with guarantees and how they affect the entire balance sheet.[1] I think it would be a useful paradigm for us to review here, and you will see how it casts everything in a different light.

If you think of the market value of a stock insurance firm as the value of its stock, it is comprised of three elements: the franchise value (or as some call it, the going concern value), the liquidation value, and the put option value (Figure 1). This is true for any financial institution.

| Market Value of Stock | = | Franchise Value | + | Liquidation Value | + | Put Option |
|---|---|---|---|---|---|---|

*Figure 1.* Market value of insurance stock.

[1] Dr Staking wrote his doctoral dissertation on this topic. A recent paper summarizing the research appeared in the December 1995 issue of the *Journal of Risk and Insurance*, under the title 'The relation between capital structure, interest rate sensitivity, and market value in the property-liability insurance industry'. I have written a discussion of the paradigm in 'A perspective on model investment laws for insurers', *C.L.U. Journal*, September 1994.

These three elements have the following components (Figure 2). The franchise value stems from what economists call economic rents. This is the present value of the rents that an insurer is expected to garner because it has scarce resources, scarce capital, charter value, licenses, a distribution network, personnel, reputation, and so forth. It includes renewal business and that sort of thing.

Liquidation value is simply the market value of tangible assets, less the present value of liabilities. This liquidation value is independent of what kind of assets an insurer has. Put option value is the value of issuing debt (i.e. insurance policies, the debt of an insurance company) at rates below market due to the insurance insolvency guarantee program. It's the value to equity holders of capturing upside earnings while not incurring all the downside costs of default.

Let us look at each of these three components of value, as a function of risk. Liquidation value appears as flat line (Figure 3). It doesn't matter how much risk the insurer has. If it has $4 billion in government securities, duration, and convexity matched to its $3 billion in liabilities, it has $1 billion in liquidation value. The insurer can put the same $4 billion in pork belly futures, yet it would still have $1 billion in current liquidation value. Liquidation value is completely independent of firm risk. Franchise value, on the other hand, is dependent on firm risk. The less firm risk there is, the more likely the firm is to stay in business and capture all these available economic rents arising from its renewal business, its distribution network, its reputation, and so forth.

Put option value, which is derived from the option that an insurer gains as a result of the insolvency guarantee provided by its competitors, becomes valuable only when the insurer takes on more risk. Because the value of this option is measured as the difference between what the liabilities would be

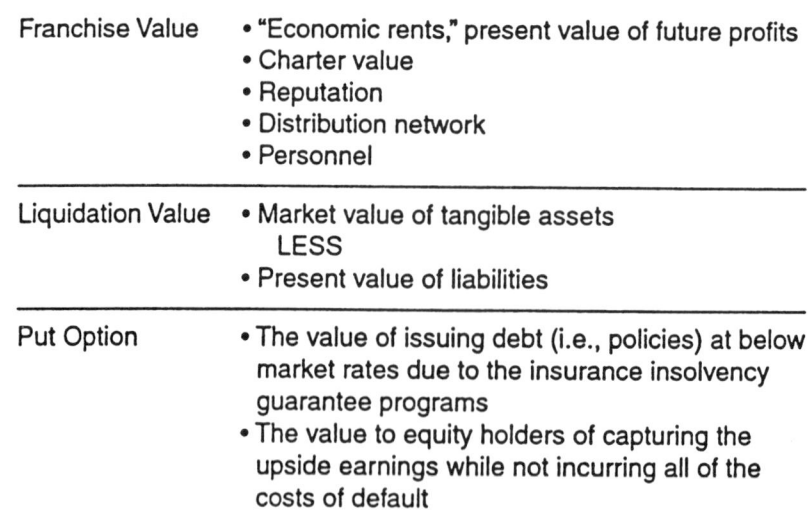

| Franchise Value | • "Economic rents," present value of future profits<br>• Charter value<br>• Reputation<br>• Distribution network<br>• Personnel |
|---|---|
| Liquidation Value | • Market value of tangible assets<br>    LESS<br>• Present value of liabilities |
| Put Option | • The value of issuing debt (i.e., policies) at below market rates due to the insurance insolvency guarantee programs<br>• The value to equity holders of capturing the upside earnings while not incurring all of the costs of default |

*Figure 2.* Coponents of insurance stock market value.

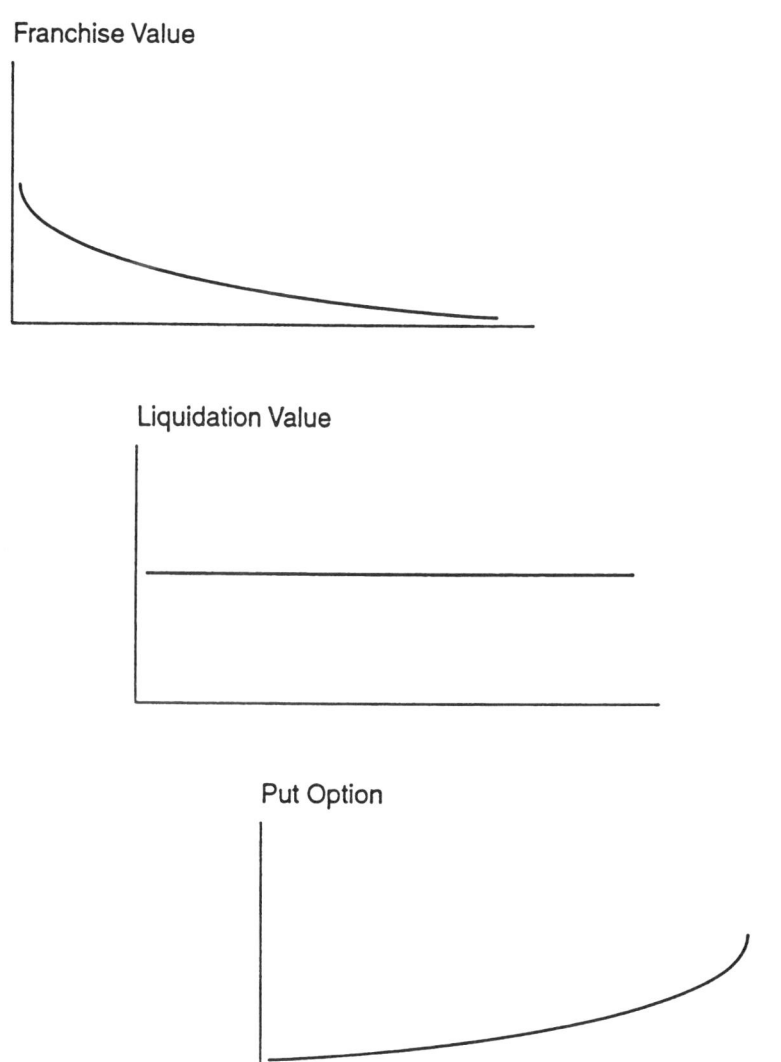

*Figure 3.* Risk and the components of value.

worth if they were backed only by the insurance firm's own assets, as a standalone enterprise versus what they are worth when they are guaranteed, it has value only if there is a difference between the values of nonguaranteed and guaranteed liabilities. If the insurer is not a risky firm, there may be no difference between these values, but if it is a risky firm it obtains a substantial benefit from its competitors who are guaranteeing the liabilities.

When these three elements are displayed together, you can see the market value of the firm. The ratio shown on the vertical axis is the market value divided by liquidation value. When market value equals liquidation value, this ratio is unity: the shaded area in Figure 4 represents the liquidation value of the firm. As the firm increases in risk, there is a higher ratio of market value to liquidation value; and, as it decreases in risk, again there is a higher ratio. This is not just a theoretical construct, but has been accepted wisdom in the financial institutions' literature for quite a few years: Kim Staking showed with data from 200 observations over an 8-year period that the insurance company values were consistent with this model. In fact, he showed that the average increment to the market value of surplus over liquidation value is about 47% in the multiline insurance industry, predominantly characterized by property-casualty lines. (We have not yet conducted a similar study for life insurance companies, but have no reason to suspect a different general result.) This equity market value premium over liquidation value stems either from put option value or from franchise value, or from some combination of the two.

This insight has important implications for the discussion of fair value of insurance liabilities, which should be considered in the context of guarantees. Let us return to my earlier comment about the difference between the corporate finance and the financial institutions' economic literature. In Figure 5, I have placed at the top an equation that gives market value of net worth [MV(NW)] as market value of assets [MV(A)] less market value of liabilities [MV(L)]. This is true by definition. Let us view this first from the point of view of the corporate finance economic literature. If you were to add pure risk to the asset side of a nonfinancial corporation but maintained the same market value of assets, it drives down the value of your liabilities. Because you are a risker firm, there is a greater chance you won't be around to repay them, so people discount the bonds that you have already issued (and require higher coupon rates on any new bonds). Your liabilities go down while your assets stay the

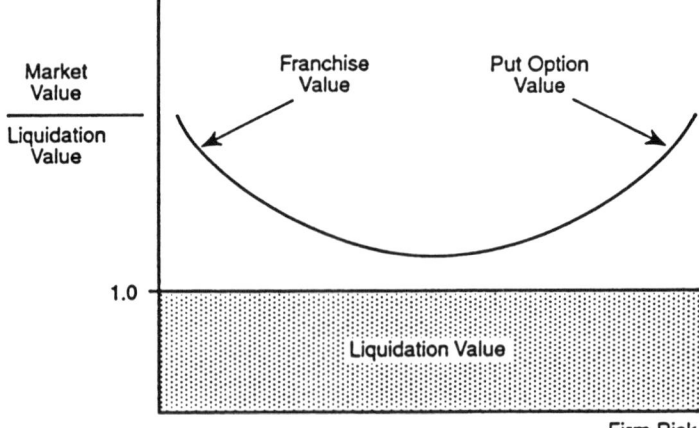

*Figure 4.* Components of value combined.

## General Condition

$$MV(A) - MV(L) = MV(NW)$$

*add pure asset risk...*

## Nonfinancial Corporations

$$MV(A) - \downarrow MV(L) = \uparrow MV(NW)$$

## Financial Institutions

$$\uparrow MV(A) - PV(L) = \uparrow MV(NW)$$
(includes put)

*Figure 5.* Market value equations and risk.

same; therefore, your stock value goes up. This well-known result from the finance literature explains the motivation for a lot of risky behavior, such as leveraged buyouts and that sort of thing.

In the financial institutions' economic literature, if we add pure risk to the firm, again holding constant the value of tangible assets, the present value liabilities doesn't change at all. This will really simplify our task in valuing them. What happens is that the market value of assets has changed, because the put option suddenly gains value, and that's one of your assets. At the same time, the franchise value, another asset, is reduced. To the extent that the increase in put option value exceeds the decrease in franchise value, the market value of net worth rises.

Let us now turn to a couple of items that the Task Force paper discussed. We will substitute the term 'economic surplus' for 'net worth' because we are going to be talking about insurance companies.[2] We will also substitue the term 'present value of liabilities' for 'market value of liabilities', since the liabilities are generally not freely traded items. The market value of economic surplus $[MV(S)]$ is comprised of franchise value (FrV), liquidation value $[\equiv MV(TA) - PV(L)]$, and put option value (P), as was shown in Figure 1. $MV(TA)$ denotes the market value of tagible assets. The present value of liabilities $[PV(L)]$ encompasses all liabilities, so these other items must necessarily go on the asset side of the balance sheet. Because some of the valuation methodologies reviewed by the Task Force do not carefully keep track of which side of the balance sheet an item is on, you have divergence of opinion, and

---

[2] We use the modifier 'economic' because we do not wish to confuse statutory surplus with net worth.

different answers on what the market value of liabilities is. Let us look at the deductive method.

### Insurance Company

$$MV(A) \quad - \quad PV(L) \quad = \quad MV(S)$$

$$\begin{Bmatrix} FrV \\ MV(TA) \\ P \end{Bmatrix} \qquad \{PV(L)\} \qquad \begin{Bmatrix} FrV \\ MV(TA) - PV(L) \\ P \end{Bmatrix}$$

### Deductive Method

$$MV(TA) \quad - \quad MV(S) \quad = \quad PV(L) + FrV + P$$

### Constructive Method

$$PV(L) \quad + \quad ???$$

*Figure 6.* Comparison of definitions.

The deductive method derives its version of the fair value of liabilities by taking the market value of tangible assets and subtracting from it the market value of surplus, which is estimated by computing the present value of distributable earnings. The present value of liabilities is thereby purportedly deduced. But the math shows what they are really inferring is the present value of liabilities plus going concern value (i.e. franchise value), which is an asset, plus the put option value, which is also an asset.

The constructive method, by way of contrast, focuses directly on the liabilities, but then it starts altering things. For example, it may bump up the discount rates because the firm might go bankrupt, and it may include a portion of going concern value. Depending on how it is applied, it takes elements of franchise value or (implicitly by using a higher discount rate) put option value, or even some of both, and adds them in. So you estimate different measures for liabilities because you are confounding assets with liabilities. In this manner you can go through each of the methodologies reviewed and find out where the mischief is happening.

It is relatively easy to estimate market value of tangible assets. You call your broker or, if it's a private placement, there are algorithms commonly available to do that. The present value of liabilities is also relatively easy to estimate. The difficult items are the franchise value and the put option to default. Depending on the methodology used, widely diverging values could be estimated for them. By including them as contra liabilities instead of the assets

– by including them on the wrong side of the balance sheet – that is the cause of much of the problem in my view. Why not let the asset valuation people deal with valuing the assets? Let us deal with what our task is: valuing the liabilities. Indeed, a correct valuation of liabilities is a necessary first step before the franchise value and put options can be properly valued.

I have a few other comments to make. The Task Force paper says: "While both methods are theoretically defensible and appealing, they can produce different answers and do not yield identical answers except in the simplest, most contrived, hypothetical case. But then why should they be consistent?" Dr Reitano doesn't think they need to be consistent because the liabilities are not liquid; accordingly, arbitrage will not force them to be consistent. That could all very well be true, but I do not think it is necessary to resort to that kind of explanation. I think the main problem is that you have different definitions of liabilities, and they are therefore, not consistent. In finance, we almost always get reasonably consistent answers in corporate finance, when we use four or five different ways to value something. If we are really careful in applying the methodologies, we should come up with the same values. Valuing insurance liabilities is one case where you apparently fail to achieve this convergence, but it is because you are using inconsistent definitions of liabilities. Therefore, values should not be consistent.

Two of my comments are of a technical nature. Dr Reitano referred to one of them briefly. In the Task Force discussions of simulations, it is not always clear that they are not simulating interest rate processes; rather, they are simulating risk-neutralized measures of interest rate processes. He mentioned this later on in his talk. I just wanted to reinforce the point by mentioning it again. You don't just simulate interest rates. You have to subtract out the market price of risk from the drift term or incorporate it into the coefficient on the drift term if it happens to be a function of interest itself.

Second, in discussing some of these other valuation methodologies, the Task Force talked about taking Treasury yields and bumping them up for various things to arrive at appropriate discount rates. In finance, we do not usually value interest-sensitive securities by discounting their cash flows by a Treasury yield plus a spread. Rather, we use lattices or simulations to discount interest-sensitive cash flows. Those are the only ways that work. If you want to determine appropriate yield to maturity, you first have to know the price. Yield is unique to an instrument and cannot be applied to other instruments with any precision at all. For instance, just noting Moody's recent bond yields, if you look at their three-year Aa bonds, you will see a 400 basis point range of yields. That is for the same maturity and ostensibly the same quality, yet you have a 400 basis point difference. In the finance field we have learned that we cannot use yield-to-maturity to value anything with precision. Indeed, we can come up with yield-to-maturity on an instrument only after we have already valued it using something else. So all of these methods that just add spreads to a yield are not going to give you precision. Sure, they give you ballpark notions, but nothing more. On Wall Street, sometimes we talk about spreads

– but that is only after we have determined price. We say, "This translates into a spread," but we would never use the spread to come up with what the price should be.

On the third page of their report, the Task Force says, "We further concede that we have no consensus on which method is more appropriate currently." Well, I have come to a consensus: obviously, it is far easier for a single individual to arrive at one than for a group of fifteen authors, but in my case, it was not certain that I would ever reach closure. Anyway, these are the conclusions that I have reached. First, you should use stochastic valuation models directly for liabilities and use Treasury-based rates for lattices or simulation paths. Second, the market value does not depend on one's assumptions – it depends on the market. Your assumptions are irrelevant to what the markets think, and I cannot emphasize that enough. We will revisit this in a moment. Third, it is easy to determine the term structure of interest. I suggest that you base your lattices or your simulations on Treasury rates. Everyone can agree on what they are; there is no ambiguity. Fourth, all liabilities within the limits under the guarantee programs are ultimately backed by NOLHGA (National Organization of Life and Health Guarantee Associations) and they ought to be treated as such. Other elements are all on the asset side of the balance sheet. So let us not complicate liability valuations by putting these other elements on the liability side.

The present value of liabilities is needed: it tells us the amount of tangible assets needed today in order to satisfy our liabilities. (We may be able to satifsy them with fewer assets, if we get lucky, by taking interest rate, equity, or low credit quality bets, but hope should not be confused with expectation.) This present value, properly computed via Treasury rate based lattices or simulations, takes into account any interest rate sensitivities in the cash flows. Mortality and morbidity are factored in only on an expectation basis, although interest rate sensitivities are included to the extent that, via interest-sensitive policy surrenders and lapses, adverse selection is expected. (In practice, most companies do not currently take into account interest rate sensitivities of mortality and morbidity. As more reliable data become available, I suspect that they will.) Surplus needed to cushion variations from these interest-sensitive projections is not included in the valuation of liabilities. This would be applicable to all policies under the guarantee, and in my view it would also be applicable to policies not under the guarantee with some adjustments.

In this vein, I would like to discuss an actuarial practice which I have noticed at times that I believe is an incorrect application of these principles. Occasionally we encounter in an actuarial valuation or appraisal something along the following lines. (Figure 7) An insurer has liabilities of, say, $100 million in present value and an equal amount of assets. The assets promise to return $12 million annually but are expected to spin off only about $10 million per year. The liabilities, valued at an 8% Treasury rate, are expected to cost $8 million annually. Suppose that these cash flows are perpetual annuities; therefore, the expectation is to net $2 million per year *ad infinitum*. When this

|  | Market Value of Assets | Present Value of Liabilities | Market Value of Economic Surplus |
|---|---|---|---|
|  | 100 | 100 | 0 |
| Year |  | Annual Cash Flows |  |
| 1 | 12 | 8 | 2 |
| 2 | 12 | 8 | 2 |
| 3 | 12 | 8 | 2 |
| 4 | 12 | 8 | 2 |
| ⋮ | ⋮ | ⋮ | ⋮ |
| n | 12 | 8 | 2 |
| ⋮ | ⋮ | ⋮ | ⋮ |

Value of Firm @ 8%: $25.0 million
Value of Firm @ 15%: $13.3 million
Value of Firm @ 80%: $2.5 million

*Figure 7.* Valuation of an insurance firm – a simplified example

perpetual net income stream is valued, regardless of whether an 8%, the proverbial 15%, or even an 80% discount rate is used, you get a positive value for the enterprise. It does not matter how you adjust the discount rate for risk, a positive firm value will result. (Depending on which of the aforementioned interest rates is used, you would estimate a firm value of $25 million, $13.3 million or $2.5 million, respectively.) But according to accepted finance principles, the enterprise is worthless. You have assets worth $100 million and liabilities with a present value of $100 million, so the economic surplus, correctly valued, is zero. (We are ignoring any insolvency guarantee programs here.) The error occurs in attempting to adjust for risk after netting expected cash flows. But first, the expected cash flows should be adjusted for their riskiness, and the risk-adjusted certainty-equivalent cash flow on assets is $8 million annually, exactly the same as the certainty-equivalent cost of the liabilities, which were properly valued using lattices or simulations based on Treasury rates. Thus, the certainty-equivalent annual net cash flows are zero.

Up to this point my discussion has focused on valuing liabilities guaranteed by NOLHGA. How about something like a GIC that either is not guaranteed or is so large that most of it is not guaranteed by NOLHGA? Suppose it is actually trading in the marketplace at something less than its price would be if you discounted its promised cash flows by Treasury rates. Suppose further that the originating insurer could purchase it back from the investor, if it so desired. I think we could, and perhaps should, still value it by using the Treasury rates. That is the value we need to have if we expect to satisfy the obligation, unless we get lucky or, alternatively, exercise our option to repurchase the liability in the marketplace at a discount. But that option to repurchase the GIC can be placed on the asset side of the balance sheet. While we have lost the default put option value, because the liability is not guaranteed by NOLHGA, we have replaced it with a repurchase option – an option to buy back the liability at less than the value of assets we would need to fund it properly, were it to remain on our books. (The value of this option is obviously the difference between the current market or repurchase price and the present value of liabilities, where the present value calculation is based on Treasury rates.) This alternative way of viewing things is shown in Figure 8 as 'Alternative No. 2'. The usual way of viewing the situation is shown under 'Alternative No. 1'. The advantages of Alternative No. 2 are that it allows all liabilities to be valued on a consistent basis and that it maintains the interpretation of the present value of liabilities as a minimum threshold level of assets needed for solvency, on an expectations basis.

We are left with two questions. Should adjustments be made for the lack of marketability or illiquidity of insurance liabilities? Should adjustments be made for the creditworthiness of NOLHGA? My responses to these two questions are no, and I don't think so. Let me explain. The non-optimal utilization by policyowners of their options should already be reflected in the state-contingent cash flow projections embedded in the valuation model. The benefits to the insurer from issuing illiquid liabilities whose options are not optimally utilized are therefore incorporated in the estimated economic values of the liabilities.

How about the NOLHGA creditworthiness spread? A theoretical argument could be made that consumers will discount insurance promises by a rate that will reflect possible insolvency – not due to insolvency of the insurer itself (assuming the liabilities are covered under the insolvency guarantee program), but one that reflects the ultimate ability of the guarantee program to satisfy the claims of an insolvent insurer. However, I think it is better not to include such a spread in the discount rates. Doing so would reinforce the illusion that you need less money than you really do to satisfy the liabilities. By ignoring the spread for deault, what you are really doing is reducing the value of the

**Items Covered by Insolvency Guarantee Programs**

| Assets | Liabilities |
|---|---|
| Market Value of Tangible Assets<br>Franchise Value<br>Put Option | Present Value of Liabilities |

**Items Not Covered by Insolvency Guarantee Programs**

| | Assets | Liabilities |
|---|---|---|
| Alternative No. 1 | Market Value of Tangible Assets<br>Franchise Value | Market Value of Liabilities |
| Alternative No. 2 | Market Value of Tangible Assets<br>Franchise Value<br>Repurchase Option | Present Value of Liabilities |

Figure 8. A closer look at a portion of the balance sheet.

put option to default, not reducing the present value of the liabilities, but this put option is already included on the other side of the balance sheet, and its reduced value can be incorporated there.

With this framework in mind, let me just finish by commenting on the last page of the first section of the Task Force report. In their discussion of the strengths and weaknesses of the 'constructive approach' or what they refer to as the option pricing approach toward fair valuation of liabilities (this is the approach I endorse), they list five weaknesses.

1. "The method is complex and somewhat unfamiliar to many industry practitioners." That is true. However, our book on interest-sensitive valuation techniques will be published this spring, and all this research that you are doing is being published shortly; therefore, it is getting more and more familiar, and I assume we will overcome this problem very soon.
2. "The method is heavily dependent upon option-adjusted spread. Given that there is no single right answer for secondary market liabilities, a variety of results could be produced." But that is not a weakness if you use the definition of liabilities that I have proposed. The option adjusted spread is not there. It is on the other side of the balance sheet. The problem goes away insofar as our concern is valuing insurance liabilities.
3. "Fair valuation of liabilities can be developed independently of the underlying asset portfolio. This is a controversial attribute of the methodology." It is controversial only if you include assets as liabilities. So, that one goes away.
4. "Fair valuation is directly linked to market conditions and, therefore, is potentially volatile. This can be viewed as either strength or weakness, depending on one's perspective ... To the extent that one's ogjective is to observe a smooth progression of value (eliminating the 'noise'), it is probably a weakness." Well, if you are doing market value on the asset side and present value on the liabilities side, what you are really worried about is volatility of economic surplus, and you remove volatility of economic surplus if you are reasonably well matched. You can obtain that smooth progression in value in this way, and with meaningful numbers, too! If you focus not just on the liability side but on the whole balance sheet and the net effect, you do not add volatility by using this valuation method, you remove volatility. The way it is now, you are marking-to-market just one side of the balance sheet, which is introducing the unwanted volatility. If unwanted volatility is revealed when marking-to-market both sides of the balance sheet, you had better take some remedial economic (as opposed to window dressing) actions, because the effect of a change in value is real.
5. "This method ignores statutory reserves and required surplus." That's a weakness? Those things have nothing to do with market value. Those are regulatory strictures put up there to help you maintain solvency. To the extent that they have any economic effects, we already reflect them on the balance sheet. For instance, we do not offset the value of assets by their AVR because we actually own the assets and wish to reflect their true value.

This is obviously only a starting point. We are showing only the current solvency condition. We regard it as another issue to assess safety; we don't ignore the fact that additional assets should be held to provide a safety cushion against undesirable asset value fluctuations and defaults, and undesirable actuarial experience. Nothing in the method I have proposed to value and report liabilities precludes additional requirements to promote or ensure safety. But at least we start the process with economically meaningful numbers.

If I were a regulator, I would endorse the constructive valuation approach and provide to insurers the basic market parameters for the valuation process, be it simulation or lattice approaches that are to be used in all reported valuations. Naturally, these parameters would be identical for all companies, for they are designed to capture market processes which are virtually independent of the actions taken by a given insurer. I would specify the current volatility of short-term interest rates. I would specify long-run volatility to which it reverts, which is roughly 12 percent historically. I would specify reversion speed. I would specify the short-term rate of interest. Then, I would let the companies specify their assumptions for lapse rates, mortality behavior, loan utilization, withdrawals, all that sort of thing, with appropriate justifications, all of which would reflect any interest rate sensitivities. They understand their own companies better than the outsiders do and would be best equipped to handle this part of the problem. With this as my base of information, I would then overlay conditions designed to promote solvency, such as reserves and capital standards. But by beginning the process with meaningful numbers, I suspect that we would already be well along the path toward fostering financial solidity among insureres, while reducing their reliance on gimmicks designed to mask their true financial position.

Finally, if I were a regulator, I would first run these ideas by the Task Force or another group of similar capabilities. They could find the weaknesses of my approach, help me to refine it, and, if the end product passes muster, help design a way to implement it.

DENNIS CARR
*ARM Financial Group*

# 4. Experience in implementing fair value of insurance liabilities

*Comment: The next three papers properly carry the same title. They represent the experience of insurance companies and auditing firms which are actually calculating a Fair Value of Insurance Liabilities. Mr Carr is with the ARM Financial Group, which owns two life insurance companies, and Mr J. Peter Duran is with Ernst & Young who are their auditors. The first two papers then view the problem from the two necessary perspectives. The third paper views it from the points of view of the company involved. Mr Crowne's company does not publish the results of the Fair Value calculation; thus the auditing problem is reduced. The companies have undertaken to calculate these Fair Values because they believe that this provides necessary information for the management of and investment in companies. Coupled with the remark of Mr Kirkland, that without consideration of Fair Value of Liabilities, the usefulness of GAAP Equity for investment analysis is compromised, we have strong arguments that such calculations are not only desirable but also possible in the present environment. – Ed.*

I will begin with some background on ARM Financial Group and how we operate. That will lead into how we became involved in calculating the fair value of liabilities. I will then discuss how we developed our approach to fair value, and I will conclude with a brief list of possible refinements to our approach. Peter Duran will then comment on our approach from an auditor's perspective.

Let me begin with a brief history of ARM Financial Group. ARM was derived from Analytical Risk Management, which was a predecessor limited partnership. It does not stand for 'adjustable rate mortgage.' We were formed in November of 1993. Our majority owner is a fund managed by the merchant banking group of Morgan Stanley. Many of the management group worked together at Capital Holding and were involved in the formation of their accumulation product group in the late 1980s. ARM Financial Group came into existence with the purchase of Integrity Life and National Integrity Life in November of 1993, so we have a fairly short history. In May 1995 we purchased SBM Life. With that background, let me discuss briefly the strategic principles which guide the way we operate at ARM.

ARM focuses on the long-term savings and retirement marketplace. We use life insurance companies as a platform, but we are not really in the life insurance business. We consider ourselves to be integrated spread managers. We look at both the assets and the liabilities. Our objective is to manage the spread on our business.

We are active asset managers in that we swap assets one for another, to increase our statutory income while keeping the risk characteristics relatively unchanged. We segment our asset portfolios based on major liability type and characteristics, and we frequently model our inforce business over stochastic interest rate scenarios. We understand and monitor our risk exposures and are reasonably well matched on an overall duration and convexity basis.

On the asset side of our balance sheet, we invest primarily in liquid, fixed income investments – bonds, mortgage backed securities, etc. More that 80% of these assets are available for sale because of our active management style. We do not invest in commercial mortgages, real estate, or common stocks, although we have inherited some small positions with our acquisitions. In summary, the asset side of our GAAP balance sheet is primarily composed of FAS 115 mark-to-market type assets.

Because of our focus on the retirement savings and accumulation business, our liabilities are primarily annuities of various types. For the purposes of this discussion, I have divided the liabilities into three major groups. First, are the accumulation liabilities. These would be single premium deferred annuities (SPDA), flexible premium deferred annuities (FPDA) and single premium endowment (SPE), also known as single premium life (SPL). We also have payout liabilities. These are primarily structured settlements along with some other immediate annuity lines. Finally, we have separate account variable annuity business, which I have labeled as 'other'.

With that basic description of our balance sheet in mind, I'd like to describe for you how ARM's GAAP balance sheet changed between year-end 1993 and year-end 1994. At 12/31/93, ARM had total assets of $2.4 billion and GAAP equity of about $112 million. By 12/31/94, ARM still had about $2.4 billion of assets; however, GAAP equity had declined to negative $14 million.

What happened? ARM came into existence with the acquisition of Integrity Life and National Integrity Life near the end of 1993. Through the Purchase GAAP process our assets were marked to market at that time. During 1994, interest rates rose throughout the year, and most of our assets were marked to market under FAS 115. Liabilities were not, so the result was a large decline in GAAP equity. To be more specific about the interest rate change, from year-end 1993 to year-end 1994, the five year treasury yield went up approximately 250 basis points and the 30 year treasury yield went up approximately 150 basis points. This large change in interest rates caused our GAAP equity to disappear (under FAS 115) in a 12-month period.

Because we carefully monitor the economics of our business and run appropriate models, etc., we felt this was an unrealistic result: our equity had not disappeared at all. However, as you can imagine, this stirred up questions from various publics. Our common stock is closely held by Morgan Stanley, so there was no direct pressure on stock price, but the rating agencies did take notice. We were rated A− by AM Best and trying to make a case for getting an upgrade. We were also trying to create new distribution for our products. Distributors took notice and were asking about our change in GAAP equity. We spent a great deal of extra time and energy trying to convince these various publics that the FAS 115 GAAP equity result was not realistic.

There were several ways we could have responded to this situation. We could have moved more assets to the held to maturity category. This really went against our grain, however, because part of our core strategy is to be active managers of assets and liabilities. We felt we would give up real economic value in making a move like that. We could have educated various publics, and we did, however, education by itself was not enough. In the end, we decided to develop a fair value balance sheet (with both assets and liabilities marked to market) and disclose that alongside of our FAS 115 balance sheet.

Obviously, our biggest challenge in developing a fair value balance sheet was to create the fair value of liabilities. What resources were available in the middle of 1994 to deal with this? A very important resource was the American Academy of Actuaries draft paper. I managed to get a copy of an early draft of that paper and tried to educate myself. This was a very good resource, but the methods described were very diverse and left a lot of room for judgement. We also used Ernst & Young, our accounting firm, as a sounding board for our ideas. Another important resource were our asset/liability models. We had existing models from the Purchase GAAP work, from our asset/liability management work and from cash flow testing. With these key resources, we created our fair value of liabilities methodology.

Before plunging into the development of our fair value methodology, we developed some overall objectives for the methodology. Number one, we wanted the methodology to produce results that would reflect the economics of the business. Also, it was important that the methodology could be implemented. The charge was to get it done: not to do a lot of research and come up with a method and create the software to do the method and then implement. We needed it now. The methodology needed to produce consistent results over time. This was difficult to test because of our short history. Where feasible, it would be a good idea to test methodologies over a historical period of several years. Finally, we felt that our methodology should produce a consistent overall balance sheet. The pattern of GAAP equity over time should reflect the economics of the business.

With these general objectives in mind, we set about to develop fair value methodologies for each of the major liability categories described earlier. Our payout liabilities are primarily structured settlements. These are very long-tailed liabilities with a duration of about 12. The good news is that there are no options involved. Policyholders have no right to surrender. It's pretty much a specified cash flow series with some possibility of mortality variation. There are significant cash flows beyond the normal investment horizon of 30 years.

Because there were no significant options contained in the liabilities, one of the direct methods seemed most appropriate and we quickly settled on a discounted cash flow approach. We tested this approach over our recent history, and it produced reasonable results in the aggregate.

The biggest issue with this method was the choice of the discount rate. We started with the general concept of treasury yields with an adjustment spread. That led us to the next issue – what is the appropriate adjustment spread? The Academy draft provided for a wide range on the adjustment spread with total discount rates ranging from a 'crediting rate' to a 'gross investment rate'. In other words, reasonable discount rates could vary by 200 basis points or more on some products. In addition to choosing an adjustment spread, we had to decide between a single interest rate 'bond' discount rate and using a series of 'spot' rates. The spot rates give a more precise answer, but is the precision worth the effort? Our choice was to use an investment type adjustment spread and a single 'bond' type rate, so our discount rate became the 30 year treasury bond rate plus 90 or 100 basis points to reflect the credit spread. At the end of each quarter we update the 30 year treasury rate and adjust the credit spread to reflect current investment markets.

I would like to make one final comment regarding the payout liabilities. Long duration liabilities have a leveraged impact on a fair value balance sheet. To illustrate this point, as stated previously, ARM's GAAP equity declined by $126 million from 12/31/93 to 12/31/94 under FAS 115. If you mark to market the payout liabilities, the effect is to reverse $106 million of that decline. Approximately 25% of our liabilities caused roughly 80% of the FAS 115 swing in GAAP equity.

Our second liability category is the accumulation liabilities. These represent the single premium deferred annuities (SPDA) and similar types of liabilities. These are shorter liabilities with a duration of two or three, however, these liabilities are loaded with options. The policyholder has the option to surrender, although he may be subject to a surrender charge. The company has the option to change the credited interest rates. The traditional SPDA liability can be described as a battle of the options. This makes for a difficult valuation problem because of the assumptions that you need to make concerning policyholder behavior.

In choosing a method for the accumulation liabilities, we started with the discounted cash flow or direct method. Because of the options involved with the liabilities, this method was rejected because of implementation concerns. Developing appropriate discount rates which reflected the options seemed an insurmountable problem. We then considered the deductive type methods, more specifically the appraisal method. Because of the availability of asset/liability models of our business, it was fairly easy to come up with appraisal values. Our management team rejected the appraisal method because they felt it was too arbitrary. We have significant experience in buying and selling blocks of business and companies. Depending on who does the appraisal and who hires them (buyer or seller), we have seen a great deal of variance in prices for a given block of business.

Moving on from the appraisal method, we considered a deductive approach based on our Purchase GAAP (P-GAAP) models. Under P-GAAP the reserve for accumulation products is set at account value, and a value of inforce (VIF) asset is established. This VIF is equal to the present value of future GAAP margins. We tested this methodology and ended up using it because it produced reasonable results and it was consistent with overall GAAP principles. In calculating our VIF, we utilized a 13% discount rate to reflect the risks associated with the accumulation liabilities. Internally we have called our methodology 'sequential P-GAAP', because the framework is based on Purchase GAAP principles. At the end of each accounting period, we update our GAAP models and recalculate the fair value VIF for the accumulation liabilities.

For our two major liability types, the payout liabilities and the accumulation liabilities, we ended up using different methodologies. We feel that's appropriate because the liabilities have very different characteristics. Thus the best method for one is not the best method for the other.

Our third liability category, the separate account variable annuities, seemed to fit best with the accumulation liabilities. We decided to use the sequential P-GAAP approach, but we did not have the asset/liability models available for these products. Since this was a fairly small line of business, we used an approximation where we substituted the deferred acquisition cost asset (DAC) for the VIF. This is a bit conservative in that we believe we have additional margins over and above our DAC amount.

Based on our fair value approach for the liabilities, let us take a look at how our GAAP equity has changed over time on a fair value basis as compared to the FAS 115 basis. Under FAS 115 our GAAP equity was $112 million at 12/31/93. As interest rates rose during 1994, GAAP equity declined to negative $14 million by 12/31/94. Interest rates subsequently declined in 1995 and at 9/30/95, our GAAP equity had increased to $100 million (adjusted for the capital infusion associated with the purchase of SBM). The substantial volatility of GAAP equity under FAS 115 clearly did not reflect the economics of our business. With the liabilities adjusted to fair value, GAAP equity was $112 million at 12/31/93; $115 million at 12/31/94; and $117 million at 9/30/95 (adjusted for SBM). Because we manage our assets and liabilities to be reasonably well matched on an overall basis, we feel this fair value of liabilities methodology provides a much truer view of the economics of ARM Financial Group.

We actually produce a fair value balance sheet in our annual report, so we had to decide how the liabilities would be presented. For the payout liabilities, the fair value is shown directly on the balance sheet. For the accumulation and separate account variable annuity liabilities, the full account value is shown as a liability with an offsetting VIF asset. Again, our attempt was to be consistent with overall GAAP principles.

There are several areas where our fair value methodology may be refined in the future. On the payout liabilities, we will consider changing to a spot rate discount approach as opposed to using the bond rate approach. We will continue to improve our VIF model for the accumulation liabilities and make sure it reflects actual experience. For the separate account variable annuities, we need to develop a VIF model. We need to continue to monitor our results for reasonableness. You can only do so much checking as you put these methods into place, and it is important to monitor results. Finally, we will continue to monitor FASB and the actuarial profession for further developments regarding fair value of liabilities.

In conclusion, I would tell you that we were able to implement a fair value balance sheet. It did not involve elegant technology, but it has been effective in presenting a better picture of the economics of our business. In turn, this has allowed us to more effectively field questions from various publics, including rating agencies and distributors. Clearly, the calculation of the fair value of liabilities is a very challenging issue. I would like to thank all of those who have developed papers for this conference and to encourage others to join in the research effort. Clearly FAS 115 is not sufficient.

J. PETER DURAN
*Ernst & Young*

# Comment on 'Experience in implementing fair value of insurance liabilities'

The principal question that I want to address is how you audit such a thing as the fair value of insurance liabilities? That is, how does the accounting firm manage to express an opinion that the calculations are done in accordance with generally accepted accounting principles (GAAP)?

Some of the hurdles we considered have become crystal clear: there are many methods, and they give different answers. There is fairly specific guidance in FAS 107 (Disclosures About Fair Value of Financial Instruments) that Denny Carr referred to about the fair value of assets. But when we consider the other side of the balance sheet, there is really very little guidance and what little there is, is very general. FAS 107 generally requires that the fair value of 'financial instruments' be disclosed in the footnotes to the financial statement and under the FAS 107 definition of financial instruments, insurance contracts are clearly financial instruments. However, FAS 107 specifically exempts insurance contracts from the disclosure requirements, because the FASB was well aware of the definitional difficulties. Nevertheless, optional disclosure is permitted, and that's what ARM has chosen to do. So ARM's approach does indeed actually fit within the existing GAAP framework and GAAP rules.

Another potential hurdle is that ARM applies different methods to different liabilities. There is one method for the payout annuities, a different method for SPDA's (single premium deferred annuities) and yet another method for the variable annuities. Of course, some would consider the assumptions to be subjective.

The practical answer to the definitional problem is actually quite straightforward, and I think this is absolutely consistent with the spirit of FAS 107, in the absence of any specific guidance, any reasonable method should be okay from the point of view of the auditing firm. What is really key, what matters to the accountants who sign the auditors' reports, is that there be a specificity of definition and that it be consistently applied from period to period.

With respect to the use of different methods for different products, this is an unfortunate fact of life in the world of GAAP for insurance, and therefore it was not viewed as a particular difficulty. And one thing to keep in mind in any practical situation is that materiality considerations are always important. If, for example, we have a line of business where we have a fair value method that we don't think is particularly good on a theoretical basis, but the line is small, that does not preclude a clean opinion on the financial statement as a whole.

One of the big issues, of course, is accepting the assumptions. The methodology we used to do that was simply to agree upfront on the process for setting the assumptions. We try, where possible, to make those assumptions as objective as we can. A good example is the use of an A-rated bond index for determining the discount rate on payout annuities. You can actually verify the index value on an objective basis. For the more 'arbitrary' assumptions, period to period consistency is key. For example, we would like to see the 13% discount rate used to discount the future profits for accumulation annuities locked in from period to period, so that management cannot change this discount rate at its own discretion. A lot of best estimate-type assumptions pervade ARM's methodology. Again, that's no particular hurdle because we have to deal with best estimate assumptions in forming opinions about GAAP all the time. A lot of professional judgement is applied in setting those assumptions.

Let us discuss the various fair value methods used by ARM beginning with the accumulation annuities which are essentially SPDA products. In his description of ARM's methodology, Denny Carr referred to the method as 'sequential PGAAP'. That's a term we coined as we talked about the method. To my knowledge, both the term 'sequential PGAAP' and the method itself are new. The method has a foundation in current GAAP practice. When a company or a block of business is bought or sold, the accountants say that both the assets and liabilities are marked to market. It is actually quite a common occurrence. At the purchase date, there is a purchase GAAP (PGAAP) balance sheet, that purports to be a fair value balance sheet. This balance sheet is derived by first marking all the assets to market. As for the liabilities, it depends on what kinds of products are involved. For account value type products such as Universal Life and deferred annuities, the policy liability is taken to be the account value. However, there is a corresponding asset which may be thought of as an offset to the liability, called the 'Value of Insurance Inforce' (VIF). It is defined as the present value at the risk rate (13% in the case of ARM) of the future GAAP profits on a best estimate basis. As an example, in the case of deferred annuities the primary source of profit is interest spread: the difference between the rate earned on assets and that credited to the liabilities. In PGAAP, assets receive a new cost basis at the purchase date equal to their then fair value. Any resulting premium or discount is amortized over the remaining life of the asset. The rate earned on assets is determined consistently with the asset values. (Note that in PGAAP deferrable acquisition costs incurred by the seller are not reflected on the acquirer's balance sheet, as these were never expenses incurred by the aquirer.)

The ARM method for deferred annuities is 'sequential PGAAP'. At each balance sheet date the invested assets are revalued at market and the VIF asset is recalculated as the present value at 13% of estimated future GAAP profits. One observation I would make about the sequential PGAAP approach is that it does not really require that all the assets be at market. It would 'work' just as well (or poorly) as PGAAP works, if some of the assets were at historical cost and some of the assets were at market. It is also worth observing that the financial statement presentation used by ARM is consistent with the PGAAP approach. The VIF is shown as an asset in the balance sheet, rather than an offset to liabilities.

For variable annuities, we have a situation where materiality considerations do come into play. This is an area that will most likely be refined in the future.

Just a few comments on the payout annuities. Obviously, in the method employed, the definition of the spread over 30 year treasuries is key. We acknowledge that spot rates would probably be a better measure than yields, but using 30 year treasury yields plus a spread certainly does not violate FAS 107 and, given the precision of the measurement process generally, is unlikely to introduce material distortion. I personally believe that linking the discount rate to the yield on the actual assets held by the company is not a good idea, because liability amounts and asset quality are inversely related in that case. For example, if you invest in junk bonds, your liabilities go way down because you appear to be earning more. That does not seem to make a great deal of sense.

Given the status of current official accounting guidance with respect to fair value of liabilities, we can probably live with lots of different variations of the approach to spreads. One could fix the spread over the 30 year treasuries, or tie it to a published index of market yields or spreads. Alternatively, one could define a hypothetical basket of assets and monitor market yields on that basket of assets.

JOSEPH E. CROWNE
*Merrill Lynch Life*

# Comments on 'Experience in implementing fair value of insurance liabilities'

At Merrill Lynch Life we do not actually publish 'fair value' financial statements at this time (other than in compliance with FAS 115). A few years ago we began to move towards fair value accounting, independent of what was going on in the insurance industry. We began looking at a market value balance sheet in 1991. The impetus for this came from a number of things that happened with regard to the insurance business within Merrill Lynch from 1989 to 1991.

In 1989, we bought out our joint venture partner in Tandem Insurance Group, giving Merrill Lynch 100% ownership of Tandem Insurance and of Royal Tandem, which was a New York company. In 1990 we purchased a $3 billion block of variable life business from Monarch Life Insurance Company. That VLI business had been produced by Merrill Lynch Financial Consultants, as was the business that was in Tandem.

Then, in 1991, we sold Family Life Insurance Company (purchased in 1973) which had operated in Seattle, Washington until this time. Before selling Family Life, we removed the business that had been produced by Merrill Lynch Financial Consultants, and then sold the company with the balance of the business to a third party.

In 1991 and 1992, Executive Life and other major insolvencies occurred and we had determined that, based on the business that had been sold by in the Merrill Lynch insurance companies, we needed to establish reserves of about $30 million to cover estimated Guaranty Fund assessments for these insolvencies. The biggest piece of which, of course, was Executive Life.

During this time, Merrill Lynch contributed additional capital to its insurance companies, and reorganized its insurance business into two companies, Merrill Lynch Life and ML Life of New York. And then really began integrating the insurance business into the Merrill Lynch & Company mainstream. The executive offices were moved to Princeton, New Jersey, and the backoffice operations to a Merrill Lynch operations center in Jacksonville, Florida. (The variable life service center, acquired from Monarch in 1992, remains in Springfield, Massachusetts.)

In addition to aligning the operations of the company with ML & Co., the financial people at Merrill Lynch began looking closely at this insurance accounting, and they noticed that insurance accounting was much different from what is done in the securities industry, particularly in that the securities industry is mark to market, basically, every day. The concern seemed to be that book value accounting within the insurance business would not adequately reveal asset/liability mismatches or other asset related problems. Therefore, in late 1991, we began to develop a market value accounting basis for the insurance group. The original plan was that it would be used internally and, possibly, if given the go-ahead by the SEC, in consolidation with ML & Co. At the time, we did not seriously consider using it for the stand-alone financial reports of the Merrill Lynch Insurance Companies. But, even so, we did want to have a solid foundation for what we were doing in order to be able to get SEC concurrence with our approach.

There were a couple of things to consider in developing our method: the first was that we do weekly estimates of earnings. Also, we do a full financial close every month. And, although the weeklies are called estimates, if our weeklies do not add up to our monthly actuals, we better have a good explanation of why. Another consideration at this time (late 1991) was that there was not much industry guidance on how we should go about doing this. One of the first questions we faced was: should we retain the current GAAP framework? It seemed to us that if GAAP worked, if we could do something within the GAAP structure, it was probably the easiest approach to take in terms of (a) getting approval from the SEC, (b) fitting into the Merrill Lynch financial reporting process; and, (c) assuring the Merrill Lynch management that we were not concocting some new, strange financial reporting method.

The first question we asked ourselves was: what would the balance sheet look like for a perfectly matched life insurance company? That is shown in Table 1. This company is not only matched as far as the durations and convexity (which you don't see here, but take my word for it), the invested assets are equal to the interest sensitive liabilities. There are no excess assets. So, under that circumstance the equity is equal to the deferred acquisition expense asset.

What would happen if interest rates changed? Say interest rates declined by such an amount that the value of the assets went up 10% and the value of the liabilities also went up 10%. What would happen to the balance sheet? Well, as seems logical, nothing would happen, if you were perfectly matched. There is no reason why you should have to write off any portion of the DAC asset, or in any way change the DAC asset. Also, if you were perfectly matched, it seems that your equity would stay the same (Table 2).

We went one step further and made it just a little bit more complicated. That is, what if we had more invested assets than interest sensitive liabilities?

*Table 1.* Initial balance sheet

| Bonds | 10 000 | Liabilities | 10 000 |
|---|---|---|---|
| DAC | 600 | Equity | 600 |
| Total | 10 600 | Total | 10 600 |

Table 2. Balance sheet after decline in interest rates

| Bonds | 11 000 | Liabilities | 11 000 |
|---|---|---|---|
| DAC | 600 | Equity | 600 |
| Total | 11 600 | Total | 11 600 |

But, otherwise, everything else was the same. In Table 3, we have $10 000 in liabilities but we have $10 400 in assets. This makes equity $1000.

Assume interest rates change by the same amount as in the first example, in such a way as to increase the assets by 10%. Liabilities also go up by 10% (Table 4). Let us assume that DAC does not change at all. Equity goes up by $40: the $40 is exactly 10% of the extra $400 in assets that we had. It seemed obvious to us that this amount represented the increase in the current value of the enterprise. So we concluded that DAC should not change in this example under market value accounting. Therefore, we could develop a basis for market value accounting that would continue to look like GAAP accounting.

We then set these objectives: first, our method would retain the existing GAAP framework. Second, it would be easy to understand. Third, it would be reasonably easy to administer. Remember, we do weekly reporting, and a full financial close monthly. We had to have a method that we could use without a great deal of difficulty. We also wanted something that would address the primary management concern regarding asset/liability mismatch.

In some ways, we do have an advantage here over many other companies: the types of liabilities that we have are shown in Table 5. We have variable annuity and variable life products that account for about 56% of our total policy liabilities. We have a market value adjusted annuity, which is another 14%, and then we have single premium whole life and single premium deferred annuities, which are another 16% of our balance sheet. Policy loans and other miscellaneous liabilities complete the picture. So we have $12.2 billion in policyholder liabilities, of which 30% are interest sensitive: the MVA (market value adjusted) annuity, the SPWL (single premium whole life) and the SPDA (single premium deferred annuity).

Table 3. Initial balance sheet 2

| Bonds | 10 400 | Liabilities | 10 000 |
|---|---|---|---|
| DAC | 600 | Equity | 1000 |
| Total | 11 000 | Total | 11 000 |

Table 4. Balance sheet 2 after decline in interest rates

| Bonds | 11 440 | Liabilities | 11 000 |
|---|---|---|---|
| DAC | 600 | Equity | 1040 |
| Total | 12 040 | Total | 12 040 |

Table 5. Merrill Lynch Insurance Group, policy liabilities (GAAP basis)

| Product | $ billions | % |
| --- | --- | --- |
| Variable annuity | 3.8 | 31 |
| Variable life | 3.1 | 25 |
| MVA annuity | 1.7 | 14 |
| SPWL | 1.2 | 10 |
| SPDA | 0.7 | 6 |
| Policy loans | 1.1 | 9 |
| Other | 0.6 | 5 |
| Total | 12.2 | 100 |

It is very interesting that, in contrast to Denny Carr's presentation, we felt that the variable products needed no further work. In other words, that 'fair value' accounting was the same as the current 'book value' accounting as far as variable products were concerned. Our product is purely a variable separate account product; there is no fixed component to it. Thus, the value of the account is marked to market daily. So we felt that the fair value for variable products was the same as the traditional book value.

The next product is the MVA annuity. This is basically a zero coupon bond, or rather, a series of zero coupon bonds. The current surrender value is based on the current credited rate for this product. If you buy a 10-year bucket at 8%, and a year later, when we are crediting 7%, say, on the 9-year bucket and you surrender, you get a value based on accumulating at 8% and discounting back at 7%. There is also a nominal surrender charge. Therefore, for this product, the 'fair value' of the liability is the 'market value adjusted' account value.

Now, products that are a little more difficult: the single premium deferred annuity (SPDA) and the single premium whole life (SPWL). How should you determine a market value? If you could trade an SPDA, what would the buyer expect in terms of a credited rate? (We called this the hypothetical secondary market.) A buyer would expect a rate that is comparable to a rate that is available on new issues at the time of the 'trade". (Since we had decided to retain FAS 97 type accounting, the 'liability' value ignored surrender charges. But, as discussed later, we did not ignore the cash surrender value.) Our first general principle was, therefore, that the fair value of a liability is the value needed today, at current interest rates, to provide the guaranteed amount under the contract.

We then decided that the minimum fair value of the liability would be the cash surrender value. Obviously, there's some discussion about this, but our thinking was that, to be consistent with our hypothetical secondary market situation, a person would not sell an SPDA for less than its 'put' value. So our opinion was that the minimum fair value for an SPDA or SPWL liability should be the cash surrender value.

A problem that you may run into is what if you have a product that has, say, a 4% minimum underlying guarantee for the life of the product, which could be 30 years or so, and interest rates drop so low that, say, a 3% rate is the current credited rate. There can be quite a bit of volatility in your valuation under that circumstance if you followed the rule that we enunciated earlier, which is you accumulate forward and you discount back without taking into account deaths or surrenders.

So, we compromised a little and decided that the fair value would be the greater of the option adjusted value, and the value based on the current period guarantee. For example, say you have a current rate of 6% guaranteed for 5 years, followed by an underlying 4% rate guaranteed until maturity. If current rates were 3%, we would only discount the accumulated value at the end of the first 5 year period back at 3%. Then we would determine the option adjusted value. The 'fair value' liability value would be the greater of the two values. This was a compromise to take into account the practical reality that rates would not be likely to stay at an extremely low level for a long period of time.

Now, recall that we have a GAAP balance sheet, and, therefore, a DAC asset. So the question was, when does the deferred acquisition cost asset change? For our perfectly matched life insurance company, we felt that there was no need to change DAC. But, what if a company is not perfectly matched? Well, we thought that the best thing to do was to follow the same procedures as if we were doing book value accounting. We made up the rules, trying to make it look like FAS97, but not necessarily following FAS 97 literally.

We decided that we would proceed as if we were doing book value DAC amortization, but using current values: fair value of the liability, fair value of the asset, current credited rates, and current new money rates. The gross profits for each period, in order to determine the amortization factor, would be discounted back at the current credited rate.

There are a few features of our approach that should be mentioned. First, it does not anticipate gains on surrender when the Fair Value of the liability is greater than the cash surrender value. We are using current credited rates, so, for an SPDA, when rates are lower than the guaranteed rate, we have a liability value that is greater than the account value and greater than the cash surrender value. However, this situation is taken into account in DAC amortization. Also, surrenders would tend to be lower when current rates are lower than existing contract rates. Nonetheless, this method does tend to overstate the liability value.

Second, the implied duration of the liability, as determined under this approach, will usually be different from the duration determined by cash flow or option adjusted modeling. For example, an SPDA with 5 years remaining on its initial guarantee period will have the duration characteristics of a 5 year zero, as long as current rates are higher than the long term guarantee and lower than the rate that would cause the minimum liability value (the cash surrender value) to 'kick in'. The option adjusted duration, generally would be lower. On the other hand, determining the duration of an SPDA is, at best, an inexact science.

As for the current status, we continue to calculate the market value of liabilities on the basis I have described. However, we do not produce pro forma financial statements on this basis. In 1993, Merrill Lynch adopted FS115, and that has taken precedence over our internal market value approach.

Now we are awaiting an industry solution. I hope that the solution is a practical one that we can deal with on a month to month or week to week basis. We need to have a solution that takes care of the concerns within the accounting profession and the securities industry about insurance accounting, and also one that is practical enough that it can be reasonably implemented.

SHYAM MEHTA
*Merrill Lynch International*

## 5. Allowing for asset, liability and business risk in the valuation of a life company*

*Comment: This is an adaptation of a paper previously published in the Journal of the Institute. It is an attempt to wed the valuation process to modern financial theory so that valuations may be based upon more realistic discount rates etc. – Ed.*

Traditional life company appraisal methods use projections of reported profit rather than of cash flow, and use discount rates typically selected without any theoretical underpinning. The theme of this paper is that life company valuation can be based on an analysis of the characteristics of the individual cash flows which form the net cash flow. Projected future cash flows may be compared with the income and gains expected from traded securities, such as common stock and government bonds, in order to assess their values. Individual rather than overall cash flows are selected for this market value based analysis because of their generally simpler distribution characteristics. Cash flow interactions are taken account of separately. Standard asset pricing models enable one to allow for lapse, mortality and other risks, and for option features. The resulting overall value is an estimate of the value of future returns discounted at risk rate(s) consistent with the estimated risk/return trade-off implicit in the capital markets.

The methodology outlined in the paper is illustrated by reference to the very different types of revenue generated by non-par, variable life and par products. It is also used, in the valuation of future new business, to allow for the risks that expected sales volumes and profitability levels will not be achieved.

The paper provides a rationale for the choice of discount rates used in the valuation of a life company and bridges the gap between actuarial techniques and modern financial theory. The latter requires one to look behind accounting conventions, to underlying cash flows. The paper facilitates the comparison of life company and alternative investment opportunities. A theoretical basis is useful since total assets and liabilities are generally large in comparison to

---

* This paper is based on Allowing for asset, liability and business risk in the valuation of a life office. *Journal of the Institute of Actuaries*, **119**, 1992, 385–455, and is included with permission of the Institute of Actuaries.

appraisal value. Small changes in the relationship between the assets and liabilities or in their risk characteristics have a geared effect on appraisal value. For these reasons the discount rate appropriate for one company cannot be used as a guide for other companies without a detailed cash flow level investigation. Similar problems arise with regard to the use of beta ratios derived from historic share price movements.

In practice, realistic estimates of value, comparable with transaction and market prices, are obtained. Extensions to the methodology have been applied to good effect in a variety of other industries, for example, property/casualty reinsurance, and fund management, and to develop business unit return on capital targets within a shareholder value framework.

## Introduction

This chapter explores how an examination of asset, liability and business risk can assist in valuing the policyholders' and shareholders' interests in a life company.

Investment in a life company is one of many possible investment choices open to investors. The proposition set forth in this paper is that an investor can examine the individual cash flows which make up the aggregate net revenue of the company and can consider the returns available on traded securities in order to obtain an assessment of comparative value. For this purpose, some individual items of life company income and expenditure can be compared directly with future cash flows from quoted securities. Other insurance cash flows have more complex characteristics and need to be valued using general asset pricing models such as those developed in modern financial theory. It is possible, having derived the value of individual cash flow components, to determine an equivalent single discount rate. If required, separate rates can be assessed for net worth, in-force value and the value of future new business. It is interesting to assess these equivalent discount rates in order to understand the overall riskiness of the life company.

The paper focuses on general methodology rather than on the particular purpose for which the valuation is used. The reader is referred to the paper by Bangert (1973) for an outline of some of the reasons for life company acquisition and merger, for a discussion of the principles of valuation, as well as for the need for pragmatism. Sherris (1987) outlines how the capital asset pricing model (CAPM) can be used to value individual cash flows. Although this chapter illustrates some points using CAPM, in principle any asset pricing model could be used, and the main focus is on developing a comparative valuation methodology.

The author believes that the approach set out in this paper has not been comprehensively applied to life company valuation in the past and should be considered for use in the future.

## Valuation of assets and liabilities

An asset is a resource from which future economic or other benefits are expected to flow.

The value of an asset can be assessed by reference to:
- Prices at which transactions in the asset have taken place.
- Values of other assets, having regard to their expected returns and risks.

Similar observations apply to the valuation of a liability, to the valuation of an interest in an asset and to the valuation of an asset which consists of a combination of various assets and liabilities, such as a life company. Where a comparative reference value is not available, it may be possible to assign individual values to the assets and liabilities which make up the combined asset.

## Life company valuation

In recognition of the different characteristics of the shareholders' interests in net worth, in-force business, and future new business, a separate valuation of each of these components of value is performed in many life company appraisals. For example:
- Net worth may be assessed as the market value of the assets less the statutory reserves.
- Future profits arising from the in-force business may be discounted using an interest rate which has some regard to the returns available on traded securities.
- The value of profits arising from all future new business ('existing structure value') may be determined by applying a multiple to the value of one year's sales. The multiple used is likely to be influenced, for example, by values implied in transactions involving other companies, having regard to differences in new business growth and other prospects.

Selection of a single rate of discount to value all future cash flows, including those from future new business, is an equally valid approach but it suffers from two main drawbacks:
- The choice of the appropriate discount rate is more difficult. The rate selected will be affected by the relative proportions of net worth, in-force business and future new business for each company being valued.
- The values derived for the individual components of value may not be valid. For example, existing structure value may be overstated and in-force value understated, compared to an open market valuation.

Before considering the subject of life company valuation in detail, it is useful to examine the nature of the cash flows and profit more closely.

## Life assurance business profit characteristics

A major difference between the business of life assurance and that of many other businesses is that cash flows arising from business sold in the year emerge over many years rather than in the year of sale. Positive cash flows arise primarily from returns on the invested assets, from future premiums expected to be paid by policyholders and from assets to be acquired out of future positive net cash flows. The future premiums can be viewed as a special type of asset, namely as a set of (typically) fixed monetary payments subject to decrement arising from lapse or from death of the policyholder. Set against the positive cash flows are negative cash flows payable to agents and employees, suppliers, policyholders and the Internal Revenue Service. The special characteristics of variable life and par business result in some degree of alignment between the interests of policyholders and shareholders so that some shareholder cash flows are proportionate to certain policyholder cash flows.

There are, however, similarities between profit for a life assurance business and for a manufacturing concern. For the latter, economic profit can be defined as:
- Achieved investment return on net worth, including realized and unrealized gains;
  **plus**
- Profit earned in the year, that is income less associated costs in respect of sales in the year;
  **less**
- Overhead costs.

For life assurance business, sales in the year generate future cash flows. The overall economic profit generated in the year may be expressed as:
- Achieved investment return on net worth plus achieved return on the value of expected future cash flows from business sold in previous years;
  **plus**
- The value of cash flows arising from sales in the year (earned profit);
  **less**
- Overhead costs.

The comparison is not taken further here, and for this reason the terms net worth, income, costs and overhead costs as applicable to a manufacturing company have not been defined. The similarities end here because net worth for a manufacturing company is not the same as net worth for a life company. Also, as seen above, cash flows derived from the in-force business have different characteristics from the returns on net worth.

The three components of life assurance business overall profit may have very different risk characteristics. For example, overhead costs could be relatively stable whereas value added from sales in the year could vary significantly from year to year.

## Valuation methodology

Individual life company cash flows exhibit generally simpler risk/return characteristics than the aggregate net cash flows of a company. First, we discuss how 'simple' cash flows can be valued by reference to the future cash flow characteristics of quoted securities. Some of the cash flows are more complex or interact with each other. Modern financial theory has developed a number of ways in which the risk and return of complex assets can be valued. These are outlined below and described in more detail in Appendix A. The relationship between the equivalent overall discount rate required to value net cash flows and the assets and liabilities of a company is then noted. The effects of establishing statutory reserves, and of holding surplus or solvency capital, are also considered.

*Simple cash flows*

For a non-par product, a company expects to receive a set of fixed payments in the future (premiums), to incur some expenses and to pay a fixed sum on maturity of the policy. The effects of policy lapse, mortality, other risks, as well as taxation, should not be ignored. They create an additional layer of complication which can be considered separately. The future premiums resemble the coupon payments and maturity proceeds of government securities, and a bond portfolio could be constructed to closely replicate the pattern of expected future premium receipts. The lack of a full complement of bond maturity dates does not present a major difficulty in the valuation because the yield curve is reasonably smooth. Since lapses and mortality are being ignored at this stage, shareholders could be expected to be largely indifferent as to whether future profits and liabilities are funded from premium receipts or government bond coupon and maturity payments. The yield curve can be analysed to assess the value of a payment at any future date.

There is an alternative way of approaching the same valuation problem. Many investors in the bond and equity markets are able to borrow, or to reduce the proportion of their portfolio invested in bonds. These investors can rearrange their portfolios in order to offset the effect of the future premium receipts. The value of these receipts can thus be assessed by reference to yields available on government bonds and the cost of borrowing. Similar considerations apply in valuing policy maturity proceeds, and expenses incurred by the company. In regard to expenses, it should be noted that fixed-interest government bond receipts are subject to inflation risk and, arguably, this risk is reflected in the level of long-term bond yields (see Appendix B.1). For this reason, to the extent that expenses are real rather than nominal monetary payments, they can be valued using an interest rate net of the premium for inflation risk.

Expected asset cash flows include income as well as proceeds arising from sale of the asset in the future. In the author's view, future asset cash flows need to be valued by adjusting market values to reflect the difference between life fund taxation and tax implicit in the market valuation of traded securities. Use of unadjusted market values could be inappropriate. For example, if a 100%

tax rate were applied to life company asset returns, a nil value, not a market value, could be attributed to these returns.

The approach adopted is to assess investment return assumptions, that is internal rates of return equating future expected asset cash flows with market values (Appendix B). These returns are assessed both for a gross investor and a net corporate investor later. The projected asset cash flows, net of allowance for life company taxation, are then valued using risk adjusted discount rates consistent with the underlying investment return assumptions. Effectively, the assets are valued at market prices and an adjustment is made in respect of the value of life fund taxation payable in addition to that assumed for direct investment by a gross or net investor.

## Asset pricing models

The methods outlined above can be used to value future cash flows, allowing for the effect of lapses, mortality and other risks on the expected level of future cash flows. Different considerations are required to adjust for the effect of these risks on the variability of future cash flows.

One approach, suggested by Sherris, to estimating the additional discount rate required to allow for risk is to use a standard asset pricing model, such as CAPM as described in Appendix A. Risk is divided into non-diversifiable and diversifiable components. The diversifiable component is that part of risk which, in the limit, does not contribute to the overall riskiness of a well diversified portfolio of assets (as the number $n$ of assets held increases, the contribution to total risk increases less rapidly than $1/n$). The non-diversifiable component of risk, 'systematic' risk, relates to returns which are correlated with a broadly based index of asset prices. If unsystematic risk were 'priced' (that is contributed towards higher expected return from an asset), portfolio investors could purchase securities with high unsystematic risk and achieve higher expected total portfolio returns for only a small addition to the variability of the total portfolio return. The price of unsystematic risk would fall as demand for securities carrying this risk increased. Similar arguments could be developed for individual cash flows.

If CAPM is true, the required return on any asset is a linear combination of the risk free rate and the expected return on the market index, weighted according to the asset's systematic risk factor, beta. Any cash flow which is not correlated with the market index has a beta of zero and is valued using the risk free rate; other cash flows can be valued using a discount rate dependent on their systematic risk. In practice, modifications to CAPM, and the arbitrage pricing theory also described in Appendix A, allow for other systematic risk factors and not just variability in market returns. If it is assumed that mortality rates and real expense levels are not correlated with the market index and other 'priced' risk factors discussed in Appendix A.1 and A.2, mortality and expense risks are entirely unsystematic and are not associated with an increase in required returns. Unsystematic risk may result in an increase in the cost of trading and in the risk of corporate failure. These effects need to be factored into the valuation process even if no addition to the discount rate is made. The concluding Section of this paper comments further on the use of a risk free rate to value cash flows subject to only unsystematic risk.

Use of an asset pricing model is one of the very few ways in which discount rates required to compensate for risks borne can be assessed. The lack of any simple and realistic alternative framework is one reason why the author would advocate greater use of these models in life company appraisal valuations. Some of the limitations of these models disappear when used to assess asset risks, rather than liability and business risks, if life company portfolio investments are reasonably well diversified.

## Option pricing theory

Some insurance cash flows accrue to shareholders only in the event of a suitably favourable or unfavourable asset return. For example, a company which has a mismatch of assets against guaranteed liabilities may only be able to continue writing new business if it achieves a sufficiently high return on its asset portfolio. The shareholders benefit from value attributed to future new business if asset returns exceed a minimum level. This example is a complicated form of a call option on an asset, a security which provides the right to purchase the asset at a prespecified (exercise) price at or before an exercise date.

Options cannot be valued accurately using standard asset pricing models because of the skewness of the return distribution of option prices. Black and Scholes (see Appendix A.3) showed that if the returns from the underlying asset have a normal or lognormal distribution, the returns from an option can be replicated instantaneously by purchasing an interest in the underlying asset and borrowing a proportion of the exercise price. From this finding they developed a general option pricing equation, solutions of which provide estimates of option values. In practice, insurance company option pricing problems are typically too complex to model and solve accurately. As discussed later, valuation entails developing simplified examples to capture the essential factors which determine the discount rate and then applying stochastic modeling techniques to incorporate the detailed asset return and liability cash flow interactions.

## Equation of value

As noted in the introduction, it is instructive to assess the equivalent overall discount rate required to value net cash flows, based on the assessed values of the assets and liabilities. This can be determined from the assumption that the value of the shareholders' interest $E$ is equal to the value of the assets less the value of the liabilities. If the assets have a value of $A$ at time 0 and provide an overall expected return of $r$, and if the liabilities are worth $L$ based on a discount rate of $g$, the discount rate $e$ required to value the shareholders' interest can be found from the equations of value at time 0 and time 1:

$$A - L = E \quad \text{and} \quad A(1+r) - L(1+g) = E(1+e).$$

Solving,

$$rA - gL = eE \quad \text{or} \quad e = r + (r-g)L/E.$$

This equation, applied in the context of a firm financed partly by equity ($E$) and partly by debt ($L$), is a standard result of modern financial theory. Its extension to insurance business follows, given the analogy which can be drawn between policyholders' guaranteed liabilities and corporate debt.

In the absence of any significant likelihood of default, the discount rate required to value net cash flows increases linearly with asset risk and with the ratio of policyholders' liabilities to shareholders' equity. The equation remains valid in the presence of corporate default risk, but $g$ and $L$ are then dependent on the ratio of policyholders' liabilities to equity. This is because an increase in shareholders' equity reduces the probability that variability of asset or liability cash flows will result in insufficient assets to meet the liabilities in full. To the extent that the relationship between $A$ and $L$ varies over time, the equivalent discount rate will also vary over time. The effect of default risk and whole company valuation is considered further later.

*Summary*

It is suggested that life company valuation should start from a consideration of the nature of the individual cash flows which make up the expected future net cash flows of the company. These cash flows are generally simpler than net cash flows, and the values of traded securities such as bonds and equities form a suitable starting point for comparative valuation. Values need to be adjusted for risks incurred by the life company. In this regard, modern portfolio theory suggests that suitable allowance can be made by dividing risk into its systematic and unsystematic components. Some insurance cash flows are contingent on the outcome of other asset returns. Option pricing theory can be used to assess the systematic risk of these contingent cash flows.

INVESTMENT RETURNS AND DISCOUNT RATES

Discount rates used in the valuation of insurance company assets and liabilities need to be consistent with the assumptions made regarding future investment returns. I will summarize the investment return assumptions used in this paper, and then consider the effect of taxation on the level of market prices and on investor risks and returns.

## Investment return assumptions

Some of the analyses of historic and other data that can be made in order to set investment return assumptions are described in Appendix B and listed in Table 1.

A further assumption is that the standard deviation of equity returns is 15% pa.

A multiplicative model is assumed, so that for example the equity return assumption is $(1.03 \times 1.03 \times 1.06 - 1) \times 100$. It is also assumed that the term premium, the difference between expected future short-term interest rates and long-term interest rates, arises from inflation risk. Since index-linked gilts are not subject to inflation risk the return on index-linked gilts is assumed to be the same as the expected future level of short-term interest rates.

The assumed level of equity return, 12½% pa, is based on an 6% pa level of treasury bill yield and a 6% pa level of equity risk premium. A standard approach in actuarial literature in the UK is to compare historic equity returns with inflation, in order to assess the prospects for future real equity returns. In contrast, the normal practice in modern financial empirical and theoretical research is to measure equity returns relative to treasury bill yields rather than to inflation rates. This is because it is believed that investors compare equity risk and return with the risks and returns of alternative investment opportunities. Thus equity risk results in investors requiring higher returns from equities than from treasury bills irrespective of the level of real treasury bill yields. The practice results in a higher estimate of total equity return than if inflation rates are used as a base and the measurement period includes a period of low real treasury bill yields such as in the UK during the period 1940 to 1980. For example, consider a period of measurement when real treasury bill returns averaged 0% pa and real equity returns were 6% pa. If the expected future treasury bill real yield is 6% pa, the traditional approach would result in an

Table 1. Investment return assumptions

|  | Long-term investment return assumptions (% pa) |
|---|---|
| Inflation | 3 |
| Real short-term interest rates (three-month treasury bills) | 3 |
| Real long-term interest rates | 4½ |
| Equity risk premium (relative to short-term interest rates) | 6 |
| Short-term interest rates | 6 |
| Index-linked gilt returns* | 6 |
| Long-term interest rates | 7½ |
| Equity returns | 12½ |

*Index-linked gilts are securities issued by the UK Government with coupons and maturity proceeds linked to the consumer prices index.

assessment of expected future equity returns of 6% pa, the same as the treasury bill yield. There would be no reward for risk. Modern financial theory would suggest use of a 12% pa real equity return assumption, based on a 6% pa level of equity risk premium. This level of equity risk premium is typical of the results of empirical research into a number of equity markets across the world.

It should be noted that the choice of equity risk premium is important because of the effect it has on the discount rates selected and on the resulting asset and liability valuations, where insurance companies invest in equities.

## Taxation

The demand and supply curves for any asset, and consequently its market price, are likely to be influenced by taxation. In terms of the bond markets, interest receipts are taxed in the hands of certain investors and the issuer of a bond generally obtains tax relief on the interest payments. The market price of an interest coupon of £100 may fall short of £100 if there is insufficient demand from gross investors or lenders for whom the coupon is worth £100. This would also be true if there is a sufficient supply from borrowers who obtain tax relief (or tax revenue, for the government), or from sales made by tax payers. Similar observations hold in relation to dividends from equities and the value placed on such dividends. Since many investors have a choice of whether to invest in bonds or in equities, there is likely to be some linkage between the effects of taxation on bond and equity prices. One factor which suggests that the effect of tax on market prices is limited, is the increasing dominance of gross investors such as pension funds and also banks and multinational portfolio investors, who pay tax only on the difference between asset returns and the amounts credited to depositors or clients. Other factors are the reduced level of government borrowing requirement, the restricted availability of personal tax relief on interest payments, the increased role of derivatives markets and the interdependence of national and international markets.

Examination of the yields available on zero coupon compared with coupon bonds, also suggests that market prices may be closer to the discounted value of gross rather than net returns. On the other hand, prices of municipal bonds clearly do exhibit a significant tax effect. Arguably, markets are segmented, with equities and bonds in the main incorporating value requirements of gross investors but with certain tax favoured investment categories reflecting the tax position of net investors. Overall, however, there is relatively little firm empirical evidence, both from the UK and the USA, on the degree to which the tax position of net or gross investors is factored into market prices. It is useful to develop both pre-tax and after-tax investment return expectations in the absence of conclusive evidence that one or other is closer to the assumption set underlying observed asset prices.

### After-tax risk and return

After-tax returns available to a net corporate investor will differ from the gross returns specified earlier. It is interesting to note that the reduction in expected net equity return for a net investor is accompanied by lower equity volatility, since a fall in equity prices will be accompanied by a reduction in any liability to tax on capital gains. For example, consider an investment which provides a return of 1 if the result of one toss of a coin is a head and $-1$ if the outcome is a tail. For a gross investor, the mean return is $0.5 \times ((1)+(-1))$, that is 0. The standard deviation is the square root of $0.5 \times ((1)^2+(-1)^2)$, that is 1. For a net investor paying 30% tax, the mean return is $0.5 \times ((1) \times 0.7 + (-1) \times 0.7) = 0$ assuming immediate tax relief for losses. The standard deviation is the square root of $0.5 \times ((1 \times 0.7)^2 + (-1 \times 0.7)^2)$, that is 0.7.

The CAPM (see Appendix A.1) market line is a straight line in a risk/return plane. It passes through the point of nil risk and a risk free return, and also the point of equity risk and an equity risk return. Equity risk is defined here as the annualized standard deviation of equity returns.

For a gross investor, this risk free return is usually taken to be the return on treasury bills. For a net investor who suffers a higher rate of tax on income than on capital gains, treasury bills and bonds are tax inefficient investments and it can be argued that the (higher) net return on high quality tax-exempt bonds represents a better measure of risk free return opportunities.

Gross and net CAPM market lines can be developed in order to assess the discount rates required to value insurance company cash flows attributable to shareholders (or to policyholders) according to the degree of systematic risk borne. If the net investor line is used, allowance should be made not just for taxes borne by the insurance company but also for the reduction in return and risk arising from taxation of gains on the investors' holding in the company. The effect of investor tax and life assurance taxation on the assessment of discount rates is considered further in Appendix C. The remainder of this paper takes the standpoint of a gross investor. The development of net investor appraisal approaches is straightforward but is not pursued further in the interests of brevity.

### Summary

This section discusses the degree to which tax is factored into market prices and the effect of tax on investment risk and return. Some of the theoretical arguments suggest that markets reflect the tax position of gross investors and borrowers. In view of the lack of conclusive empirical evidence, the sets of investment return opportunities available to both gross and net investors could in principle be considered. These sets of returns provide a framework for assessing discount rates required to value more complex assets and liabilities, such as life insurance cash flows. They are needed as CAPM input parameters, where a CAPM approach to valuation is used.

## NON-PAR PRODUCTS

For non-par products, policyholder liabilities can be likened to debt. Asset risk is borne primarily by shareholders. The liabilities result in a 'gearing-up' of asset risk and this increases the discount rate required to value net cash flows.

The valuation of liabilities and of assets is discussed. The use of option pricing theory to value policyholders' rights to guaranteed cash values, and to value corporate choice as to the interest rates credited to policies, is then discussed. Although accurate modeling of these options is likely to be difficult, the result of applying a simple model, described in Appendix D and summarized below, shows that the options can be valued approximately by valuing stochastic net cash flows using a discount rate which depends on the difference between short and long dated bond yields. A few practical modeling issues are considered.

### Valuing non-profit liabilities

A starting point for determining the discount rate required to value non-par liabilities is to use the interest rate on government bonds of similar term, as discussed earlier. To the extent that policyholders bear some credit risk, a marginal addition to the government bond yield could be used to assess the market value of the liabilities, perhaps by taking into account the yield on the company's senior debt or any available credit rating information. Where lapses are a significant characteristic of the business, a stochastic model which allows for the interaction of interest rates and lapse rates is desirable. The result needs to be adjusted to reflect riskiness introduced by any options granted to policyholders or shareholders because the expected cost, not the systematic risk cost, is allowed for in the stochastic modeling process. Option pricing theory is needed to value the systematic term premium risk embedded in the liabilities. Systematic risk in this context is the factor which gives rise to the term premium (defined in this paper as the difference between the yield on a long-term bond and the yield expected on short-term bonds over the life of the bond).

### Asset risk

The assets backing non-par liabilities are typically fixed-interest or floating rate securities. Corporate securities offer interest margins over US government stock of similar type and term for some or all of the following reasons:
- Expected default costs. This arises because historic experience of corporate securities is that there is some possibility that promised payments will not be made. Rating agency historic default cost data may provide some guide as to the level of future expected costs.
- Systematic default risk. Because defaults tend to be high during periods when, for example, equity markets are falling, corporate bonds have 'systematic' default risk. In the author's experience, the additional yield required in

respect of this risk is often of a similar order of magnitude to the expected default cost.
- Transaction costs.
- Taxation differences.
- Premium for illiquidity.

If the last three factors are assessed to have a significant impact on asset yield, it may be appropriate to use a discounted cash flow rather than market value approach to asset valuation. The discount rate selected needs to allow for systematic default risk generated by investment in corporate bonds. This risk can be estimated using correlation analysis between the interest margin over government stock and the stock market index, as discussed in Appendix A. Alternatively, the effect of the last three factors can be gauged by careful analysis of the yields on comparable securities.

The existence of fixed policyholders' liabilities results in a gearing-up of asset risk borne by shareholders. Consider an example where shareholders' equity, $E$, is 7% of policyholders' liabilities, $L$, and the total assets are invested in corporate rather than government bonds yielding an additional 0.2% pa of interest, $r$, in respect of systematic default risk. This risk increases the discount rate required to value future net cash flows by about 3% pa $(0.2 + 0.2/0.07)$, based on the equation derived earlier.

## Policyholder put and company call options

Lapse risk arises from:
- Variations in lapse rates. A method for dealing with systematic lapse risk is outlined later.
- An option against the company, for guaranteed cash value products, if interest rates increase sufficiently to offset the effect of any surrender value penalty (the policyholders' put option).

For certain types of products, the company has an option to reduce the interest rates credited to policies if interest rates fall. This is equivalent to a call option on the underlying asset with exercise price equal to the value of a bond purchased at the time of exercise. In the event of an interest rate fall, the company can reduce the credited rate and sell the original bond investment for a profit. If interest rates rise, the credited rate can be maintained and the original bond held to maturity.

## Option valuation results

Both put and call option features arise for interest sensitive single premium deferred annuity ('SPDA') products commonly sold in the USA. Appendix D summarizes the results of applying option pricing theory to value the put and call option features for an SPDA with certain simplified liability and asset characteristics, for a variety of input parameters and sensitivities. Application of the methodology to typical UK products is straightforward.

In the examples given, the call option has a high level of systematic (term premium) risk so that stochastic cash flows arising from the option need to be valued using a high discount rate. The put option has low systematic term premium risk and is valued using a low discount rate. An examination of the sensitivity results presented in the Appendix shows that the key factor determining the level of discount rates required to value the options is the term premium. Other factors, such as the volatility of bond yields, the credited rate spread and the option term, have a relatively smaller impact on the level of discount rate.

Based on the parameters used in the examples, the systematic term premium risk of the put and call options can be allowed for approximately (without the need for exact modeling of the option features) by reducing the discount rates used to value the stochastic liability cash flows by approximately 0.05% pa for the policyholder put option, and 0.25% pa for the shareholder call option, in total 0.3% pa. In other words, the total value of the liabilities, allowing for the Black–Scholes values of the put and call options, can be determined approximately by assessing the mean discounted value of the stochastic liability cash flows. The discount rate is the yield on government bonds, with term equal to the liability term, reduced by 0.3% pa. Systematic risk introduced by a term premium of 1% pa, as in the numerical examples, gives rise to the need for a 0.3% pa adjustment to the discount rate.

The examples illustrate that although exact modeling of option terms may be impractical, construction of a simplified model representing the main option features can assist in the choice of discount rate used to value liability payments. Further, there are various stochastic interest rate models, and the extent to which results depend on the particular model selected is often unclear. Use of a simplified model can highlight the key drivers affecting value.

*Modeling issues*

Valuation of complex asset/liability options requires the use of a stochastic asset model. Where an arbitrage free model is not used net cash flows need to be discounted using a risk rate selected using a process such as that outlined in this section. An alternative approach is to convert the asset model to a risk neutral framework (for a good exposition of this technique, the reader is referred to Hull, 1993). The probability of adverse environments is increased and of favourable scenarios reduced, such that expected returns on the assets calculated using these modified probabilities are equal to the expected future returns on treasury bills, rather than the return on risky assets such as dated government bonds or equities. Future net cash flows assessed in this modified probability space can then be discounted at the expected future treasury bill rates. Although use of a risk discount rate is not required, estimation of the individual risk premia is still necessary and the methods outlined in this Section may also provide useful checks on the results.

Another issue to be considered is the treatment of taxes levied on the life company. The deferred acquisition cost (DAC) tax can be valued by discounting the repayment instalments using a bond yield of appropriate term. Differences between statutory profit and the tax basis will typically be unrelated to systematic risk factors, primarily reflecting differences in underlying accounting treatment (that is, tax versus statutory reserving) rather than cash flows. The difference can therefore also be allowed for by discounting using a bond yield.

*Summary*

Use of government bond yields of appropriate term is suggested for valuing non-par product premium and liability payments. An adjustment may be required to allow for systematic lapse risk. Expenses can be valued using expected future short-term interest rates. Stochastic cash flow modeling, combined with approximate option pricing techniques, is required to value guaranteed cash value and interest rate options. Assets can be valued using discounted cash flow techniques if, for example, liquidity risk is borne by policyholders rather than shareholders.

Table 2 illustrates the equivalent overall discount rate required to value net cash flows, based on the examples of asset and liability risk premium levels discussed in this section. By 'risk premium' is meant the additional yield, required because of systematic risk, over and above the yield on a US government bond with term equal to the average term of the liabilities.

In table 2, if the government bond yield is 7.5% pa, the overall discount rate required to value net cash flows allowing for surplus is 12.3% pa (7.5% + 4.8%). The rate required to value net cash flows before allowing for surplus is 12.2% pa (7.5% + 90/10 × 0.3% + 100/10 × 0.2%). It can be seen that since the values of the assets and liabilities are both substantially larger than shareholders' equity, a relatively small addition to the level of asset or liability risk results in a significant increase in the overall discount rate required to value the shareholders' interests.

VARIABLE LIFE POLICIES

Profits from variable life products (unit-linked business in the UK) arise from a variety of sources. Some cash flow streams are relatively certain and can be

Table 2. Illustrative effect of risk for non-par business

| Source of risk | Value | Risk premium (% pa) | Effect on overall discount rate (% pa) |
|---|---|---|---|
| SPDA liability with interest rate put and call options | (90) | (0.3) | 1.8 (90/15 × 0.3) |
| Assets invested in fixed interest bonds | 100 | 0.2 | 1.3 (100/15 × 0.2) |
| Surplus invested in equities, say | 5 | 5.0 | 1.7 (5/15 × 5.0) |
| Total | 15 | – | 4.8 |

valued using a discount rate close to the yield on a government bond. Unit fee income is proportional to the market value of the linked asset portfolio and can be valued using a discount rate which corresponds to the asset return rate. These cash flow characteristics are considered first, followed by a brief examination of the effect of holding surplus assets. Variability in policy lapse rates creates additional risk and is considered separately. The final section describes how the equivalent aggregate discount rate required to value net cash flows can be found.

*Product characteristics*

Premiums payable under variable life policies are divided between amounts invested for the benefit of policyholders, accumulated in the unit fund, and amounts which accrue for the benefit of shareholders. Shareholders also benefit from unit fees and other charges deducted from the unit funds. These items of income are required to pay for policyholder benefits not covered by the unit funds, for expenses, commissions and taxation, and to provide a margin of profit.

The shareholders have a relatively limited direct interest in the unit fund since the full unit fund is usually paid out to policyholders on maturity of the policy. In order to recoup initial costs, the amount paid out on policy surrender in the first few policy years is sometimes less than the accumulated unit fund, giving rise to a profit when a policy lapses. For other types of policy, initial costs are recouped by a reduction in the allocation rate in the first few policy years. The full accumulated unit fund is then typically paid out on surrender.

Shareholders have a direct interest in non-unit reserves to the extent that such reserves are set conservatively. Any surplus will ultimately fall through to profit.

Viewed in this way, shareholders' profits arising from a variable life policy can be assessed as the sum of:
- Premiums not allocated to the unit funds.
- Expense charges less expenses.
- Mortality charges less costs.
- Lapse profits.
- Unit fee income.
- Tax deducted from the unit funds less tax payable.
- Surplus from income and gains on assets backing non-unit reserves, and releases of these reserves.

If it is assumed that tax payable is a proportion of profit, each of the first five items can be multiplied by $(1-p)$ to allow for tax. A separate adjustment is required to allow for the DAC tax, and tax basis differences, as discussed earlier. For a typical company, there is little risk of insolvency (in the UK the appointed actuary will insist on an adequate level of reserves). Because of this, the full net liability to policyholders will be paid and all the items can be valued separately. Risk of insolvency is considered later. The value of the shareholders' interest in non-unit reserves is discussed below.

### Cash flow risk characteristics

Ignoring lapses, premiums not allocated to the unit funds and also DAC tax repayments are an almost certain income stream. Expenses and mortality costs are also broadly uncorrelated with the main risk factors identified in Appendix A. Diversification and arbitrage arguments (outlined earlier) suggest that company-specific or unsystematic risk will not be priced, that is, such risks will not be reflected in the required valuation discount rate. Since the premium and other cash flows emerge over a period, it would be consistent to value them using government bond yields of equivalent term. To the extent that it is believed that real expenses are not subject to inflation risk, and that the term premium is related to this risk, expenses can be valued using expected future short-term yields rather than a long-term bond yield.

Unit fees vary in line with the market value of the linked asset portfolio. If the linked asset portfolio is considered to be a series of individual funds, one for each unit allocation, discounting at a bond rate would be appropriate prior to the unit allocation, and at a risk rate from the point of allocation to receipt of the fees. The risk rate will correspond to the riskiness of the linked asset portfolio. These discount rates need to be adjusted to allow for lapse risk.

### Non-unit reserves and surplus

Shareholder value arises in respect of non-unit reserves and surplus because the underlying assets which back these quantities generate income and gains and may eventually become distributable. Since the main liability risks are considered separately, cash flows arising from assets backing non-unit reserves and surplus can be discounted at the asset return rate, adjusted to allow for the difference between the tax position of the company and tax implicit in the capital market line.

### Lapse risk

An increase in policy lapses in a period gives rise to reductions in the value of future premiums not allocated to unit funds, expenses, mortality payments and unit fees. The increase in lapse rate in the period will also have an effect on any lapse profits in the year, arising from payments on policy lapse to the extent that these are less than the amount of the unit funds. There appears to be some correlation between adverse lapse experience and factors such as economic downturns, stock market falls and interest rate rises. In the absence of such correlation, lapse risk would be entirely 'unsystematic", that is, unrelated to the APT and CAPM risk factors, and arbitrage arguments could be developed to suggest that it should not be priced. Any agency and other costs

160   S. Mehta

associated with a poor lapse experience would then need to be allowed for purely by use of stochastic modeling techniques rather than in the use of a higher discount rate.

Based on historical lapse data obtained by the author for a number of UK life companies, a very approximate estimate of the link between regular premium policy lapse rates and stock market returns is for a market decline of 15% to be associated with an increase in the level of lapse rates of 3% (in policy year one) and 1% (for policy years three and over). Expressed differently, the correlation between lapse rates and market returns, multiplied by the ratio of the standard deviation of lapse rates to the standard deviation of market returns, is 3/15 in policy year one and 1/15 for policy years three and over.

CAPM can be used to provide an estimate of the excess return required in respect of lapse risk. From Appendix A.1, the additional discount rate required to value a cash flow stream subject to lapse risk can be assessed as:

- The equity risk premium (say, 6% pa);

   **times**
- the correlation between the market index and the value of the cash flow stream;

   **times**
- the standard deviation of changes in the value of the cash flow stream;

   **divided by**
- the standard deviation of market returns (say, 15% pa).

The risk return required to allow for lapse risk in the valuation of the premium, mortality, and unit fee cash flows can then be gauged. If a 1% increase in the lapse rate were to reduce the value of these future cash flows by 1%, the additional premium would be:

$$6\% \times 1/15 = 0.4\% \text{ pa.}$$

The premium is not required when valuing overhead maintenance costs since these are generally not affected by policy lapse.

The effect of systematic risk on the value of lapse profits can be much greater. Table 3 illustrates the effect for a policy where the penalty on lapse is

*Table 3.* Effect of systematic lapse risk

|  | Prior to market fall | | | After market fall | | |
| --- | --- | --- | --- | --- | --- | --- |
| Policy year | Lapse rate (%) | Lapse penalty (£) | Profit (£) | Lapse rate (%) | Lapse penalty (£) | Profit |
| 3 | 10 | 1000 | 100 | 11 | 850 | 93 |
| 4 | 10 | 500 | 45 | 10 | 425 | 38 |
| 5 | 10 | 500 | 40 | 10 | 425 | 34 |
| 6+ | 10 | 0 | 0 | 10 | 0 | 0 |
| Present value at 12% pa | | | 172 | | | 154 |

expressed as a proportion of the unit fund. It allows for a 1% increase in lapse rates, and a 15% market fall, at the beginning of policy year 3.

A 10% reduction in the value of future lapse profits (in the example from 172 to 154) resulting from a 15% market fall would increase the discount rate needed to value future lapse profits by 4% pa (6% × 10/15). The effect of lapses in policy year one can be allowed for in existing structure value and this is considered later.

The analysis outlined in this section suggests that risk introduced by variability in ultimate lapse rates is normally small relative to equity risk. This conclusion is consistent with the author's experience that variations in embedded values (that is, in the values of in-force portfolios) arising on account of ultimate lapse experience are typically much smaller than variations in stock market levels.

### Equation of value

The value of the shareholders' interest in a variable life company is equal to the value of the company's total assets, less the value of net liabilities to policyholders, $E = A - L$. However, the main policyholder liabilities are determined by reference to the value of the assets held in the unit funds. For this reason, it is useful to restate the equation of value by deducting the value of the unit fund assets from both $A$ and $L$. Shareholders' equity $E$ is then the value of non-unit fund reserve assets plus the value of future cash flows less the value of net cash flows into the unit funds. The equation of value becomes:

$$E = S + V_1 + V_2 + ...,$$

where $S$ is equal to non-unit reserves and surplus and $V_i$ are the values of individual items of cash flow $i$, measured net of movements into the unit funds. The equivalent aggregate discount rate used to value net cash flows is the internal rate of return at which the value of these cash flows is equal to $E$. It can be determined approximately, as the weighted average of the discount rates used to value the individual cash flows, with weights equal to the values of these cash flows. This approximation is valid only if the individual cash flow distributions are reasonably similar to each other.

### Summary

Table 4 illustrates the discount rates that could be used to value individual cash flows based on the observations made in this Section and the discount rates set out in Appendix C. It assumes that the treasury bill rate is 6% pa and that unit funds are invested entirely in equities yielding an expected return of 12½% pa. The level of additional return required in respect of lapse risk, as outlined in the section 'Lapse risk', has been rounded to ½% pa. It has been assumed that expense charges have the same variability characteristics as expenses; a fixed charge subject to inflation risk would be treated in the same

*Table 4.* Discount rates for variable life business

|  | Gross investor (% pa) |
|---|---|
| Premiums not allocated to unit funds | 8 |
| Expense charges less expenses | 6½ |
| Overhead costs | 6 |
| Mortality charges less costs | 8 |
| Lapse profits | 10 |
| Unit fee income |  |
|   Prior to allocation | 8 |
|   After allocation | 13 |

way as premium receipts. No account has been taken of the additional lapse risk in the initial period of a policy.

The equivalent overall discount rate required to value net cash flows will vary according to product design and company experience. If surrender charges are not dependent on the size of the unit fund and if all future unit fees are funded (that is, anticipated at the point of sale by weakening the reserving basis), an aggregate discount rate close to a government bond yield could be justified to value the in-force business of a large company. If overhead costs are substantial and cannot be fully recouped from expense charges, and if future surrender profits and unit fees are substantial, an overall discount rate close to the expected return on equities could be justified.

As an example, consider a company which sells products designed to recoup initial costs by having a reduced allocation rate in the first two policy years. The bid offer spread (the difference between the buying and selling prices of units in the fund) meets the cost of paying renewal commission and a part of maintenance expenses. The annual management charge provides the main source of ongoing profit. The in-force value to a gross investor for a company with total annualized premium income of 1000 could be broken down as shown in Table 5.

*Table 5.* Illustrative overall discount rate for variable products

| Value attributed to | Discount rate (% pa) | Value |
|---|---|---|
| Future premiums not allocated to unit funds | 8 | 300 |
| Expenses | 6½ | (200) |
| Mortality charges less costs | 8 | 0 |
| Lapse profits | 10 | 0 |
| Unit fee income | 10½* | 200 |
| Net cash flows | 10½ | 300 |

*In between the 8% pa rate in respect of the period prior to allocation to the unit fund and the 13% pa rate for the period after allocation.

*Valuation of a life company* 163

In the example, the equivalent overall discount rate required to value net cash flows has been calculated as a weighted average rate. In practice, an internal rate of return should be used and this will differ from the weighted average rate.

### WITH-PROFIT (PAR) BUSINESS

This section considers valuation issues for another type of life assurance business, business written with both shareholders and policyholders having a common interest in profits emerging, such as that written in the UK. For a with-profit company, the value of the long term fund assets less the net guaranteed obligations of the company can be compared with shareholders' equity in a stock company which writes non-par business. The equity is shared between policyholders and shareholders and is available for ultimate distribution in the form of bonus additions and transfers to shareholders. The overall discount rate required to value equity is considered. For a UK with-profit company, shareholders' transfers are normally linked to the cost of the bonus declarations. The discount rate required to value transfers is the same as that required to value bonuses in respect of the period prior to bonus declaration.

The following further observations can also be made:
- A consideration of cash flow risk allows the amount of surplus (estate) required to support bonus policy to be assessed.
- The level of mathematical reserves (and therefore reserving policy) has a second order effect on shareholder value compared with the amount of assets held to support the liabilities.
- Bonuses are to some extent driven by marketing considerations, and the distribution of assets needed to approximately correspond to the volatility of liability and bonus payments can be derived.
- The value of assets not required to support the in-force business, free capital, varies according to the uses to which this capital is put.

In the UK, policyholder benefits are often considered in relation to asset shares, that is the accumulation of cash flows attributable to the policy at the achieved rate of investment return. Asset shares can also be developed by accumulating the component policy cash flows separately, from policy inception, using returns from appropriately matched assets. The assessment of asset shares using risk rates of return rather than the earned rate is not considered further here.

#### *Equity in a with-profit company*

With-profits business in the UK is written on terms providing maturity values equal to the sum of guaranteed sums assured, plus reversionary bonus declared annually but paid at maturity or death, plus substantial terminal bonuses declared and paid on maturity or earlier death. Assets are invested substantially in equities, and reserves are established on a net premium method using a low rate of interest but without having specific regard to the terminal bonus component of maturity values.

Defining equity ($E$) as the value of the assets less the guaranteed component of net liabilities ($L$), the discount rate ($e$) required to value bonus payments for the period prior to bonus declaration, and to value shareholder transfers, can be found from the equation

$$e = r + (r - g)L/E$$

where $r$ is the earned rate on the assets, and $g$ is the aggregate rate of discount required to value the guaranteed component of net liabilities (non bonus payment related cash flows net of premium receipts).

As noted below, a different rate of discount needs to be applied for the period between bonus declaration and bonus payment, since the level of bonus is then fixed.

For some companies equity is substantial and is used to support new business, or to smooth bonuses by holding back surplus in order to mitigate the effect of asset value fluctuations. For these companies a closer analysis of the discount rate needed to value bonuses is required.

*Assessment of discount rates*

Use of close to a long-term government bond yield is suggested for valuing future premiums, sums assured and bonuses after declaration. This is because the main risk affecting these cash flows is lapse risk, and lapse risk after the initial period is estimated to be small. The correlation between real expense levels and other economic factors may be small, so that their systematic risk is low. If it is believed that the term premium is related to inflation risk, expenses could be valued using expected future short-term bond yields, that is long-term government bond yields net of the term premium.

Cash value payments and bonuses prior to declaration should also be discounted using rates which reflect the variability of these payments. It is useful to construct a simplified model and to introduce complexities gradually, as in the following paragraphs.

*Mutual company*
Consider a mutual company in which the guaranteed element of liability (for sums assured and declared bonuses, less future premiums) and also expenses have been fully reassured (or are matched against appropriate investments and excluded from further consideration). No new business is being written and reversionary and terminal bonus payments will be set to exhaust the fund. Bonuses once declared are reassured. The variability ('risk') of bonus declarations is similar to the variability of the fund's assets: any reduction in asset values will result in an equal expected reduction in aggregate bonus payments and any increase in asset values will be fully reflected in increased bonuses. The company can choose, for any individual policy or policy type and for any

individual year of bonus declaration, to depart from a matching of bonuses with asset returns. However, it cannot do so once all years and all policies are taken into account.

*Proprietary company*
Consider next a proprietary with-profit company which in other respects is similar to the mutual described above. Transfers to profit and loss are a proportion of the cost of bonuses and the two together will be set to exhaust the fund. As for the mutual fund, bonus payments would need to be reduced in the event of any reduction in value of the asset portfolio. To the extent that asset appreciation is also reflected in the bonus payments, the variability of bonus declarations and shareholder transfers is equal to that of the asset return. In practice, companies smooth bonus declarations and this is considered next.

*Symmetrical bonus smoothing policy*
Bonus smoothing policy is described here as symmetrical if the change in bonus levels due to a fall in asset prices relative to expectations is equal and opposite to the change arising from an increase in asset prices. A company with a large estate can choose the degree to which it smooths bonus declarations. The choice may depend on marketing or other considerations, not just financial ones. At one extreme, bonus declarations can be fixed in advance. Shareholders' transfers would then also be fixed and could be valued using a government bond yield. Use of a discount rate between the bond rate and the asset return rate could be justified if a company maintains a bonus smoothing policy under which a change in asset prices results in a less than proportionate change in bonuses.

At the opposite extreme, a company may have no surplus of assets beyond the amount required to meet future expected bonus payments. If, as before, the guaranteed liabilities are matched by government bonds, shareholders' transfers and bonuses prior to declaration can be valued using a discount rate equal to the expected return on the assets backing these payments. The effect of taxation is considered in Appendix C.

More generally, the degree of smoothing of bonuses will depend on the variability of the returns on the underlying assets and on whether any surplus is available to mitigate asset return variability. The discount rate required to value shareholders' transfers can be determined by assessing the proportion of bond investment in a notional portfolio, such that the aggregate variability in the return on the notional asset portfolio is equal to the variability of bonus declarations. Companies are likely to smooth reversionary bonus rates to a greater extent than terminal bonuses. Consequently, a discount rate closer to the bond yield than to the equity return rate may be appropriate to value future reversionary bonuses.

A substantially higher link is likely between terminal bonus rates and equity returns, requiring use of a discount rate closer to the equity return rate to value terminal bonus payments. Assessment of the risk and discount rate for terminal bonus payments needs to be consistent with the overall variability of policy maturity proceeds. The latter is likely to depend on the variability of policy asset shares. Because terminal bonuses can be viewed as balancing items required to track asset shares to a greater or lesser extent, the discount rate required to value them may be high unless a heavy smoothing policy is adopted.

*Asymmetrical bonus smoothing policy*

An alternative bonus smoothing policy is for bonus declarations to follow asset price increases but to be maintained if asset prices decline. For example, terminal bonuses could be set such that the proceeds on maturity of a policy are a proportion, say 90%, of the asset share, subject to a minimum maturity payment equal to the sum assured and accumulated reversionary bonuses. Reversionary bonus rates could be fixed. For a company which adopts this bonus smoothing policy the value of shareholders' transfers can be assessed using option pricing theory. The terminal bonuses are given by:

$$\max(0.9A - G, 0) \quad \text{or} \quad 0.9 \times \max(A - G/0.9, 0),$$

where $A$ is the (variable) asset share on maturity of the policy, and $G$ is the sum assured and accumulated reversionary bonuses.

The expression is that for a call option on an asset which provides the asset return in excess of an exercise price, if asset returns exceed the exercise price. The cost of the bonus declaration can then be assessed as the value of a call option on the asset portfolio, plus the reversionary bonus payments discounted using a government bond yield. Option pricing theory enables an approximate value of the call option to be assessed.

In practice, bonus policy is likely to be complex and complex option pricing formulae, as well as simulation techniques, are likely to be needed.

*Required surplus*

Required surplus is defined here as the value of assets required to meet future payments to existing policyholders and shareholders, and expenses, less the amount of mathematical reserves. Future payments to policyholders include expected future bonuses and may be assessed, for example, by projecting policy asset shares. In other words, required surplus is the amount of estate needed to support expected future bonus or other payments. The estate is defined as the excess of the value of assets over the mathematical reserves. The amount of required surplus can be determined by discounting future cash flows at the relevant risk rates discussed above. There is an element of circularity in the calculation of required surplus because the risk rates themselves may depend on the amount of available surplus. The amount of required surplus depends on the extent to which a company adopts a policy of smoothing bonus rates. Higher surplus is required, and a lower discount rate is used to value future bonuses, if policyholders and shareholders are to be insulated from the effects of a decline in asset prices.

This methodology generally results in a higher estimate of required surplus than traditional methods, because a lower rate of discount (closer to the bond yield than to the earned rate) is used to value future expenses, sums assured and reversionary bonus payments. This has a greater impact than the use of the lower rate to value future premium receipts. This is because the value of future expenses, sums assured and reversionary bonus payments generally exceeds the value of future premiums.

### Statutory valuation basis

Assets backing both required surplus and the mathematical reserves are required to meet future payments to existing policyholders and shareholders. For this reason, the valuation methodology disregards the strength of the reserving basis except insofar as this affects the total of required surplus and reserves. In the UK the valuation basis is also used to determine the amount transferred to shareholders. The appraisal valuation needs to reflect expected future levels of the valuation basis, so that the amounts of transfer can be projected. It may also need to reflect systematic risk, if future changes in the valuation basis are assessed to be correlated with common economic factors.

### Asset matching

A company may have a bonus smoothing policy which results in terminal bonuses and reversionary bonuses prior to declaration exhibiting variability characteristics equal to some factor times that of equities. Other cash flows may have a relatively low variability. The proportion of the asset portfolio which needs to be invested in bonds in order to match approximately the variability characteristics of a company's net liabilities can be found. If the estate falls short of required surplus, values should be based on bonus smoothing policy and bonuses limited to reflect the amount of the estate and the long-run target asset mix. The discount rate used to value bonus cash flows would be increased to reflect the restriction on bonus smoothing.

### Free capital

Free capital is defined here as the value of assets less the amount of mathematical reserves and required surplus.

Free capital can be used for some or all of the following:
(1) Reducing investment mismatching risk
(2) Subsidising future new business through bonus rate or bonus smoothing policy
(3) Maintaining a 'free asset' ratio higher than needed for (1) and (2) in order to promote new business sales.

It should be noted here that these uses are not necessarily residual to bonus policy. For example, a company may prefer to limit bonus smoothing than to reduce new business subsidies. For this reason it is necessary to quantify the amount of capital required for each potential use. The total needs to be compared with the amount of available estate in order to avoid double counting.

The first of the uses of free capital is considered next.

### Free capital required for asset/liability mismatching

Mismatching gives rise to risk of 'failure', that is the possibility that asset values will fall below the level required in order that new business can be sold. Free capital held to reduce the risk of failure has value to shareholders because it reduces the risk that existing structure value will be lost. Risk of failure is discussed further later.

Companies may use equity and property investments to back guaranteed liabilities. The variability of bonus payments may differ from the variability of returns on the backing assets. These mismatch policies result in:

- Higher expected bonus declarations, arising from the higher expected returns on the investments.
- A corresponding increase in the riskiness of bonus declarations, because of the riskiness of equity/property investment returns.
- Tax issues, since different investments have different tax treatments.
- A risk of failure, and a need to hold free capital to reduce this risk.

The higher expected maturity proceeds may also result in increased new business sales.

The first two factors result in an increase both in expected shareholders' transfers and in their variability. These offset each other and consequently guaranteed liabilities can be valued using fixed interest bond yields, irrespective of the actual investment policy. For the same reasons, bonuses can be valued using discount rates depending on bonus smoothing policy rather than on investment policy.

A mismatching strategy results in a gain to shareholders if higher expected maturity proceeds facilitate new business sales. On the other hand, from the shareholders' viewpoint, risk of failure is undesirable because shareholders could lose their interest in future new business and perhaps a part of their interest in the in-force business. These two factors result in a need to assign shareholder value to free capital held to offset risk of failure. The cost of failure, and the value of reducing it, can be assessed using option pricing techniques. The value generated by enhanced new business sales can, in principle, be calculated directly.

### Free capital required to support sales distribution capability

Besides free capital needed for mismatching purposes, a part of future cash flows may be set aside to enhance the company's sales distribution capability.

To the extent that these cash flows are not distributed, they do not directly generate value for shareholders or policyholders. A separate value can, however, be assigned to these cash flows for embedded value purposes, for example by considering the opportunity cost of alternative uses. The discount rate required to value future new business sales prior to the point of sale can be reduced for a company with capital which is used to support the sales distribution capability and to which no separate value is assigned. This is because uncertainty as to whether future expected sales will in fact be achieved is reduced if the company is able, if necessary, to increase new business subsidies. This is likely to be an inefficient use of capital from the point of view of shareholders since they only benefit if circumstances prove adverse. If the discount rate is not reduced, then it would be appropriate to assign a (discounted) value to this capital when calculating an appraisal value.

*Summary*

The overall discount rate used to value terminal bonuses and reversionary bonuses prior to declaration should be consistent with the amount of available estate. A high degree of bonus smoothing policy will require a higher proportion of bond investment, a lower discount rate to value bonuses and hence result in a greater utilization of the estate. For example, consider a company with the characteristics shown in Table 6. The discount rates shown in Table 6 to value the expense cash flows were based on short-term rather than long-term bond returns. A small addition has been made to the discount rates shown for the premium, expense and liability cash flows, to allow for lapse risk.

The discount rate required to value equity is the internal rate of return at which net cash flows are valued at 8000. In Table 6, for the sake of simplicity, the weighted average discount rate has been calculated although it is recognized that this may not equal the internal rate of return.

The company is approximately matched in that the value of the guaranteed obligations and expenses is equal to the value of the gilt portfolio and future premiums. With a 100% equity portfolio, the weighted average discount rate required to value bonus declarations and shareholders' transfers would increase

Table 6. Illustrative overall discount rate for with-profit business

| Value attributed to | Discount rate (%) | Value |
| --- | --- | --- |
| Equity assets | 12½ | 8000 |
| Bond assets | 7½ | 2000 |
| Future premiums | 8 | 3000 |
| Future expenses | 6½ | (200) |
| Sum assured related liability payments | 8 | (3000) |
| Bonus declared to date | 8 | (1800) |
| Equity | 12.4 | 8000 |
| Future bonuses and shareholder transfers | 12.4 | 8000 |

to 13.7% pa. Expected future bonuses and their volatility would increase. If the company had assets worth 5000 invested entirely in equities (not, as in the table above, assets of 10 000 invested partly in gilts), the weighted average discount rate would become 15.6% pa; bonus levels would need to be reduced and the company would not be able to maintain its bonus smoothing policy.

If the assets are worth 20 000, leading to equity of 18 000, the company can smooth bonuses and use a part of the estate to support new business. The weighted average discount required to value the whole equity, assuming a 100% equity investment policy, is 13.0% pa. The increase in available equity enables the company to adopt a greater degree of bonus smoothing. If bonuses are smoothed so that the level of risk is in between that of gilts and equities, a discount rate of 10.0% pa would be appropriate (that is, approximately halfway between the discount rate required for bonds, 7.5% pa, and for equities, 12.5% pa). The value of future bonuses and transfers is increased to, say, 10 000. The remaining equity, 8000, could be valued using a discount rate of $(18\,000 \times 13.0\% - 10\,000 \times 10\%)/8000 = 16.8\%$ pa. This rate of discount would need to be factored in when assessing value attributed to alternative uses of the estate.

An option pricing valuation method may be needed to value future bonuses, if the amount of estate is relatively small and if the assets and liabilities are not matched. Terminal bonuses are likely to have different risk characteristics from reversionary bonuses and can be valued using a higher discount rate or using option pricing techniques.

Although the data discussed here refer primarily to UK with-profits (par) business, they also have relevance to non-par and variable life business where free capital is used to support new business activities or to offset risk arising from mismatching assets and liabilities.

EXISTING STRUCTURE VALUE

Existing structure value (also known as 'goodwill') is value attributed to future new business. Future sales are uncertain and a different rate of discount is required to value profits in respect of the period prior to the point of sale than from the date of sale. New business sales and lapse risks result in a need to apply a higher discount rate to value future gross profit margins up to the point of sale than to value overhead costs and future initial expenses. Lapse risk arises because initial expenses may not be recouped if a policy lapses. For a with-profit company, the existence of an estate can substantially reduce lapse and sales risk borne by shareholders. I also review the special considerations required for with-profit companies distributing business through a direct salesforce (that is, tied agents) and through brokers (independent agents), respectively.

*Table 7.* Sales and lapse risks

|  | Value prior to market fall | Value after market fall — Reduced sales | Value after market fall — Increased first-year lapse rates |
|---|---|---|---|
| Earned profit gross of initial expenses | 100 | 90 | 87 |
| Marginal initial expenses | (60) | (54) | (54) |
| Acquisition overhead costs | (10) | (10) | (10) |
| Earned profit | 30 | 26 | 23 |

### New business risk

Future earned profits are subject to a variety of risks. A number of such risks impinge on expected levels of earned profit and can be allowed for in assessing the level of future growth. Other risks can be divided between unsystematic risks, those unrelated to common market factors, and systematic risks. Both types of risk increase costs. This is because policyholders, agents, staff and suppliers may require better terms from a company which exhibits volatile results and which could cease to trade. For the reasons discussed earlier, unsystematic risks may not give rise to an increase in required discount rates.

Systematic risk arises because sales may fall and lapse rates may increase in an economic downturn. These two effects are compounded by the existence of overhead costs and initial expenses, as illustrated in Table 7. We have already considered some of the effects of holding free capital to support the sales distribution capability of a company.

### Non-par business

For non-par and variable life business, the gearing introduced by overhead costs and first-year lapse risk can be allowed for by developing separate existing structure multiples for earned profit gross of initial expenses, marginal initial expenses, and acquisition overhead expenses. Estimates of the required multiples can be derived using CAPM, based on an examination of historic new business sales and first-year lapse rates relative to stock market returns or other economic factors. For example, a decline of 10% in new business sales (relative to prior expectations) and an increase of 3% in first-year lapse rates might be associated with an equity market return of 15% below expectations. With these assumptions, the additional discount rates, based on an equity risk premium of 6% pa are shown in Table 8. In practice, overhead costs are also subject to systematic risk since in a severe economic downturn a company may cease to transact new business. For the purpose of illustration, it is assumed that the level of this risk is one-third of the level of new business sales risk, resulting in a 1¼% pa additional discount rate.

*Table 8.* Additional discount rates for sales and lapse risks

|  | Gross investor (% pa) |
|---|---|
| New business sales risk | 10 × 6/15 = 4.0 |
| Lapse risk | 3 × 6/15 = 1.2 |

The overall discount rates, assuming a risk free rate of 6% pa are given in Table 9. The overall multiples required for a company where sales margins and expenses are increasing with inflation at 3% pa are illustrated in Table 10.

The effect of adjusting for systematic risk in first-year lapse rates and in new business sales is to dramatically reduce estimated existing structure values (in the example, to £117 million).

The low values shown in Table 10 result from high initial expenses relative to the value of gross earned profit. An increase in gross earned profit to £110m with no increase in expenses, for example, would increase existing structure value to £238 million. The lower the responsiveness of new business sales to a market decline, the higher the calculated level of existing structure multiples. For a large efficient company, acquisition overhead costs would be spread over a larger number of policies, and higher multiples apply. For a less efficient company, overhead costs may form a larger proportion of total costs, but possibly these costs should be discounted at a rate which reflects higher systematic risk (the company might be more likely to be closed to new business in a severe recession), rather than the riskless rate shown in Table 10. Existing structure multiples are also increased if a portion of initial expenses are clawed back on policy lapse (such expenses should be deducted from profit and not included in initial expenses in deriving the multiples), or through the use of persistency bonuses, volume overrides and share option schemes. On the other hand, it should be noted that there may be a significant delay between a decline

*Table 9.* Discount rates to value existing structure

|  | Gross investor (% pa) |
|---|---|
| Earned profit gross of initial expenses | 6 + 4 + 1.2 = 11¼, say |
| Marginal initial expenses | 6 + 4 = 10 |
| Acquisition overhead costs | 6 + 1¼ = 7¼ |

*Table 10.* Derivation of existing structure multiples

|  | Value (£m) | Gross investor |
|---|---|---|
| Earned profit gross of initial expenses | 100 | 1/(11.25 − 3) = 12.1 × |
| Marginal initial expenses | (60) | 1/(10 − 3) = 14.3 × |
| Acquisition overhead costs | (10) | 1/(7.25 − 3) = 23.5 × |
| Earned profit and existing structure value | 30 | £117m |
| Overall multiple | – | 4 × |

in sales and management action to reduce costs, resulting in a higher effective level of overhead expenses than a strict analysis might suggest.

### With-profit company – direct salesforce

For with-profit companies, somewhat different considerations apply in the assessment of existing structure multiples. Assume that new business sales depend largely on salesforce size and productivity rather than on bonus subsidy. The gearing from overhead costs and first-year lapse risk, needs to be allowed for primarily in assessing the cost to the estate of writing new business, rather than in assessing the value of profit and loss transfers. Because of this, the existing structure multiples are relatively high. Against this, the assessed cost of writing new business is also higher.

For assessing the value of shareholders' transfers a multiple of 12 times (gross investor) could be appropriate, based on the following analysis and on the new business sales and lapse risk levels assumed previously (see Table 11).

For some companies, new business sales may require support from the estate. In practice, there is a possibility that sales would reduce if the new business subsidy is eliminated, particularly if the subsidy is cut before similar action is taken by other similar companies. A lower multiple is appropriate for that part of total sales which is dependent on the estate in this way, reflecting investment risk of the underlying assets and the expected period of support.

### With-profit company-broker distribution

New business sales subsidy may represent a significant portion of the estate since companies are under pressure to maintain bonus levels. Whilst the subsidy continues, a high level of sales may be achieved. Sales arising as a result of the subsidy are subject to sales and first-year lapse risk. They are also subject to asset risk, since a reduction in the amount of estate available to subsidise new business will reduce the period during which the subsidy continues. The discount rate applied to values arising from the subsidy should reflect the impact of all three risks. At some point the subsidy may cease. If this occurs before similar action is taken by competitors, new business volume is likely to substantially reduce (or the company may close to new business), and bonus rates will

Table 11. Existing structure multiples for a with-profit company

|  | Gross investor (% pa) |
| --- | --- |
| Risk free rate | 6.00 |
| New business sales risk | 4.00 |
| First-year lapse risk | 1.20 |
| New business growth | (3.00) |
| Net discount rate | 8.20 |
| Multiple | 12 × |

reduce. These features should be incorporated in any projection of expected future new business. Alternatively, the derivation of existing structure value can be based on the projected ultimate level of sales and a reduced existing structure multiple applied in respect of the temporary additional volumes and higher bonuses.

For the last companies to eliminate the subsidy, new business sales may continue at an undiminished level because there will presumably always be some demand for with-profit products. For these companies, the existing structure value should reflect the impact of the eventual decline in bonus rates. In practice, a company needs a relatively strong estate in order to pursue a policy of subsidising new business. The interaction of bonus policy, new business subsidy, and estate size is a complex subject which is not considered further in this paper.

*Summary*

This section shows how a consideration of systematic risk leads to the assessment of separate multiples for gross earned profit, acquisition costs and overhead expenses, rather than a single multiple as is currently common in appraisal valuations. The special considerations needed for with-profit companies are investigated. It should be noted that in any appraisal, the value placed on existing structure is likely to involve considerable exercise of judgement. This is because existing structure multiples are sensitive to small changes in assumptions and because of the need to interpret transactions and other data. It should also be noted that further research is required into the magnitude of systematic sales and lapse risks.

WHOLE COMPANY VALUATION

A company with an insufficient amount of capital may be unable to make the best use of its other resources. On the other hand, too much capital may lead to inefficiencies. The concept of target surplus is introduced, and the use of option pricing theory to assess the optimal level of surplus or estate required to ensure that a company will be able to continue writing new business is then discussed. The market valuations of quoted life companies, supported by analyses of transactions in insurance companies, can be used to validate the component approach to valuation. Such analysis is useful because transaction prices provide objective evidence as to the value placed on insurance companies by investors. I will briefly consider the uses and, particularly, the limitations of beta analysis in the process of validation.

*Target surplus*

The level of assets in relation to the liabilities has a number of implications for company valuation. Surplus can be defined as the excess of the value of assets over reserves calculated on a statutory minimum basis. Target surplus can be defined as management's long-term desired level of surplus, expressed, for example, in relation to statutory minimum reserves or solvency margin requirements. The value of liabilities (for a with-profit company, net guaranteed liabilities) can be defined as the value of policyholder and other liabilities discounted at appropriate risk-adjusted rates of return as derived previously.

Both target surplus and reserves in excess of the value of liabilities are similar to the extent that neither will be distributed. Nevertheless it may be appropriate to operate a target surplus policy based on statutory reserves rather than value of liabilities, because the former may be a better guide to minimum surplus requirements set by regulators and capital needs resulting from agency costs. Agency costs arise because a more risky company, with a lower level of surplus, may find it more difficult and costly to attract staff, policyholders and intermediaries and to arrange reinsurance or financing. These costs, as well as inefficiencies which may arise if capital exceeds an optimal level (perhaps assessed as suggested below) can be allowed for directly, in the valuation of net worth, in-force business and existing structure.

The ratio of target surplus to reserves is in some ways analogous to an equity/debt ratio since policyholder liabilities have a number of similarities to debt. Operating a target surplus policy is then similar to targeting a particular level of debt to equity. Of course, capital market theory would suggest valuing debt at market value and disregarding regulatory valuation rules, so that the surplus/reserve ratio needs to be interpreted with care.

### Risk of failure

Failure here is defined as the event that asset values fall below minimum regulatory standards, resulting in a company being unable to continue writing new business and in shareholders losing existing structure value. An increase in surplus reduces the risk of failure. Insolvency is a special case of failure, and arises when a company is unable to meet its guaranteed obligations in full. The risk of insolvency for UK life companies is generally small and so can normally be ignored in the valuation process.

Consider only existing business. All liabilities are payable at time 1. Maximum shareholder value at time 1 is given by:

$$\max i(Ai - Li, 0),$$

where $i$ is the set of alternative management strategies at time 0, $Ai$ is the (variable) asset return at time 1, $Li$ is the amount payable to policyholders at time 1, and it is understood that the mean of a stochastic process is being assessed.

Shareholder value in this example is a call option on the underlying asset $Ai$, with exercise price $Li$. Shareholder value is maximized by choosing an asset with high return variability and by minimising the amount of asset utilized against the specified level of policyholders' liability (that is, minimising target surplus). For, the shareholder gains by the full amount of asset appreciation, whereas policyholders meet the cost of any excess asset depreciation (in the event of bankruptcy).

Introducing new business, assume that the shareholder will lose the value of future new business, $B$, if asset values fall below a minimum level, $Ri$. Shareholder value is given by:

$$\max i(Ai - Li, 0) + (\text{if } Ai > Ri)B$$

Consider an example where the policyholders' liability $Li$ is 950 and is equal to $Ri$. The value of the asset is 1000 and the potential loss of existing structure value, $B$, is 100. The asset consists of the payoff from a gamble which provides 1100 if a head is thrown, and 900 on a tail. Time 1 is the time it takes to throw the coin.

Shareholder value is $0.5 \times 250 + 0.5 \times (0) = 125$.

If the policyholders' liability is reduced to 900 and surplus is increased from 50 to 100, shareholder value is increased to $0.5 \times 300 + 0.5 \times 100 = 200$. Injecting 50 of surplus adds 75 of value. Further increases in surplus do not create additional shareholder value (beyond the amount injected). Optimal target surplus is an increasing function of risk of failure and of agency costs. A higher level of surplus reduces the probability that assets will fall below the level required to continue writing new business, and hence preserves existing structure value.

If the company matches its liabilities, or has sufficient surplus to ensure that its assets will always exceed the minimum required level, there is no risk of failure. Shareholder value can be assessed by taking the difference between the market values of the assets and the liabilities and adding in existing structure value. If the risk of failure is increased, an option pricing approach is needed to value the shareholder's call option, as seen above.

*Insurance company beta ratios*

Under CAPM (Appendix A), the beta of an asset determines the discount rate required to value the asset. The quoted UK life companies have beta ratios averaging approximately one (see, for example, the beta ratios published quarterly by London Business School Financial Services). The ratios are influenced by gearing introduced by holding company debt so that the beta for a typical ungeared UK quoted life company could be approximately 0.9. This ratio is the weighted average of beta ratios applicable to net worth, in-force business and existing structure value. Table 12 illustrates the relationship:

The existing structure discount rate is a composite of the rate required to value business in-force (that is, from the point of sale) and new business up to the point of sale. If these have an equal weight, the discount rate required to value new business up to the point of sale is 17% pa (gross investor). This corresponds to a multiple of 7 times for a company with expected future long-

*Table 12.* Beta ratios for a UK life company

| Component | Illustrative proportion of total value | Beta ratio | Gross investor discount rate (% pa) |
|---|---|---|---|
| Net worth | 0.1 | 1.0 | 12.5 |
| In-force value | 0.7 | 0.8 | 11.0 |
| Existing structure value | 0.2 | 1.3 | 14.0 |
| Total | 1.0 | 0.9 | 11.8 |

term growth equal to 3% pa. In practice, as discussed previously, beta ratios for the individual components of value could differ significantly from the ratios shown in Table 12. For example, much lower ungeared beta ratios generally apply in the USA, since the level of equity investment is much lower than in the UK.

Observed insurance company beta ratios provide one possible means to assess discount rates. These discount rates may be a useful check on the results of the analyses suggested earlier. However, beta ratios suffer from substantial measurement error and also only indirectly take account of the risks to which companies are exposed. A close analysis of the risk/return characteristics of the individual cash flows which make up the overall return to shareholders facilitates understanding of the sensitivity of company values to changes in company structure or circumstances. The approach to valuing individual assets and liabilities by comparing their risk characteristics with those of traded securities, and the use of option pricing arbitrage relationships where options exist, should enable the derivation of more reliable discount rates than those derived from beta analysis.

*Summary*

As seen previously, different types of insurance business and different risk factors can cause substantial variations in the amount of risk borne by shareholders and in discount rates which would compensate for this risk. A particularly important risk factor is the level of surplus held by the company in relation to the amount of its liabilities. If surplus is sufficiently high, the company is not likely to fail and full allowance can be given to the existing structure in an assessment of the total appraisal value. Analysis of the beta ratios of quoted companies can provide a guide to the overall levels of discount rate required to value in-force business and existing structure. However, beta analysis is subject to substantial measurement error and this limits its usefulness.

CONCLUSION

The approach developed in this chapter provides a practical framework for assessing the value of a life company. Value is assessed in the context of the risk and return tradeoff implicit in the market valuation of securities traded on the principal securities exchanges. The method proposed is to examine each cash flow separately and, where possible, to draw a comparison between these cash flows and the cash flows expected from traded securities such as conventional and index-linked bonds and equities. For example, premium, expense and guaranteed liability payments are compared with bond coupon and maturity payments; unit fee income and bonus payments are compared with the returns from the underlying life company assets. The cash flows can then be valued using discount rates based on the investment return assumptions selected for each traded security. In general, the value of future net cash flows is assumed to equal the sum of the values of the individual cash flows.

In principle, discount rates could be assessed on both a net and a gross investor basis. There is relatively little firm empirical or theoretical evidence as to the extent to which taxation of investment returns affects the level of market prices. However, particularly for US companies given the US tax code, pragmatic considerations favour use of a gross basis and this is the basis selected in this paper. Use of general arbitrage arguments, and of asset pricing models such as CAPM and APT, is suggested to allow for mortality, lapse and other risks. Risks are divided into systematic and unsystematic components, the former being those related to common economic factors such as stock market returns, industrial production, personal consumption, inflation and the term premium. Modern portfolio theory suggests that cash flows subject to systematic risk may need to be valued using discount rates in excess of a risk free rate whereas no such excess is required to value cash flows subject only to unsystematic risk. For this reason, an addition to the discount rate is required to allow for lapse risk but no addition is made for mortality risk since this is assumed to be broadly uncorrelated with the principal economic factors. This risk does, however, adversely affect the value of a company.

Valuation of risky cash flows which are subject to only unsystematic risk using a risk free rate seems counterintuitive. It may be felt that, not withstanding diversification and arbitrage arguments to the contrary, potential investors in an imperfect market will in practice require a risk return for bearing unsystematic risk. The same argument could, however also be applied to suggest that an investor may require more than a market return from any asset. Just as potential investors will seek to achieve a transaction price below a fair price, a seller will strive for a higher price. The eventual outcome will depend on the balance of supply and demand rather than necessarily on assessed value, although it is the author's view and experience that markets are generally more efficient than a first examination suggests.

We have examined risk in relation to the valuation of future new business. Gross profits from new business sales are subject to sales risk, with a high systematic risk component, whereas overhead costs have low systematic risk. Similarly, first-year lapses affect gross profits but not acquisition expenses. Because of this, separate valuation of gross profit margins, marginal initial expenses and acquisition overhead costs is suggested for the determination of existing structure value.

For some companies, surplus levels may be insufficient to ensure that regulatory approval for continued new business sales will be forthcoming under all realistic scenarios. This may be true even though the risk of insolvency is negligible. Existing structure value is retained in circumstances when the value of the assets exceeds the value of the liabilities by a sufficient margin, in much the same way as a call option on an asset provides a payoff in the event that the asset price exceeds the exercise price. For other companies there is little likelihood that existing structure value is at risk, and an additive rather than an option pricing approach can be used to assess company value. The total value of the company is then the sum of its in-force and existing structure values.

The author has had the opportunity to consider the relationship of transaction and market prices with appraisal values for many companies, UK and overseas, over a number of years. In his view, application of the techniques outlined in the paper, with suitable exercise of judgement, is likely to provide realistic estimates of value. Any individual transaction value may of course also depend on other factors, such as voting or control structure. The methodologies explored result in a closer degree of alignment with empirical and theoretical research work in the field of finance undertaken in the last 40 years. The techniques have been used successfully not just in the appraisal of life company but also for other financial institutions such as property/casualty and fund management companies.

An interesting application is in the setting of return on capital targets for different lines of business in a financial services institution. Currently, relatively unsophisticated approaches are often used, for example based on the company level aggregate cost of capital. Modern financial theory provides many insights into the relationship between price, risk and return. A few of these insights have been used in developing the valuation approaches explored in this paper. However, the theory has much wider application, for example in product development and pricing, bonus philosophy, investment policy, profitability assessment, profit recognition and financial control. The author looks forward to the start of a more extensive debate within the profession on the uses and limitations of modern financial theory.

## Acknowledgements

I would like to thank my colleagues Alan Botterill, Chris Fordham, Niall Franklin, Jeremy Goford, David Keeler, Peter Needleman and Geoff Westall for their comments on various drafts of this paper. The views expressed in the paper are entirely my own and should not be taken as representing those of my firm.

## REFERENCES

There is an extensive range of literature on the subject of asset pricing models and modern financial theory. For a general introduction and overview, the reader is referred to the books by Chew and Stern, Copeland and Weston, Elton, Gruber and Platt.

Bangert, R.M. (1973). Valuation of a life assurance company for purchase. *Journal of the Institute of Actuaries*, **99**, 131.

Beenstock, M. and V. Brasse (1986). Using options to price maturity guarantees. *Journal of the Institute of Actuaries*, **113**, 151.

Black, F. and M.J. Scholes (1973). The pricing of options and corporate liabilities. *Journal of Political Economy*, **81**, 637.

Breedon, D. (1979). An intertemporal asset pricing model with stochastic consumption and investment opportunities. *Journal of Financial Economics*, **7**, 265.

Burrows, R.P. and G.H. Whitehead (1987). The determination of life company appraisal values. *Journal of the Institute of Actuaries*, **114**, 411.

Chew, D.H. and J.M. Stern (1986). *The Revolution in Corporate Finance*. Oxford: Basil Blackwell.

Clarkson, R.S. (1989). The measurement of investment risk. *Journal of the Institute of Actuaries*, **116**, 127.

Copeland, T.E. and F.J. Weston (1983). *Financial Theory and Corporate Policy*. Addison-Wesley.

Cox, J., Ingersoll, J. and S. Ross (1981). A reexamination of traditional hypotheses about the term structure of interest rates. *Journal of Finance*, **36**, 769.

Cox, J. and M.V. Rubinstein (1985). *Option Markets*. New York: Prentice-Hall.

Elton, E.J. and M.J. Gruber (1991). *Modern Portfolio Theory and Investment Analysis*. Chichester: John Wiley & Sons.

Fama, E.F. (1977). Risk-adjusted discount rates and capital budgeting under uncertainty. *Journal of Financial Economics*, **5**, 3.

Hull, J.C. (1993). *Options, Futures, and Other Derivative Securities*. New York: Prentice-Hall.

Lintner, J. (1965). The valuation of risk assets and the selection of risky investments in stock portfolios and capital budgets. *Review of Economics and Statistics*, **XLVII**(1), 13.

Markowitz, H.M. (1952). Portfolio selection. *Journal of Finance*, **VII**, 77.

Merton, R. (1973). Theory of rational option pricing. *Bell Journal of Economics and Management Science*, **4**, 141.

Miller, M. and F. Modigliani (1958). The cost of capital, corporation finance and the theory of investment. *American Economic Review*, **53**, 261.

Miller, M. and F. Modigliani (1961). Dividend policy, growth and valuation of shares. *Journal of Business*, **34**, 411.

Pepper, G.T. (1984). The long-term future of interest rates both real and nominal. *Journal of the Institute of Actuaries*, **39**, 145.

Platt, R.B. (1986). *Controlling Interest Rate Risk: New Techniques and Applications for Money Management*. Chichester: John Wiley & Sons.

Report of the Maturity Guarantees Working Party (1980). *Journal of the Institute of Actuaries*, **107**, 101.

Ross, S.A. (1976). The arbitrage theory of capital asset pricing. *Journal of Economic Theory*, 341.

Sharpe, W.F. (1964). Capital asset prices: a theory of market equilibrium under considerations of risk. *The Journal of Finance*, **XIX**, 425.

Sherris, M. (1987). On the risk adjusted discount rate for determining life company appraisal values. *Journal of the Institute of Actuaries*, **114**, 581.

Wilkie, A.D. (1987). An option pricing approach to bonus policy. *Journal of the Institute of Actuaries*, **114**, 21.

Wise, A.J. (1984). The matching of assets to liabilities. *Journal of the Institute of Actuaries*, **111**, 445.

APPENDIX A: ASSET PRICING MODELS

The last few decades have seen a number of breakthroughs into the understanding of how risk affects asset prices. In 1952 Markowitz noted that investors are concerned primarily with the return on their whole portfolio of assets, and that the risk of any individual asset is of concern only to the extent that it contributes to the risk of that portfolio. Since Markowitz' original pioneering work, several asset pricing theories have emerged. The capital asset pricing model, arbitrage pricing theory, and option pricing theory stand out and are the most widely used. These theories enable the market price of an asset to be estimated once the cash flow distribution and risk characteristics of the asset have been assessed. A brief description of each theory follows.

*Capital asset pricing model*

Sharpe, Lintner and Mossin developed the Capital Asset Pricing Model (CAPM) in 1964 and 1965, based on the observation that many institutional portfolios are well diversified and that the risk of an individual asset can be assessed by measuring its contribution to the standard deviation of returns on the market portfolio ('systematic' or 'non-diversifiable' risk). CAPM states that the required return on an asset depends solely on its systematic risk and equals:

$$r(f) + b(\tilde{r}(m) - r(f))$$

where $r(f)$ is the return on a risk free asset, $\tilde{r}(m)$ is the expected return on some broadly based index of asset prices (the market index) and $b$ is the asset's systematic risk factor, beta.

Beta is equal to:
- the correlation coefficient between returns on the asset and the market index;
**times**
- the standard deviation of returns on the asset;
**divided by**
- the standard deviation of returns on the market index.

The beta of the market index is, by definition, 1.0 and the beta of an asset measures the responsiveness of the asset price to changes in the market index. An asset which is expected to rise or fall in price by 5% when the market index rises or falls by 10% has a beta of 0.5.

CAPM draws considerable strength from two empirical observations:
- Individual share prices tend to rise or fall in tandem (that is, systematic risk is large).
- The returns from a relatively small reasonably diversified portfolio of shares are likely to be close to that of the market index (95% of unsystematic risk is likely to have been diversified away in a portfolio of 40 shares chosen at random).

The empirical evidence for a strict and stable linear relationship between expected return and systematic risk relative to a single market index is mixed.

There is rather more evidence for a modified form of CAPM, the two-factor or zero beta model, under which the risk free rate is replaced by the return on a minimum variance portfolio uncorrelated with the market index. The zero beta version can be derived using more realistic assumptions than those required for the single index model. Another criticism levied at CAPM is that not just variance but also skewness of returns contribute towards investor risk/return preferences and that some degree of skewness is exhibited in typical asset return distributions. These criticisms have led to a number of alternative versions of CAPM, including multi-factor models to allow for industry specific risk and the effects of tax, and models which seek to correct for possible misspecification of the market index (the consumption based CAPM attributable to Breedon).

One effect which has not so far been fully explained is the small company effect. Many studies have found that returns on small companies exceed the CAPM equilibrium levels. Some research has been undertaken which suggests that the excess return may be attributed to marketability or liquidity effects. Other research suggests that traditional tests have understated small company betas.

In the author's view, CAPM provides a useful benchmark with which to assess expected returns on an asset.

*Arbitrage pricing theory*

Ross presented the arbitrage pricing theory (APT) in 1976. Under APT, expected returns on an asset depend linearly on the responsiveness of the asset's return to one or more of an unspecified number of common factors. Examples of factors which have been suggested include the market index, industrial production, inflation and the differentials between the yields on short- and long-term government bonds (the term premium) and on low grade and high grade corporate bonds.

APT is more general than CAPM in that asset prices may depend on a variety of factors. Under the conditions of riskless arbitrage used to derive the APT model, shares which are priced at a discount to their expected price will be bought to replace shares or combinations of shares with similar risk characteristics not priced at a discount. The evidence in favour of APT is stronger than for CAPM. However, there is only a limited volume of data on the number, size and type of the APT factors and risk premia. For this reason, examples in this paper are based on CAPM rather than APT.

## OPTION PRICING THEORY

In 1973 Black and Scholes published their paper on 'Pricing of options and corporate liabilities'. A call option on an asset is a security consisting of the right to acquire the asset for a pre-specified price (the 'exercise' price) at (sometimes on or before) the option expiry date. A put option provides the right to sell the asset at the exercise price. Black and Scholes showed that if the asset return is normally or lognormally distributed, it is possible to replicate the return distribution of a call option by buying shares in the asset and borrowing a proportion of the exercise price. The value of the option is given by the value of the shares bought less the amount of borrowing. The proportions of shares and borrowing need to be continuously rebalanced during the life of the option in order to maintain instantaneous replication of the option return distribution. Black and Scholes noted that opportunities for riskless arbitrage limit departures of the price of a traded option from its theoretical price.

The expected value of an option can be assessed using a stochastic model of the asset return distribution. However, the Black–Scholes (B–S) valuation approach is required in order to allow for the option's systematic risk. The risk neutral approach, briefly described earlier, provides a very general and powerful method of valuation of complex assets and asset/liability interactions.

Option pricing techniques have been applied in the valuation of many different securities including shares, fixed interest securities and convertible bonds. For example, ownership of the equity in a firm can be considered to be a call option on the firm with exercise price equal to the amount of debt financing. It can be used for everyday capital budgeting decisions where a positive value is achieved only if costs are recouped, and in the evaluation of natural resource investments.

The B–S theory is more robust than CAPM and APT in that the B–S estimated value of a contingent claim on an asset depends on the price of the asset and on the construction of a portfolio which matches the return distribution of the option. Estimated values are dependent on the expected variability in the asset return, not on the expected return. Finally, it should be noted that estimated option prices are known to be reasonably accurate (relative to observed transaction prices) for short-term contracts. The range of comparisons conducted for long-term contracts is more limited although the results to date appear encouraging (see, for example, the valuation of equity notes in the article by Courtadon and Merrick in *The Revolution in Corporate Finance*, edited by Chew and Stern).

### APPENDIX B: INVESTMENT RETURN ASSUMPTIONS

The methodology explored in this paper requires that discount rates selected to value future cash flows be consistent with investment returns available on equally risky investments. The level of available investment return therefore plays an important part in the valuation process.

This Appendix sets out some of the analyses of historic and other data that can be made in order to obtain an informed assessment of future asset returns.

### Real short-term interest rates

Pre-tax real returns on 3-month treasury bills in the UK, measured by taking the geometric average of treasury bill returns divided by the consumer price inflation index, have been as follows:
- In the 116 years between 1824 and 1939: over 3% pa.
- In the 41 years between 1940 and 1980: minus 0.9% pa.
- In the 14 years between 1981 and 1994: 4.8% pa.

Data on interest rates in the UK since 1970 can be found in the CSO publication 'Financial statistics'. The publication 'The British Economy Key Statistics 1900–1970' (London and Cambridge Economic Service) provides data since 1900. Pepper, in a lecture to the Faculty of Actuaries on 20 February 1984 'The long-term future of interest rates both real and nominal', provides a useful discussion, as well as the information on real rates since 1824.

Factors which may have impinged on the level of real yields in the period between 1940 and 1980 include the Second World War, exchange controls, the operation of interest rate policy, credit restrictions and the effect of severe inflation from about 1970. Since 1980, the absence of exchange controls has led to an expectation that real returns in the UK will match those in other countries, subject to differences arising from purchasing power or other deviations in currency rates. The average real return on short-term instruments for the leading industrialized nations in the period 1979 to 1994 was 3.5% pa.

If, as the author believes, investors and issuers focus on real rather than nominal yields, analysis of the structure of interest rates can provide input into anticipated future real yields:
- Short-term bond yields can be compared with available inflation forecasts.
- Long-term bond yields net of a term premium adjustment (to obtain an equivalent expected average future short-term bond yield) can be compared with inflation forecasts derived from survey data, historic trend analyses or from an economic model. The term premium is considered below.
- Analysis of the index-linked yield curve may provide a best estimate, particularly if it is believed that these bonds do not incorporate a term premium. This might be true, for example, if the existence of a term premium is related to inflation risk.

The results of an analysis conducted along these lines are likely to depend on the relative weight given to the level of real yields in the period 1940 to 1980 compared with the other evidence. In the author's view, bond market prices at the time of writing are broadly consistent with short-term real treasury bill yields of perhaps 3% or 3½% pa in the longer term.

### Term premium

The term premium, defined here as the difference between expected future short-term interest rates and long-term interest rates, measures the additional return expected from investing in long-term bonds. In practice, measurement of the term premium is usually based on the difference between current short- and long-term rates. As noted by Pepper, the term premium tends to be high during periods when real short-term interest rates are low and vice versa. Thus, in the UK, there was only a small term premium during the 1980s, in contrast to the high premium experienced in the fifty-year period to 1979 (1.9% pa). Similar results have been experienced in the USA.

In the context of a real yield on treasury bills of say 3% pa, a term premium of 1½% pa would result in a real yield on long-term government bonds of 4½% pa.

*Long-term inflation assumptions*

Long-term inflationary expectations can be assessed by deducting from long-term bond yields the assumed real long-term bond yield. As defined above, the real long-term bond yield is the sum of the forecast real short-term bond yield and the term premium. It has been assumed that government bond yields reflect the requirements and expectations of gross investors. Because of this, no adjustment for tax has been made when comparing yields and inflation levels. The examples used in this paper assume that long-term inflation expectations amount to about 3% pa and that the real yield on long-term government bonds is 4½% pa.

*Equity returns*

A guide to prospective returns on the equity market can be found from:
- An assessment of corporate growth prospects.
- A consideration of return on capital employed.
- An analysis of historic returns.
- Consensus forecasts.

These are considered in turn.

*Real economic growth*

It can be argued that corporate sector growth will bear some relation to growth in the economy as a whole. An assumption as to future growth in the economy, say 1½% pa, can then be used to assess prospects for future profitability and equity returns. Analysis of these, consistent with growth prospects, could be made as in the following example for the UK.

Consider a firm which is expected to grow in real terms at 1½% pa, and to pay a gross of tax dividend of 5% pa. Capital employed is 1500 at the start of the year, made up of 500 of debt and 1000 of equity taken at market value. These levels of debt to equity ratio and dividend yield are similar to the average for large companies quoted on the London Stock Exchange. Inflation is assumed to equal 3% pa and bond and equity yields are assumed to remain constant over time. Tax is assumed to be paid on real earnings, and the effect

*Table 13.* Inflation and growth

| | |
|---|---|
| Inflation adjusted profit pre-tax and interest | 135 |
| Interest (8½% of 500) | (43) |
| Tax (33% of 135–43) | (30) |
| Equity earnings | 62 |
| Net dividend (5% × 1000, less tax) | (40) |
| Retained earnings | 22 |

of capital or other tax allowances is ignored. In order to have grown at a 1½% pa real rate, the company value at the end of the year needs to be 1,567, an increase of 67 made up of 45 (inflationary growth) and 22 (retained earnings). The level of inflation adjusted pre-tax profit required to achieve this growth is 135 (9% of capital employed) as shown in Table 13.

The 4½% increase in total company value, to 1567, has a geared effect on the value of equity. Debt is still worth 500 at the end of the year and consequently equity has increased to 1067 (+6.7%). The equity return in this example is 12%, made up of a 5% dividend yield and 6.7% growth. If the company does not issue further debt, its debt/equity ratio declines over time, resulting in a declining level of equity risk and return. If the company maintains a target debt/equity ratio of one-half by reducing its equity base and issuing debt, its equity return will be a constant 12% pa. The equity return derived depends on the level of debt/equity ratio as well as on the profitability, interest rate, inflation, dividend and tax assumptions. A company which has a lower (higher) level of target debt/equity ratio is likely to achieve a lower (higher) rate of return on equity, corresponding to a reduced (increased) overall level of equity risk.

*Return on capital employed*
The average inflation adjusted pre-tax return on industrial capital employed (measured at replacement cost) in the UK in the period since 1963 has been approximately 8% pa to 9% pa (source: Bank of England Quarterly Bulletins); the current level is approximately 10% pa. A 9% pa return equates to a 12% pa equity return using the gearing level and other assumptions stated in the previous example, and assuming that replacement cost is equal to the market value of the total debt and equity capital base. The assessment of prospective returns on capital can be supported by consultation with investment analysts or experts specialising in the various sectors of the equity market.

*Historic returns*
The geometric average risk return on equities in the UK, derived by dividing equity returns by the return on treasury bills, during the 76-year period between 1919 and 1994, was 6.3% pa. The arithmetic mean excess return was about 2% pa higher (source: the annual equity-gilt study by BZW). Research is not yet conclusive as to whether the geometric or the arithmetic mean provides the better measure of the equity risk premium. Similar results obtain in the US. If treasury bills have a real yield of 3% pa and inflation is 3% pa, the

total equity return based on a 6% pa equity risk premium would be 12½% pa (1.06 × 1.03 × 1.03).

*Consensus forecasts*
An alternative approach to assessing future return prospects is to use estimates prepared by equity market analysts and fund managers. These estimates tend to be lower than the results produced from the analyses suggested above. For example, at the time of writing, typical fund manager forecast long-term returns for the UK are:
- Inflation                              – 3% pa to 5% pa.
- Real yield on treasury bills           – 2% pa to 4% pa.
- Real yield on long-term bonds          – 3% pa to 5% pa.
- Risk premium on equities               – 3% pa to 6% pa.
  (relative to treasury bills)

*Volatility of investment returns*

For option pricing and stochastic modeling purposes, estimates of the volatility of asset yields and returns are required. The annualized standard deviation of stock market returns in the UK during the last 70 years has a 'normal' level of approximately 15% pa which, however, varies significantly from time to time. For example, volatility was much higher at times during 1974 and 1987 (so that estimates of volatility based on shorter measurement periods including these years are higher than 15% pa). The distribution of equity returns has a 'tail' which is fatter than lognormal, resulting in extreme returns occurring more frequently than for a lognormal distribution.

There is some evidence that share prices regress towards levels based on long-run average corporate earnings, that is, there is some normal level of earnings yield. If return is measured as the logarithm of the ratio of the value of a share portfolio at the end and beginning of a period, the standard deviation of eight-year returns, for example, could be 0.8 or 0.9 times the standard deviation that would be observed if there were no mean reversion. In other words, mean reversion appears to reduce long-term volatility and risk. However, it is not yet clear either whether this effect has diminished over time or if other effects, for example related to asset price shocks, mean that it is appropriate to reflect the shorter run overall volatility in modeling work.

One method which can be used to measure the volatility of bond yields is to assess the standard deviation of a series of the natural logarithm of yield rates. If the standard deviation is $sY$, where $Y$ is the expected yield, the one standard deviation range of yields in one year's time is $Y\exp(-s)$ to $Y\exp(s)$. Yields typically exhibit some degree of mean reversion. Thus, the one standard deviation range of the expected yield in $n$ years' time could be less than $Y\exp(-s\sqrt{n})$ to $Y\exp(s\sqrt{n})$. For example, the reduction over a 20-year period might be one-third. Under typical investment market conditions, the parameter $s$ could be 0.25 for treasury bills and 0.15 for ten-year bonds. In some periods, volatility is much higher than these levels.

188  S. Mehta

In the author's view, allowance for a mean reversion effect, and for shocks, should be considered in all long-term option pricing and stochastic modeling work.

APPENDIX C: DISCOUNT RATES AND TAXATION

Life company taxation may result in double taxation of returns to shareholders and consequently may affect the discount rates required to value the shareholders' interest in a life company.

*Capital market line*

As discussed earlier, net and gross capital market lines can be developed to represent the investment opportunity set for net and gross investors (Table 14). The risk free rate for a net investor has been set to a rate somewhat higher than 65% of the gross rate, given opportunities for tax efficient investment (for example in tax exempt bonds). Similarly, the net return on equities assumes some level of dividend exemption and deferral effects of capital gains taxation. Standard capital market text books provide the formulae required to adjust for tax.

As noted earlier, it is not clear which of these two lines more closely represents the risk/return profile implicit in the principal securities markets.

*Net investor discount rates*

In order to value life company gross asset returns using the return requirements of a net investor, it is necessary to use the net capital market line. Since the investment return in a US life company is exempt from tax, the volatility of returns is higher than the volatility of direct investment. Based on a risk free rate of 6% pa and a net equity risk premium of 4½% pa, and assuming that this effective rate of tax on capital gains is 25%, the return required by a net investor on an equity investment held in a life company is:

$$1.06 \times (1 + \tfrac{4}{3} \times 0.045) - 1 = 12\tfrac{1}{2}\% \text{ pa}$$

Table 15 summarizes the position for other types of asset, based on the same risk free rate and equity risk premium assumptions. The net asset returns shown reflect the tax position of the life fund, whereas the required returns reflect the tax position of a net corporate investor.

Table 14. Illustrative net and gross capital market lines

|  | Net investor (% pa) | Gross investor (% pa) |
| --- | --- | --- |
| Risk free rate | 5 | 6 |
| Equity return | 10 | 12½ |
| Variability of equity return | 10 | 15 |
| Equity risk premium | 4½ | 6 |

*Table 15.* Asset return and net investor required return assumptions

|  | Asset return (% pa) | Required return (% pa) |
|---|---|---|
| Short-term bonds | 6 | 5 |
| Long-term bonds | 7½ | 6½ |
| Equities | 12½ | 12½ |

*Table 16.* Asset return and gross investor required return assumptions

|  | Asset return (% pa) | Required return (% pa) |
|---|---|---|
| Short-term bonds | 6 | 6 |
| Long-term bonds | 7½ | 7½ |
| Equities | 12½ | 12½ |

For the net investor, returns available via investment in bonds through the life company exceed the returns available on alternative direct investments even after allowance is made for the dampening effect on risk caused by taxation. Overall, tax effects result in net investor discount rates being about 1% pa lower than the asset yield, for bonds held in the life company. The discount rates derived above are those that could be appropriate for net investors or for a market dominated by net investors.

### Gross investor discount rates

The methodology used to determine net investor discount rates can also be used to derive gross investor rates. Discount rates required to value returns to a gross investor are shown in Table 16.. Gross investor discount rates are the same as the asset yield, since both the company and the investor are not taxed on the investment return. Clearly, this applies to assets backing policyholder liabilities, rather than surplus. The discount rates derived above could be appropriate for gross investors or for a market dominated by gross investors.

## APPENDIX D: PUT AND CALL OPTION FEATURES OF A SINGLE PREMIUM DEFERRED ANNUITY

The examples in this Appendix are based on a single premium deferred annuity (SPDA) product, and the policyholder put and company call options described earlier.

### Policy characteristics

Key SPDA product and experience characteristics typically include:
- A high premium (resulting in sensitivity to interest rate considerations).

190    S. Mehta

- Accumulation of the initial premium with credited interest which can be a function of various factors including the initial yield on the portfolio, competitor (new money) rates and surrender rates.
- After the first year, credited rates might equal the lesser of the portfolio yield minus 1.5% pa and 0.5% pa above the competitor rate. The second of these two terms gives rise to the company call option. The company has an option to reduce credited rates further, subject to a minimum guarantee of say 4% pa, but the value of this option may be limited if existing structure value is to be maintained.
- Surrender penalties in the first six years (for example, 6% of the accumulated premium declining to 1%).
- Low surrender rates in the first six years followed by a mass lapse on expiry of the surrender value penalty period and by high surrenders thereafter.
- High surrender rates if the credited rate falls significantly below the competitor rate. This feature is the policyholder put option. High surrender rates are also associated with companies which experience bad publicity (for example, arising from a decline in surplus or in asset values).

*Simplified model*

The SPDA has an initial face value FV of 100 and initial term $N$ equal to 6 years. The credited rate, $C1$, is $CS1$ (1% pa) below the yield $Y1$ on a zero coupon $N$ year government bond. At duration $T$ years, the policyholder has an option to surrender his policy for the accumulated value times a surrender value factor SV and to switch into a new product with term $N-T$. The company has an option to reduce the credited rate. The new credited rate at time $T$, $C2$, is $CS2$ below the yield at time $T$ on a zero coupon $N-T$ year bond. For the company call option a yield margin $M$ is also credited and included in $C2$. A proportion $W$ of policyholders take advantage of the option to switch if it is to their advantage to do so. The company is assumed to always take advantage of its option. The company has surplus $E$ in excess of the value of the $N$ year bond ($S$) at the outset of the policy.

*Yield curve characteristics*

At the outset of the policy, the expected annual return from treasury bills (that is, exclusive of any term premium) is $R1$ over the $N$ year period and $R2$ during the first $T$ years. The total return on the $N$ year bond is $Y1$ including a term premium of $P1$ ($R1 + P1 = Y1$). The total return on the $T$ year bond is $Y2$ including a term premium of $P2$ ($R2 + P2 = Y2$). The expected term premium in $T$ year's time on an $N-T$ year bond is $P3$. The expected yield on the $N-T$ year bond in $T$ years is $Y3$, where

$$(1 + Y3 - P3)^{N-T} = (1 + R1)^N / (1 + R2)^T.$$

The standard deviation factor of $N-T$ year bond yields is $V$ (see Appendix B) so that the one standard deviation range of the yield in $T$ years' time is

$$V1 = Y3 \times \exp(\pm V \times \sqrt{T}),$$

and the standard deviation of bond price in $T$ years is approximately

$$Z = Y3 \times V \times \sqrt{T} \times (N - T).$$

The expected return on the $N$ year bond over $T$ years, $Y4$, is given by

$$(1 + Y4)^T = (1 + Y1)^N/(1 + Y3)^{N-T}.$$

*Option statistics*

The initial value of the bond matching the expected maturity proceeds is

$$S = FV \times ((1 + C1)/(1 + Y1))^N.$$

The option exercise price in $T$ years' time is

$$K = FV \times SV \times (1 + C1)^T \times ((1 + C2)/(1 + Y3))^{N-T},$$

where $SV$ is set to 1 if the value of the company call option is to be assessed.

The value of the put option granted to policyholders, $P$, is $W$ times the Black–Scholes put option price evaluated with input parameters $S$, $Z$, $K$, $T$ and $Y2$.

The Black–Scholes put option price based on these parameters is:

$$SN(-d_1) - K^1 N(-d_2)$$

where $d_1 = (\ln(S/K^1) + Z^2/2)/Z$, $d_2 = d_1 - Z$, $K^1 = K \exp(-TY2)$ and $N(x)$ is the probability that a normally distributed variable with mean zero and variance 1 is less than $x$.

The expected value of the put option at time $T$, $P^1$, is $W$ times the Black–Scholes put option price evaluated with input parameters

$$S \times (1 + Y4)^T, \quad Z, K \times (1 + Y2)^T, \quad T \text{ and } Y2.$$

Similar input parameters are used to assess the value and expected value of the call option. The Black–Scholes value of the call option is $SN(d_1) - K^1 N(d_2)$.

The discount rate required to value the put and call options is given by

$$(1 + D)^T = P^1/P \quad \text{and} \quad C^1/C.$$

The overall discount rate, $I$, required to value future maturity and surrender cash flows is solved by iteration. The value of the policyholders' liability, $L$, is given by $S + P$ and $S - C$. The value of the shareholders' interest, $MV$, is $E - P$ and $E + C$.

*Model results*

The put option results shown in Tables 17 and 18 include:
- The value of a bond ($S$) required to meet the maturity proceeds assuming no surrender option.

Table 17. Policyholder put option

| | | Examples | | | | | | | | | | | |
|---|---|---|---|---|---|---|---|---|---|---|---|---|---|
| | | 1 | 2 | 3 | 4 | 5 | 6 | 7 | 8 | 9 | 10 | 11 | 12 |
| Input | | | | | | | | | | | | | |
| Bond term | N | 6.000 | 6.000 | 6.000 | 6.000 | 6.000 | 6.000 | 6.000 | 6.000 | 6.000 | 6.000 | 6.000 | 6.000 |
| Option term | T | 3.000 | 3.000 | 3.000 | 3.000 | 3.000 | 3.000 | 3.000 | 3.000 | 3.000 | 5.000 | 1.000 | 1.000 |
| Risk free rate $N$ years | R1 | 0.080 | 0.080 | 0.080 | 0.080 | 0.080 | 0.080 | 0.080 | 0.080 | 0.080 | 0.080 | 0.080 | 0.080 |
| Risk free rate $T$ years | R2 | 0.080 | 0.080 | 0.080 | 0.080 | 0.080 | 0.080 | 0.080 | 0.080 | 0.080 | 0.080 | 0.080 | 0.080 |
| Term premium $N$ years | P1 | 0.010 | 0.010 | 0.010 | 0.010 | 0.010 | 0.010 | 0.010 | 0.010 | 0.010 | 0.010 | 0.010 | 0.010 |
| Term premium $T$ years | P2 | 0.005 | 0.010 | 0.005 | 0.010 | 0.005 | 0.005 | 0.005 | 0.005 | 0.005 | 0.005 | 0.005 | 0.005 |
| Term premium $N-T$ year bond in $T$ years | P3 | 0.005 | 0.010 | 0.010 | 0.005 | 0.005 | 0.005 | 0.005 | 0.005 | 0.005 | 0.005 | 0.010 | 0.010 |
| Volatility factor ($N-T$ year bond yield) | V | 0.150 | 0.300 | 0.150 | 0.150 | 0.300 | 0.150 | 0.150 | 0.150 | 0.150 | 0.150 | 0.150 | 0.150 |
| Credited rate spread to $N$ year bond | CS1 | 0.010 | 0.010 | 0.010 | 0.010 | 0.010 | 0.005 | 0.010 | 0.010 | 0.010 | 0.010 | 0.010 | 0.010 |
| Credited rate spread to $N-T$ year bond in $T$ years | CS2 | 0.010 | 0.005 | 0.010 | 0.010 | 0.010 | 0.010 | 0.005 | 0.010 | 0.010 | 0.010 | 0.010 | 0.010 |
| Surrender factor | SV | 0.970 | 0.970 | 0.970 | 0.970 | 0.970 | 0.970 | 0.970 | 0.980 | 0.970 | 0.990 | 1.000 | 0.950 |
| Initial face value | FV | 100.000 | 100.000 | 100.000 | 100.000 | 100.000 | 100.000 | 100.000 | 100.000 | 100.000 | 100.000 | 100.000 | 100.000 |
| Withdrawal rate | W | 0.300 | 0.600 | 0.300 | 0.300 | 0.300 | 0.300 | 0.300 | 0.300 | 0.600 | 0.300 | 0.300 | 0.300 |
| Surplus (excess over the asset value $S$) | E | 5.000 | 5.000 | 5.000 | 5.000 | 5.000 | 5.000 | 5.000 | 5.000 | 5.000 | 5.000 | 5.000 | 5.000 |

## Valuation of a life company 193

Table 17. Continued

| Calculation | | Examples | | | | | | | | | | | |
|---|---|---|---|---|---|---|---|---|---|---|---|---|---|
| | | 1 | 2 | 3 | 4 | 5 | 6 | 7 | 8 | 9 | 10 | 11 | 12 |
| N year bond yield | Y1 | 0.090 | 0.090 | 0.090 | 0.090 | 0.090 | 0.090 | 0.090 | 0.090 | 0.090 | 0.090 | 0.090 | 0.090 |
| N year credited rate | C1 | 0.080 | 0.080 | 0.080 | 0.080 | 0.080 | 0.085 | 0.080 | 0.080 | 0.080 | 0.080 | 0.080 | 0.080 |
| T year bond yield | Y2 | 0.085 | 0.090 | 0.085 | 0.090 | 0.085 | 0.085 | 0.085 | 0.085 | 0.085 | 0.085 | 0.085 | 0.085 |
| N–T year bond in T years: yield | Y3 | 0.085 | 0.090 | 0.090 | 0.085 | 0.085 | 0.085 | 0.085 | 0.085 | 0.085 | 0.085 | 0.090 | 0.090 |
| Return on N year bond over T years | Y4 | 0.095 | 0.090 | 0.090 | 0.095 | 0.095 | 0.095 | 0.095 | 0.095 | 0.095 | 0.091 | 0.090 | 0.090 |
| N–T year bond in T years: credited rate | C2 | 0.075 | 0.085 | 0.080 | 0.075 | 0.075 | 0.075 | 0.080 | 0.075 | 0.075 | 0.075 | 0.080 | 0.080 |
| N–T year bond price volatility at T | Z | 0.066 | 0.140 | 0.070 | 0.066 | 0.133 | 0.066 | 0.066 | 0.066 | 0.066 | 0.029 | 0.068 | 0.068 |
| N year bond asset value | S | 94.620 | 94.620 | 94.620 | 94.620 | 94.620 | 97.279 | 94.620 | 94.620 | 94.620 | 94.620 | 94.620 | 94.620 |
| Exercise price | K | 118.845 | 120.518 | 118.860 | 118.845 | 118.845 | 120.503 | 120.511 | 120.070 | 118.845 | 144.123 | 103.136 | 97.979 |
| Value of put option | P | 0.421 | 2.397 | 0.462 | 0.293 | 1.126 | 0.310 | 0.572 | 0.529 | 0.842 | 0.265 | 0.778 | 0.248 |
| Value of put option at T | P′ | 0.276 | 3.105 | 0.439 | 0.267 | 1.083 | 0.191 | 0.398 | 0.362 | 0.552 | 0.082 | 0.776 | 0.239 |
| Discount rate to value surrender payments | D | −13.11% | 9.00% | −1.72% | −3.02% | −1.32% | −14.83% | −11.43% | −11.87% | −13.11% | −20.91% | −0.22% | −3.42% |
| Overall discount rate for cash flows | I | 8.96% | 9.00% | 8.98% | 8.98% | 8.94% | 8.97% | 8.95% | 8.95% | 8.92% | 8.96% | 8.99% | 8.99% |
| Total value of liability to policyholders | L | 95.041 | 97.018 | 95.082 | 94.913 | 95.747 | 97.589 | 95.192 | 95.149 | 95.462 | 94.885 | 95.398 | 94.868 |
| Policyholder liability valued using bond yield | L1 | 94.836 | 97.018 | 94.964 | 94.826 | 95.468 | 97.429 | 94.931 | 94.904 | 95.052 | 94.675 | 95.335 | 94.841 |
| Value of shareholders equity | MV | 4.579 | 2.603 | 4.538 | 4.707 | 3.874 | 4.690 | 4.428 | 4.471 | 4.158 | 4.735 | 4.222 | 4.752 |
| Net cash flows discounted at 12% | | 4.070 | 2.211 | 3.960 | 4.076 | 3.548 | 4.125 | 3.991 | 4.014 | 3.891 | 4.203 | 3.644 | 4.062 |

Table 18. Company call option

| Input | | Examples | | | | | | | | | | | |
|---|---|---|---|---|---|---|---|---|---|---|---|---|---|
| | | 1 | 2 | 3 | 4 | 5 | 6 | 7 | 8 | 9 | 10 | 11 | 12 |
| Bond term | N | 6.000 | 6.000 | 6.000 | 6.000 | 6.000 | 6.000 | 6.000 | 6.000 | 5.000 | 6.000 | 6.000 | 6.000 |
| Option term | T | 3.000 | 3.000 | 3.000 | 3.000 | 3.000 | 3.000 | 3.000 | 3.000 | 3.000 | 5.000 | 1.000 | 1.000 |
| Risk free rate $N$ years | R1 | 0.080 | 0.080 | 0.080 | 0.080 | 0.080 | 0.080 | 0.080 | 0.080 | 0.080 | 0.080 | 0.080 | 0.080 |
| Risk free rate $T$ years | R2 | 0.080 | 0.080 | 0.080 | 0.080 | 0.080 | 0.080 | 0.080 | 0.080 | 0.080 | 0.080 | 0.080 | 0.080 |
| Term premium $N$ years | P1 | 0.010 | 0.010 | 0.010 | 0.010 | 0.010 | 0.010 | 0.010 | 0.010 | 0.010 | 0.010 | 0.010 | 0.010 |
| Term premium $T$ years | P2 | 0.005 | 0.010 | 0.005 | 0.010 | 0.005 | 0.005 | 0.005 | 0.005 | 0.005 | 0.005 | 0.005 | 0.005 |
| Term premium $N$–$T$ year bond in $T$ years | P3 | 0.005 | 0.010 | 0.010 | 0.005 | 0.005 | 0.005 | 0.005 | 0.005 | 0.005 | 0.005 | 0.010 | 0.010 |
| Volatility factor ($N$–$T$ year bond yield) | V | 0.150 | 0.300 | 0.150 | 0.150 | 0.300 | 0.150 | 0.150 | 0.200 | 0.150 | 0.150 | 0.150 | 0.300 |
| Credited rate spread to $N$ year bond | CS1 | 0.010 | 0.010 | 0.010 | 0.010 | 0.010 | 0.005 | 0.010 | 0.000 | 0.010 | 0.010 | 0.010 | 0.010 |
| Credited rate spread to $N$–$T$ year bond in $T$ years | CS2 | 0.010 | 0.005 | 0.010 | 0.010 | 0.010 | 0.010 | 0.005 | 0.000 | 0.010 | 0.010 | 0.010 | 0.010 |
| Margin over competitor yield (if exercised) | M | 0.005 | 0.005 | 0.005 | 0.005 | 0.005 | 0.005 | 0.005 | 0.000 | 0.005 | 0.005 | 0.005 | 0.005 |
| Initial face value | FV | 100.000 | 100.000 | 100.000 | 100.000 | 100.000 | 100.000 | 100.000 | 100.000 | 100.000 | 100.000 | 100.000 | 100.000 |
| Surplus (excess over the asset value $S$) | E | 5.000 | 5.000 | 5.000 | 5.000 | 5.000 | 5.000 | 5.000 | 5.000 | 5.000 | 5.000 | 5.000 | 5.000 |

## Valuation of a life company

Table 18. Continued

| Calculation | | Examples 1 | 2 | 3 | 4 | 5 | 6 | 7 | 8 | 9 | 10 | 11 | 12 |
|---|---|---|---|---|---|---|---|---|---|---|---|---|---|
| N year bond yield | Y1 | 0.090 | 0.090 | 0.090 | 0.090 | 0.090 | 0.090 | 0.090 | 0.090 | 0.090 | 0.090 | 0.090 | 0.090 |
| N year credited rate | C1 | 0.080 | 0.080 | 0.080 | 0.080 | 0.080 | 0.085 | 0.080 | 0.090 | 0.080 | 0.080 | 0.080 | 0.080 |
| T year bond yield | Y2 | 0.085 | 0.090 | 0.085 | 0.090 | 0.085 | 0.085 | 0.085 | 0.085 | 0.085 | 0.085 | 0.085 | 0.085 |
| N−T year bond in T years: yield | Y3 | 0.085 | 0.090 | 0.090 | 0.085 | 0.085 | 0.085 | 0.085 | 0.085 | 0.085 | 0.085 | 0.090 | 0.090 |
| Return on N year bond over T years | Y4 | 0.095 | 0.090 | 0.090 | 0.095 | 0.095 | 0.095 | 0.095 | 0.095 | 0.093 | 0.091 | 0.090 | 0.090 |
| N−T year bond in T years: credited rate | C2 | 0.080 | 0.090 | 0.085 | 0.080 | 0.080 | 0.080 | 0.085 | 0.085 | 0.080 | 0.080 | 0.085 | 0.085 |
| N−T year bond price volatility at T | Z | 0.066 | 0.140 | 0.070 | 0.066 | 0.133 | 0.066 | 0.066 | 0.088 | 0.044 | 0.029 | 0.068 | 0.135 |
| N year bond asset value | S | 94.620 | 94.620 | 94.620 | 94.620 | 94.620 | 97.279 | 94.620 | 100.000 | 95.496 | 94.620 | 94.620 | 94.620 |
| Exercise price | K | 124.238 | 125.971 | 124.246 | 124.238 | 124.238 | 125.971 | 125.971 | 129.503 | 124.813 | 146.256 | 105.546 | 105.546 |
| Value of call option | C | 1.774 | 4.576 | 1.915 | 2.382 | 4.238 | 2.397 | 1.314 | 3.337 | 1.147 | 0.653 | 1.576 | 4.058 |
| Value of call option at T | C' | 3.927 | 5.927 | 3.202 | 4.010 | 7.153 | 5.069 | 3.054 | 6.287 | 2.877 | 3.176 | 1.891 | 4.619 |
| Discount rate to value the call option | E | 30.33% | 9.00% | 18.69% | 18.96% | 19.06% | 28.35% | 32.46% | 23.50% | 35.86% | 37.20% | 19.98% | 13.84% |
| Overall discount rate for cash flows | I | 3.76% | 9.00% | 8.89% | 8.86% | 8.75% | 8.71% | 8.80% | 8.72% | 8.75% | 8.73% | 8.97% | 8.97% |
| Total value of liability to policyholders | L | 92.846 | 90.044 | 92.705 | 92.238 | 90.382 | 94.882 | 93.306 | 96.663 | 94.349 | 93.967 | 93.044 | 90.563 |
| Policyholder liability valued using bond yield | L1 | 91.545 | 90.044 | 92.113 | 91.524 | 89.020 | 93.311 | 92.229 | 95.078 | 93.244 | 92.508 | 92.877 | 90.363 |
| Value of shareholders equity | MV | 5.774 | 9.576 | 6.915 | 7.382 | 9.238 | 7.397 | 6.314 | 8.337 | 6.147 | 5.653 | 6.576 | 9.058 |
| Net cash flows discounted at 12% | | 6.790 | 8.137 | 6.349 | 6.843 | 8.877 | 7.528 | 6.225 | 8.317 | 6.287 | 5.994 | 5.722 | 7.849 |

- The surrender value ($K$) at the time of option expiry.
- The value of the put option given to policyholders at policy inception, and expected value at the time of option expiry ($P$ and $P^1$).
- The discount rate ($D$) consistent with the option pricing value of the surrender payments.
- The overall discount rate ($I$) required to value policyholder cash flows.
- The value of liabilities to policyholders ($L = S + P$, that is, the value of the bond plus the value of the put option) compared with stochastic payments discounted using government bond yields ($L1$).
- Shareholder value assessed on an option pricing basis ($MV = E - P$, where $E$ is surplus measured by reference to the bond price $S$ and $P$ is the cost of the put option) compared with the value of net cash flows discounted at, say, 12% pa.

The call option results are similar in format. The value of policyholder liabilities is the value of the bond less the value of the company call option ($L = S - C$) and shareholder value is equal to surplus plus the value of the call ($MV = E + C$).

The calculated value of policyholders' liabilities ($L$) allowing for the put option, is up to 0.4% higher than the value that would be calculated by multiplying stochastic cashflows by discount factors derived from an analysis of government bond prices ($L1$). This is because systematic risk inherent in the put option results in a reduction in the discount rate required to value the policyholder liabilities, and in a consequent increase in the value of these liabilities. There is no such increase if the expected return on the $N$-year bond ($Y4$) over the $T$-year period equals the return on a $T$-year bond ($Y3$) that is, there is no term premium.

The calculated value of policyholders' liabilities ($L$), allowing for the call option, is up to 1½% higher than the value that would be calculated by applying government bond discount factors to the stochastic cashflows. The call option has a relatively high systematic risk. This high risk reduces the value of the option compared with the expected cost discounted at the bond rate. The value of the policyholders' liabilities is correspondingly higher than the level derived from a stochastic model discounted using a government bond yield. In practice, the expected future lapse rate $W$ may depend on the term structure of interest rates and therefore may also carry systematic risk. Further research is required to model this feature.

PHELIM BOYLE
*Centre for Advanced Studies in Finance, University of Waterloo*

# Comments on *'Allowing for business risk'*

In my view, the ideas and paradigms that provide the intellectual foundations to tackle the problem posed at this conference stem in large measure from financial economics. This discipline has generated some powerful new theories in the last thirty years: theories that have been translated into a host of practical applications. The whole intellectual underpinning of pricing and hedging derivatives is based on these theories. Hence, I am quite confident that we have the tools available to solve the problem of estimating the market value of insurance liabilities.

If we look at the papers presented at this conference, we see that they tend to cover four main topics. These are:
1. Problem formulation
2. Conceptual framework
3. Description of paradigms and models
4. Implementation details

My comments will tend to focus on item 3. It is exciting to see the application of new paradigms to the solution of important practical problems in accounting and actuarial science. I applaud this development, and my comments will focus on some aspects of these models that are often not as well explained as they should be. One of these is the intuition behind the risk neutral pricing approach in modern finance and the connection between the 'real' probability measure and the risk neutral measure. Another is the role of complete markets in the application of the no-arbitrage pricing strategy. Both of these can conveniently be discussed within a one period discrete time model.

We assume a one period model. At the end of this period the economy will be one of $N$ distinct states. In this model a security is a contract which is defined by its payouts in each state. At time zero, the security can be purchased for its initial price and its owner is entitled to the subsequent payments. We assume no frictions of any kind. There is a market for securities where they are purchased and sold by the agents in the economy.

A generic traded security has different payouts in each state. It is useful to consider a special type of security that pays one unit at time one if and only if state n occurs. These primitive securities are known as Arrow Debreu securities. If there are $N$ such securities, we say the market is complete. The market will be complete if there are $N$ traded securities with linearly independent payouts. In this case, we can reconstruct the payouts of Arrow Debreu securities using the existing traded securities. If the market is not complete, we say that it is incomplete. If the market is incomplete, there will be some payout configurations that cannot be obtained using the existing traded securities. This has important implications for pricing by arbitrage.

Suppose that the market is complete and that there is no arbitrage. We can construct the Arrow Debreu securities. Suppose the time zero price of the $n$th such security is $\phi_n$. Since there is no arbitrage, it can be shown that these prices are positive. Since the market is complete, these prices will also be unique. We can use these Arrow Debreu securities to value any payoff. For example, the current price of the security which pays off $x(n)$ in state $n$ is:

$$x_0 = \sum_{1}^{N} \phi_n x(n)$$

Suppose we consider the security pays just one unit in each state. This corresponds to the risk-free one period bond. Its current price is:

$$\frac{1}{1+r} = \frac{1}{R} = \sum_{1}^{N} \phi_n$$

Guided by this result we define:

$$q_n = (1+r)\phi_n$$

The values of $q$ are all positive and they sum to one. We can interpret them as probabilities. However these are not the 'real' probabilities otherwise known as nature's probabilities. They have been induced by the market prices. The price of security $x$ in terms of $q$ is:

$$x_0 = \frac{1}{R} \sum_{1}^{N} q_i x(i) = \frac{1}{R} E_Q[x]$$

The price is equal to the discounted value of the expected future payoff under the $Q$ measure. Note that the expected return on security $x$ is equal to the risk-free rate. This result carries over to continuous time. For example the Black–Scholes–Merton formula for a European call option can be recast as a discounted expectation over the risk neutralized density of the terminal stock price. The expected return on the stock under this measure is the risk-free rate. In the Black–Scholes formula the 'true' expected return on the stock does not appear.

We can also derive a valuation formula in terms of nature's measure. In this case suppose that the probability of state $n$ occurring is $p_n$. Define the positive random variable $z$ as follows:

$$z_n = \frac{q_n}{R p_n}$$

The price of security $x$ can be written as:

$$x_0 = \frac{1}{R}\sum_n^N q_n x(n) = \sum_1^N p_n \frac{q_n}{Rp_n} x(n) = E_P[zx]$$

Note that we now have written the price of the security in terms of nature's measure. The $z$ term can be interpreted as a risk adjustment factor and has a direct economic interpretation in a general equilibrium framework.

The distinction between these two measures is important and it is often obscured. The usual approach to option pricing concentrates on the risk neutral measure. This can generate the impression that stochastic interest rate models are confined to this set. If one uses these risk neutral models to generate future interest rate scenarios the resulting paths appear 'strange'. However, it is inappropriate to use this measure for projecting realistic future interest rate paths. These should be projected under nature's measure: the $P$ measure. To give another illustration, the Black–Scholes European call option formula is based on the $Q$ measure. However, if we want a realistic estimate of the probability of the call option ending up in the money, we should use the $P$ measure.

I now turn to discuss some of the specifics of Shyam Mehta's paper. Shyam does a good job of visiting the major issues and he suggests clear and practical proposals for the valuation of insurance liabilities. He advocates the use of option pricing models and also the capital asset pricing model (CAPM) to help value the liabilities at market.

The CAPM has the advantage that it is intuitive and simple to apply. It provides a methodology for pricing systematic risk. The model discussed in the paper is the single period model. One needs some strong assumptions of staionarity to apply it in a multi-period case. Mark Rubenstein (1976) has developed the framework for a multi-period extension of the CAPM. The CAPM approach is widely recommended in the basic finance texts as a tool for valuation and appraisal of capital investment projects. However it does not deal adequately with what are called growth options. Many investments involve choices at future times which impact the current value of the project. The incorporation of this aspect into valuation models is a live issue in the finance literature at the present time. For a discussion of some of the issues involved see Dixit and Pindyck (1994). In the context of an insurance firm these options might correspond to new investments such as the opening of a new line of business or the purchase of a subsidiary. On the empirical side the support for the CAPM is mixed. Recently researchers have found that the ratio of market value to book value explains as much of the risk as the traditional beta measure. However it is not clear that the APT should be used since it lacks the simple intuitive appeal of the CAPM.

The other finance paradigm recommended in Shyam Mehta's paper is the option pricing model. In particular, this approach can be used to value securities and contracts whose payoffs depend on the evolution of stochastic interest rate models. It is quite fitting that these tools should move into the mainstream of actuarial science.

I have just a couple of comments on the application of the Single Premium Deferred Annuity (SPDA) described in some detail in the Appendix. This is a popular contract in the United States and any proposed scheme for the valuation of liabilities must be able to handle it. In proposing a model to do this there is a trade-off between simplicity and complexity. The paper employs the Black model to deal with stochastic interest rates. The Black interest rate model is very simple and because of its close similarity to the Black–Scholes model it has gained wide acceptance for pricing such contracts as caps and swaptions. However it also has limitations. Some of these are mentioned in John Hull's book. The Black model is theoretically unappealing for interest rate applications. In addition it cannot be used for American style securities. I appreciate that it was chosen for its simplicity rather than as a recommended method for the valuation of SPDA contracts.

To summarize, it seems to me that the theoretical models are in place to estimate the market value of insurance liabilities. There will be some teething problems as we develop the precise details of the implementation. Conferences like this can play a useful role in this endeavor.

## References

Dixit, A. and R. Pindyck (1994). *Investment Under Uncertainty.* Princeton University Press.
Hull, John C. (1997). *Options, Futures, and Other Derivatives.* Third Edition. Prentice Hall.
Rubinstein, M. (1976). The valuation of uncertain income streams and the pricing of options. *Bell Journal of Economics and Management Science,* 7, 407–425.

MARK W. GRIFFIN
*Goldman Sachs & Co.*

# 6. A market-value accounting framework for insurance companies

*Comment: The paper by Mark Griffin was originally published in The Financial Reporter in March of 1992. It is an early view of the subject and undoubtedly had some effect in stimulating this conference. The remarks by Joan Lamm-Tennant are intended to not only relate to Mr Griffin's paper, but also are an overview of all earlier papers.*

In North America, book value accounting for insurance companies is a basic tenet. For many, the very idea of replacing book value accounting with market-value accounting is heresy. However, a number of recent developments should help to motivate serious consideration of a market-value approach.

1. The AICPA has recently proposed new accounting rules for financial institutions, including stock insurance companies, which involve marking assets to their current market value. Many people, including actuaries, are quick to argue that this would be inappropriate, because there is no 'market' for existing insurance liabilities and therefore no market value of liabilities to compare to the market value of assets. Nonetheless, public statements by members of Congress, consumer groups, and others on the need to market-value insurance company assets, with no mention of the liability side, are becoming more frequent. Therefore, it may behoove actuaries to think about how to 'market-value' insurance liabilities because the worst possible outcome would be to have to market-value the assets without being able to 'market-value' the liabilities.

2. New York State and the NAIC are beginning to test the use of a risk-adjusted capital ratio for insurance companies on an experimental basis. Experimental or not, the capital ratios resulting from the New York State/NAIC formula are already appearing in the press. Examination of the C-3 component of the formula reveals that it is a very simple calculation based on the type of business written, with no regard for either the duration of the liabilities or the maturity structure and price behavior of the assets! While it would be convenient to measure C-3 risk using statement information, those with hands-on experience will recognize how misleading such a calculation could be.

3. Both US and Canadian insurance companies will soon have Appointed Actuaries. Hopefully, Appointed Actuaries will apply the complete set of actuarial skills to the topic of insurance company solvency.

Perhaps a market value approach to accounting would provide better information to Appointed Actuaries, regulators, rating agencies, and all those concerned with the insurance industry. Certainly we do not need another accounting method unless it provides significant information not currently available or replaces one or more methods currently in use. The purpose of this article is not to provide a complete 'cookbook' on how to implement market value accounting, but to introduce a framework for market value accounting in the hope that it will stimulate thought, experimentation, and discussion of the subject among actuaries.

## Example

The mechanics of a market value approach are best illustrated by a simple example. Suppose that on December 31, 1991 an insurance company receives $1 000 000 and agrees in return to make a single payment of $1 469 328 on December 31, 1996. The maturity amount translates to a guaranteed rate of 8.00%, which we will assume is 0.50% above the prevailing 5-year US Treasury zero-coupon rate at time of issue. All interest rates in the example are annual effective. Assume that up-front expenses plus commission are $10 000 and that, for simplicity, the only other expenses are $1000 on the maturity date. The market value of assets at the time of issue is $990 000 ($1 000 000 single premium minus $10 000 commission plus up-front expenses). The rate that discounts the single liability payment of $1 470 328 in five years to the market value of assets is calculated as follows to be 8.23%.

$$\$990\,000 = (\$1\,469\,328 + \$1000) \div (1.0823)^5$$

The discount rate of 8.23% represents a spread of 0.73% above the 5-year Treasury zero rate. For lack of a better name, let us call this spread the accounting spread for this policy. Once calculated, the accounting spread will stay with the block of liabilities. Note that the accounting spread is a function of the product's pricing and is independent of the investments chosen to the back the product.

Assume that the insurer invests the $990 000 in a 5-year zero-coupon corporate bond with a yield of 8.70%, 1.20% above the 5-year zero-coupon Treasury. The asset maturity amount of $1 502 391 will pay the contract maturity amount plus expenses as well as a profit of $32 063. Table 1 shows:

- **Applicable Treasury rate.** The rate for the zero-coupon Treasury (zero) maturing on the date of maturity of the liability. At time one year this will be a 4-year zero; at time two years this will be a 3-year zero; and so on.
- **Market value of assets (MVA).** The market value of the asset assuming it continues to trade at a spread of 1.20%.
- **Market value of liabilities (MVL).** The present value of the $1 470 328 liability payment using the applicable Treasury rate plus the accounting spread of 0.73%.

Table 1. Market value accounting. Example: 5-year asset, 5-year liability

|  |  | Applicable Treasury rate | | | | |
| --- | --- | --- | --- | --- | --- | --- |
| Time | | 5.50% | 6.50% | 7.50% | 8.50% | 9.50% |
| 1-year | MVA ($) | 1 159 112 | 1 116 658 | 1 076 130 | 1 037 424 | 1 000 443 |
|  | MVL | 1 154 497 | 1 112 030 | 1 071 498 | 1 032 796 | 995 826 |
|  | MVS ($) | 4615 | 4628 | 4632 | 4628 | 4617 |
| 2-year | MVA ($) | 1 236 772 | 1 202 640 | 1 169 753 | 1 138 054 | 1 107 491 |
|  | MVL | 1 226 445 | 1 192 452 | 1 159 704 | 1 128 144 | 1 097 719 |
|  | MVS ($) | 10 327 | 10 188 | 10 049 | 9910 | 9772 |
| 3-year | MVA ($) | 1 319 636 | 1 295 244 | 1 271 522 | 1 248 446 | 1 225 992 |
|  | MVL | 1 302 877 | 1 278 690 | 1 255 171 | 1 232 294 | 1 210 038 |
|  | MVS ($) | 16 759 | 16 554 | 16 351 | 16 152 | 15 954 |
| 4-year | MVA ($) | 1 408 051 | 1 394 978 | 1 382 144 | 1 369 545 | 1 357 173 |
|  | MVL | 1 384 073 | 1 371 165 | 1 358 497 | 1 346 060 | 1 333 849 |
|  | MVS ($) | 23 978 | 23 813 | 23 648 | 23 485 | 23 324 |
| 5-year | MVS ($) | 32 063 | 32 063 | 32 063 | 32 063 | 32 063 |

- **Market value of surplus (MVS).** MVA − MVL. At the time of issue this will be zero. At five years MVS is the net maturity payment of the assets over the liabilities.

Notice how the market value of surplus is very stable for considerable changes in Treasury rates.

Table 2 is an example of how the market value of surplus behaves when a 7-year zero-coupon asset is substituted for the 5-year zero-coupon asset. The 7-year zero is assumed to yield 0.2% more than the 5-year zero and is market-valued at 0.2% higher than the 5-year zero in each situation. At the 5-year point the asset is assumed to be sold.

Tables 1 and 2 demonstrate how the MVS reflects changing market conditions and the consequences of two different investment strategies with different risks and rewards. Through two simple examples, Tables 1 and 2 show that market value accounting does not cause unstable results, it merely reflects management decisions. In the case where the 7-year asset was used, current

Table 2. Market value accounting. Example: 7 year asset, 5 year liability

|  |  | Applicable Treasury rate | | | | |
| --- | --- | --- | --- | --- | --- | --- |
| Time | | 5.50% | 6.50% | 7.50% | 8.50% | 9.50% |
| 1 | MVS ($) | 50 439 | 27 437 | 6612 | −12 223 | −29 239 |
| 2 | MVS ($) | 61 632 | 37 032 | 14 358 | −6534 | −25 774 |
| 3 | MVS ($) | 74 077 | 47 923 | 23 382 | 355 | −21 250 |
| 4 | MVS ($) | 87 891 | 60 251 | 33 848 | 8622 | −15 484 |
| 5 | MVS ($) | 103 202 | 74 170 | 45 935 | 18 467 | −8261 |

statutory accounting could hide the economic results of taking interest rate risk for at least five years. Currently statutory accounting creates a disincentive to rebalance a risky position that has moved against an insurance company.

ASSET SPREAD CONSIDERATIONS

The market value of the bond in our 5-year bond, 5-year liability example is affected by changes in Treasury levels and changes in the bond's spread to Treasuries. One reason for a change in the spread is an upgrade or downgrade of ABC's credit-worthiness. Suppose that just prior to the end of the third year, the ABC bond is upgraded/downgraded, which causes the spread at which it trades to tighten/widen by 0.20%. Table 3 shows how the market value of assets, liabilities, and surplus behaves for both situations. Table 3 assumes no change in the applicable Treasury rate since time zero, although a change in Treasuries would have little effect on the results, as shown in Table 1.

Notice that if the ABC bond continues to be held and the maturity payment is made in full, the terminal MVS is unchanged from Table 1. In this case, the terminal MVS is unchanged, but the upgrade/downgrade affects the accretion pattern of the MVS.

Suppose that at the time of the upgrade/downgrade, the insurer sold the ABC bond and used the proceeds to buy a two-year zero-coupon bond with the pre-upgrade/downgrade credit rating and spread of the ABC bond. Table 4 shows that this strategy would effectively 'lock in' the marginal gain/loss resulting from the upgrade/downgrade.

It is also possible for the spread on the ABC bonds to change, apart from any change in the credit-worthiness of ABC. Changing demand and supply for similar or competing securities is the most common explanation of this phenomenon. Assume that this spread change also happens at the end of three years. In this situation, the insurer's expectation of receiving the net cash flow of $32 063 at the end of 5 years has not changed, so it would follow that the MVS at time three years should not change materially. Table 5 shows that the MVS

Table 3.

| Time | Credit upgrade | Credit downgrade |
|---|---|---|
| 3-year MVA ($) | 1 276 214 | 1 266 856 |
| MVL | 1 255 171 | 1 255 171 |
| MVS ($) | 21 043 | 11 685 |
| 4-year MVA ($) | 1 384 692 | 1 379 606 |
| MVL | 1 358 497 | 1 358 497 |
| MVS ($) | 26 195 | 21 109 |
| 5-year MVS ($) | 32 063 | 32 063 |

Table 4.

| Time | Credit upgrade | Credit downgrade |
|---|---|---|
| 3-year MVA ($) | 1 276 214 | 1 266 856 |
| MVL | 1 255 171 | 1 255 171 |
| MVS ($) | 21 043 | 11 685 |
| 4-year MVA ($) | 1 387 245 | 1 377 072 |
| MVL | 1 358 497 | 1 358 497 |
| MVS ($) | 28 748 | 18 575 |
| 5-year MVS ($) | 37 607 | 26 550 |

Table 5.

| Time | Spread tightens 0.10% | Spread widens 0.10% |
|---|---|---|
| 3-year MVA ($) | 1 273 865 | 1 269 186 |
| MVL | 1 257 494 | 1 252 855 |
| MVS ($) | 16 371 | 16 331 |
| 4-year MVA ($) | 1 383 417 | 1 380 874 |
| MVL | 1 359 753 | 1 357 243 |
| MVS ($) | 23 664 | 23 631 |
| 5-year MVS ($) | 32 063 | 32 063 |

has no material change if we allow the accounting spread to be changed in accordance with the change in the spread of the ABC bond.

To allow the 'logical' result shown in Table 5, there must be a mechanism to change accounting spreads when 'market' spreads change. Although it is feasible to attach an accounting spread to a block of liabilities (this is analogous to the way that certain liabilities are reserved now), it is not feasible to pair particular assets with the liabilities. Therefore, measurable market indexes would have to be used to determine the appropriate change in accounting spreads for existing liabilities from period to period.

As a simplistic example of how the appropriate change in accounting spreads might work, consider the following. The insurer has 40% and 60% in A- and BBB-rated securities, respectively. The market indexes for spreads on A- and BBB-rated securities are 0.80% and 1.20%, for a weighted spread of 1.04% (40% of 0.80% plus 60% of 1.20%). Suppose that a year later the market indexes for spreads were 0.70% and 1.00%, giving a weighted spread of 0.88%. The calculation would indicate that a decrease in accounting spreads of 0.16% is warranted. In reality, calculation of this 'accounting spread index' would have to recognize at least two other possibilities.

- Market spreads vary significantly by maturity.
- The changing composition of the insurer's portfolio by credit rating can be a result of upgrades/downgrades as well as changes in the distribution of new investments.

## Illiquid assets

There will be certain assets for which obtaining periodic market values will be difficult. These include private placement debt, commercial mortgages, real estate, reinsurance receivables, and the like. For those assets for which fixed expected cash flows can be identified, a spread can be calculated at the point of purchase of the asset and used again periodically to recalculate the asset's market value as Treasury rates change and time passes. In fact, the same technique can be used for assets with interest-sensitive cash flows whenever there is an identifiable link between the expected cash flows and prevailing interest rates. It is possible that different methods would have to be used for different classes of illiquid assets. Any asset whose market value is calculated rather than observed should be part of the illiquid assets classification of the assets on the market value balance sheet.

## Interest-sensitive liabilities

For liabilities for which cash flows are interest-sensitive, discounting a stream of expected cash flows using the prevailing Treasury rates plus the accounting spread is not appropriate. This problem is currently addressed through cash-flow testing along a small number of deterministic interest rate scenarios. To market-value these interest-sensitive liabilities, the New York Deterministic Seven should be replaced by a set of scenarios that might be called the 'NAIC Stochastic 100'. A properly calculated set of stochastically generated interest rate paths would be consistent with prevailing Treasury rate environment at the valuation date and therefore consistent with the market value of the assets. The easiest way to progress the evolution from the use of deterministic paths to stochastic paths is probably for some regulator like the NAIC to produce a diskette quarterly containing the set of interest rate paths to use for 'market valuing' interest-sensitive liabilities.

Many of the finer points of constructing such a set of interest rate paths would continue to be debated by academics and theoreticians. (These points include: how many factors are necessary, how to incorporate correlations and volatilities, the existence of mean reversion, and so on.) Regardless of the existence or intensity of this debate, stochastic sets of interest rate paths can be generated that are consistent with prevailing asset market values, while deterministic sets of rate paths cannot. In projecting interest-sensitive liability cash flows, many assumptions are necessary and would have to be disclosed.

One important assumption that would have to be made in many situations is how credited rates would change over time in different interest rate environments. Disclosure of this assumption would be a means of imposing discipline in a situation where a 'bait and switch' strategy is necessary to realize profits.

Another important assumption for interest-sensitive liabilities is the interest-sensitive withdrawal behavior of policyholders. One way to approach this is to prescribe an interest-sensitive withdrawal function to be used. The function could depend on: prevailing surrender charges, the degree of uncompetitiveness (if any) versus some index representative of new money rates for comparable products, and how the product was sold. The function should be conservative and other functions should be permitted if it could be shown that they were more appropriate. The appropriateness of any function would have to be monitored over time.

Some may argue that the lack of a scientifically proven interest-sensitive withdrawal function is sufficient to dismiss market value accounting. However, any plausible function selected will certainly do a better job of addressing the value of policyholder's surrender rights than current statutory accounting. Also, the exercise of valuing interest-sensitive liability cash flows has a cousin on the asset side, the mortgage-backed securities (MBS) market. Mortgage holders have a valuable option in their right to prepay, but exercise of this option is far from efficient. The MBS market does not have a scientifically proven formula for interest-sensitive behavior by mortgage holders, but this has not prevented billions of dollars of MBS from trading every week!

## CONSERVATISM

In the simple example shown in Table 1, the market value of surplus at the inception of the policy is zero, that is, no reserve strain. There are a number of ways conservatism could be incorporated into the market value balance sheet.
- **Assets.** An asset default reserve could be established. The most logical formula approach would be based on a quality assessment of the various assets (such as the new NAIC rating categories) and their remaining time to maturity.
- **Liabilities.** Conservative assumptions could be used for projecting uncertain liability cash flows. Prescribing mortality and morbidity tables to be used for specified situations would increase uniformity and comparability.

In addition, market value accounting should either include or facilitate certain types of stress testing. Stress tests would simply show how the market value surplus would behave in certain situations, such as:
1. **Increased asset defaults.** A number of approaches are possible. One approach would be to measure the effect of a credit downgrade on a portion of the portfolio. The portion of the portfolio could be chosen to reflect the degree of credit diversification.

2. **Liability cash-flow variability.** A specified shock would be applied to any (or all) of the assumptions used to project uncertain cash flows.
3. **Interest rate changes.** Asset and liability market values would have to be calculated for specified parallel and nonparallel changes in the yield curve applying to the valuation date (initial yield curve).
4. **Significant withdrawals.** The market value of surplus would be recalculated by assuming significant policyholder withdrawals had occurred. In many cases, maximum withdrawal activity would be the most detrimental to the market value surplus. However, it is also possible that the cash surrender provisions for certain products and the degree of liquidity in the asset portfolio could be such that a smaller, more selective pattern of withdrawals would hurt the market value surplus more. Presumably, liquid assets would be assumed to be sold first to meet withdrawals. To the extent that illiquid assets would need to be used, the method of calculating the proceeds from such sales would have to be disclosed. Other sensitivities that could be stress-tested include: real estate, values, equity values, inflation, etc.

ITEMS TO BE RESOLVED

1. **Participating products.** The best approach to participating products would seem to be to project cash flows based on product guarantees plus expected dividends. Disclosure of expected dividends would enable a comparison to illustrated dividends.
2. **Treasury zero coupon rates.** The Treasury zero-coupon rates implied by the on-the-run Treasury coupon curve (which can be calculated unambiguously) should be used as the rates to which appropriate spreads are added for discounting purposes. Although Treasury zero-coupon instruments exist, the market is much smaller and less liquid than the on-the-run coupon market.
3. **Future premiums.** When future premiums are guaranteed, the net liability cash flows should be discounted. When future premiums are not guaranteed, only the liability cash flows arising from the existing policy should be discounted. In this situation, however, it would have to be assumed that subsequent premium payment behavior would maximize the value of the existing policy to the policyholder.
4. **Liability blocks.** Reasonable latitude would have to be given in the procedure for determining what constitutes a block of liabilities and when the accounting spread is calculated. To the extent possible, the procedure chosen by a company should be disclosed and used consistently over time.
5. **Where to start.** How does one assign an accounting spread to existing business? One simple approach would be to simply dictate the spread to be used for all existing business. Another approach would be to calculate the accounting spread for existing business such that at the point in time when market-value accounting began to be used, the market value of surplus was equal to the traditionally calculated statutory surplus.

While politically feasible, the latter approach would be dangerous, because it would invite the selective harvesting of capital gains (one of the largest problems with current statutory accounting) in the meantime.

### Resources required

Conversion to market value accounting would be a very large job. Preparing, or auditing, such a statement would be very computer-intensive. However, with all the recent publicity about the safety of financial institutions (and the new cottage industry of ratio calculation), not allowing accounting methods to evolve, and sticking with existing methods to save money may be very short-sighted. Few people would advocate immediate implementation of market value accounting, but with a reasonable advance warning, the major wrinkles in the new approach could be ironed out.

### Advantages

Market value accounting gives an appraisal of an insurance company's value reflecting current market conditions. Perhaps the greatest advantage of market value accounting is that it would enable insurance company asset portfolios to be managed on an economic risk/reward basis without the capital gain/loss constraints imposed by current statutory accounting.

### Conclusion

Market value accounting is the next step in the regulatory evolution that has produced dynamic solvency testing in Canada and scenario testing in the USA. While this article only scratches the surface of many of the considerations of market value accounting, I hope it will stimulate thought, experimentation and discussion on the topic.

JOAN LAMM-TENNANT
*Villanova University*

# Comments on 'A *market-value accounting framework for insurance companies*'

Mark Griffin admits that his work is intended to "introduce a framework for market-value accounting in the hope that it will stimulate thought, experimentation, and discussion of the subject among actuaries." This has been effective as we are most assuredly in the midst of stimulating thought and experimentation. My only comment is that he underestimated the impact of your work as he invited not only the thoughts of actuaries but also financial economists.

Let us recount the methodologies discussed sofar and summarize their strengths and weaknesses. James Hohmann and Robert Reitano provided a comprehensive overview of the methodologies for fair valuation of liabilities. Given the extensive body of literature, they have performed an exemplary service by providing us with a document that is inclusive yet comprehensible. Hohmann and Reitano began by stating that there are two pricing paradigms. Within each paradigm we have a sequence of methodologies ranging from simple to complicated. The appeal of simplicity is clouded with judgment whereas the more complicated methodologies offer objectiveness. The first paradigm presented is constructive – evaluating liabilities directly as one values assets. That is, we value the series of payments contractually defined as well as the embedded options of both parties. The second paradigm is deductive – first we evaluate the insurance nenterprise and then deduct the value of the liabilities from the value of the insurance enterprise and the known value of assets. Under the deductive or appraisal method, a feasible set of distributable earnings are projected and then discounted by rates reflecting the risk-free time value of money plus an appropriate risk spread. As in the risk-adjusted present value approach, defining the risk spread introduces complications. However, in the appraisal valuation approach it is typical to explicitly model individual risk and, in essence, remove the discount rate charge for these risks. For example, if one option-adjusts the initial valuation to produce the option-adjusted value of distributable earnings (OAVDE), then one has removed option risk from the risk spread and need only consider other risks such as mortality, morbidity, asset credit risk, expense risk, and other life contingencies.

On one hand, Hohmann and Reitano indicated preference for the constructive methodology since it is more consistent with asset valuation and reflective of valuations in the secondary GIC market. Alternatively, the distributable earnings approach is more reflective of valuations in the company or block acquisition market. They are up-front about the strengths and weaknesses of the alternative methodologies and clearly acknowledge that, given their framework, the methodologies do not converge on one solution. Hohmann and Reitano admit that we simply do not have a consensus on which mthod is more appropriate.

In the review of Hohmann and Reitano's work, David Babbel provided insights explaining the divergence between the deductive versus constructive methods. He concluded that the appropriate method for fair valuation of liabilities is to use stochastic valuation models directly for liabilities and use Treasury-based rates for lattices or simulation paths. Babbel began the justification for his conclusion by first identifying the three elements of the market value of a stock insurance company; namely, the franchise value, the liquidiation value, and the put option value. Using these elements of the market value, Babbel identified differences in the effect of risk behavior on the market value of net worth for a nonfinancial corporation versus financial institutions. Herein lies the contradiction. In the case of the financial institution adding pure risk to the firm does not effect the present value (market value) of liabilities. Instead, the addition of pure risk creates value for the put option which is one of the firm's assets, not liabilities. Likewise, the franchise value (an asset, as well) is reduced. The net effect of the franchise value and the put option value will dictate whether the market value of net worth increases and by what amount. In any event, the market value of the liabilities are unchanged. Babbel attributed the disparity in market value of liabilities within a deductive versus constructive framework to confounding assets and liabilities. One aspect of general agreement is that regardless of the chosen methodology, any attempt to standardize the underlying assumptions regarding mortality, profits, credited rates, and surrender behavior would defeat the objjective of establishing a 'fair value'. These estimates must take into account product and company specifics to capture fair value.

Shyam Mehta suggested that life company valuation should start by considering the individual cash flows which make up the expected future net cash flows of the company. In essence, Mehta examines each cash flow separately and, where possible, draws comparisons between these cash flows and the cash flows expected from traded securities such as index-linked bonds and equities. Therefore, the discount rate may be based on the investment return assumptions selected for each traded security. An interesting 'bonus' identified by Mehta is that this methodology leads directly to the identification of by-line of business return on capital targets. This leads to interesting capabilities in terms of product development, pricing, and financial control.

Phelim Boyle commented on Mehta's paper by citing the limitations of the CAPM as it is a single-period pricing model which needs heuristic assumptions to support a multiperiod analysis. Mehta acknowledges the limitations of the CAPM, although dismisses the problem to measurement errors and remains an advocate of the literature that provides support of its underlying tenets.

Moving beyond the constructive-deductive paradigm, Hohmann and Reitano presented a series of methodologies categorized as migration methods. I would place the market value accounting framework of Mark Griffin within the set of migration methods. Using a simple example, Griffin has communicated the mechanics of a market-value accounting approach. I congratulate Mark for providing such a simple, yet accurate perspective and, more so, for being the genesis of our deliberations.

In time we may reach a consensus on the appropriate methodology for fair valuaiton of liabilities. For the moment, our comprehensive review of the possibilities and their implications will serve our deliberations well. Let me conclude by saying we are in an experimental stage. Our pursuit for the appropriate methodology for deriving the fair valuation of liabilities will also provide us with a more meaningful assessment of the insurer. This will have far-reaching implications for the financial community. I must tell you that I feel as if my role in this experiment is that of the lab attendant, although I consider it a privilege. I thank the master scientists, their critics, and the student participants. I also thank Ed Altman and Irwin Vanderhoof who are in a league of their own for orchestrating this laboratory experiment.

DAVID N. BECKER

*Lincoln National Life Insurance Company*

# 7. The value of the firm: the option adjusted value of distributable earnings

*Comment: This paper could be considered the one most rich in original thought and insight. Like the Academy paper presented by Mr. Hohman and the Dicke paper it includes a review of the underlying accounting principles as well as the introduction on new ideas. The Staking comments are quite useful and incisive. – Ed.*

### Abstract

The goal is to maximize the value of the insurance firm. The first step is to develop the right objective function to measure the firm's value. The second step is to use the objective function to identify and quantify the risks to which the firm is exposed. The third step is to use the objective function to analyze proposed strategies to maximize the value of the firm relative to risk, i.e. either maximize value given a fixed risk or minimize risk given a fixed value. Such strategies are to be applied to the pricing of new business, the management of in force business and the acquisition/divestiture of blocks of business or entire companies. The challenge is more difficult when the firm is exposed to multiple stochastic risks, many having embedded options and not all of which are independent. The fourth step is to use the objective function to provide management information about the performance of the firm during each time period and to allocate capital to future and existing projects. It would be ideal if the external financial reporting of the firm's performance could be presented on this basis. In this way the owners of the firm would know its value and income for a given period and be able to assess the impact of management's actions on that value.

This paper defines such an objective function, demonstrates its properties and shows how the different steps above can be carried out. Since the current accounting environment less accurately quantifies the value and performance of the firm over time, the paper first presents background on the goals and evolution of current accounting systems for life insurance companies, culminating with the environment after the enactment of Financial Accounting Standard 115 and prior to the resolution of the issue of the market value of liabilities.

An overview is provided of several methods of adapting the current accounting structure to accommodate a market value of liabilities. Two of these approaches are examined in some detail. Second, a brief, intuitive presentation on option pricing for assets is given and used to provide the foundation for several potential market values of liabilities. Clarifications between the application of market value concepts to accounting and asset/liability management are given. Limitations of the applicability of these solutions to the issues described above are identified. Third, the proposed objective function is then motivated, defined and explored. Fourth, several concrete examples are provided that demonstrate the capabilities of the tool. Alternative ways of evaluating results are demonstrated and their relationships are shown. Fifth, various general applications of the tool are given that complete and augment the goals stated in the first paragraph.

Although the focus of the paper is on interest rate risk, extensions to other stochastic risks are indicated.

## CURRENT ACCOUNTING ENVIRONMENT

### Introduction

The terms 'market value of liabilities', 'market value of surplus' and 'economic surplus' are used in similar but not necessarily identical ways when referencing the issues of market value accounting and asset/liability management. Because of this ambiguity and the attention being given to market value accounting as an alternative solution to a decreasingly credible accounting system, this section presents some general concepts regarding accounting systems used for the insurance industry, a brief history of the evolution of certain GAAP accounting concepts, the market value accounting issue and proposed solutions together with issues that each raise. Insights into these issues relative to asset/liability management are presented in the next section.

### Accounting systems

Accounting systems quantify the financial state of a firm via the balance sheet, what the firm owns (assets) and the claims on what is owned (liabilities and surplus), and the financial progress of the firm via the income statement, how those values change from one accounting period to the next. 'Surplus' represents both the amount of the firm's assets owned by shareholders and the amount of funds in excess of the liabilities that are available to cover obligations of the firm should the provision for liabilities be inadequate. Accounting systems employ a system of standardized rules so that the financial results of two firms are comparable and that the financial results of firms are comparable over time. Inherent in these rules must be a basis for the estimation of the values of assets and liabilities.

The transactions of a life insurance company consist of activities such as collecting premiums, investment income and investment maturities and paying claims, surrender values, commissions, expenses, taxes and shareholder dividends, if the company is a stock life insurance company. Such transactions must be recorded on the general ledger of the firm. In this sense, the accounting system is transaction driven. In an insurance company the products or services provided by the firm result in transactions over many accounting periods. Its liabilities are referred to as long-duration contracts. Utilizing the valuation basis for assets, the reserving system for liabilities and the transactions for a given accounting period, accounting systems allocate profit or loss to each accounting period.

In the USA there are two principal bases for accounting systems for insurance firms: these are referred to as statutory and GAAP. Statutory accounting is based on statutory accounting principles (SAP) and GAAP accounting is based on generally accepted accounting principles. The legal bodies responsible for SAP are the state insurance departments and, indirectly, the NAIC. The legal bodies responsible for GAAP are the Securities Exchange Commission (SEC), the Financial Accounting Standards Board (FASB), and the American Institute of Certified Public Accountants (AICPA).

### Statutory accounting

Statutory accounting principles emphasize solvency, i.e. the ability of the firm to provide for its policyholder obligations. SAP is referred to as being 'balance sheet' oriented. Thus it tends to overstate liabilities and understate surplus and income. Key examples of this conservatism can be seen in the valuation of liabilities through conservative mortality/morbidity and interest assumptions and in the treatment of acquisition costs, which are immediately expensed or charged against income. Other examples of conservatism are the rules for deficiency reserves, the interest maintenance reserve for interest-related capital gains and losses, the asset valuation reserve and the requirement of conservative risk based capital requirements. The values of many assets are 'not admitted', so that the assets of the firm are understated. The rules for asset valuation do not always ensure conservatism as many investments are carried at amortized cost rather than market value. Market values may be either higher or lower than amortized cost. The use of book values for assets was consistent with the accounting tradition of holding assets at historic cost and the fact that insurance enterprises typically have held securities to maturity (in light of the long duration nature of their liabilities) and did not engage in active trading. Statutory accounting has a liquidation orientation for valuing the company. Revenue is annualized premiums plus earned investment income. SAP applies to both stock and mutual life insurance companies.

SAP can result in counterintuitive financial performance for insurance companies. For example, an insurance company experiencing rapid growth will report a pattern of lower statutory earnings than it would under normal growth.

An insurance company experiencing a decline in new business or no new business will show higher statutory earnings than it would under normal growth. The use of statutory accounting poses problems for those needing to analyze the performance of stock life insurance companies.

*GAAP accounting: a brief history of DAC, FAS 60, FAS 97 and FAS 115*

The problems posed by statutory accounting were addressed in 1973 when GAAP reporting principles were required for stock life insurance companies. The goal was to account for insurance companies as 'going concerns' with the emphasis on a realistic income statement. All assets were admitted, liabilities were valued on a 'conservatively realistic' basis and acquisition costs, both internal and external, that were primarily related to and varied directly with the production of new business were not immediately expensed, but instead were capitalized and amortized over the life of the block of business. As a result of this approach the 'matching principle' was fully implemented in GAAP accounting. These issues are treated in the *Audits of Stock Life Insurance Companies*, first published in 1972 and in *Statement of Financial Accounting Standard Number 60* (FAS 60), published in 1982. In 1974 Ernst and Young, then Ernst and Ernst, published the text GAAP: Stock Life Companies [37].

Originally, GAAP accounting only applied to stock life insurance companies. In the past, mutual insurance companies contended that for them GAAP was SAP and declared that their statutory statements were in compliance with GAAP. FAS 120, *Accounting and Reporting by Mutual Life Insurance Enterprises and by Insurance Enterprises for Certain Long-Duration Participating Contracts*, issued in January, 1995, extends the requirements of FAS 60, FAS 97 and FAS 115 to mutual life insurance companies effective for fiscal years beginning after December 15, 1995. For insurance contracts not covered by FAS 120, the AICPA's *Statement of Position 95-1, Accounting for Certain Insurance Activities of Mutual Life Insurance Enterprises*, will apply for fiscal years beginning after December 15, 1995.

The hallmarks of FAS 60 were:
- insurance contracts were (mainly) long duration contracts; revenue was defined to be earned investment income and premium, where premium is recognized in proportion to performance under the contract;
- capitalized acquisition costs (also known as 'deferred acquisition costs' or DAC) were to be amortized in proportion to premium revenue over the life of the block;
- liabilities were valued using all relevant applicable assumptions where such assumptions were chosen as 'best estimate' plus a provision for adverse deviation;
- those assumptions, once chosen, were 'locked in' (the lock-in principle), i.e. could not be changed unless severe adverse experience developed in the future.

With this definition of revenue, DAC was amortized in proportion to premium income. Profits would emerge as a level percent of premium revenue, plus a portion due to release from risk which would occur as actual experience emerged more favorably than that assumed in the reserve basis and from any deviation of actual experience from expected. With this reserving system for liabilities profits would emerge over the entire life of the block of business.

The DAC was termed recoverable at issue if there were sufficient future revenues in the business to amortize the DAC after providing for all future benefits and expenses. Subsequent to issue, if experience deteriorated to the extent that based on then current best estimates of future experience the net GAAP liability, i.e. the GAAP benefit reserve less the DAC, together with future premiums would not provide for future benefits and expenses, then a state of 'loss recognition' was said to exist. This meant that the business would have to be revalued on the revised, new best estimates of future experience. The changing of the assumptions was termed 'unlocking'. In this event, the DAC was reduced by the deficit. If the deficit was larger than the amount of outstanding DAC, then additional benefit reserves were established. The amount of write down of DAC plus the amount of any extra benefit reserves established was an immediate charge to GAAP earnings. If future experience exactly equalled the new assumptions, then no further GAAP losses (or gains) would be reported.

The mechanism by which a loss recognition situation is determined is the computation of a gross premium valuation (GPV). For a block of business a GPV is the present value of all future policyholder benefits and company expenses less the present value of future premiums where the present value is computed at the net earned rate of the assets supporting the block. If the GPV is less than or equal to the net GAAP liability, then no loss recognition exists. If the GPV exceeds the net GAAP liability, then a loss recognition situation exists and the magnitude of the loss is that excess.

FAS 60 worked well for many years, but the mechanism was stressed by two events that occurred in the 1980s. First, some insurance companies applied the letter of the law of FAS 60 when preparing GAAP financial statements for single premium deferred annuities. Often, little provision for adverse deviation was present, thus the majority of profit was released in proportion to premium which meant released in the year of issue. This approach 'front-ended' earnings. The concern raised by this was heightened by the fact that one of the companies using that practice became insolvent. Second, universal life, with its flexible premiums, became a major life insurance product. Since premiums were flexible, their use as the basis of revenue would create volatility in the reported earnings of insurance companies selling significant amounts of these products. There was a disconnect between the flow of premium and the actual source of earnings of the insurance company for this type of product.

In 1987 the Financial Accounting Standards Board adopted Financial Accounting Standard Number 97 (FAS 97) which dealt with these issues. FAS

97 was effective in 1988 and applied to deferred annuities and universal life policies in particular. It did not apply, in general, to traditional fixed premium, fixed benefit life insurance. The hallmarks of FAS 97 were:
- a new definition of revenue;
- a new method for amortizing DAC;
- a new principle called 'unlocking';
- defining the GAAP benefit reserve to be the account value.

Revenue was defined to be the sum of interest earned and the various loads and fees charged against the product, e.g. pure mortality charges, policy fees, premium loads, administrative charges, front end loads and surrender charges. DAC would be amortized by a level percent of 'estimated gross profits', i.e. the periodic revenues above less expenses associated with those revenues, e.g. pure mortality costs, general expenses and interest credited. The GAAP benefit reserve was the account value. The assumptions underlying the estimated gross profits were to be best estimates with no provision for adverse deviation.

If there were any material deviation of actual experience from assumed, then the company would be required to 'unlock' its assumptions by adopting new best estimates from that date going forward and recompute the amortization of DAC since the inception of the block. This resulted in a new amortization percentage for amortization of DAC. The difference between the prior period DAC and the recalculation of the prior period DAC resulting from the application of the new amortization percentage to the historic actual estimated gross profits would be an immediate charge or credit to earnings; and the resulting DAC balance would be amortized by that new percentage of the revised future estimated gross profits. FAS 97 excluded realized gains and losses from the definition of estimated gross profits.

In 1991 the AICPA promulgated Practice Bulletin Number 8 (PB 8) which declared that for products accounted for under FAS 97 realized gains and losses were part of a product's investment returns and their inclusion in estimated gross profits should be considered if it would materially impact DAC amortization. The motivation was that if an insurance company realized a significant interest related capital gain, then that gain front ended the excess of the coupon on the sold security over that from a similar security that could be purchased with the proceeds. If the security had not been sold, then that excess investment income would have been included in future estimated gross profits and resulted in amortization of DAC. If no action were taken, then the realized capital gain would go through earnings, but there would be no change in the DAC. Therefore, equality of treatment (holding the original security with its higher coupon versus realizing the capital gain and owning a security with a lower coupon) motivated the inclusion of the realized capital gain in estimated gross profits and in the amortization of DAC. Of course, there should be symmetrical treatment for interest related realized capital losses. Realized losses result in reduced amortization or, possibly, negative amortization of DAC. There is an 'income statement geography' issue as the realized capital gain is reported in net income and the amortization of DAC due to the gain is reported in operating income.

By itself, FAS 97 exposed insurance company earnings to new levels of volatility due to DAC amortization mechanics, the unlocking provision and the use of best estimate assumptions. PB 8 created even more potential volatility as companies realized capital gains in 1991 through 1993 and then capital losses in 1994 and 1995.

The issue of a fully market valued balance sheet (and therefore income statement), had been in discussion for some time during the late 1980s and 1990s. The impetus for this issue may have been heightened due to the insolvencies in the savings and loan industry during the 1980s where it was believed that if financial statements had been prepared on a market value basis, then the financial problems would not have become so severe. When FASB was discussing market value accounting issues many from the insurance industry argued that it was important that both sides of the balance sheet be marked-to-market or else significant swings in surplus could occur from having assets marked-to-market but liabilities accounted for at book. For many industries this is not a severe problem as they do not have liabilities which are interest sensitive or as long a duration as those of insurance companies..

In 1993 FASB issued FAS 115, to be effective in 1994 and optionally at year end 1993, which generally called for marking assets to market, but did nothing to change the financial reporting of liabilities. FAS 115 requires a company to segregate its applicable assets (FAS 115 does not apply to all assets, e.g. commercial mortgages and real estate are excluded) into three accounts or classes: the held-to-maturity (HTM) account; the available-for-sale (AFS) account; and the trading (T) account. Securities in the HTM account are valued at amortized cost, but, effectively, they may never be traded. Securities in the AFS account are valued at market with the change in market value being directly added to equity, or surplus, i.e. not going through the income statement. ('Below the line' is the phrase used for this type of treatment by the insurance industry.) Securities in the T account are valued at market with the change in market value reflected in the income statement. For changes due to the AFS account and the T account there are corresponding GAAP deferred tax offsets.

FAS 115, by marking the assets to market but leaving the accounting for liabilities at book, created even further potential for volatility in both insurance company earnings and surplus values. In addition, it made comparability of results for two insurance companies more difficult. For example, consider three companies with identical assets and liabilities, but the first puts all its assets in the HTM account, the second all into the AFS account and the third into the T account. If all three companies are managed in the same manner, then the reported financial results could be extremely different for each company due to changes in the interest rate environment, although the underlying financial transactions of all three companies are identical.

In December of 1993 the SEC realized the potential impact in financial reporting for financial institutions due to FAS 115. As a result, the SEC issued instructions that insurance companies should make two adjustments to their financial reporting process. The first was that for assets supporting FAS 97 liabilities and held in the AFS or T accounts each company should compute the unrealized capital gain or loss of those assets and then determine the change in DAC that would have occurred due to PB 8 if those assets would have been sold. This change in DAC would be offset against the surplus adjustment for AFS account unrealized gains and losses and against income for the T account unrealized gains and losses. For each of these there would be corresponding GAAP deferred tax adjustments. This, essentially, created a new type of DAC on the balance sheet. It is sometimes referred to an 'imaginary DAC' or 'virtual DAC', although the former term is a more accurate description.

The second adjustment called for the insurance company to compute a gross premium valuation for each of its lines where FAS 60 or FAS 97 applied and where assets were held in either the AFS account or the T account. This gross premium valuation would be computed as if the FAS 115 applicable assets in the supporting portfolios were sold (thereby realizing all the unrealized capital gains and losses) and new assets purchased. If there would be any loss recognition resulting from the GPV computed using a net earned rate reflecting the hypothetical asset structure after the restructure, then a reduction in 'DAC' and, if necessary, an increase in a liability for such unrealized or imaginary loss recognition would be established.

The changes caused by PB 8, FAS 115 and the SEC instructions created a higher probability of negative amortization of DAC, both real and imaginary. There was not any significant accounting literature in this area; but it was a reasonable position to allow both positive and negative amortization as long as three conditions were satisfied. First, the amount of DAC should not become negative. Second, the amount of DAC at any time should not exceed the amount originally capitalized on the then in force business accumulated with interest. Third, the DAC should be recoverable. Volatility in surplus would be dampened by the creation of imaginary DAC and the taking of unrealized loss recognition. Thus was the state of GAAP accounting in 1994.

Contemporaneous with these events members of the insurance industry had been attempting to create a basis for adjusting GAAP accounting to reflect the market value of liabilities. It is now possible to give an outline of some of the proposed solutions.

*Proposed solutions for market values of liabilities*

There are five major proposals for addressing the problems created by FAS 115's marking the assets to market but leaving the liabilities at book. They are treated in turn from the simplest to the most complex. The first three proposals are included here for completeness of the discussion, with the primary focus being on the last two proposals.

The first proposal is that nothing further needs to be done. This position asserts that the SEC's creation of imaginary DAC and unrealized loss recognition provides sufficient relief from the volatility of surplus created by FAS 115 and that further action is unnecessary given the difficulty of determining a basis for a market value of liabilities. As events stand in 1995, this approach is not likely to be adequate.

The second proposal is for the creation of a GAAP analogue to the interest maintenance reserve (IMR) in statutory accounting. Much of the logic that supports the IMR in statutory accounting is applicable in a GAAP environment. A GAAP IMR would remove the problem that when an interest related capital gain is realized, the gain net of taxes flows through net income in the current period. The future earnings from that gain might be needed to support the product line. The proposed treatment would not allow the gain to be released immediately, but would add it to the IMR and then release it over the time-to-maturity of the original asset that was sold. The change in the IMR due to the gain and the subsequent amortization of that portion of the IMR due to the gain would be an element of operating income, thus eliminating the 'geographic' difficulty in the income statement. This would also apply to realized interest related capital losses and the GAAP IMR would be allowed to become negative.

Implementing this approach would eliminate the need for PB 8 adjustments, i.e., reflecting realized capital gains and losses in the revenue stream for the amortization of DAC, and for reflecting unrealized capital gains and losses in imaginary DAC. For the latter situation one would create an imaginary GAAP IMR that would offset the change in unrealized capital gains and losses. It would actually simplify the existing situation.

The third proposal, made by Richard S. Robertson, would be to determine a method for valuing the GAAP liability and the DAC using interest rates current as of the date of the valuation and not the rates in place when the liability was established. This method is described more fully by Dicke (1993). This proposal remains the closest in spirit to the current GAAP accounting for life insurance companies. It is transaction based with a reserve system that allocates earnings over the lifetime of the block. Note that this method, however, does not reflect the value of embedded options, e.g. guaranteed surrender values, interest rate guarantees, loan provisions, flexible premium provisions or fixed/variable transfer provisions, in the value of the liability. Thus it is not exactly comparable to the market value of assets which does reflect the impact of embedded options. A further challenge is that although a theoretical basis for the adjustments can be described, resulting applicable calculations are not easily describable.

The fourth proposal is to define a market value of liabilities based upon an analogy to assets, i.e. value the liability as if it were a fixed income security by using option pricing techniques. This method has the advantage of reflecting the presence of embedded options in the value of the liability. This requires many new assumptions to be made in valuing the liability than are extant in the current GAAP accounting environment. Since the market value of the liability is similar to a gross premium valuation (which is comparable to a realistic value of the net GAAP liability) it would imply that DAC and its offshoots would be discarded. Credit for the DAC is embedded in this market value of the liability and its amortization is implicit. This method has several difficulties. First, the market value of surplus so obtained does not represent an estimate of the intrinsic or fair value of the insurance enterprise. It will not necessarily provide a value of what a willing buyer would pay a willing seller in an arms-length transaction. Second, although the market value of the liability is a gross premium reserve which provides for the strain of new business, this effect might or might not be completely realized depending on the spread used to discount the liabilities. The question about spreads is part of a larger issue regarding the provision, if any, for adverse deviation. Third, there is no unambiguous definition of the market value of a liability. As will be seen, this stems from the lack of a clear choice in the spread used to discount the liabilities. A more complete discussion on this issue is provided later.

In each of the four methods discussed above the value of surplus is obtained by subtracting the value of liabilities from the value of assets, although the values would now be market values. The fifth method is to define the market value of surplus directly as the value of the firm based on what a willing buyer would pay a willing seller (see Dicke, 1993). This value is computed using classical actuarial appraisal techniques. In this scheme, the market value of liabilities is the market value of assets less the market value of surplus. This is a significant shift in the accounting architecture. Profits no longer emerge over time; but the present value of profits emerge when the business is written. (This could be mitigated, as in FAS 60, by the use of conservatively realistic assumptions instead of best estimates.) This approach would remove the need for FAS 60, FAS 97, PB 8, FAS 115 and imaginary DAC and unrealized loss recognition. An approach based on what a willing buyer would pay a willing seller automatically puts all the assets on a mark-to-market basis. Like the fourth method, many new assumptions are needed. The difficulty in the fourth method stemming from lack of clear choice of a spread by which the liability cash flows are to be discounted has an analogue here. The question is what discount rate should be used in the appraisal. Also, this approach does not reflect the value of the embedded options in the liabilities. From the above one can conclude that the current GAAP accounting environment is subject to ambiguity and inconsistency with regard to the underlying economics of transactions, can result in significant volatility of earnings and/or surplus, is losing the goals of company comparability and comparability over time, is not capturing all the risk exposures of the company and so is not reflecting what has really transpired and the impacts of company management actions on the firm. In the sense of Khun (1970) the stage is set for a 'paradigm shift' in the accounting environment.

## The market value of liabilities

### Introduction

This section is divided into three parts. The first part describes the computational architecture for applying the theory of option pricing to estimating the market value of assets and then specializes it to liabilities. It will be seen that the only 'free variable' in this architecture is the spread at which the asset or liability cash flows are to be discounted. The second part of the section examines accounting consequences from the adoption of a number of potential choices for the spread. The third part considers certain approaches to asset/liability management that result from the market value of liabilities. Cautions and limitations to these approaches are then identified and explored.

### Option pricing architecture

Fixed income securities contain a variety of guarantees and embedded options which create interest rate risk. Examples are: guarantees of performance; bond put and call options; sinking fund acceleration provisions and/or call provisions; and prepayment features in mortgages and mortgage derivatives, e.g. mortgage pass-throughs and collateral mortgage obligations (CMO). In general, the principle of no riskless arbitrage requires that it is impossible for an investor to make an investment with zero net outlay which has a positive probability of positive return now or in the future.

The valuation or pricing of fixed income securities is based on arbitrage pricing theory and utilizes the concepts of no riskless arbitrage (the law of one price), complete markets and risk neutral valuation. Sources on these topics can be found in Cox *et al.* (1979), Cox and Rubinstein (1985), Jarrow (1988) and Pedersen *et al.* (1989). The theoretical assumptions required for arbitrage pricing to hold include: information is freely available; borrowing and lending take place at the same interest rate; the market continuously trades with no transaction costs, no taxes, and no restrictions on short sales; investors are price takers, acting rationally based on all available information and preferring more wealth to less wealth; and markets are complete. A complete market implies that all combinations of securities are available and are perfectly divisible within the market.

The concept of arbitrage pricing implies that two securities, A and B, having the same cash flows in all possible future states of the world, must have the same price. If the price of A, for example, were greater than the price of B, then an investor could sell A, purchase B, use the future cash flows from B to meet the obligation to the buyer of A and pocket the difference in initial price as riskless profit. The foundation for assuming no riskless arbitrage is that if such discrepancies in prices were significant, then they would be observed and trading would commence to take advantage of the difference. Once commenced, however, trading would result in the convergence of the prices of A and B. The result of efficient market trading ultimately drives away discrepancies in price.

Suppose B is a 'basket' of securities whose net cash flows in all possible future states of the world equals those of A. B is said to be a replicating portfolio for A. Thus the arbitrage-free price of A must equal the price of B, which equals the sum of the prices of the individual securities. For this to be true in general it is required that the market be complete, i.e. any asset can be represented by the sum of individual assets from some basic group that spans the entire set of future outcomes. (As an analogy consider this special set of assets as similar to the basis of a vector space, i.e. a set of vectors that both span the space and are independent.) In this case A is said to be priced (or valued) consistently relative to B, A's replicating portfolio. Note that if A is valued consistently relative to B and B is valued consistently relative to C, then A is valued consistently relative to C.

A further consequence of no riskless arbitrage and the other assumptions is that the values obtained for securities must be independent of individual investors' preferences. This is not to say that investors do not have different views of the future states of the world or have the same aversion to risk, it says that the price obtained is the same no matter what those views and levels of aversion are. Since all preferences are equally valid and lead to the same price, then it makes sense to choose the preference in which the computations are the easiest. The simplest frame of reference is that of an investor who is risk-neutral, i.e. not risk averse and not a risk seeker. For a risk-neutral investor the value of the security is the expected present value over all paths of its future cash flows discounted at the risk free rate.

To value a security with fixed cash flows requires a set of fixed income securities free from default and without embedded options which are traded in a market that is active, robust in volume, liquid with ease of trading at narrow bid/ask spreads and covering a large range of maturities. From this ideal set it is possible to infer the prices of zero-coupon bonds. Since any security's cash flows can be considered the sum of a series of zero-coupon bonds, then it is possible to use the law of one price to compute the price of the given security as the sum of the prices of the respective amounts of zero-coupon bonds from the ideal set. The security is priced consistently relative to the collection of zero-coupon bonds. This ideal set of reference securities is the discount bills and coupon notes and bonds issued by the United States Treasury. From this set of Treasury securities it is possible to infer the prices and corresponding yields of hypothetical Treasury zero-coupon bonds. The set of interest rates corresponding to these zero-coupon bonds is referred to as the Treasury spot rates and constitutes what is known as the term structure.

Market forces will eliminate arbitrage opportunities from the market for Treasury securities. Thus it is possible to value a security with fixed cash flows consistently relative to the implied Treasury zero-coupon bonds. Because of risk-neutral valuation the value of the security is the present value of the security's cash flows discounted at these risk-free rates. Since there is no arbitrage opportunity among the Treasury zeros, then there are no arbitrage opportunities among several securities each valued consistently relative to the Treasuries.

Barring unusual circumstances, the price obtained in this way for a security with fixed cash flows is larger than the market price. This is because the market demands a premium for assuming default and liquidity risks as well as other risks. To adjust for this, a spread is added to the Treasury spot rates such that the resulting price equals the market price. This spread, called the spread-to-Treasuries, represents the market's expected incremental return over investing in Treasury securities. It is the reward for taking on risk. In this manner, two securities with fixed cash flows can be compared. If an investor has a desired target for the spread-to-Treasuries then it is possible to compute the price necessary to obtain that incremental return.

The cash flows of a fixed income security that are not fixed, but depend only on the level of interest rates (path independent) or the particular sequence of interest rates over time (path dependent) are called contingent cash flows. Even if the default and liquidity aspects of two such securities are the same it may not be possible to compare them by examining their prices, nominal coupons or yields due to the presence of the embedded options. The goal is to value them in a manner that removes the impact of the embedded options.

The process of determining the spread on this type of security is based on solving for the spread which equates average price of the security to the market price. This average price equals the probability weighted net present values of the security's cash flows over a large number of potential future interest rate paths. The present values are computed using the one period future risk-free rates for each path plus a spread. The paths must have the property that they correctly reprice the Treasury zero-coupon bonds at the date of valuation. Paths satisfying the necessary conditions are said to be arbitrage free at the date of valuation. The resulting spread obtained from solving the algorithm above represents the spread to be earned net of the impact of embedded options. Thus one can compare two securities on the same basis, net of the impact of any embedded options. In this case the spread is called the option adjusted spread (OAS).

The details of how such paths are generated are beyond the scope of this paper. The following provide references for the interested reader: Black et al. (1990), Hull (1993), Ho and Lee (1986), Heath et al. (1990), Jacob et al. (1987), Miller (1990, 1991, 1992), Pedersen et al. (1989) and Tilley (1992).

The following describes the mathematics of the process.

Definitions:
    Let $i_0$ denote the initial term structure of Treasury spot rates.
    Let $p$ be the index for paths ($p$ ranging from 1 to $P$).
    Let $t$ be the index for the time period ($t$ ranging from 1 to $N$).
    Let $j$ be a general index.
    Let $\text{prb}_p$ be the probability of path $p$.

Let $r_{p,t}$ be the one period future rate for path $p$, time $t$.
Let $\text{ACF}_{p,t}$ be the asset cash flow for path $p$, time $t$.
Let OAS be the option adjusted spread.
Let $\text{MVA}(i_0)$ be the market value or price of the asset.

$$\text{MVA}(i_0) = \sum_{p=1}^{P} \text{prb}_p * \left\{ \sum_{t=1}^{N} \left[ \text{ACF}_{p,t} \middle/ \prod_{j=0}^{t-1} (1 + r_{p,j} + \text{OAS}) \right] \right\}. \tag{1}$$

Following Reitano (1991), for a security with fixed cash flows under the assumption of a flat term structure, i.e. $i$ is constant for all maturities, let $P(i)$ be the function that assigns to each value $i \geq 0$ the value of the future cash flows. The rate $i$ can be specified in any system of units. Assume $P(i)$ is twice differentiable with a continuous second derivative. The modified duration, $D(i)$ is defined as

$$D(i) = -\frac{dP}{di} \middle/ P(i). \tag{2}$$

The convexity function, $C(i)$, is defined to be:

$$C(i) = \frac{d^2 P}{di^2} \middle/ P(i). \tag{3}$$

Using first and second-order Taylor series expansions, the following two equations are approximations to the value of $P(i)$ resulting from a small shift in rates from $i_0$ to $i = i_0 + \Delta i$:

$$P(i)/P(i_0) = 1 - D(i_0)\Delta i \tag{4}$$

$$P(i)/P(i_0) = 1 - D(i_0)\Delta i + \tfrac{1}{2} C(i_0)(\Delta i)^2 \tag{5}$$

These equations can be generalized to the case of a non-flat term structure where $\Delta i$ becomes a parallel shift to the term structure $i_0$.

For assets with contingent cash flows it is possible to calculate an option adjusted duration and an option adjusted convexity. Following Fabozzi (1994) these are called effective duration (OAD) and effective convexity (OAC), respectively. In this paper they will be referred to as just duration and convexity for simplicity and are computed assuming a parallel shift in the term structure (the implied Treasury spot curve).

Let $\Delta i$ be a small, positive change in the level of the term structure of interest rates from $i_0$ to $i_0 + \Delta i$. Let $\text{MVA}(i_0 + \Delta i)$ be the market value that results from shifting the initial term structure upward by the amount $\Delta i$ and valuing the resulting cash flows. The computation uses the value of OAS computed from the original term structure. Let $\text{MVA}(i_0 - \Delta i)$ be defined similarly. The following definitions can be made:

$$\text{OAD} = -\frac{\text{MVA}(i_0 + \Delta i) - \text{MVA}(i_0 - \Delta i)}{2*\Delta i*\text{MVA}(i_0)}, \quad (6)$$

$$\text{OAC} = \frac{\text{MVA}(i_0 + \Delta i) - 2*\text{MVA}(i_0) + \text{MVA}(i_0 - \Delta i)}{(\Delta i)^2 * \text{MVA}(i_0)}. \quad (7)$$

The equations preceding these hold for OAD and OAC in place of $D$ and $C$, respectively.

Insurance liabilities may be analyzed in a manner similar to fixed income securities by substituting liability cash flows for asset cash flows in equation (1). In this case one needs a cash flow model that describes the liability cash flows in terms of management and policyholder behavior along a set of arbitrage free interest rate paths.

Nearly all insurance liabilities grant guarantees and options that expose the company to interest rate risk. The list includes, but is not limited to:
- single premium and flexible premium deferred annuities;
- immediate annuities;
- guaranteed interest contracts;
- terminal funded annuities; universal life;
- non-participating and participating ordinary life;
- disability income and long term care.

The features that create risk include:
- cash surrender at book value;
- minimum crediting rate guarantees;
- flexible premium or 'dump in' provisions with or without 'window' limitations;
- bailout provisions;
- return of premium provisions;
- partial withdrawals both with and without penalty;
- benefit responsive options in institutional pension products;
- fixed account/variable account transfer options;
- policy loans, both regular and wash loans.

These expose the insurance company to reinvestment and disintermediation interest rate risks.

Define the following additional terms.

Let $\text{LCF}_{p,t}$ be the liability cash flow for path $p$, time $t$.
Let LS (liability spread) be the spread chosen for discounting liabilities.
Let MVL be the market value of liabilities at the given spread.

$$\text{MVL}(i_0) = \sum_{p=1}^{P} \text{prb}_p * \left\{ \sum_{t=1}^{N} \left[ \text{LCF}_{p,t} \bigg/ \prod_{j=0}^{t-1} (1 + r_{p,j} + \text{LS}) \right] \right\}. \quad (8)$$

As with assets one can compute duration and convexity, $D_L$ and $C_L$ respectively, for liabilities. The formulae for them are similar to the above with $\text{LCF}_{p,t}$ in place of $\text{ACF}_{p,t}$. The subscripts $A$ and $S$ (instead of $L$) are later used for assets and surplus.

## The market values of liabilities

Unlike many fixed income securities and common stock, insurance liabilities have no corresponding secondary market on which they trade. As a result there is no market price with which an option pricing model can be used to determine a liability's spread. One is forced to arbitrarily choose a spread for discounting liability cash flows. In this section several choices for the spread will be considered. The implications of each choice with regard to market value accounting will be examined. The notation $i_0$ denotes the initial term structure. Note that assets and liabilities are valued consistently using the same interest rate paths.

### $LS = 0$

The MVL resulting from discounting the liability cash flows at the risk-free rate, i.e. a spread equal to zero, would be a conservative estimate of the amount of funds that the insurance company should hold such that those funds together with future premiums and investment income would mature the obligations.

$$\text{MVL}(i_0) = \sum_{p=1}^{P} \text{prb}_p * \left\{ \sum_{t=1}^{N} \left[ \text{LCF}_{p,t} \bigg/ \prod_{j=0}^{t-1} (1 + r_{p,j}) \right] \right\}. \tag{9}$$

Advantages of this definition include the following. It is a simple and unambiguous choice that is not subject to manipulation. It is responsive to changes in market interest rates and reflects the value of the embedded options. There is less volatility over time as this choice of spread is always zero, and the spread may change over time for other choices.

Disadvantages are that it is overly conservative, may result in materially understating surplus and earnings and does not relate the underlying value of the assets to the liabilities as does, for example, the choice for the spread defined next.

### $LS = OAS$

The OAS is the option-adjusted spread-to-Treasuries of the asset portfolio supporting the liabilities. The principal use of this application would be as an option-adjusted gross premium valuation if, as is usually the case, expenses are included in the cash flows.

$$\text{MVL}(i_0) = \sum_{p=1}^{P} \text{prb}_p * \left\{ \sum_{t=1}^{N} \left[ \text{LCF}_{p,t} \bigg/ \prod_{j=0}^{t-1} (1 + r_{p,j} + \text{OAS}) \right] \right\}. \tag{10}$$

The advantages of this choice are:
- it is explainable;
- it relates the MVL to the character of the asset portfolio that supports the liabilities;

*The value of the firm* 231

- it is responsive to changes in market interest rates and reflects the value of the embedded options;
- it should be relatively free of manipulation;
- it would provide a more realistic value;
- and it is useful for loss recognition purposes.

Disadvantages are:
- it requires the computation of an OAS for the asset portfolio, which may contain securities for which it is difficult to obtain a reliable value and, hence, exposes itself to subjectivity and manipulation;
- it can expose the MVL to volatility if the OAS of the asset portfolio changes dramatically due to restructuring or other causes;
- it could understate the MVL (and so overstate surplus and income) if the size of the OAS is large due to taking significant credit risks or duration risks in the asset portfolio. Some might argue that it is too generous.

*LS = Default Spread (DS)*

DS is the default spread that can be assigned to the insurance company. It may be based upon debt ratings of itself or its parent, the claims paying ability/financial strength ratings assigned by ratings agencies or a combination of the two.

$$\text{MVL}(i_0) = \sum_{p=1}^{P} \text{prb}_p * \left\{ \sum_{t=1}^{N} \left[ \text{LCF}_{p,t} \bigg/ \prod_{j=0}^{t-1} (1 + r_{p,j} + \text{DS}) \right] \right\}. \qquad (11)$$

The advantages of this method are:
- it values liabilities in the manner most similar to assets, i.e. where the spread reflects the default costs;
- it is responsive to changes in market interest rates and reflects the impact of embedded options;
- it is understandable in that it relates to the risk of the insurance company.

The disadvantages are:
- debt ratings and financial strength ratings are not consistent nor is either consistent across rating agencies;
- there is a potential problem in relating the value of DS to the debt/financial strength rating; DS has no provision for liquidity as the OAS does in assets;
- it is contrary to accounting for assets in that the borrower must carry the debt on the balance sheet at book, not market;
- it is not likely to be viewed as having any relation to the amount the insurance company should hold to mature its obligations;
- it has the property that lower ratings lead to higher surplus, a counter intuitive result.

Consider two insurance companies with identical liabilities. Company A has its entire assets invested in Treasury securities and is cash matched to its liabilities. Company B has an equal market value of securities that are invested in call protected C rated corporate bonds whose expected cash flows are matched to the liabilities. Because the quality of B's bond portfolio, B is viewed as riskier than A. B, accordingly, has been assigned a lower credit rating. This lower credit rating translates into a higher DS for company B than for company A. Therefore, $MVA_A = MVA_B$ and $MVL_A > MVL_B$. Let MVS be the market value of surplus and be defined by $MVS = MVA - MVL$, then $MVS_A < MVS_B$. This result is not incorrect given the definition of DSs and a truly economically based balance sheet. This is due to the fact that the excess surplus in B reflects the positive value of B's put option in the event of insolvency which places the assets and liabilities in the hands of the state guarantee associations and/or ultimately back to the policyholders. This result, even if economically rational, does not seem to be an acceptable basis for an accounting system.

*LS = cost of funds spread (COF)*

COF is the spread-to-Treasuries that discounts the future liability cash flows back to the initial cash flow of the block at issue. COF is then assumed fixed for all time. If market interest rates change causing embedded options in the liabilities to become more valuable, then the MVL will rise. COF can be thought of as the cost of funds, i.e. the cost to the insurance company of acquiring the business from the policyholders.

$$MVL(i_0) = \sum_{p=1}^{P} prb_p * \left\{ \sum_{t=1}^{N} \left[ LCF_{p,t} \bigg/ \prod_{j=0}^{t-1} (1 + r_{p,j} + COF) \right] \right\}. \quad (12)$$

Its advantages are that it is responsive to changes in market interest rates and reflects the value of embedded options in the liabilities and provides an innovative method to manage profitability and interest rate risk.

Disadvantages are:
- one must determine the COF for each block of business, which may pose problems for companies with large existing blocks;
- it is not related to the amount that the insurance company needs to hold to support its liabilities;
- it reflects a limited view of profitability;
- it creates the situation where for two companies with otherwise identical circumstances, the one with the higher acquisition costs could have the greater MVS.

This last result reduces the method's utility as a basis for market value accounting, and is somewhat similar to the situation for the default spread. Assume insurance companies A and B have identical assets, liabilities and management strategies for the business. Assume that company A has higher acquisition costs than company B. This means that the initial net cash flow for A's block was smaller than for B's block. Since future benefits and expenses are the same, then $LS_A > LS_B$ as the liability cash flows have to discount to a smaller number for A than for B. Thus $MVL_A < MVL_B$, and so $MVS_A > MVS_B$.

*Asset/liability management applications of the market value of liabilities*

Up to this point the discussion involving the market value of liabilities has centered on its use as a basis for a market value accounting. The concepts underlying the market valuation of liabilities originally arose from efforts to improve asset/liability management. These concepts and their applications to asset/liability management are presented here. Cautions and limitations to these applications are presented in the next part of this section. The concepts are applied, in a different context, see later.

The term market value analysis is used here to represent the totality of various devices by which a firm measures and/or controls interest rate risk. The 1980s witnessed a major innovation among insurance companies in the measurement of interest rate risk and techniques to control it. The innovation was to treat the insurance liability as a fixed income security and to apply fixed income security analysis and management techniques, including option pricing theory, to the assets and liabilities of the firm. In particular the concepts of market values, duration, convexity and immunization were applied to the assets and liabilities of insurance companies. Progress was made in bringing these concepts into the design and pricing of insurance liabilities. Further, the theory of duration and convexity was generalized beyond parallel shifts in the yield curve (Reitano, 1991a; Ho, 1990). Further, Reitano has extended most of the classical work into the very general domain of arbitrary movements in the term structure. For simplicity of exposition, examples in this section will be stated from the perspective of parallel shifts in the term structure.

From the perspective of funds management the risk posed by reinvestment and disintermediation is that the insurance enterprise does not have the funds available to pay its obligations without incurring a loss. This is what is meant by interest rate risk. The most conservative approach would be to cash match the assets with the liabilities. Cash matching would typically employ the use of assets with no embedded options and little or no default risk. Reinvestment risk would be diminished by assuming a conservative reinvestment rate. Market risk would be eliminated by holding the securities to maturity. Mathematical algorithms can be used to choose the portfolio that cash matches with least cost.

There are two problems with this. It is extremely costly in terms of sacrifice in return and it may be difficult or impossible if the liability and/or asset cash flows are not fixed but have embedded options.

Another approach is to relax the cash match criteria and manage the market values so that a change in the term structure of interest rates results in changes in market values such that the market value of assets remains larger than the market value of liabilities. If the market value of assets exceeds the market value of liabilities, then the insurance enterprise can liquidate assets necessary to pay its obligations and the remaining market value of assets still exceeds the remaining market value of liabilities. One wants the following equation to be valid at any time $t$ and remain valid for reasonable shifts in the term structure:

$$\text{ACF}_t + \text{MVA}(i_t) \geq \text{LCF}_t + \text{MVL}(i_t). \tag{13}$$

The exposure of a portfolio of liabilities and its supporting assets to interest rate risk is often displayed via market value diagrams. A typical example is shown in Figure 1.

Simply put, the degree of interest rate risk is smaller the larger the value of MVS for a wider range of parallel shifts in the term structure. This quantification is really a relative measure because, as noted in the prior section, there is freedom in the choice of the definition of the spread to be used for discounting the liabilities. Different choices of spread result in different values of MVL and MVS. Once a basis is chosen, however, one can analyze the situation and take management action. The term economic surplus is sometimes used to denote this market value of surplus, and is used to distinguish it from accounting surplus.

Immunization theory for fixed income portfolios provides that under suitable conditions and restrictions it is possible to immunize the value of the portfolio and its rate of return from changes in interest rates that occur over an investment horizon (Bierwag et al., 1953, Bierwag, 1987). More precisely, if a portfolio of securities is chosen such that its duration equals the investor's time horizon, then the portfolio is immunized so that the annual realized rate of return can never fall below the initial yield to maturity at which the securities were purchased. Some of the restrictions are that the yield curve is flat, the change in rate is a parallel shift occurring instantaneously with no further changes over the horizon, no external cash in flows or out flows, investment cash flows can be reinvested at the same rate as that earned by the portfolio and the original securities have no embedded options and have positive convexity. Bierwag (1987) defines the notion of a duration window for which the above results hold. The fact that the rate of return on the portfolio is the yield at the initial point in time can be seen from Babcock's formula (1984). Market and reinvestment risk are balanced around that duration window.

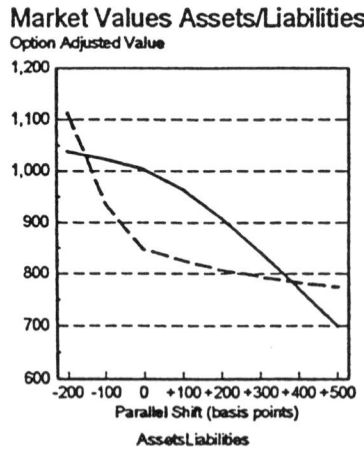
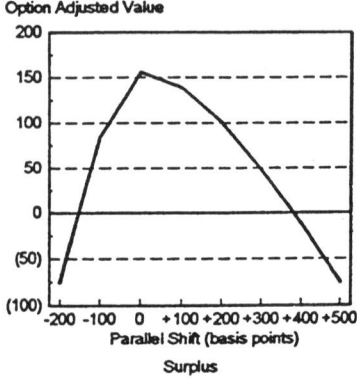

*Figure 1.* Market value analysis.

This work can be extended to insurance enterprises by treating liabilities as fixed income obligations. As a special case assume that at time $t$, $S_t = A_t - L_t \geq 0$, $D_A = D_L(L/A)$ and $C_A > C_L$. Let $S'_t$ denote the value of surplus immediately after an instantaneous parallel shift to the term structure. Use similar notation for $A'_t$ and $L'_t$. Then $S'_t > S_t$. Using equation (5)

$$S'_t = A'_t - L'_t = A_t[1 - D_A \Delta i + \tfrac{1}{2} C_A (\Delta i)^2]$$
$$\quad - L_t[1 - D_L \Delta i + \tfrac{1}{2} C_L (\Delta i)^2]$$
$$= A_t - L_t + [L_t D_L - A_t D_A]\Delta i$$
$$\quad + \tfrac{1}{2}[A_t C_A - L_t C_L](\Delta i)^2 > A_t - L_t$$
$$= S_t.$$

In the second line of the equation above the first bracketed expression is zero because the condition on the durations of $A$ and $L$ implies that $AD_A = LD_L$. In the second bracketed expression the fact that $S_t = A_t - L_t \geq 0$ and $C_A > C_L$ justify the inequality.

Note that $SD_S = A_t D_A - L_t D_L$. This case says that if $D_S = 0$ and $C_A > C_L$, then the dollar amount of surplus is instantaneously immunized against small parallel shifts in the term structure.

For a second special case assume that at time $t$, $S_t > 0$, $D_A = D_L$ and $C_A > C_L$. Then the ratio of surplus to assets is immunized at time $t$, i.e. $r'_t = S'_t/A'_t > r_t = S_t/A_t$. Again using equation (5)

$$r'_t = S'_t/A'_t = [A'_t - L'_t]/A'_t$$
$$= 1 - L'_t/A'_t$$
$$= 1 - L_t/A_t \frac{1 - D_L \Delta i + \tfrac{1}{2} C_L (\Delta i)^2}{1 - D_A \Delta i + \tfrac{1}{2} C_A (\Delta i)^2} > 1 - L_t/A_t$$
$$= r_t.$$

By the conditions given, the expression in brackets above is less than 1.

Reitano (1991a,b) generalizes the results of Bierwag et al. (1983) and Bierwag (1987) to non flat term structures with non parallel shifts in the term structure. Instead of Bierwag's duration window, Reitano defines an immunization boundary. Reitano proves that the immunization boundary gives rise to a minimum annualized return $i(k)$ on investment over every investment period $[0, k]$ for which a yield vector exists so that $P(i)$ is immunized at time $k$. This can be applied to $S$ of an insurance enterprise. Reitano also derives the two results given above in this more general setting. The minimum annualized return is, of course, more complex in this general setting.

A hybrid between cash matching and full immunization is that of cash matching for liability cash flows out to a certain number of months and immunization for the remaining liability cash flows. This situation can be relaxed even further to allow for a degree of active management through contingent immunization (Bierwag, 1987). In this case the investor stipulates the degree of risk tolerance at the start of the investment. If errors develop over the period of the plan, the investor can move the current duration closer to the remaining time horizon of the plan. If $r$ is the initially promised rate of return and $x$ the maximal tolerable loss, then $r_f = r - x$ is the floor to the rate of return, i.e. the minimally acceptable rate of return. The maximum tolerable loss, $x$, is the safety margin. Over time the closer the projected return is to $r_f$, the greater the danger that the realized rate may fall below $r_f$. If the projected rate falls to $r_f$, then strict immunization over the remaining planning horizon is triggered. Essentially, the investor is willing to trade off the safety margin $x$ for the potential of obtaining excess returns.

A different application of the market value of liabilities concept was made by Griffin (1990). His paper uses the cost of funds method coupled with the techniques from option pricing theory to analyze a liability and set targets for asset performance. This approach solves for the required spread on assets (RSA). It is computed as follows. First, create a set of arbitrage-free interest rate paths based on the current Treasury term structure. Second, using the features built into the proposed liability (e.g. crediting rate strategy, book value surrenders, surrender charge design, interest rate guarantees, bail outs, or return of premium features) calculate the present value of the liability cash flows along each path at a tentative value of the RSA. Third, compute the weighted average present values (weighted according to the path probabilities). Fourth, if that average equals the initial net cash flow, then the estimated RSA is the RSA. If not, iterate the process to find the RSA which produces an average equal to the net initial cash flow. This part of the RSA represents the amount the insurance enterprise must pay to acquire the business. Thus the RSA includes the cost of funds for the insurance enterprise. (The cost of funds is the amount COF defined earlier.) To this RSA must be added amounts for the credit risk, investment expenses and the profit target. In this case the profit target is expressed in basis points. The final value of RSA is the spread that the asset portfolio must earn for the insurance enterprise to achieve its desired profit level.

Over time, the relative performance of the asset and liability portfolios will not track with what was anticipated at issue. The RSA can then be recalculated by using the then current market value of assets as the amount to which the future liability cash flows must be discounted. The new RSA, adjusted for the effect of any expenses, can then be subtracted from the spread-to-Treasuries actually being earned on the assets to determine the excess spread available to the insurance enterprise.

A slightly different market value approach is taken by Ho et al. (1992). In this case the quantity COF (the cost of funds spread defined earlier) is determined for a new block of business. It is held fixed for all future time periods. On this basis, the market value of liabilities is computed at each future point in time according to equation (12). Based on the liability cash flows and the market values of liabilities it is possible to calculate the total return on liabilities. This method presupposes equality between the asset value and the liability value, i.e. a zero surplus on a market value basis. The net return to the insurance enterprise equals the total return on assets supporting the block less the total return required by the liabilities.

If at the end of a period the MVA exceeds the MVL, then net return earned by the insurance enterprise reflects that excess. Although the authors do not state this explicitly, that excess would then be considered transferred to surplus, i.e. funds not associated with the product. Other things being equal, if the change in MVL exceeded that for MVA, then that would contribute to a negative total return and would require an infusion from surplus so that MVA = MVL going into the next period. By holding the COF constant for the block of business, the change in value of embedded options in the liabilities is reflected by increases or decreases in the MVL.

The methods describing immunization can be overlayed on these approaches. It should be noted that if one is immunizing the dollar amount of surplus and its return over a long holding period, then the duration of surplus will have to equal that length of time. Thus the market value of surplus will be more volatile over the time period as its duration is large. If one shortens the duration of surplus, then one not only reduces the volatility but also reduces the rate of return locked in by the immunization. One is trading risk for return.

A method of interest that does not directly depend on market values is that of Miller et al. (1989). First, a set of interest rate paths is determined. Second, the liability cash flows are projected along each path. The return that must be earned on the assets in order to satisfy the liability cash flows is called the required return (RQ). The realized return (RR) on the assets depends on the value of the assets at the beginning and the end of the period, the cash flows received during the period and the reinvestment income earned on the cash flows received during the period. These amounts will depend on the interest rate environments at each point in time along each interest rate path. The asset cash flows will reflect any embedded options contained in them. Mathematical programming techniques can be used to identify assets which, ideally, will provide a RR in excess of the RQ for each time period. Some compromises, however, may have to be made. For all portfolios that satisfy the required conditions the one with the highest expected realized return would be selected.

*Cautions and limitations in market value analysis*

There are cautions that one should be aware of when using these forms of market value analysis. For some asset classes, e.g. private placements, residential and/or farm mortgages, commercial mortgages, real estate, defaulted securities and over-the-counter derivatives, there may be considerable uncertainty about the market values. Insurance enterprises tend to hold significant quantities of these assets. Market values are subject to volatility from uncertainty in borrower behavior, policyholder behavior and insurance enterprise (asset and liability management) behavior. The calculated market values may be subject to the nature of the option pricing model used.

Duration and convexity measures are local measures. Their use is valid over small changes in interest rates. Some assets with embedded options are path dependent and the way the change occurs may not be captured in the duration and convexity measures used. It is necessary to maintain the duration and convexity conditions at all times. Even if interest rates do not change the duration and convexity of assets and liabilities will change as time passes. Thus rebalancing will have to be performed frequently, which increases costs. Rebalancing will also be required as there are always new external cash flows entering the picture due to new business and the fact that cash flows from existing assets may not be reinvested at the same rate of return as the asset portfolio itself.

Market values, duration and convexity of liabilities require the ability to accurately predict policyholder behavior. Such prediction is reasonably valid for fixed liabilities, e.g. guaranteed interest contracts (GICs), immediate annuities and terminal funded annuities, but is not as valid for deferred annuities and life insurance. It is important to sensitivity test the policyholder behavior functions used in modeling the liabilities. There is a tendency to micro-manage to the 'numbers' (e.g. market values, durations and convexity) for assets and liabilities. This may be risky unless the policyholder behavior function is known with a high degree of certainty or the results are generally insensitive to policyholder behavior misspecification. Management decisions based on such micro-management may not be robust. Market value analysis uses single-point option pricing, i.e. at the date of valuation only. The asset cash flows are those from existing assets. It does not reflect the reinvestment behavior of the insurance enterprise over time. As such, it presents a serious problem for interest sensitive liabilities using a portfolio crediting strategy.

As seen earlier in this section there is no unambiguous definition of the market value of a liability. There is, therefore, no unambiguous definition of the market value of surplus or economic surplus. Different choices of liability spread (LS) lead to different market values for the same liability. These different market values result in different option adjusted durations for the liability. Thus, the option adjusted duration of a liability is a function of LS. Using choices for LS as described earlier in this paper for a block of single premium deferred annuities results in option adjusted durations which vary by more than a factor of seven (7) from smallest to largest. This stems from the fact that there is no secondary market for insurance liabilities. And with the exception of viatical settlement companies (which buy the policies of terminally ill individuals) there is not likely to be due to underwriting, tax and public policy (insurable interest) issues. Some refer to other insurance companies as buyers of liabilities via assumption reinsurance. It is important to clarify that the assuming company is not just buying the liabilities, it is buying the liabilities and either the supporting assets or cash. The assuming company is entering into the transaction in order to receive the earnings from the net activity of the assets and the liabilities. It is not likely that the market value of surplus as described above would equal what a willing buyer would pay a willing seller for the liabilities and supporting assets.

Market value analysis also does not consider all relevant cash flows. First, if a realized capital gain must be taken to meet a liability cash flow, then tax on the capital gain will need to be paid. But there is no provision in the analysis for this tax. Second, the insurance enterprise is itself subject to income taxes. There is no provision for these cash flows. Third, there is no provision in the analyses for the payment of shareholder dividends. Market value analysis also does not recognize the cost of capital that the insurance enterprise incurs in maintaining statutory reserves, deficiency reserves, interest maintenance reserves, asset valuation reserves and risk based capital. Market value analysis treats the assets and liabilities separately. It does not look at the enterprise as an integrated whole. This may lead to suboptimization in managing interest rate risk. For example, an insurance enterprise may engage in a hedge transaction to mitigate interest rate risk. Because market value analysis does not reflect all relevant transactions and costs it may result in either a costly hedge (buying too much interest rate risk insurance) or an ineffective hedge with regard to the value of the firm.

In summary, this definition of market value of surplus or economic surplus does not equal the value of the firm. Thus the challenges of measuring interest rate risk, managing interest rate risk and pricing new business, blocks of business or entire companies with regard to the value of the firm remain open.

## Conclusions

For this method of market valuation of liabilities there are major issues. First, the resulting market value of surplus does not relate to the fair value of the firm from buyer/seller perspective. Second, the definition of the market value of liabilities is inherently ambiguous. Of several not unreasonable choices for the spread to define MVL, none are immune from difficulties. Application of fixed income theory to insurance liabilities and assets results in a much higher level of sophistication in asset/liability management, but there are cautions and limitations in the theory, and the theory is still incomplete with regard to the value of the firm.

## THE OPTION ADJUSTED VALUE OF DISTRIBUTABLE EARNINGS

### Introduction

The goal is to define the appropriate objective function, i.e. the proper measurement of the value of the firm and determine how to compute it. The work in this section represents a fusion of finance theory and option pricing theory applied to the insurance enterprise. It is an extension of the author's earlier work (Becker, 1991).

### The price of a security

The price of a security reflects its inherent risk. From finance theory the price or value of a security, also known as its intrinsic or fair value, is the risk-adjusted present value of the security's free cash flows. Free cash flows are amounts of money that can be freely transferred to the owner of the security. The owner must be able to dispose of those amounts in any way he or she desires.

If the security is a bond, then in exchange for the purchase price the owner receives the coupon income, any call premium (if the bond is called) and the maturity value. The owner is free to dispose of the income, call premium or maturity value in any way. Any default, liquidity, interest rate risk due to the level and/or volatility of interest rates or other risk is reflected in the price of the bond. Option pricing theory is required for the valuation of bonds with contingent cash flows due to the embedded options. Option pricing theory also provides for consistent valuation of securities on a relative basis.

For a firm, the goal is to maximize the wealth of its shareholders. Copeland and Weston (1988) state this to be the same as maximizing the present value of shareholders' lifetime consumption and no different than maximizing the price per share of stock. Shareholder wealth, or the price of the stock, is the discounted value of after-tax cash flows paid out by the firm. The after-tax cash flows available for consumption are shown to be the same as the stream of dividends paid to shareholders. Shareholder dividends are the free cash flows of common stock. The discount rate is the market-determined rate of return on equity capital (common stock) or opportunity cost of capital for equivalent income streams.

A question arises about capital gains. Shareholders receive both capital gains and dividends from ownership of stock. Why does the above statement refer only to dividends? Copeland and Weston (1988) show that this formulation does include capital gains in that if the firm reinvests funds at the cost of capital that it could have paid as shareholder dividends, then the resulting value of the stock is the same value as if all funds had been distributed as dividends. If the firm in which the security represents ownership is an insurance enterprise, then it is necessary to determine the free cash flows, i.e. shareholder dividends, that can be paid by the insurance enterprise. Unlike other industries, state law regulates the amounts of shareholder dividends that can be paid. This law ties shareholder dividends to statutory accounting. This fact often causes people to turn away from the use of statutory net income as a basis for economic value on the basis that the conservative nature of statutory accounting does not reflect the true economic value or economic reality of the firm. But the fact is that statutory accounting does affect the true economics of the insurance enterprise. Cash flows within the insurance enterprise that are not capable of being paid to shareholders are not free cash flows. So they can not be used either as shareholder dividends or to fund new business projects.

Statutory accounting imposes another restraint. The insurance enterprise is required to hold an asset valuation reserve (AVR). Although not funded from statutory net income, increases in the AVR are charged against surplus and can not be used to pay shareholder dividends or fund new business. If the increase in the AVR reduces surplus below the company's desired level, the ability to pay the statutory net income as a shareholder dividend is diminished. In addition to the limits of statutory accounting, the amount of capital that needs to be held either due to internal required surplus formulae or to satisfy external capital requirements, e.g. rating agencies or a desired level of NAIC risk based capital ratio, will impose a limitation on the ability of the firm to pay shareholder dividends. The insurance enterprise needs to hold such capital and provide shareholders an adequate return on it. In light of the required surplus component, the amount of AVR, described above, that must be managed equals the excess, if positive, of the AVR over the asset default component of required surplus.

The free cash flow or shareholder dividend that the insurance enterprise can pay in a given time period is referred to as distributable earnings and is given by the following formula. For time period $t$, let DE be the distributable earnings, SNI be statutory net income, AVR be the excess, if positive, of the asset valuation reserve over the asset default component of the required surplus, and RS be the level of required surplus (however determined) that the company wishes to hold. Assume that the level of surplus is at the desired level the insurance enterprise desires to hold.

$$DE_t = SNI_t - \Delta_t AVR - \Delta_t RS. \tag{14}$$

If the surplus is at a high enough level, then the term involving the AVR can be ignored.

For background purposes three appendices are included. Appendix A provides background on deterministic insurance pricing, especially with regard to the role of required surplus and the impacts of required surplus and taxes. Appendix B provides some additional commentary about the perceived difficulties in using statutory accounting as a basis for value. It is presented in a question and answer format. Appendix C provides deeper insight into the differences between market value analysis and OAVDE analysis and related issues.

Figure 2, following, shows sample free cash flow patterns for several types of securities. The presence of a call option in a bond affects its price relative to a noncallable bond as interest rates change. This is demonstrated graphically in Figure 3.

Since the assets and liabilities of the insurance enterprise have embedded options, the distributable earnings represent a series of contingent cash flows to the shareholders. As a result, option pricing techniques must be used in order to compute their present value. In this case a set of arbitrage-free paths repricing the initial term structure is obtained and the actual operations of the insurance enterprise are projected out along each path into the future. The asset, liability and distributable earnings cash flows will reflect the actual management of the business from the date of valuation into the future. They involve the nature and behavior of the assets (affected by borrower behavior), the nature and behavior of the liabilities (affected by policyholder behavior and company management behavior, e.g. credited interest rate), results of

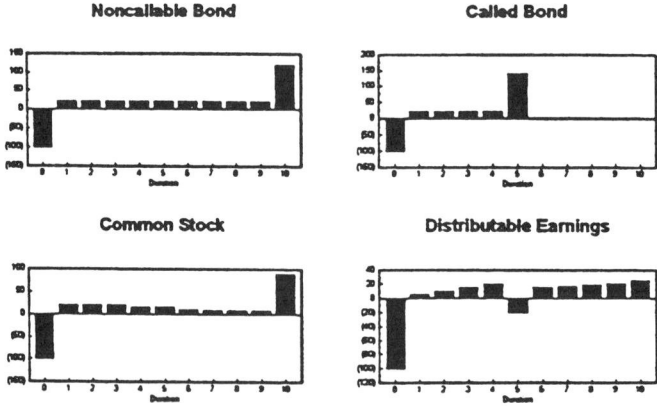

*Figure 2.* Free cash flow diagram.

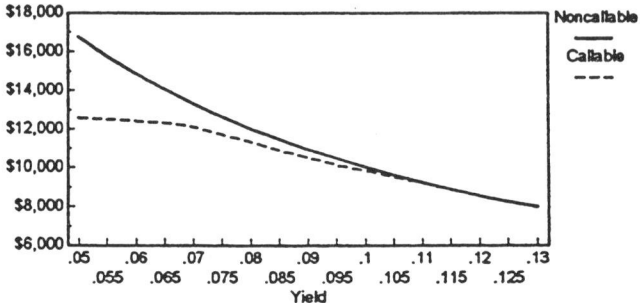

*Figure 3.* Bond prices.

reinvestment and disinvestment (to cover negative cash flows) and other demands of statutory accounting and required surplus.

Unlike market value analysis, which is single point option pricing, this situation requires multipoint option pricing. This means that at each time interval on each interest rate path one has to be able to purchase or sell securities. These decisions must be made in an arbitrage free environment; thus at each combination of path and time interval one must perform an option pricing exercise from the term structure extant at that point in time. If certain restrictions are placed on disinvestment and range of securities that can be purchased, it is possible to avoid the need for multi-point option pricing, e.g. if future asset purchases are limited to assets without embedded options and disinvestment is accommodated by borrowing.

The weighted average of the present values of distributable earnings discounted along each path is called the option adjusted value of distributable earnings (OAVDE). It is the intrinsic or fair value of the insurance enterprise. Thus, OAVDE is the mark-to-market value of the firm.

If a price is specified, it is possible to solve for the spread that the investor earns at that price. Alternatively, if a spread is specified, the price the investor must pay to earn that spread can be solved for. The following notation will be used.

Let $i_0$ be the initial term structure.
Let $t$ be an index for time ($t = 0, 1, ..., N$).
Let $p$ be an index for the path ($p = 1, ..., P$).
Let $j$ be a general index.
Let $r_{p,t}$ be the risk-free future one period rate corresponding to path $p$ at time $t$.
Let $\text{prb}_p$ be the probability of path $p$.
Let $\text{tr}_{p,t}$ be the federal income tax rate at time $t$ on path $p$.
Let $\text{DE}_{p,t}$ be the distributable earnings corresponding to path $p$ at time $t$.
Let OAS be the option adjusted spread for distributable earnings.

The liabilities are supported by assets whose book value equals the sum of statutory reserves, deficiency reserves (if any), interest maintenance reserve, required surplus and the excess, if positive, of the AVR over the asset default component of required surplus.

$$\text{OAVDE}(i_0, \text{OAS}) = \sum_{p=1}^{P} \text{prb}_p * \left\{ \sum_{t=1}^{N} \left[ \text{DE}_{p,t} \bigg/ \prod_{j=0}^{t-1} (1 + r_{p,j} + \text{OAS}) \right] \right\}. \quad (15)$$

If it is desired to find the OAS for a proposed block of new business, set $\text{OAVDE}(i_0, \text{OAS}) = -\text{DE}_0$, i.e. the initial or 'time 0' distributable earnings for the block. The negative sign is needed as the initial distributable earnings is almost always negative.

It is also possible to solve for an option adjusted yield (OAY) instead of an option adjusted spread. It is sometimes useful to express results in this manner or to compute an OAVDE based on a level discount rate. For example, one choice for OAY is the insurance enterprise's cost of capital. Another choice might be a target rate of return in excess of the cost of capital that the firm wishes to earn.

$$\text{OAVDE}(i_0, \text{OAY}) = \sum_{p=1}^{P} \text{prb}_p * \left\{ \sum_{t=1}^{N} [\text{DE}_{p,t}/(1 + \text{OAY})^t] \right\}. \quad (16)$$

To solve for OAY for a new block set $\text{OAVDE}(i_0, \text{OAY}) = -\text{DE}_0$, as above.

Results can be analyzed on a path-by-path basis. For each path $p$, it is possible to determine a spread-to-Treasuries, $s_p$, and a yield, $y_p$. Statistics about the sets $\{s_p\}$ and $\{y_p\}$ can be determined. These would be the minimum, maximum, the mean, standard deviation, skewness (measuring degree of symmetry) and kurtosis (measuring peakedness and length of the tails of the distribution). Similarly if the spread or yield is fixed, it is possible to examine the distribution of $\{\text{PVDE}(i_0, s_p, p)\}$ or $\{\text{PVDE}(i_0, y_p, p)\}$ where PVDE means the present value of distributable earnings for the term structure $i_0$ and path $p$ and the discounting is done with a spread-to-Treasury $s_p$ or a constant yield $y_p$, respectively. OAS and OAY may not equal the means of $\{s_p\}$ and $\{y_p\}$, respectively.

The pattern of distributable earnings shown in Figure 2 includes a second negative quantity. The first negative quantity represents the initial negative distributable earnings amount that is assumed covered by shareholder investment. Unlike other securities where the cash flows are contractual, distributable earnings represent a transfer from the insurance enterprise to the shareholder. If a second negative distributable earnings occurs, there is no contractual ability for the firm to demand it from the shareholders. The firm must cover it from the surplus of the insurance enterprise. But this represents funds which can not be paid to shareholders, so it is a second investment. Such events can happen in a volatile interest environment and they can happen (and do) when interest rates are unchanging. The generalized net present value and generalized internal rate of return algorithms developed by Becker (1988) resolve the problem of evaluating a stand-alone project that requires multiple shareholder investments. This is described more fully in Appendix A on deterministic pricing.

The formulae for computing OAVDE with the generalized net present value algorithm are given below. Additional notation is defined first. PVB stands for present value balance.

Let $\text{PVB}_{p,N}(i_0, i) = \text{DE}_{p,N}$ and $\text{PVB}_{p,t}(i_0, i) = \text{PVB}_{p,t+1}(i_0, i)/(1+r) + \text{DE}_{p,t}$ for $t = N-1, N-2, \ldots, 1$ or 0, if there is an initial distributable earnings amount; where $r = i$ if $\text{PVB}_{p,t+1}(i_0, i) \geq 0$, and $r = (1 - \text{tr}_{p,t}) * r_{p,t}$ if $\text{PVB}_{p,t+1}(i_0, i) < 0$.

Here $i$ is chosen to be $r_{p,t}$ + OAS if the discounting is to be done as a spread-to-Treasuries or OAY if a level discount rate is desired. This formula may be summarized as:

$$\text{OAVDE}(i_0, i) = \sum_{p=1}^{P} \text{prb}_p * \text{PVB}_{p,1}(i). \tag{17}$$

In formula (17), if the prior PVB term is negative, then the discount rate used is $r = (1 - \text{tr}_{p,t}) * r_{p,t}$, which is consistent with option pricing. This only arises if multiple shareholder investments occur that cause a present value balance to become negative. It is assumed that the insurance enterprise either has other profitable projects or sufficient retained earnings (which could be paid to shareholders) so that the firm can cover a negative PVB. The insurance enterprise will have to earn the amount needed on a pretax basis to cover the negative PVB and the amount of tax due. This is most easily done by tax-effecting the risk-free rate. This is equivalent to discounting the negative PVB grossed up to account for the tax due at the risk-free rate.

The use of arbitrage free paths is important for several reasons. First, as already noted, the paths must provide for the consistent relative valuation of security prices at the valuation date and, in general, the same will be required at each point in time along each path. Second, it provides for valuing OAVDE consistently relative to fixed income securities. Third, it provides for consistent relative valuation of OAVDE over time to prior values of OAVDE. Fourth, if non arbitrage free paths are used, it is possible to misidentify an investment or disinvestment strategy as being favorable when it may not really be so because it has actually identified an arbitrage.

The results of the computations may be interpreted as follows. If an investor pays OAVDE for the insurance enterprise, the OAS represents the option adjusted spread-over-Treasuries that he or she expects to earn. OAY is interpreted similarly. Alternatively, if an investor desires a return of OAS over Treasuries or a level OAY, the OAVDE is the fair value or intrinsic value that he or she should pay. This also applies to issuing a new block of business. The OAVDE computation must be adjusted for the associated federal income tax implications if the assumption of a block is being considered.

### Evaluation of alternative strategies

A liability, crediting, investment or disinvestment strategy is defined to be a management plan of action with regard to liability design and management, crediting rates, investment (including any hedges) or a disinvestment, respectively. A block of business requires the insurance enterprise to choose a management plan for each of the four items. Define a strategy as a management plan of action that consists of one each of strategies for liability design/management, crediting, investment and disinvestment.

For $s = 1, ..., S$, let $s$ represent a distinct strategy. Taken together they represent a universe of possible management plans of action for the block of business. The following describes a method to evaluate these alternative strategies. Let $DE_{p,t,s}$ be the distributable earnings resulting at time $t$, on path $p$ following strategy $s$.

Define the resulting OAVDE value obtained for strategy $s$ by:

$$OAVDE(i_0, OAS, s) = \sum_{p=1}^{P} prb_p * \left\{ \sum_{t=1}^{N} \left[ DE_{p,t,s} \bigg/ \prod_{j=0}^{t-1} (1 + r_{p,j} + OAS) \right] \right\}. \quad (18)$$

For the generalized net present value algorithm the formula is:

$$OAVDE(i_0, i, s) = \sum_{p=1}^{P} prb_p * PVB_{p,1,s}(i). \quad (19)$$

Recall that $i$ means either discounting at $r_{p,t} + OAS$ or at OAY. For either equation (18) or (19) the OAS or OAY, respectively will depend on $s$.

To evaluate alternative strategies one can compare the following results for each strategy.
- the OAS, the spreads by path and their distribution, if given the initial distributable earnings amount for new business or price for an existing block;

- the OAY, the yields by path and their distribution, if given the initial distributable earnings amount for new business or price for an existing block;
- the OAVDE, present values of distributive earnings and their distributions, if given a specific spread to the risk-free rates, the cost of capital or other hurdle rate;
- a mean variance diagram of any of the quantities, e.g. mean spread versus the standard deviation of spreads, mean yield versus standard deviation of yield, mean present value of distributable earnings versus the standard deviation of distributable earnings;
- the risk adjusted value for OAVDE computed using an exponential utility function;
- cumulative distribution functions which display the distribution of any of the profit parameters, e.g. spread, yield, present value of distributable earnings.

Examples of these are provided in the next section.

### The insurance enterprise as a giant CMO

The difficulty of understanding the use of statutory accounting in computing the fair value of an insurance enterprise may be eased if one thinks of an insurance enterprise as a giant CMO. This analogy can be described in the following manner. A CMO is composed of underlying collateral with associated cash flows and tranche rules which determine how owners of tranches are paid. For an insurance enterprise, the underlying collateral consists of net effects of the asset cash flows and the liability cash flows. The tranche rules consist of statutory accounting constraints, tax accounting constraints and the insurance enterprise's desired level of risk based capital. There is only one tranche and that tranche's cash flows are the distributable earnings. The analogy is not as complex as the actual situation as the tranche rules impact additional cash flows, e.g. federal income tax and shareholder dividends, for which provision must be made. Figure 4, assists in understanding the influence of the actions taken by various parties within the operation of an insurance enterprise. It relates the results of the actions to distributable earnings.

## ILLUSTRATIONS OF OAVDE

### Introduction

This section will present five examples analyzed by the OAVDE methodology. In these examples the presentation uses the techniques developed in the previous section.

The value of the firm 247

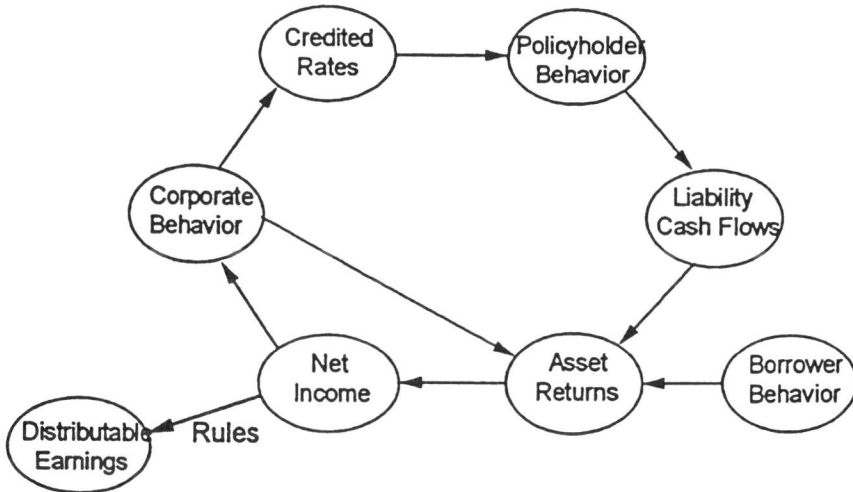

*Figure 4.* Insurance company flow diagram.

*Evaluation of investment strategies*

For simplicity, this example assumes that three of the four components of the strategy have been chosen. Those three are: the liability design, the crediting rate strategy and the disinvestment strategy. The only component allowed to vary is the investment strategy. The goal will be to choose the best investment strategy from a set of five choices. These choices are meant to be illustrative only.

The liability is a single premium deferred annuity. It provides for surrender at book value less a surrender charge that grades off over the first seven years. It has a minimum guaranteed crediting rate of 4%. The interest crediting strategy is the portfolio rate less a spread. The current rate is guaranteed for one year at a time and then reset. The disinvestment strategy is to liquidate assets. The interest margin or spread is set so that with a flat yield curve (deterministic pricing) the internal rate of return on distributable earnings is 15%. This spread represents that needed for the insurance enterprise to recover its investment in the block of annuities, maintenance expenses, commissions, benefits and cost of capital it must hold in doing so at a profit of 15%. (See Appendix A for more information about deterministic pricing.)

The investments will be limited to noncallable, default free bonds. There are no embedded options in the investments. Thus, any resulting financial impacts to the insurance enterprise can only result from the policyholders exercising the option to surrender at book value and any effects of the 4% minimum crediting rate guarantee. Five investment strategies will be examined. These strategies are followed consistently at any point where positive cash flow is to be invested. They are: invest long (IL) in 25 year bonds; invest in assets having a duration at purchase of 4.6 (TDP for target duration of purchase); invest in a ladder (L3/15) of 3 to 15 year bonds in fixed proportion; invest as closely as possible to maintain a portfolio duration of 3 (PD3); and invest as closely as possible to maintain a portfolio duration of 5 (PD5). The March 31, 1994 yield curve was used. The initial distributable earnings is covered by the insurance enterprise. Figure 5 displays the spreads and the OAS that the block of annuities returns to the insurance enterprise. This graph indicates that for each investment strategy the distribution of spreads about the mean is negatively skewed (data farther away from the mean negatively than either positively or equally distributed) with positive kurtosis (data clustered about the mean more so than for a normal distribution, but with longer tails than a normal). That means that for each strategy there is more downside risk than upside potential, that financial results tend to cluster about the mean more often than they would if normally distributed, but large (negative) deviations occur more frequently than would be expected with a normal distribution. This is typical for interest rate risk. This also implies that pricing products with a flat yield curve (deterministic pricing) provides results that are optimistic. The graph shows that the ladder is the best performing strategy. It has the highest OAS and mean spread, the smallest range and the highest minimum over all paths. Investing long has almost the lowest OAS, but has the largest range and the lowest spread of any of the strategies. The OAS differs from the mean spread in that the OAS is the spread that solves the equation over all paths simultaneously. The mean spread is the probability weighted algebraic mean of the spreads of the individual paths.

Table 1 below displays some of the statistical measures that can be computed from the projections. The statistics are computed for the spread-to-Treasuries variable and are shown for the invest long and ladder investment strategies. Similar statistics can be computed for any of the other measures described in

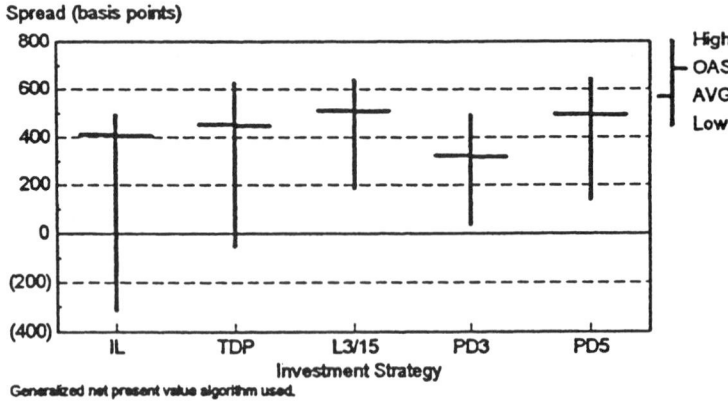

*Figure 5.* Option adjusted spreads: distribution of spreads.

# The value of the firm 249

Table 1 Statistics for spread-to-treasuries (basis points) random variable

| Strategy | OAS | Min | Mean | Max | Std. Dev. | Skewness | Kurtosis |
|---|---|---|---|---|---|---|---|
| Invest Long | 407 | −312 | 412 | 492 | 167 | −2.92 | 11.37 |
| Ladder | 510 | 187 | 512 | 636 | 97 | −1.37 | 4.72 |

this paper. Note that the skewness and kurtosis values are standardized so that values outside the range of ±2 would indicate rejection of the hypothesis that the variable in question is normally distributed.

Figure 6 presents the distributions of yield. Again, the distributions are not normal. The strategy with the best characteristics is again that of the ladder. For the ladder the option adjusted yield is 12%. The yield on a deterministic pricing basis was 15%. Therefore, deterministic pricing overstated the yield by 3%. This is a relative error of 25%. Not all relationships remain constant when comparing spreads and yields. The comments regarding the relationship of the OAS to the mean spread apply analogously to the OAY and the mean yield.

Figures 7 and 8 present the distributions of present values of distributable earnings at the risk-free rates and cost of capital, respectively. For the examples in this section the cost of capital is assumed to be 12%. These results are

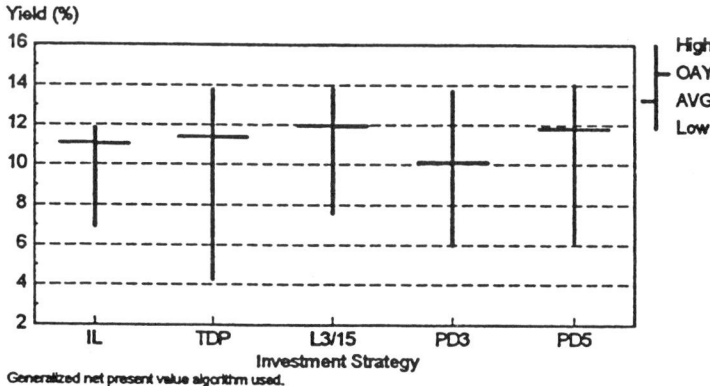

Figure 6. Option adjusted yield: distribution of yield

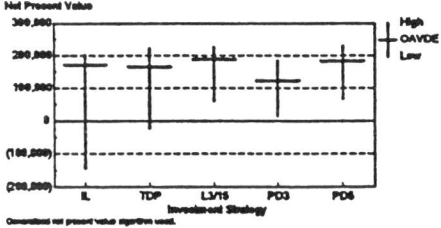

Figure 7. Option adjusted value of distributable earnings: present value at RFR.

250  D.N. Becker

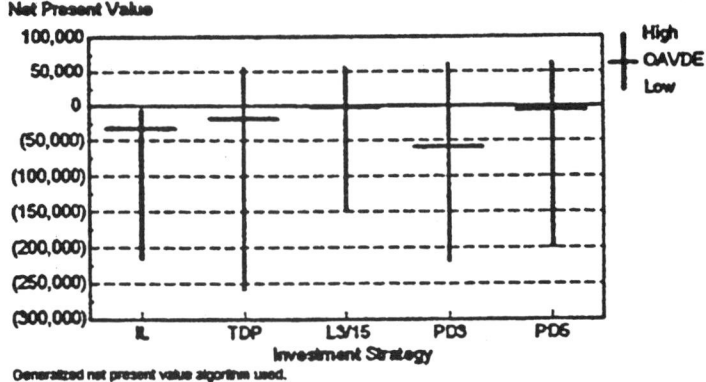

*Figure 8.* Option adjusted value of distributable earnings: present value at cost of capital.

consistent with the graphs for spreads and yields. The OAVDE at the cost of capital for the ladder is at zero. This is consistent with the OAY of the ladder being 12%.

These results can also be analyzed by using a mean/variance diagram. In this case the vertical axis represents the mean of the spread and the horizontal axis the standard deviation of the spread. Figure 9 compares the results of the five strategies in the mean/variance diagram. Again the ladder is the best choice. The invest long strategy has the worst trade off between risk and return. There is some risk in using this diagram. First, the user must make an intuitive trade off between risk and return. Second, the use of variance (standard deviation) as an adequate proxy for downside risk is only valid if the return distribution is normal or if the investor's utility function is quadratic (see Markowitz, 1959).

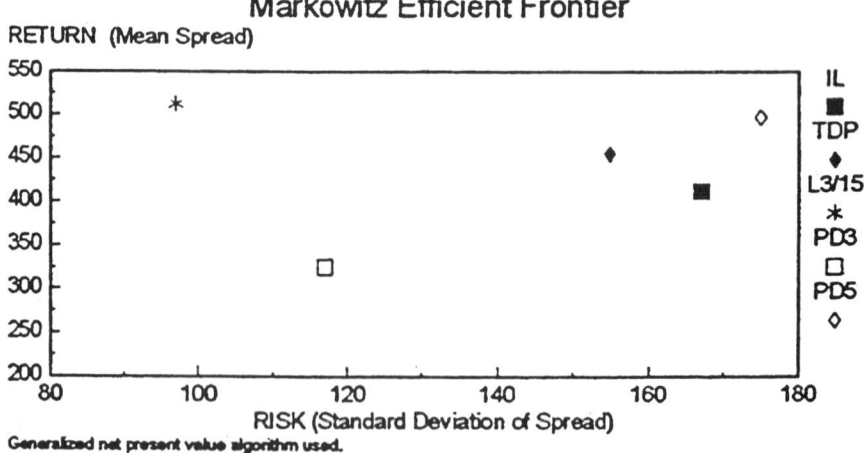

*Figure 9.* Risk/return diagram: mean/variance criteria.

Quadratic utility functions are difficult to defend and the distribution of results differs substantially from a normal distribution. Third, the method only uses the first two moments of the distribution Caution in using this type of diagram for these problems is warranted.

Another method of comparing many strategies is the concept of risk adjusted value (RAV) described by Cozzolino (1979). The method uses an exponential utility function and requires an estimate of the insurance enterprise's or product manager's aversion to risk. But once done, this method linearly rank orders all of the strategies. This method uses all moments of the distribution; thus no important information is omitted and there is no need to make intuitive trade offs. Figure 10 shows the results for the five investment strategies at two discount rates, the risk-free rate and the cost of capital. No matter which discount basis is chosen, the best strategy is the ladder.

A final method of comparison is to graph the cumulative distribution function of a given statistic for each strategy. One can analyze the percentage of paths for which outcomes are greater than a prespecified comfort level. This method may be preferred if there is difficulty in reaching a consensus about the insurance enterprise's risk aversion factor and/or the insurance enterprise is interested in controlling the behavior near the tails of the distribution. Additional insight can be gained by overlaying the graphs on one another. As an example, Figure 11 shows the cumulative distribution function (CDF) for the yield by path for both the invest long and ladder strategies. The CDF for the ladder strategy everywhere outperforms the CDF for the invest long.

Do the results attributable to the ladder strategy depend on the slope and steepness of the initial term structure, which was steeply increasing? Additional tests were done with shallow positively sloped, shallow negatively sloped and steeply negatively sloped term structures. The results are shown in Figure 12. Instead of the raw data, the table has been scaled so that 100 represents a base line for the ladder strategy and other results are multiples of it. The slope and steepness of the term structure is denoted by '+' and '−' signs and the number of repetitions of the sign. The robustness of the ladder strategy is clear. The figure also includes data on the market value of liabilities. These market values were computed on the same basis as the OAVDE values. The spread used for

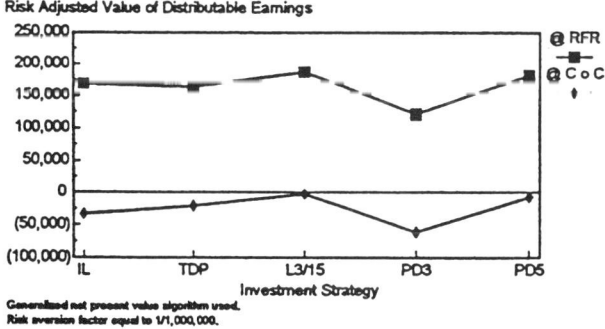

*Figure 10.* Risk adjusted value: risk certainty equivalent.

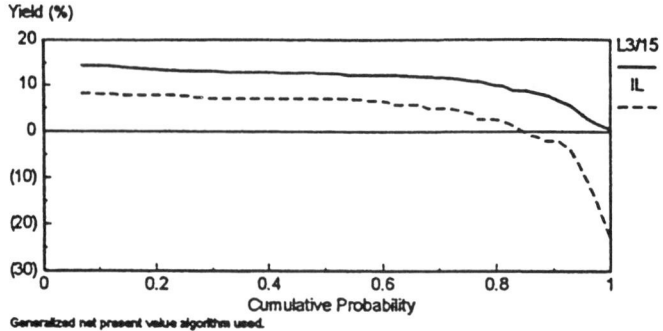

*Figure 11.* Cumulative probability distribution yield on distributable earnings.

## OAVDE and MVL
### @ Risk Free Rate

|  |  | IL | TDP | L3/15 | PD3 | PD5 |
|---|---|---|---|---|---|---|
| O A V D E | +++ | 83 | 82 | 100 | 72 | 96 |
|  | + | 103 | 89 | 113 | 81 | 104 |
|  | - | 215 | 77 | 153 | 164 | 115 |
|  | — | 216 | 39 | 139 | 131 | 99 |
| M V L | +++ | 104 | 99 | 100 | 99 | 99 |
|  | + | 103 | 99 | 98 | 98 | 99 |
|  | - | 102 | 100 | 101 | 100 | 100 |
|  | — | 103 | 102 | 102 | 103 | 102 |

Generalized net present value algorithm used.

*Figure 12.* Relative comparison of investment stratagies and initial yield curves: OAVDE and MVL.

discounting the distributable earnings and the liability cash flows was zero, i.e. discounting was performed at the risk-free rates. These results persisted even for parallel shifts in the term structure.

A test was performed with a slightly different ladder strategy. The new ladder (L2/10) involved bonds with maturities from 2–10 years, instead of the 3–15 years. The results for spreads and yield are shown in Figures 13 and 14, respectively. Differences are not large.

These results are a function of all the assumptions for the liability, the crediting strategy, the disinvestment strategy, the investment strategy and, especially, the policyholder behavior assumption. The universe of assets consisted of noncallable bonds. If the universe of investments had been larger to include callable bonds, sinking funds, mortgage pass-throughs, CMOs, mortgages, etc. then the results could have been entirely different. This example is for illustration only.

*The value of the firm* 253

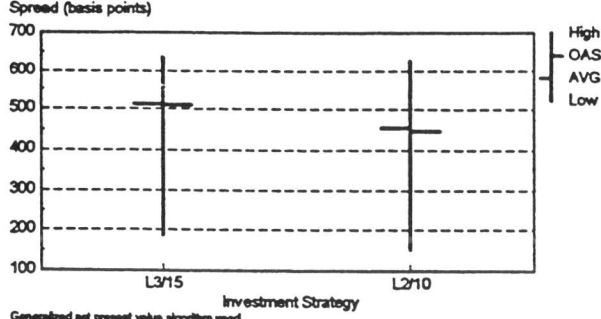

*Figure 13.* Option adjusted spread: distribution of spreads.

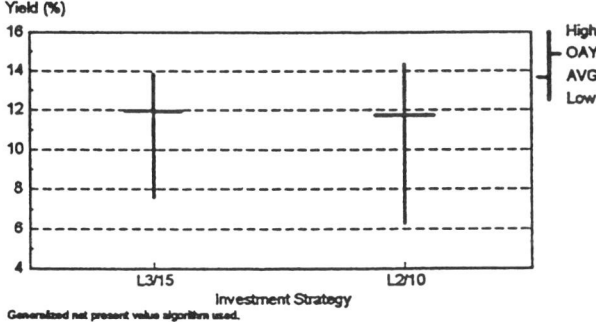

*Figure 14.* Option adjusted yield: distribution of yields.

## Evaluation of liability design

The second example focuses on liability design. This determines the costs to the insurance enterprise to provide additional liability options. In this example the crediting strategy is the portfolio rate less a spread, the investment strategy is the ladder of 2–10 year bonds (L2/10) and the disinvestment strategy is to liquidate assets. The only strategy allowed to vary is the liability design.

The first liability is the simple single premium deferred annuity with a 4% guaranteed minimum crediting rate. It is denoted in the following figures as 4. The second liability is the above annuity with a return of premium (ROP) feature which places a floor on the cash surrender value equal to the premium paid. This annuity has a slightly higher deterministic spread as a result of having to hold a higher reserve and risk based capital level than the simple annuity. The return of premium feature eliminates taking credit for the full surrender charge during the time the return feature is effective. A return of premium feature is a limited duration option as once the interest credited exceeds the surrender charge there is no value to the option. Note that the extra margin does not represent the full cost of the option; it only represents the cost of holding additional capital. The third liability is the simple annuity above but with a bail out feature (BO) that allows the policyholder to surrender without surrender charge if the credited rate ever drops more than 1% below the initial credited rate. It is also an option with life limited to the surrender charge period. Again the interest margin was adjusted to reflect the fact that if the annuity has a bail out feature, then the reserve must be the account value and the margin must be increased to return the deterministic profit back to 15%. The fourth liability is the simple annuity above but with a temporary interest rate guarantee of 6% for the first 5 years and 4% thereafter (6/4).

Figure 15 shows the spreads for the four liability designs. Figure 16 shows the yields for the four liability designs. As in the first example the distributions of spreads and yields are non normal with negative skewness and positive kurtosis. There is a small reduction in OAS for the ROP, but considerable reductions for the BO and 6/4. The same situation holds for OAY.

Table 2 shows the loss in yields and spreads that occurs if the extra liability features are added to the base case annuity. Figure 17 shows the risk adjusted values for the four annuity designs. The results of this graph are consistent with those of the graphs for spreads and yields.

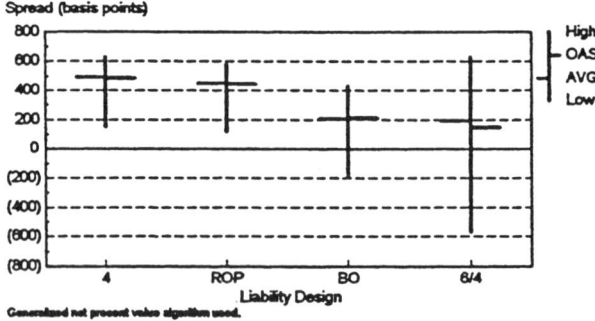

*Figure 15.* Comparison of liability designs: spread analysis.

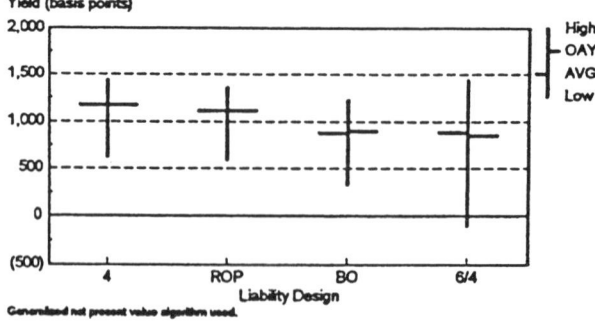

*Figure 16.* Comparison of liability designs: yield analysis.

The value of the firm 255

Table 2. Loss of OAY/OAS on OAVDE due to liability options

|  | OAY | OAS |
|---|---|---|
| 4 | 0 | 0 |
| ROP | (63) | (42) |
| 6/4 | (323) | (338) |
| BO | (278) | (274) |

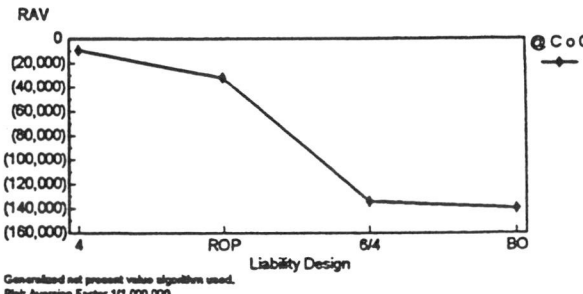

Figure 17. Comparison of liability designs: risk adjusted value.

Figure 18 shows the OAVDE results for the four designs if plus and minus 100 basis point shifts in the term structure occur. OAVDE is the fair value of the blocks of annuities. This graph demonstrates their relative value and how much that value can change due to instantaneous shifts in the term structure. The ROP annuity has almost the same characteristics as the base case. If interest rates rise, its value is just slightly higher than for the base case as the cost of the ROP option is reduced and the ROP has a higher margin.

For the BO and 6/4 annuities the OAVDEs, like that for the ROP, rise for the upward shift, but by a much larger amount. This is due to the fact that if rates shocked upwards, the value of the bail out option and the temporary interest rate guarantee would diminish considerably. The bail out, having an additional margin, also elevates the value of OAVDE. The 6/4 annuity does not have any additional margin, but it also carries no extra reserve or required

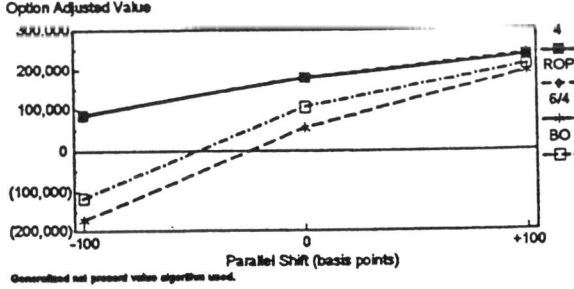

Figure 18. Comparison of liability designs: OAVDE at risk free rate.

256  D.N. Becker

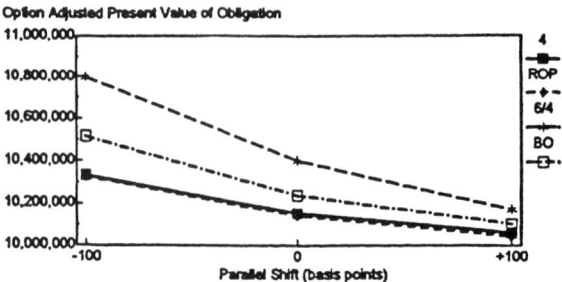

*Figure 19.* Comparison of liability designs: market value of liabilities at risk free rates.

surplus. For a downward shift, however, the values of OAVDE fall materially as each option becomes ever more valuable. Figure 19 shows the market value of liabilities for the four products. Both the distributable earnings for OAVDE and the liability cash flows are discounted at the risk-free rate, i.e. a zero spread-to-Treasuries. The market value results are consistent with what would be expected.

*Evaluation of hedge strategies*

OAVDE analysis can be used to identify an optimal hedging strategy. If there are a number of hedge strategies that have acceptable market values of surplus, the optimal strategy can be found by applying OAVDE analysis to them. One can then choose the best one based upon the criteria described and demonstrated above.

This example consists of a large block of single premium deferred annuities. The annuities are straight forward in design with a 4% minimum interest rate guarantee and no other features. The interest crediting rate follows a portfolio strategy. Disinvestment consists of borrowing short. The assets supporting the block consist of noncallable bonds, sinking funds, mortgages, mortgage pass-throughs and CMOs.

Management is considering four courses of action. The base case is to do nothing. Option 1 is to buy interest rate caps as 'interest rate insurance' for the insurance enterprise, i.e. the shareholders. The idea is that since the insurance enterprise sold the put option to the annuity policyholders, it will hedge that risk by buying interest rate caps. The caps are designed with strike levels that will only pay off for a run up in interest rates of 200 to 300 basis points. This is stop-loss interest rate risk insurance. The annuities' prior interest margin is increased by the amount needed to repay the cost of purchasing the caps at the insurance enterprise's cost of capital. If the caps pay off, the cap income goes to the benefit of the shareholders.

Option 2 is to buy a program of interest rate caps as 'interest rate insurance' for the policyholders. The same cap structure is used. The caps and the income from the caps are included in the asset portfolio supporting the annuities. The company takes its regular margin plus an increment to cover the cost of the caps from the portfolio.

Option 3 is to self insure, i.e. raise the margin but do not buy the caps. The extra profit accrues to the shareholders via higher distributable earnings. This is analogous to not buying automobile insurance and putting aside what it would have cost to protect against an accident.

Figure 20 shows the results on OAVDE for the initial term structure and instantaneous parallel shifts of $\pm 100$ and $\pm 200$ basis points. Here the OAVDE values are computed at the insurance enterprise's cost of capital. Note that a new option pricing projection is performed for each shift in the term structure.

As can be seen from Figure 20, the OAVDE of the block declines if interest rates rise and rises if interest rates fall. Option 3, self insure, has greater OAVDE values than the base case as it has a higher margin. Note that all the options have a higher value of OAVDE at the 0 basis point shift. This is due to the fact that the extra margin to cover the caps was deducted for the entire length of the projection and its present value exceeded the cost of purchasing the caps on the valuation date.

Option 2 presents an interesting situation. It would appear that it is better to 'share the wealth' of the caps as the profits in this case exceed those of Option 1 until $+200$ basis points. It might be thought that the extra income is derived from keeping policyholders with the insurance enterprise and that is the source of the extra OAVDE. In fact, that is not the case. What is happening is that for $-200$ bp, $-100$ bp, 0 bp and $+100$ bp the impact of the caps on the portfolio rate effectively increases the insurance enterprise's margin. To see this consider the 0 basis point shift. The caps are purchased and the margin increased to cover the caps. Now compare the asset portfolios under Option 1 and Option 2 that support the liabilities. The asset portfolio in Option 2 is larger as it contains the book value of the caps. On many of the paths emanating from the initial term structure, i.e. the 0 bp shift, the caps do not pay off as they have high strike levels. On these paths the investment income for Option 2

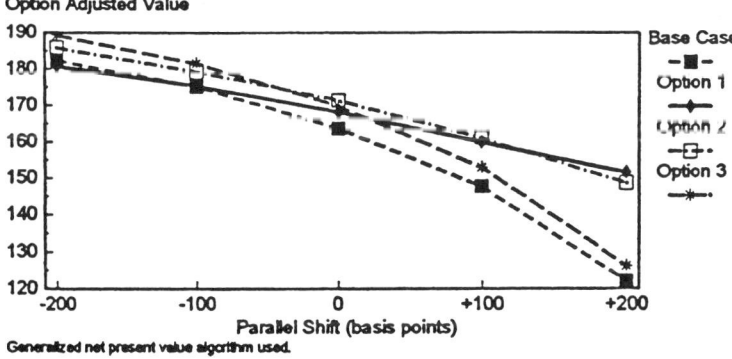

*Figure 20.* Portfolio hedge: OAVDE at cost of capital.

is less than for Option 1 as the investment income from the caps is negative due to the drop in book value over time. Thus the portfolio rate calculated for Option 2 is less than that for Option 1. In addition, the insurance enterprise takes its margin. So the effective margin for Option 2 is higher than for Option 1.

Once the interest rates have shifted upward enough the caps begin to pay off with sufficient frequency that there is a positive impact in the portfolio rate and the cap income does go to the policyholders. That is why the OAVDE for Option 2 is lower than for Option 1 at +200 basis point shift, but it is less effective for protecting the net worth (OAVDE) of the insurance enterprise. Thus Option 1 is the best hedge strategy against rising interest rates.

Figure 21 shows the results for the market value of surplus where the market value of liabilities is discounted at the risk-free rate. A deterministic appraisal of this block of business at the insurance enterprise's cost of capital produces a value of $185 million. The OAVDE at the cost of capital is $165 million. Thus, if a buyer paid $185 for the block of business, the or she would have overpaid by $20 million if they managed the business using the base case strategy. The impact of the embedded options in assets and the liabilities reduced the value of the deterministic appraisal by the $20 million.

Since OAVDE is the fair value of the insurance enterprise, it is possible to compute a duration and convexity for it. These are the numerical measures which capture the behavior of the 'price curve' of OAVDE from instantaneous parallel shifts in the term structure. Tables 3 and 4 show duration and convexity for both OAVDE and the market value of surplus at the 0 basis point shift and at the +100 basis point shift, respectively. Numerically the goal of the hedge strategy would be to reduce the duration and maximize the convexity of OAVDE. As can be seen, Option 1 achieves both of these in comparison with either the base case or the other options.

Figure 22 displays the distribution of present values of distributable earnings for each of the strategies using the initial term structure. Note the closeness of the ranges of the results for Option 1 and Option 2. Without consideration of

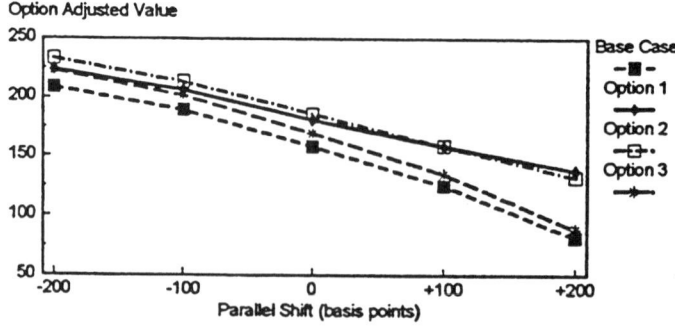

*Figure 21.* Portfolio hedge: OAV of surplus.

*Table 3.* Portfolio hedge at basis point shift

|  | OAVDE (12%) |  | OAV of surplus |  |
|---|---|---|---|---|
|  | Duration | Convexity | Duration | Convexity |
| Base case | 8.4 | (280.6) | 20.3 | (113.1) |
| Option 1 | 4.6 | (63.6) | 13.3 | 191.3 |
| Option 2 | 5.3 | (129.0) | 14.5 | 69.3 |
| Option 3 | 8.4 | (308.2) | 19.8 | (104.4) |

*Table 4.* Portfolio hedge at +100 basis point shift

|  | OAVDE (CoC) |  | OAV of surplus |  |
|---|---|---|---|---|
|  | Duration | Convexity | Duration | Convexity |
| Base case | 12.7 | (645.6) | 24.1 | (819.2) |
| Option 1 | 4.9 | (8.4) | 11.9 | 107.2 |
| Option 2 | 6.6 | (142.6) | 14.4 | (56.9) |
| Option 3 | 12.9 | (639.3) | 23.8 | (857.7) |

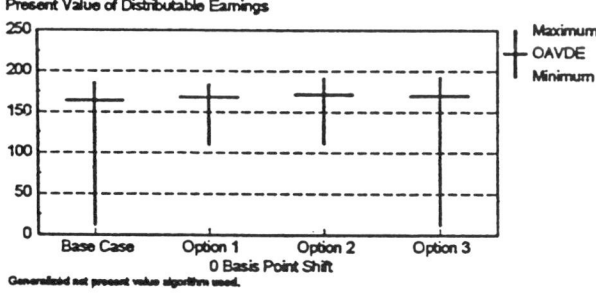

*Figure 22.* Portfolio hedge: distribution of present value.

the shifts in interest rates one could not discern all the impacts of each of the two strategies. Figure 23 displays the distribution of present values of distributable earnings for Option 1 under the initial term structure and parallel shifts of ׀ 100 and ׀ 200 basis points. The horizontal bar denoting the average value is the OAVDE value. The OAVDE gradually falls as the level of rates rise and the range of the distribution widens as the level of rates rise.

In this example the duration and convexity of OAVDE was computed. A situation that can arise with the market value of surplus approach is that atypical values for the duration and convexity for the market value of surplus occur for new blocks of universal life. Depending on the liability design these values can be either extremely positive or even negative. This is often explained away by noting that it is not unusual in the asset market for derivatives to have extremely positive durations or negative durations. This explanation is

260  D.N. Becker

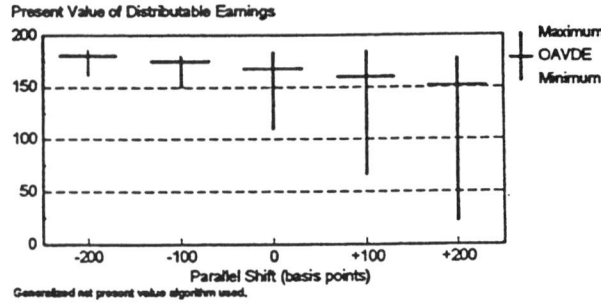

*Figure 23.* Portfolio hedge: distribution of present values (option 1).

strained when applied in this case. It is not likely that people would view universal life insurance as being a 'derivative' liability. This situation is not limited to universal life but applies to participating and nonparticipating life, disability income and long term care insurance. It has to do with the liability design (level premium), the level of acquisition costs, and increasing magnitude of benefit payments over time. The application of the market value of surplus as defined does not work well for all liabilities. OAVDE works equally well for all products.

*Portfolio restructure*

For this example the liabilities consist of a combination of GICs and terminal funded annuities. They are managed together as a single entity. The assets supporting the liabilities consist of noncallable bonds, sinking funds, mortgages and CMOs. Generally, the management strategy has been to cash match for some period and duration match the rest. It is noticed that the existing structure has downside risk to the OAVDE of the block if rates rise. Due to the nature of the liabilities one can not take any management action regarding them. The current structure of the asset portfolio, however, can be changed. Figures 24

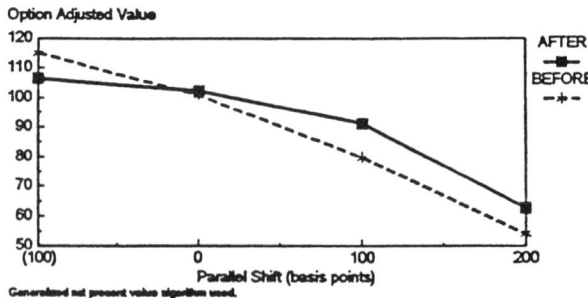

*Figure 24.* Portfolio restructure: OAVDE at cost of capital.

*The value of the firm* 261

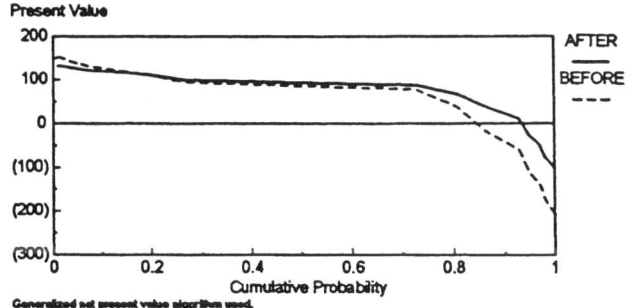

*Figure 25.* Portfolio restructure: cumulative distribution of PV of distributable earnings at +200 basic point shift.

and 25 demonstrate how OAVDE can be used to test asset portfolio restructures.

Figure 24 demonstrates how OAVDE was used to validate the results of portfolio restructures. There is a major improvement in the value of the block after the restructure for positive shifts in the term structure. There was, however, a decline for a negative shift. This was to be expected in the trade off. Figure 25 shows the cumulative distribution function for the present value of distributable earnings by path for both before the restructure and after. There is some sacrifice in value at the high end with relatively small probability in return for superior values over the greater range of the paths.

*Hedge trade-offs*

This example focuses on the evaluation of trade-offs that can arise from different hedge strategies. The liability is a block of single premium deferred annuities with an initial surrender charge of 7% grading to zero by year eight. The crediting strategy is an asymmetric strategy that is independent of the portfolio earned rate. The strategy follows market interest rates down quickly, but lags market rates on the way up. The baseline investment strategy is to invest in five year noncallable A rated bonds. The disinvestment strategy is to borrow at 100 basis points (bp) over the 90 day Treasury bill. The liability spread for the annuities is 75 bp and the distributable earnings are valued at 300 bp over Treasuries.

The block of $100 million in deposits is received and invested as of August 1, 1995. Figure 26 shows the market values of surplus and the OAVDE values for the block as of September 1, 1995 for the then current yield curve and for parallel shifts of ±100, ±200, +300 and +400 bp. As is seen, there is significant interest rate risk and loss in value of the block from rising rates.

The first alternative (SWAP) is to hedge the risk by implementing a synthetic swap. The insurance enterprise sells a seven year callable bond (no call protec-

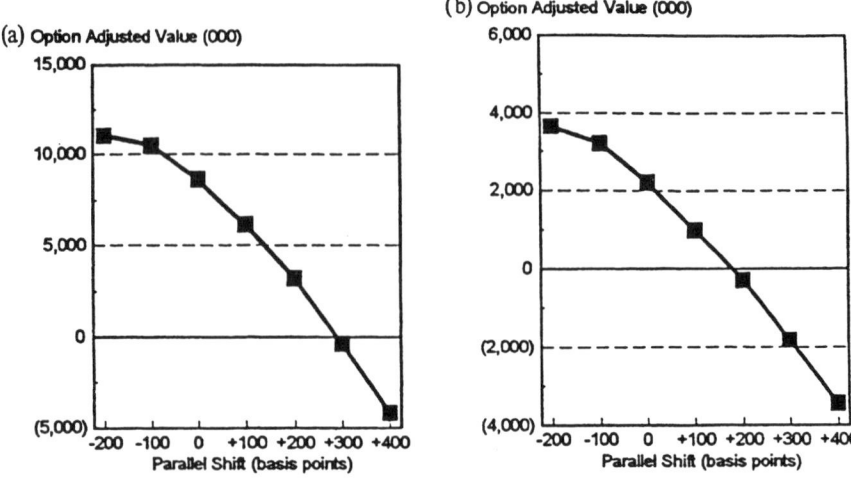

*Figure 26.* OAV of surplus (a) and distributable earnings (b).

tion period) and uses the proceeds to purchase a floating rate note that pays 6-month LIBOR. The second alternative (CAP) is to use a 10-year interest rate cap whose notional amount is $95 million and rate index is the five year constant maturity Treasury with a strike level of 8%. The market values of surplus for the base case and the two alternatives are shown in Figure 27; the OAVDE values for the same are shown in Figure 28. An examination of the these two figures shows that either hedge significantly improves both the value of the block (OAVDE) and the market value of surplus. For either measure the flattening of the two curves demonstrates the trade-off between reduced performance if rates drop and improved performance if rates increase. The SWAP nicely flattens the OAVDE curve (thus immunizing OAVDE); but the surplus curve begins to fall at the +200 bp shift and above. The CAP results in a flat surplus curve out to +400 bp; but the OAVDE curve underperforms

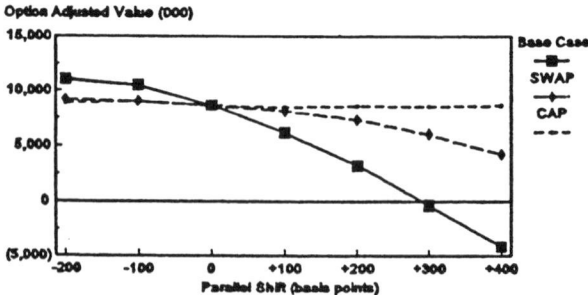

*Figure 27.* OAV of surplus.

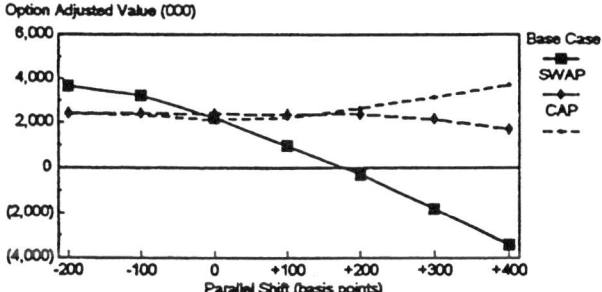

*Figure 28.* OAV of distributable earnings.

the SWAP if rates do not rise more than about 125 to 200 bp. If rates rise more than 200 bp, then the CAP materially outperforms the SWAP in OAVDE.

From a pure risk control perspective the CAP would be the choice as the diminished performance below shifts of less than +125 bp does not seem as significant as the gain from shifts greater than +125 bp. Recall that these graphs are based on instantaneous shifts in the yield curve. The graphs do not indicate the relative likelihood of such shifts occurring; they only indicate the results if they did occur. Empirical studies based on the forty year period from 1955 through 1994 show that the frequency of 200, 300 and 400 bp increases in the 90 day Treasury bill over a period of a year are 12.8%, 4.9% and 2.1%, respectively. The frequencies for the longer maturities are less than these. (The frequencies for similar increases over a 2-year period are 21.1%, 10.9% and 8.1%, respectively; but the insurance enterprise has considerable time to adjust its position.) It should be noted that the frequencies above are only driven to these levels by the experience in 1978 to 1981. In this light it is fair to ask if the reduction in value from the use of the cap is offset by the increased protection afforded by the cap against an event which may occur with a frequency less than 13%.

Examining the shapes of the curves in Figures 27 and 28 one concludes that the SWAP is effective for medium shifts in the yield curve and the CAP is effective at the extreme upward shifts, but penalizes the insurance enterprise for intermediate shifts. Is it possible that one could combine the two hedge concepts and arrive at a better overall result? Consider the hedge SCAP where the SWAP is combined with the above cap at a $25 million notional amount. The results are shown in Figures 29 and 30.

SCAP produces a market value of surplus curve almost identical to that of CAP and an OAVDE curve superior to either SWAP or CAP for the initial yield curve and all upward shifts with only a modest concession for downward shifts. Thus SCAP is superior to either of the other two hedges. It is important to note that the superiority of SCAP would not be apparent from examining just the market value of surplus diagrams. In fact, CAP would have been chosen if the only criteria had been surplus. The choice of the proper metric is

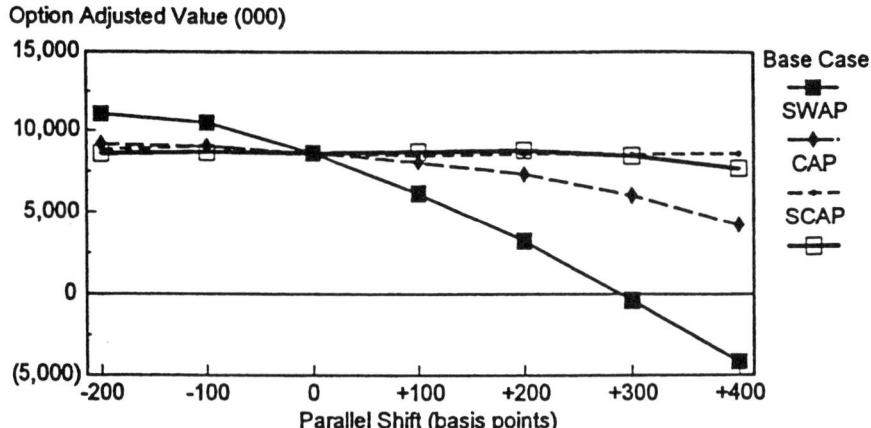

*Figure 29.* OAV of surplus.

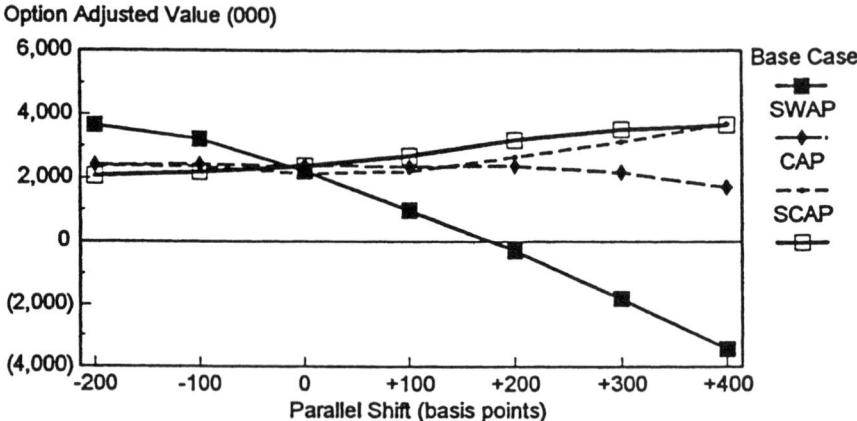

*Figure 30.* OAV of distributable earnings.

important. The "OAVDE" metric captures elements of economic reality, i.e. the free cash flows of the firm, that the "market value of surplus" metric does not.

## APPLICATION OF OAVDE

### General applications

As seen in the previous section, OAVDE can be used to identify and quantify interest rate risk. It can be used to evaluate different strategies, and so discover strategies that optimize the risk/return posture of the block of business or the company as a whole. There are other risks that are stochastic in nature, e.g.

asset default, mortality, morbidity, term conversion and lapsation, but are traditionally treated as deterministic. The OAVDE model can be enhanced to reflect the stochastic nature of these other risks. Specific recognition of AIDS or random fluctuations in mortality due to epidemics can be modeled. Also, not all of these risks are independent, e.g. mortality and lapse. It is possible to incorporate these risks as random variables and incorporate the user's perception about the correlation between higher rates of lapse and the resulting higher mortality among the persister group (Becker, 1984; Becker and Kitsos, 1984; Dukes and MacDonald, 1980; Shapiro and Snyder, 1988). This has the added utility of adequately reflecting the fact that if increases in interest rates cause higher interest-sensitive lapses then the model reflects higher mortality among the persisters.

With regard to morbidity in disability income products there is significant historical experience that during recessions disability incidence rates increase and termination rates decrease. The opposite occurs during economic recoveries. If it were possible to correlate economic states with the pattern of change in the interest rate environment, then one could model dynamic incidence and termination rates implied by the change in interest rates.

As regulators and rating agencies become more comfortable with this more sophisticated financial projection methodology it is possible that hedging, whether it be through investment strategy, liability strategy or reinsurance strategy, will allow the insurance enterprise to hold less risk based capital.

A special case of this methodology can be used to determine economically sound risk based capital requirements for interest rate risk. Choose a comfort level, e.g. 95%. As of the date of valuation create a set of arbitrage free interest rate paths. For each path $p$ and each $t$, $t = 1$ to $N$, calculate $\text{PVSNI}_{p,t}$, the present value of the statutory net income from $j = 1$ to $j = t$, where the discounting is done at the after-tax risk-free future one period rates along that path. The statutory net incomes are computed on a 'profits released' basis, i.e. they do not include any interest on surplus or retained earnings of the block.

$$\text{PVSNI}_{p,t} = \sum_{j=1}^{t} \left\{ \text{SNI}_{p,j} \bigg/ \prod_{k=0}^{j-1} [1 - \text{tr}_{p,k}] * r_{p,k}] \right\}. \tag{20}$$

Let $\text{RBC}_p$ equal the maximum of the sequence of 0 and the negative of each of the present values above.

$$\text{RBC}_p = \max\{0, -\text{PVSNI}_{p,1}, -\text{PVSNI}_{p,2}, \ldots, -\text{PVSNI}_{p,N}\}. \tag{21}$$

Rank order the $\text{RBC}_p$ from lowest to highest. Choose the value of $p$, $p^{95}$, such that 95% of the values are less than or equal to $\text{RBC}_p^{95}$. The level of risk based capital as a percent of statutory reserves is equal to the ratio of $\text{RBC}_p^{95}$ to the statutory reserve.

$$\text{RBC}_{95} = \text{RBC}_p^{95}/\text{SR}_0. \tag{22}$$

From capital budgeting theory, if a firm has several projects available in which to invest, then the order in which the projects should be pursued is found by ranking the projects in descending order by their net present value or, more accurately, their generalized net present value. Because the OAVDE of a block of business computed using the generalized net present value at the cost of capital is the measure of its fair value or net worth to the shareholders, it is an appropriate device on which to allocate capital to existing lines or to new ventures.

OAVDE analysis can be applied at the insurance enterprise level or at the line of business level. If applied at the enterprise level, the firm can take credit for all offsetting risks that arise from combining all the liabilities and assets. In this way hedging is first performed within the company with any net risk accommodated by either reinsurance or investment vehicles. Although this would be the most efficient approach, it is more likely that management (and external audiences such as regulators and rating agencies) would want each major product line to be self sufficient. When liabilities with offsetting interest rate risk characteristics are combined to take advantage of the offset there is the risk that the balance of the two liabilities may not be able to be maintained into the future. This additional challenge may make management shy away from relying too much on such combinations.

Another facet of this is the explicit use of the ability to sell new liabilities as a tool in risk management. If one can sell new liabilities at an attractive, or at least acceptable, price, then this can be a useful tool in asset/liability management and shareholder wealth maximization. This should be used as a tactical method not a strategic method. There is the risk of becoming a 'new business junkie' whereby the insurance enterprise must acquire the new liability cash income in order to meet other liability cash expense. The continuing ability to do it at favorable terms may not exist.

*Investment strategy and benchmarking*

In Section III the process of evaluating strategies was discussed. At its most basic level, if it is possible to identify a robust strategy, then one can simply follow the associated investment strategy. That investment strategy may not be optimal for each path but it will perform well over the spectrum of paths that can occur. The strategy would be revalidated from time to time and adjusted if necessary.

Another approach is to use the strategy to create a model of the business. One can then take the asset portfolio (built from the generic investments used in the model) that results from the application of the investment strategy and determine its associated cash flow characteristics, e.g. cash flow patterns under different interest rate scenarios, duration, partial or key rate durations, convexity and partial convexities. These parameters can serve as the benchmarks for the real asset portfolio. The portfolio manager can then engage in various techniques that will generate the highest return consistent with the benchmarks. It also allows the portfolio manager to take 'bets' if he or she has a belief as to how the future interest rate environment will move. Experience analyses will show if value was added or lost by the tactical bets. As experience develops the model is updated for the actual liability cash flows. This results in an update of the model asset portfolio which is then used to measure the next set of benchmarks.

If the portfolio manager has made bets and deviated from the investment strategy, the actual current portfolio and investment strategy can be put in the model to see if it produces either an OAVDE of greater or lesser value or an OAVDE having more or less volatility than that from the original investment strategy. If the results are superior, the bets have been good; if poorer, then bad and the portfolio can be restructured. This last step closes the loop to ensure that OAVDE has been optimized. Again the strategy should be revalidated from time to time.

The various immunization techniques described earlier can also be applied to the value of OAVDE. Further, the application of mathematical programming as proposed by Miller et al. (1989) can be used to identify the investment portion of the strategy that results in the optimal values for the spread and/or yield along each path, which process would also result in a robust value of OAVDE.

Does OAVDE optimization imply a buy-and-hold investment strategy or a total return investment strategy? In and of itself the OAVDE methodology says nothing about this. The person performing the financial projections defines the investment strategy that he or she wishes to use within the OAVDE model. Such strategies may be buy-and-hold based or total return based. Choose the one which optimizes OAVDE.

*Option adjusted appraisal values (OAAV)*

The investment income on assets in classic appraisal values of insurance enterprises is computed in one of two ways. The first assumes a constant portfolio net earned rate. The second assumes the yield curve at the date of the appraisal remains constant and projects the book yield on the existing asset portfolio into the future. The resulting book yield together with a reinvestment assumption is used to compute the future statutory earnings. These earnings are then discounted at a hurdle rate. More recently, the actual assets are modeled and an explicit reinvestment assumption is made. Many interest rate scenarios are run and the weighted average of the present values of statutory earnings is computed. While the latter is superior to the classical approach, there are still difficulties with the approach.

Let $i_0$ be given together with a strategy $s$. The corresponding option adjusted appraisal value for a block of business is given by $\text{OAVDE}(i_0, i, s)$ where the OAVDE value is computed at a hurdle rate, $i$, expressed either as a desired option adjusted spread-to-Treasuries or as an option adjusted yield. Let free surplus equal the excess, if positive, of the market value of total capital and surplus and items in the nature of surplus over the required surplus needed to support the liabilities, their associated assets and the assets backing required surplus. The AVR is treated as an item in the nature of surplus except for the excess, if positive, of the AVR over the asset default component of required surplus. Not admitted assets may or not may not be included in free surplus. If the value of a not admitted asset is realizable and such realization is not reflected in the future distributable earnings, then it should be included in free surplus. If its realization is reflected in future distributable earnings, it should not be counted in free surplus.

The OAAV equals the sum of free surplus, the $OAVDE(i_0, i, s)$ of the existing blocks of business and an estimate of the franchise value, or the value of new business. The OAVDE values are computed using the hurdle rate of the evaluator. The franchise or new business value may be omitted or included. The computation of OAVDE for new business beyond that expected in the next period presents a challenge as the value at issue on a future date will depend on the path taken. Attention should be paid to new business as it is possible that the OAVDE of new business could be negative.

For a stock life insurance company it is possible to compute the return (expressed either as an option adjusted spread-to-Treasuries or option adjusted yield) implied by the market using the market value of the stock as of a given date. It would be the value of i that equates the OAAV with the market value of stock.

### Option adjusted value added (OAVA)

For a block of business define its option adjusted value (OAV) at the end of period $t$ after the release of any distributable earnings to be:

$$OAV_t = OAVDE_t. \tag{23}$$

Define the option adjusted income (OAI) for period $t$ as:

$$\begin{aligned} OAI_t &= DE_t + OAVDE_t - OAVDE_{t-1} \\ &= DE_t + \Delta_{t-1}(OAVDE) \\ &= DE_t + \Delta_{t-1}(OAV). \end{aligned} \tag{24}$$

Define the option adjusted value added (OAVA) as:

$$OAVA_t = OAI_t - h*OAV_{t-1}, \tag{25}$$

where $h$ is the insurance enterprise's cost of capital.

If the OAVA is positive for the period, then shareholder value has been added; if negative, then shareholder value has been depleted.

Define the option adjusted total return (OATR) earned by the block as:

$$OATR_t = OAI_t/OAV_{t-1}. \tag{26}$$

If the period over which the OATR is calculated is less than one year, it can be converted into an annualized rate.

Other adjustments can be made to formula (26) to reflect the changing basis of value over the year. Since distributable earnings are received over the course of the year, the following approximates the return for the year:

$$\text{OATR}_t = (2*\text{OAI}_t)/(\text{OAV}_t + \text{OAV}_{t-1} - \text{OAI}_t). \tag{27}$$

If OAV represents the option adjusted value for all product lines and FS represents the market value of free surplus, i.e. those assets not included in the computation of OAV, the enterprise total return is

$$\text{ETR}_t = (\text{OAI}_t + \text{aftertax total return on } \text{FS}_{t-1})/(\text{OAV}_{t-1} + \text{FS}_{t-1}). \tag{28}$$

The OAVA and OAI can be analyzed in the following way:
- external environment:
    change in level and slope of yield curve;
    change in volatility of interest rates;
- internal environment:
    change in investment and/or disinvestment strategy;
    change in crediting rate strategy or liability management strategy;
- new business;
- existing business performance; and
- shareholder dividends paid.

Within this framework it is natural to define the fair or market value of surplus, MVS, of the insurance enterprise as:

$$\text{MVS}_t = \text{FS}_t + \text{OAV}_t. \tag{29}$$

Then it is possible to define the fair or market value of liabilities (MVL) as:

$$\text{MVL}_t = \text{MVA}_t - \text{MVS}_t.$$

The quantity MVL represents all liabilities of the firm, not just those related to the products manufactured by the firm. The market value of product liabilities would be MVL less the non product liabilities. The fair or market value of income is the change in MVS.

This approach would fully implement the mark-to-market of the insurance enterprise via the appraisal method in a manner that correctly reflects the presence of embedded options in the assets and liabilities and on a basis that is comparable between firms and over time if an appropriate discount rate can be found. While this may seem to be a difficult challenge, there are two reasonable approaches. First, McKinsey and Company (1994) has estimated the cost of capital for insurance enterprises manufacturing life insurance, annuities and reinsurance to be from 10.9% to 11.8%. It would be possible to pick an intermediate rate, e.g. 11.5%, and simply define that rate to be used by all insurance enterprises for external reporting. Second, Childs (1994) presents research that suggests a cost of capital for an AA rated firm of 3% to 4% over the AA long bond yield for insurance enterprises. For an insurance enterprise with higher or lower quality, appropriate adjustments would be made. To stabilize the rate from year to year a moving average of long bond rates could be used. In either case, the methodologies used to estimate the cost of capital could be applied periodically to determine if the chosen cost of capital value remains current or if revision is called for.

Within this framework a fair value accounting basis can be constructed that provides the best information on the performance of the firm on both an absolute basis and in comparison with other firms and pre-determined goals, allows an appraisal of management performance, and serves as framework for making economic decisions. This methodology presents exposure to the key risks of the insurance enterprise and results and risk posture by major product line and the company as a whole in a manner communicable to and understandable by management, shareholders, securities analysts and regulators. The position of the firm, its performance, analysis of performance and sensitivity to risks in the environment can be displayed numerically and graphically using the criteria discussed previously.

In light of the comment in the last paragraph regarding sensitivity to risks please recall that both OAAV and OAV depend on the OAVDE algorithm. The OAVDE value, and so the OAAV, OAV and other values derived from OAV as described above, are the means of probability distributions. As such, they are point estimates and do not reflect the dispersion of results, e.g. the standard deviation or higher moments of the distribution. This is to some extent provided for if one is discounting at the cost of capital or other risk adjusted rate. Alternatively, one could derive risk adjusted values for OAAV and OAV (and other values dependent on OAV) by using techniques presented in Section IV. The benefit of this is that when considering a change in strategy or evaluating the results of a change in strategy the use of a risk adjusted measure might indicate that a result with a lower mean is superior due to a reduction in the dispersion of the distribution; essentially one has traded off an acceptable amount of expected value for a commensurate reduction in uncertainty in that value. Such indication might be missed if a risk unadjusted measure is used.

As an example, consider the use of utility theory. Assume that the insurance enterprise (or product line) has a utility function $U(X)$. One can define the risk adjusted option adjusted value, $OAV^{RA}$, in the following manner:

$$OAV_t^{RA} = E[U(\{PVDE_t(i_0, p)\})], \tag{29}$$

where $E$ is the expectation operator applied to the distribution over all paths $p$.

In the above expression for the present value of distributable earnings the choice of discounting at a constant $y$ or a spread $s$ is omitted; and it is assumed that the present value is computed using the generalized net present value algorithm. Using this definition for $OAV^{RA}$ one can then derive the remaining quantities in this section on a risk adjusted basis. While the challenges of implementing such a fair value basis can not be ignored, it would mean the demise of DAC, imaginary DAC, PB 8, FAS 60, FAS 97, deferred taxes and other accounting issues as they are known today.

In this section it is assumed that all discounting is performed at the firm's cost of capital which is expressed as a level amount. It is also possible to perform the discounting on a pathwise basis using each path's risk-free rates plus a spread, or OAS. In this case the firm's cost of capital or hurdle rate must be expressed as an add-on to the one period risk-free rate. This approach is more consistent with the finance of option pricing; but there is difficulty in determining an appropriate OAS. Also, since the one period risk-free rate can be volatile, the resulting cost of capital would be volatile. It is not generally thought that firms' costs of capital are that volatile.

*Other application*

This framework is built around the appropriate choice of an objective function. If circumstances change, all that is required is to ascertain the new objective function for free cash flows. By the use of the appropriate objective function the methodology can be applied to other firms and firms in other legal jurisdictions.

## REFERENCES

Anderson, J.C.H. (1959). Gross premium calculations and profit measurement for non-participating insurance. *TSA*, **XI**, 357–94, Discussion, 395–420.

Atkinson, D.B. (1990). *Introduction to Pricing and Asset Shares*. Society of Actuaries Study Note 210-25-90.

Babcock, G.C. (1984). Duration as a link between yield and value, *Journal of Portfolio Management*, Summer, 58–65 and Corrections, Fall 1984: 97–98.

Becker, D.N. (1988). A generalized profits released model for the measurement of return on investment for life insurance. *TSA*, **XL**, 61–114.

Becker, D.N. (1991). A method for option-adjusted pricing and valuation of insurance products. Product Development News, Society of Actuaries, **30**, 1–6.

Becker, D.N. (1984). Pricing for profitability in ART. *Best's Review*, (September), 26–28, 154–155.

Becker, D.N. and T. Kitsos (1984). Mortality and lapse assumptions in renewable term insurance. *Reinsurance Reporter*, **104**, 9–14.

Bierwag, G.O. (1987). *Duration Analysis: Managing Interest Rate Risk*. Cambridge, MA: Ballinger Publishing Company.

Bierwag, G.O., G.G. Kaufman, and A. Toevs (1983). Duration: its development and use in bond portfolio management. *Financial Analysts Journal*, (July–August), 15–35.

Black, F., E. Derman, and W. Toy (1990). A one-factor model of interest rates and its application to treasury bond options. *Financial Analysts Journal*, **46**, 33–39.

Childs, J.F. (1994). *Common Stock Cost – The Mystery in Cost-of-Capital*. Working paper, Kidder, Peabody & Company, Inc.

Copeland, T.E. and J.F. Weston (1988). *Financial Theory and Corporate Policy*, 3rd edn. Reading, MA: Addison-Wesley Publishing Company.

Cox, J.C., S.A. Ross and M. Rubinstein (1979). Option pricing: a simplified approach. *Journal of Financial Economics*, **7**, 229–263.

Cox, J.C. and M. Rubinstein (1988). *Options Markets*. Englewood Cliffs, NJ.

Cozzolino, J.M. (1979). New method for risk analysis. *Sloan Management Review*, (Spring), 53–66.

Dicke, A. (1993). Fair-valuing of insurance liabilities – actuarial approach. *Financial Reporter*, (June), 14–15.
Dukes, J. and A. MacDonald (1980). Pricing a select and ultimate annual renewable term product. *TSA*, **XXXII**, 547–584.
Fabozzi, F.J. (1990). *Valuation of Fixed Income Securities*. Summit, NJ: Frank J. Fabozzi Associates.
Griffin, M.W. (1990). An excess spread approach to non-participating insurance products. *TSA*, **XLII**, 229–246.
Heath, D., R. Jarrow, and A. Morton (1990). Bond pricing and the term structure of interest rates: a discrete time approximation. *Journal of Financial and Quantitative Analysis*, **25**, 419–440.
Ho, T.S.Y. and S.-B. Lee (1986). Term structure movements and pricing interest rate contingent claims. *Journal of Finance*, **41**, 1011–1029.
Ho, T.S.Y. (1990). *Strategic Fixed Income Management*. Homewood, IL: Dow Jones-Irwin.
Ho, T.S.Y., A.G. Scheitlin. and K.O. Tam (1992). *Total Return Approach to Performance Management*. Working paper, Metropolitan Life Insurance Company.
Hull, J.C. (1993). *Options, Futures, and Other Derivative Securities*, 2nd edn. Englewood Cliffs, NJ: Prentice-Hall.
Jacob, D.P., G. Lord, and J.A. Tilley (1987). A generalized framework for pricing contingent cash flows. *Financial Management*, **16**, 5–14.
Jarrow, R.A. (1988). *Finance Theory*. Englewood Cliffs, NJ: Prentice-Hall, 1988.
Kuhn, T.S. (1970). *The Structure of Scientific Revolutions*. Chicago, IL: The University of Chicago Press.
Lee, D.S. (1979). A conceptual analysis of nonparticipating life insurance gross premiums and profit formulas, *TSA*, **XXXI**, 489–509, Discussion, 511–531.
Lorie, J. and L.J. Savage (1951). Three problems in rationing capital. *Journal of Business*. **28**, 229–239.
McKinsey & Company, Inc. (1990). *Cost of Equity Capital Discussion*. Working paper.
Markowitz, H. (1959). *Portfolio Selection*. New Haven, CT: Yale University Press.
Miller, L., U. Rajan, U and P. Shimpi (1989). Liability Funding Strategies. In: F. Fabozzi (ed), *Fixed Income Portfolio Strategies: State-of-the-Art Technologies and Strategies*. Probus Publishing.
Miller, S. (1990). A continuous arbitrage-free interest rate model, part 1. *Risks and Rewards*, **7**, 4–7.
Miller, S. (1991). A continuous arbitrage-free interest rate model, part 2. *Risks and Rewards*, **10**, 5–7.
Miller, S. (1992). A continuous arbitrage-free interest rate model, part 3. *Risks and Rewards*, **13**, 2–6.
Pedersen, H.W., E.S.W. Shiu and A.E. Thorlacius (1989). Arbitrage-free pricing of interest-rate contingent claims. *TSA*, **XLI**, 231–265.
Posnak, R. (ed.) (1974). *GAAP: Stock Life Companies*. Ernst and Young.
Reitano, R.R. (1991a). Multivariate duration analysis. *TSA*, **XLIII**, 335–376.
Reitano, R.R. (1991b). Multivariate immunization theory. *TSA*, **XLIII**, 393–441.
Shapiro, R. and J. Snyder (1988). Mortality expectations under renewable term insurance. Proceedings, Conference of Actuaries in Public Practice, **XXX**, 592–614.
Smith, B.M. (1987). Pricing in a return-on-equity environment. *TSA*, **XXXIX**, 257–272.
Solomon, E. (1956). The arithmetic of capital budgeting decisions. *Journal of Business*, **29**, 24–29.
Sondergeld, D.R. (1982). Profitability as a return on total capital. *TSA*, **XXXIV**, 415–429, Discussion, 431–433.
Tilley, J.A. (1992). An actuarial layman's guide to building stochastic interest rate generators. *TSA*, **XLIV**, 509–564.
Teichroew, D., A. Robichek, and M. Montalbano (1965). An analysis of criteria for investment and financing decisions under certainty. *Management Science*, (November), 51–79.

### APPENDIX A: DETERMINING PRICING

Atkinson (1990) describes the early development of insurance pricing. In the nineteenth century and as late as the 1960s in some cases, gross premiums were calculated by loading or grossing up valuation net premiums for expenses. In 1919 E.E. Cammack developed the equation-based gross premium formula with mortality its only decrement. W.A. Jenkins in 1932, introduced a second decrement for lapse. Deterministic assumptions were made for all experience, including interest rates, which were assumed constant. (This is what is meant by deterministic pricing.) With these methods profits emerged as release from risk. In some cases this approach used more realistic assumptions than valuation assumptions but the formula then included an explicit provision for profit. It might be loading the gross premium by a constant × dollars per thousand or a percentage of premium loading. Only indirectly, if at all, does the basis of the accounting system play a part and there is no relation of the profitability measure to the period by period emergence of earnings under the accounting system.

The next step forward was the change to an accumulation type of formula where premiums less benefits and expenses are accumulated with interest to some point in the future. The value of this accumulation is divided by the number of surviving units at the end of the projection and the quotient is called the asset share. J.E. Hoskins used the following profit objective: the asset share at the end of a given number of years must equal the cash value or reserve plus some margin, e.g. 10% of the cash value. The accumulations were projected using expected, deterministic experience. These models often included a charge for the increase in the statutory reserve on which interest was then credited. By tying the profit target to the reserve at the end of the pricing horizon the accounting system was recognized, but again the emergence of profit did not figure into the premium decision. The year by year change in the asset share was not a key element. Federal income taxes were not included.

In 1959 J.C.H. Anderson recognized the implication of accumulating the profits within the product line up to the end of the pricing horizon, i.e. the asset share model profits as they emerged were retained with the product and not considered available to or released back to surplus until the end of that horizon. Anderson changed the focus to that of profits released where the initial surplus strain of new business is viewed as an investment by surplus and the future accounting profits were repayments to surplus each year. These profits released were not accumulated but discounted. Thus each period's profit did not include any investment income on retained earnings but only on the opening reserve and cash flow during the period. He designated these profits as 'book profits'. They were viewed as a return of both principal invested and interest on this invested amount. Anderson treated the writing of new business as an investment and applied the methods of capital budgeting to determine the return on that investment, where such return could be compared to a predetermined return on investment target. In this manner the accounting system and the emergence of earnings under that system were explicitly recognized. In this methodology interest rates earned by the insurance enterprise remain deterministic (along with all other assumptions), although interest rates are allowed to change each year. Again federal income taxes were excluded.

This ultimately gave rise to an array of profit measures based on book profits besides the return on investment. Examples are: the net present value of book profits; the net present value of book profits divided by the present value of premium (a levelized profit/premium ratio); the net present value of book profits divided by an annuity (a levelized statutory profit per unit in force); and breakeven year, i.e. the first year in which the net present value of book profits turns positive and remains positive. Profit targets were often expressed as a combination of these. In many cases the present values were calculated by discounting the book profits at the pretax asset investment rate earned by the insurance enterprise. In this event the measures expressed the profitability in the product in excess of the return afforded by investable assets. Another choice for the discount rate was the insurance enterprise's cost of capital. If the profit measures were not positive, the insurance product was not earning back its cost of capital. Sometimes a higher target rate was used for the discounting. Here if the measures were zero or positive, the product earned a return at or above the target.

Lee (1979) added two innovations to Anderson's approach. First, he allowed the fund that earned interest to be more general than the statutory reserve. He allowed, in a very general way, for a portion of the book profit not to be released, but accumulated with the product itself. Second, he incorporated federal income tax into the computation. Sondergeld (1982) extended the nature of the fund that was associated with the product to include what has come to be known as required surplus. The total capital required to support the business should include required surplus. If this is not factored into the pricing, the insurance enterprise's return on total capital will be less than anticipated in the pricing. The products will be underpriced relative to the desired return on total capital. This is commented on more fully below.

The concept of required surplus emerged as the amount of funds that the insurance enterprise must hold in order that the enterprise will remain solvent at some confidence level of possible adverse future experience. The risks became identified as the asset default risk $(C-1)$, obligation risk $(C-2)$, interest rate risk $(C-3)$ and general business risk $(C-4)$, the 'C' standing for 'contingency'. (Subsequently, this concept was embraced by the rating agencies and later the National Association of Insurance Commissioners as expressed in their risk based capital requirements.) This meant that not all of an insurance enterprise's capital was available for distribution but that a portion of it must be earmarked to support the liabilities and associated assets.

The more assets an insurance enterprise has in surplus, the lower its return on capital will be as assets backing surplus will not provide a return as large as that of the insurance liabilities. Therefore, it is better to hold as little as is prudent. With prudence necessitating the holding of surplus at an amount equal to at least the required surplus level, this created a drag on the return on capital. In order to provide the shareholders with a target return on all capital employed by the business, the pricing of the individual liabilities had to provide for a return not only on the amount of surplus invested in the liability, but also an extra return such that when it is combined with the aftertax investment income on assets supporting required surplus, the return on the totality equals or exceeds the cost of capital or target return, if higher. Thus the product must earn back its investment and pay rent on the required surplus. The pricing does not provide for the insurance enterprise to ever pay out the required surplus, merely to provide a differential return on it.

Smith (1987) presented an insightful analysis regarding why the average GAAP return on equity that emerges over time might not equal the statutory internal rate of return priced into the product. Becker in a discussion to Smith's paper presented an additional reason for this to occur and identified a solution for it. This is examined below. The method developed by Anderson is based on a policy year approach. Profits are computed assuming the product is issued at the beginning of the year. The formula explicitly assumes that negative cash flows are covered by borrowing at the net earned rate of the insurance enterprise and that the charge for the reserve (or change in reserve) occurs at the end of the year. This means that the shareholder investment occurs at the end of the year, not when the product is issued; and the reserve is only established for those persisting into the subsequent year, which reduces the magnitude of the investment. In reality, insurance enterprises must invest capital and be solvent when the product is issued and must set up reserves for all new business. Without taking these issues into account it is possible to overstate the internal rate of return. For this reason this paper makes special note about the initial distributable earnings at time 0. The earliest form of distributable earnings was given by: statutory book profit, plus aftertax investment income on the opening balance of required surplus, less the change in required surplus. The old mandatory securities valuation reserve (MSVR) was generally ignored. Subsequently, the MSVR was replaced by the AVR and a new reserve, the IMR, was added. IMR effects are automatically included in statutory net income. The excess, if positive, of AVR over the asset default component of required surplus must be considered.

The last issue facing deterministic pricing was the emergence of products whose distributable earnings showed multiple changes in sign. This situation might signify the need for more than one shareholder investment. Historically, most insurance products had an initial investment (negative distributable earnings) followed by positive distributable earnings. More recently product features were added to designs that created multiple sign changes in distributable earnings, e.g. cliff surrender charges, reversionary interest rate bonuses and/or mortality and expense charge give-backs and compensation bonuses. Such sign changes also could occur in the pricing of disability income and long term care products. There is also the possibility that the product is not adequately priced and it has a pattern of alternating and/or late duration negative distributable earnings. The classical algorithms for net present value and internal rate of return are not capable of determining the net present value or internal rate of return for a stand alone project which requires multiple shareholder investments.

The classical net present value and internal rate of return algorithms used in capital budgeting demand a well behaved series of cash flows (one change in algebraic sign) in order to guarantee that both net present value and internal rate of return are economically meaningful. The problem that arises when there is more than one investment, i.e. negative quantity, was originally demonstrated in 1955 by the 'pump project' of Lorie and Savage which had two internal rates of return. An interpretation for this special case was given in 1956 by Solomon. In 1965 Teichroew *et al.* developed a classification scheme that classifies all projects by whether they are simple consumers of capital, investment projects, non users of capital, financing projects, or complex investment projects, mixed projects, which have repeated investment elements. They could not provide a complete analysis for mixed projects. In 1988, Becker provided a general solution to the problem of mixed projects that enables all projects to be classified as either financing or investment and generalizes the classical net present value and internal rate of return algorithms making them economically meaningful in all situations. The application of the generalized net present value to the pump project is shown Figure A.1.

The various deterministic profit measures noted previously can be redefined using the refinements described above.

APPENDIX B: OBJECTIONS TO DISTRIBUTABLE EARNINGS AS A BASIS FOR FAIR VALUE

In this section several objections are presented that people have in using distributable earnings as a basis for fair value estimation.

First, it is common in finance texts to adopt pure cash flows as the basis of the economic reality as accounting earnings have non cash items, e.g. depreciation, in them. The accounting system doesn't necessarily give a real picture of the economic reality. Why should the accounting system be used here? The first part of the statement is true. But most firms do not have limitations placed

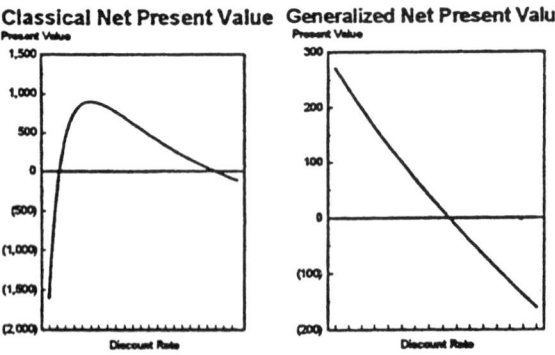

*Figure A.1.* The pump project.

on them with regard to the payment of free cash flows, i.e. shareholder dividends, similar to insurance enterprises. For them, a pure cash flow basis may be appropriate. But due to the statutory limitation on shareholder dividends from insurance enterprises statutory accounting does impact the economic reality. The payment of income taxes is a result of statute; but that does not make that economic fact of taxes any less real.

Second, for a growing company it is known that the statutory net income for the financial reporting period understates the real earnings of the firm. How can that be reconciled? As noted in the response to the first question, state statute limits shareholder dividends, i.e. free cash flows. But OAVDE does recognize the entire value of existing and new business. It does so by recognizing the present value of the future distributable earnings not just the current period's earnings. OAVDE takes into account all the earnings and when they will be available to shareholders. If the insurance enterprise could invest distributable earnings in new business whose generalized internal rate of return substantially exceeded its cost of capital, then the straight forward application of OAVDE analysis would understate the value of the firm as OAVDE would look at the original distributable earnings. This can be remedied by adding the new business to the model for a given number of future years production and computing the resulting OAVDE.

Third, everybody knows statutory accounting is too conservative and doesn't reflect economic reality. That is why GAAP accounting was developed. Why isn't GAAP the right basis? Consider two insurance enterprises, A and B. A has GAAP earnings of $100 million and B has GAAP earnings of $150 million. Both A and B have statutory net income of $75 million. While company B has half again as much GAAP earnings as company A, both of them are limited to the same amount of free cash flows, i.e. shareholder dividends, namely $75 million. Possibly due to AVR and required surplus issues A and B don't have the same final distributable earnings, but one can see that GAAP doesn't change the rules when it comes to paying out shareholder dividends. Also, A and B are both limited to only investing $75 million in new business unless they have free surplus in excess of the AVR and the level of required surplus they need to maintain.

Fourth, the method is tied to free cash flows, i.e. shareholder dividends. What about an investor who is looking for growth stocks? They are expecting appreciation in value, not cash to spend. As noted in the paper, in Chapter 2 of Copeland and Weston the authors address the fact that amounts not paid as shareholder dividends but reinvested in new projects at the firm's cost of capital have the same effect on stock price as if they had been paid out in cash. Also, over long periods of time growth stocks that never pay out dividends will have declines in stock value. As a parallel consider a life insurance policy whose death benefit is a paid up life insurance policy on the life of the beneficiary, whose death benefit is a paid up life insurance policy on the life of its beneficiary. And so on. Somebody at sometime will demand to be paid.

Next, are there not other sources of value that are not recognized by the distributable earnings concept? For example, what about management talent, investment expertise, superior data processing systems, good risk control? The beneficial effects of management talent, investment expertise and good risk control should already have been reflected in the OAVDE amount in terms of such items as expense management and higher productivity, extra investment returns, lesser claim levels. Consider superior data processing systems. The value of this item also should already be reflected in lower operating expenses that are incurred by the insurance enterprise. There may be additional value in that the insurance enterprise could perform third party administration and realize a profit. But if so, the use of the data processing capability should be part of the strategy of the firm. Its value, then, would be reflected in the distributable earnings of the insurance enterprise via the associated revenues less expenses that could be realized from third party administration. If there is added value and it is not in the distributable earnings, then it is not being realized.

Then what if unused capacity exists or if there are undervalued assets? This is somewhat similar to the prior question. If either of these issues exist, it means that the current strategy is not optimal. If the current strategy is the basis of the OAVDE computation, then a better strategy exists which will reflect the unused capacity or undervalued assets. Find it.

Statutory accounting only recognizes 'admitted assets'. GAAP recognizes all assets. Doesn't that mean that statutory accounting isn't the right basis? If a not admitted asset is such that its value will only emerge into statutory income over time, then its value is not realizable now. It will increase the OAVDE. If the not admitted asset's value can be realized now and isn't limited to emergence over time, then its value is already reflected in free surplus. An example of the latter is the value of furniture and equipment. A possible example of the former is agents' debit balances that are not realizable through factoring or securitization.

Another point is that of a prospective buyer of an insurance company knows of actions that could be taken that would add value, then the OAVDE amounts already computed won't reveal that value. Can't the OAVDE value therefore understate the value of the firm? The OAVDE value depends on the strategy being implemented. Under current management the OAVDE value may be all that is realizable to them. The buyer has his or her own strategy. Under that strategy the buyer's OAVDE will be higher assuming both have the same cost of capital. The increase in OAVDE represents the value added by the expertise of the buyer. Merely because the buyer's OAVDE or fair value is higher than that of the current owner/management doesn't mean the buyer should pay it to them! After all, the buyer is the one who will have to deliver on the new strategy. But the new OAVDE can tell the buyer if the asking price is rich or cheap and it puts a ceiling on what the buyer should be willing to pay the seller.

So what happens to OAVDE or the value of the firm if statutory accounting changes? If changes are made in statutory accounting principles or if management changes the level of required surplus deemed prudent, then there will be a discontinuity in OAVDE and in the value of the firm; but, other things being equal, OAVDE will proceed normally under the new rules thereafter. Similar events have occurred with the significant accounting changes in GAAP and SAP and changes in the surplus requirements of rating agencies. These events can also be driven by tax law changes. For example, consider an insurance enterprise whose business is substantially noncancellable disability income. When the federal government adopted the DAC tax, the value of that firm dropped immediately as the firm had no way of passing on the reduction in distributable earnings due to the DAC tax with regard to the then current in force block.

How does OAVDE apply to a defined benefit pension plan? It doesn't. There are two reasons for this. First, there are no shareholder dividends and no need to use surplus to fund growth, both of which are applicable to a stock insurance company and the latter to a mutual company. Second, these plans do not pay federal income tax and are not affected by statutory accounting concepts, e.g. IMR, AVR, reserves or deficiency reserves. In this case the objective function provided by the market value of surplus may be more appropriate to measure the risk posture of the plan. But note that market value analysis is a 'time 0' analysis for the risk posture and does not show how the situation unfolds over time as reinvestments are actually made.

The term 'surplus' is often used with different meanings. How does one keep track of them when analyzing a given situation? The term 'surplus' is defined as the value of assets less the value of liabilities where the values for assets and liabilities are computed under a given set of assumptions. 'Surplus' has three major interpretations: as a redundancy or cushion against adverse experience to the company in meeting its obligations; as a residual or shareholder liquidation value; and as the value of the firm in the sense of what a willing buyer would pay a willing seller. These interpretations are not only different; but the significance they have depends on the particular situation. Consider a firm whose product or service is one for which the entire results of the economic transaction are known within a short period of time. For this firm, the redundancy interpretation of surplus is of small significance as the liability items on the balance sheet are mainly small period accrual items. The residual value interpretation is of large significance as long as the assumptions underlying the accounting system when considered in light of the assets do not produce asset values materially different from market values, i.e. the liquidation must be actually feasible. Next consider a firm for which the results of the economic transaction are only known over a long period of time. In this case the redundancy or cushion interpretation of surplus is meaningful; but the residual value has less meaning as the value of the liabilities will be dominated by the value of the performance obligation arising from the incomplete economic transactions. If there is no liquid and robust market for selling those obligations, then the residual value is hypothetical and vague. In either case, the interpretation of surplus as value of the firm may bear no relation to the actual value of the firm for a going concern. In the case of the firm whose economic transactions are completed quickly, the franchise value of the firm, at least, is ignored. In the other case, not only is the franchise value ignored but also ignored is the value of future distributable earnings arising from the incomplete economic transactions. It is not likely that any set of assumptions, 'market' or 'book', can provide for an accounting system for which all three interpretations of surplus are simultaneously realized in one number. To avoid confusion an accounting system should be designed to focus on one of these interpretations. If the interpretation chosen for surplus is the value of the firm, then the value of liabilities is the balancing item. It may not bear a simple relationship or any fixed relationship to the value of liabilities resulting from the design of an accounting system where surplus is defined to reflect either a redundancy value or a residual value.

Finally, while its true that there is no direct third party market for liabilities, isn't it the case that the market for the purchase of blocks of insurance or entire companies is not that large and so it is hard to infer a discount rate to be used? As noted earlier, one basis that can be used is the insurance enterprise's cost of capital. This can be approximated in either of the manners described in Section V or by deriving a marginal cost of capital. Management might want to use a hurdle rate in excess of the cost of capital. But the market for 'acquisitions' in a broader sense is not as thin as might be expected. Every day reinsurance transactions take place for both new business and existing blocks of business where the terms of the transactions reflect the price that is reached by a willing buyer and a willing seller. These transactions are not priced on an assessment of the market value of assets less the market value of liabilities, but on the present value of the distributable earnings that result from the interaction of the assets and liabilities, the resulting cash flows and the rules governing their distribution. These present values are evaluated using costs of capital, hurdle rates or profit criteria expressed as return in excess of what can be obtained from other investments.

## Appendix C

This appendix elaborates on certain structural and methodological differences between market value analysis and OAVDE analysis, the issue of their ultimate convergence and provides comments on the 'two paradigms' concept articulated by Robert R. Reitano in 'Market Value of Liabilities: Two Paradigms'.

### Market value analysis and OAVDE analysis

First, consider what may be termed 'pure' market value analysis. In this approach one compares the market value of existing assets at the date of the valuation to the market value of liabilities at the same date. Alternatively, one could compute the value of the existing assets after a hypothetical restructure or hedge is established; but it still represents the present value of asset cash flows from assets actually held or that could be held at time 0. Note that it does not reflect any investment strategy applicable beyond time 0. Thus it can not be a simulation of the anticipated total performance of the business over time.

The liability and expense cash flows are similarly projected based on time 0 considerations and their market value determined. In this case the interest rate crediting strategy must be constrained to be a function of an index. The index may utilize only exogenous variables, i.e. the future yield curves and, possibly, the prior credited rates. The pure market value analysis approach can not be applied to an interest sensitive liability whose credited rate reflects to any degree the performance of the assets supporting the liability as that performance is not being explicitly or implicitly modeled in the pure approach.

Second, consider a 'modified' market value analysis. In this case the market value of assets is similar to the above. But an actual simulation of the performance of the business is performed which reflects how the business is to be actually managed along the future interest rate paths, i.e. it utilizes all the information in the strategy. From this simulation it is possible to extract the data to determine the liability cash flows and their market value. This method must be used if the actual portfolio earned rate is used in any way in determining the interest crediting rate. The other information generated from the simulation is not needed for the market value analysis. In either case, the market value analysis presents a snapshot of the business at time 0 and does not represent a simulation of the total performance of the business. By design it utilizes single point option pricing, i.e. at time zero only.

OAVDE analysis, on the other hand, reflects the total performance of the business by using a complete simulation of the operation of the business. Thus it utilizes all the information in the strategy and can model all liabilities, including those interest sensitive liabilities whose interest crediting strategy depends on actual asset performance. At each point in time along each path decisions are required about asset investment or disinvestment. Multi-point option pricing is employed to provide relatively consistent security prices needed for investment or disinvestment decisions at each path/time point. As noted in the text, certain simplifying assumptions may be made that do not require the use of option pricing at each path/time point. OAVDE analysis produces the resulting distributable earnings that would emerge along each path/time point based on how the business is to be managed. The path-wise vectors of distributable earnings can then be analyzed using the initial set of arbitrage-free paths to provide the option adjusted value of distributable earnings at time 0.

*Convergence of the two methods?*

Is it possible that both processes eventually lead to the same result? It is difficult to rationalize how this might occur. First, the objective function for each methodology is entirely different from the other. Second, the issues raised in an earlier section would have to be resolved. For example, cash flows occurring due to capital gains taxes, federal income taxes and shareholder dividends are not considered in market value analysis. Third, based on the description above, there are significant methodological differences between the two approaches.

Is it possible that the market value analysis could be modified to determine the distributable earnings? In the case of the modified market value analysis the additional information, in principle, could be made available to compute the distributable earnings at each path/time point because the modified market value analysis is a simulation using all elements of the strategy. Such a model can be augmented, if necessary, so that any additional items for the determination of distributable earnings are computed. The OAVDE value could be directly determined. In this case, one is simply performing an OAVDE analysis.

In the case of pure market value analysis the additional information for a total simulation is not available in principle. Never-the-less it is possible to define a formula that will approximate a cash flow for distributable earnings. Such a computation is only approximate as the model is not a total simulation and many items required for actual determination of distributable earnings at each path/time point are not available. But even more significant is that interpreting the result of such a computation as a distributable earnings amount is fraudulent in that distributable earnings are only meaningful in the context of an actual simulation of total business performance, i.e. it must utilize the complete strategy. For example, formulae for the distributable earnings cash flows that can and have been derived implicitly from a pure market value analysis assume reinvestment is based on the one period future rate and disinvestment is based on unlimited ability to borrow at the one period future rate because this is all that is available in the pure market value approach. The 'add-on' approach that can be done for modified market value analysis does not work for pure market value analysis.

*Two paradigms*

For market value analysis the market value of insurance liabilities (MVL) is directly determined. In the case of OAVDE analysis the market value of all liabilities is indirectly determined and is given by the formula MVL = MVA − OAVDE. The market value of insurance liabilities is then found from subtracting the market value of non insurance liabilities from the total. Reitano (1995) noted above, calls this dichotomy the 'two paradigms'. The principle thesis of his paper is that if there existed separate deep and liquid markets for each of the buying/selling of insurance companies and/or blocks of business and for the buying/selling of individual insurance liabilities by third parties, then any differentials between the two markets would be arbitraged away. If so, then he asks which paradigm would change? His answer and argument are as follows: "In general, we expect it would be the distributable earnings approach. That is, if liability contracts on individuals were as easily and actively traded as are assets currently, we expect that the presence of this market would fundamentally change our notion of 'earnings', to a basis that is more reflective of total returns in the mutual fund or investment banking industries. That is, in this environment it would be entirely inconsistent for statutory accounting to proclaim book value earnings during a period in a market where participants could actually earn, through trading, the change in the asset market value less the change in the liabilities market value, all tax adjusted. This accounting change would then redefine distributable earnings of a firm in terms of future cash flows, which would create implied liability values with the indirect methodology effectively equal to those provided by the direct methodology. In summary, the direct methodology below provides a valuation of liabilities that is more consistent with current asset valuation ..."

There are several observations that are important to fully appreciate this complex issue. First, there is the assumption that statutory book value earnings differing from market value earnings will change. This seems unlikely because statutory book value accounting principles and the resulting earnings are determined by authorities whose mission is unrelated to these market value issues but is related to insuring the protection of policyholders through multiple conservative accounting principles. When the asset/liability management risk is contemplated neither statutory nor GAAP accounting is an adequate basis on which to base the insurance enterprise's balance sheet or income statement. An accounting system based on OAVDE analysis does provide an adequate basis.

It may be that the possible confusion of statutory earnings for the economic earnings under OAVDE and/or the concerns about the underlying use of any existing accounting system (especially statutory accounting) in determination of economic earnings are key mental barriers to understanding OAVDE as an economic accounting basis. These misconceptions often occur because it seems straightforward to conclude that as statutory accounting heavily influences the OAVDE computation, then the economic earnings under OAVDE analysis are the statutory earnings. An earlier section elaborated on the accounting basis and the definition of earnings that emerges from OAVDE and, as shown, the basis is not statutory accounting and the earnings are not statutory earnings. The OAVDE analysis methodology defines the basis. OAVDE does reflect market values, specifically the intrinsic or fair value of the insurance enterprise computed from fundamental financial principles. The intrinsic or fair value itself incorporates the market values of the assets of the insurance enterprise insofar as they result in earnings that may be distributed to shareholders at future times.

Second, the phrase 'all tax adjusted' does not make clear that many tax related issues are not addressed by the current state of the art of market value analysis. In fact, current immunization theory is not comprehensive with regard to taxation. There are unresolved issues here. As noted above, there are significant economic realities that are not reflected in market value analysis.

Third, if there were such a deep and liquid market, then the values of the insurance liabilities would be computed by the direct method from models that reflect only insurance obligation cash flows. As insurance enterprise maintenance expenses, renewal commissions, premium tax, etc. are irrelevant to the owner of the insurance liability, there is no need or reason to reflect them as is done in the models currently used to compute a market value analysis. Thus the direct approach paradigm would change at least to eliminate those unnecessary items.

Fourth, the conclusion asserts that it is the distributable earnings paradigm that changes. The rationale for this position might result from a confusion of statutory accounting and the economic accounting system based on OAVDE. Since OAVDE defines a new basis that, while reflecting certain aspects of statutory accounting is not equivalent to statutory accounting, the rationale is not applicable. The discussion of the first item in this section may also be relevant here.

Fifth, market value analysis considers the value of the liability from the perspective of a liquid and deep direct third party market. The market among insurance companies and blocks of business is based on future earnings from the company or block in question to the acquiring insurance company. Here the market value of liabilities is indirectly inferred from the basic accounting equation. In this case the indirect market value of liabilities is a logical construct. Must that indirect market value equal the third party market value? Is it even the case that a directly computed market value from the perspective of an insurance enterprise must equal the third party market value?

Consider a medically standard individual with an annual renewable term policy. In any third party market the market value of that policy must be non-negative, i.e. greater than or equal to zero. Suppose that the policy in question was issued by an insurance company that writes only annual renewable term insurance and that the premium scale is more than adequate at each attained age to cover the expected benefits and associated expenses. In this case a pure market value analysis of the block would result in a negative direct market value of liabilities assuming that future premiums are considered as negative cash flows to be combined with the benefit and expense positive cash flows. There is a contradiction as the third party market value is non-negative but the internally computed direct market value is negative.

A work-around to the contradiction posed by the negative market value of the liability is to separate the liability cash flow stream into two streams: the benefit and expense stream; and the premium stream. Add the present value of the premium stream to the asset side of the basic accounting equation and define the direct market value of the liability as just the present value of only the benefit and expense cash flows, i.e. only the liability cash out-flows. (This technique can be applied to the general case of any liability having renewal premiums. Such renewal premiums must be considered if all the embedded options in a liability are to be valued.) The resulting market value of the liability is now a positive number.

Even if this separation is made it is extremely unlikely that the actual third party market value of the policy would equal the internally computed direct market value based on the insurance company's best estimate of future mortality and expense, the collection of arbitrage free interest rate paths used and any of the choices for spread-to-Treasuries considered earlier. The only way that the internally computed direct market value will equal the third party market value is if the spread-to-Treasuries used in the computation is explicitly solved for so that the computed value equals the third party market value. (This is the same situation that exists with fixed income securities where the market price is used to calibrate the model.) This spread will be volatile and will not equal, other than by chance, any of the types of spreads considered above. This means that, in general, if a real third party market exists, then the internally computed direct market value derived using conventional choices for the spread will not equal the third party market value. (Spreads are important because, as there is no third party market, they are the likely candidates for actual use.)

The argument for the convergence of the two methods was that given a real third party market, then the indirect method market value would change to equal the third party market value, which implicitly assumes that the internally computed direct market value equals the third party market value if the two methods are to converge. But the exposition above demonstrates that this implicit assumption is not necessarily valid.

The scheme of separating the liability cash flows used above creates another layer of complexity in direct market value computations. In the example given let the liability cash flows be so separated. Now consider the computation of the liability spread as defined earlier for the benefit and expense cash flows. All these future liability cash flows are positive. The initial cash flow equals the initial premium less external acquisition costs (commissions and overriding commissions) and internal acquisition costs (underwriting and issue). This initial cash flow is negative for term policies issued today. What spread can be added to the Treasuries such that the present value of the positive liability cash flows equals this negative number? If there are problems such as these, then there are problems with market values and derived duration and convexity computations as well. One might argue that the above example is not conclusive as it involves a pure insurance product, i.e. one without investment characteristics. But a similar example could be constructed using cash value life insurance.

For products with renewal premiums the separation of liability cash flows poses the added problem of adjudicating the appropriate duration of assets, especially in the early durations of a block of business. This is due to the fact that while the duration of liabilities is based on outflows only, the duration of assets will depend on the mix of real assets and the 'virtual' assets representing future premium payments. For a considerable period of time the virtual assets will dominate the real; thus the duration of assets will be dominated by the duration of virtual assets. One could initially invest in assets with significantly different duration characteristics, but the duration of the virtual assets would overwhelm the final computation. This creates problems in deciding how to invest and makes rebalancing decisions more difficult as the actual situation only unfolds over time and prior decisions possibly may have been inappropriate as they were based on assets dominated by virtual assets.

Situations described above also lead to unusual durations for life insurance during the early years. This and the above issues may indicate the strain of extrapolating too far the analogy of insurance liabilities with fixed income securities. OAVDE analysis is not susceptible to the problems here or noted earlier.

Sixth, Michael S. Smith, FSA has shown that the present value of distributable earnings can not be optimized without knowing the investment income earned by the insurance enterprise. This fact and the fact that a pure market value analysis does not provide information on the future investment income (because it is a time 0 computation and not a simulation of future performance) imply that it is unlikely that decisions would both optimize and/or immunize the market value of surplus and optimize and/or immunize OAVDE to the same value. Essentially, the same is true for the modified market value analysis. Recall that for the examples in Section IV the market values of surplus do not equal the OAVDE values.

Seventh, the direct method seems simple and compelling, a straightforward analogy to the market for fixed income securities. But it does so at the expense of implicitly assuming that all insurance liabilities are identical in all ways to bonds, e.g. legal, regulatory, taxation to both the policyowner and company, etc. and that one can ignore the capital requirements of insurance enterprises. The market for fixed income securities provides prices which are used to calibrate the option pricing models. Unless a real deep and liquid third party market for individual insurance liabilities exists which would allow the calibration of the model, it is not possible to test how far the analogy can be meaningfully extended and there can be no unambiguous definition for the market value (or the 'fair' value) of a liability. In short, no market, then no market values.

Applying finance and option pricing theory directly to liabilities is a powerful and useful analogy; but it is not a completely valid analogy for insurance enterprises. The further the analogy is extended the more speculative are the conclusions. What appears very attractive about market value analysis is that it seems to provide an elegantly simple way to decompose liabilities and assets to provide guidance on how to invest for those liabilities to minimize interest rate risk. While market value analysis does provide insight as to the risk posture, it does not provide all the insight into the risk/reward posture of the value of the firm that OAVDE analysis does. This is due to the omission from market value analysis of significant economic variables and their timing that affects the value of the insurance enterprise. Similarly, total return measures based on market value analysis fall short of the mark.

Eighth, this discussion is predicated on the assumption of the existence of the deep and liquid third party market. For a theoretical discussion this is satisfactory when subject to the limitations in market value analyses and the caveat at the beginning of the prior paragraph. But how reasonable is this assumption? The majority of insurance liabilities are sold to individuals. In nearly all cases the owners are the insureds or others who have a financial dependency on the insured; and the products are purchased to meet a particular need which may have little relevance to another individual. What would be the motivation for the widespread trading of such liabilities? These products have favorable federal income tax treatment. This treatment may be lost upon sale. The income tax free status of the death benefit to the beneficiary of a life insurance policy is often lost in transfers for value. State laws and regulations impede the development of such a market due to insurable interest and public policy requirements. Tax qualified products and SEC registered products create additional problems. Deferred annuities, which would have the least problems in terms of a third party market, rarely have embedded options that are not available in newly issued products. New and innovative products from one company are quickly replicated by others.

The investment aspect of most general account insurance liabilities may be characterized as having a put option at book value, a floor crediting rate, perhaps premium flexibility and a floating credited rate not tied to any index, but set at the discretion of the insurance enterprise. Fixed income securities in active markets do not resemble these. Note that there is no similar third party market for certificates of deposit, savings accounts and other non insurance savings vehicles for which there are fewer problems to overcome. Similarly, there is no third party market for mutual fund shares except closed end funds which were designed with that in mind.

While thin, there is a market for the buying and selling of insurance companies and blocks of business. Also, there is a large number of stock life insurance companies for which it is possible to estimate costs of capital. It is then possible to create a reasonable proxy for the cost of capital for stock insurance enterprises overall and this can be used as the benchmark for OAVDE computations for all insurance enterprises.

KIM B. STAKING
*Inter-American Development Bank*

# Comments on 'The value of the firm: the option-adjusted value of distributable earnings'

INTRODUCTION

I believe that the subject of this conference is important, and I am especially pleased to see the growing collaboration and cross fertilization between professionals in the actuarial and finance/investment fields. About 7 or 8 years ago, when working on my dissertation at the Wharton School, I was invited to spend a summer consulting with the investment management group of a major New York based property-liability insurance company on improving their asset-liability management (with the emphasis on understanding better the liability side of the balance sheet). One of my first requests was to meet with the actuaries in order to see how they were managing and pricing risk and how they were determining the technical reserves and the expected timing of the liability cash flows. I was told that the actuarial and investment side of the company did not communicate; they didn't know each other and didn't speak the same language. I almost hesitate to admit that by the time I left at the end of the summer, I had never met with the actuaries. The two sides of the insurer continued to operate independently. I spent the time applying some financial concepts to some basic actuarial models for generating aggregate claims estimates. While interesting and useful in my dissertation, I remain convinced that the process could have been more valuable and more efficient if the two sides of the business had been able to communicate effectively. I understand that the degree of communications has traditionally been better in the life insurance industry, but it is heartening to attend a conference of the Society of Actuaries and note that the critical issues of finance and actuarial science are coming together.

I very much enjoyed reading through David Becker's article (which is important as I found that I had to go back and read it several times as there is a lot of information contained therein). The paper makes a positive contribution to understanding some very difficult financial management issues and has much to offer as a first step to resolving some important problems that must be addressed by an insurer's management. The issues are adroitly and comprehensively addressed. I would encourage you to look carefully at the paper. Indeed, if for nothing more, the illustrations of how the proposed methodology can be applied to some very specific management problems are, in and of themselves, worth careful analysis.

While I believe that the paper merits careful attention, I do nonetheless believe that it could be improved with some reorganization. Indeed, one of the suggestions that I would make is that Mr. Becker should split the paper into two or three separate papers. Some of the impact of what he is trying to say may be lost by his trying to cover too wide a variety of subjects. In addition, Mr. Becker has also incorporated several brief reviews of the central tenants of financial economics, including option pricing, the concept of arbitrage, and duration/convexity analysis. Possibly some of these have been included under the assumption that the reader is not familiar with these concepts, but I found that they more often interferred with the core development of the paper. Most of these asides seemed too brief to provide any real value to someone not already familiar with the subjects, and the occasional technical flaws serve to distract the reader. I would be interested in knowing whether this discomfort is shared by those with less formal training in financial economics, for I am not certain how to best handle the need for cross-fertilization between the fields of finance and actuarial science, other than to continue the process of educating insurance and actuarial professionals regarding the central tenants of finance (and vice versa).

The paper can be split into four major sections. Mr. Becker provides a good review of the evolution of the accounting treatment of insurance assets and liabilities (and therefore surplus) and the lingering limitations of the accounting treatment; suggests a methodology for estimating the market value of both assets and liabilities (evaluating the strengths and weaknesses of several approaches); extends the suggested approach of valuing assets and liabilities to provide direct estimates of the value investors would place on a firm (the OAVDE noted in the title); and provides some very useful illustrations of how this methodology can be incorporated into an insurance firm's financial management.

I will concentrate my remarks on the last three of these areas. I have little to add to the discussion of the recent developments in both statutory and GAAP/FASB accounting for investment income and changes in liabilities. As a trained economist, I have a fairly strong bias against the use of accounting systems which do not reflect market values. Worse still, the accounting treatment of insurance assets and liabilities provides neither consistency nor transparency. Thus, they are of little use to management, consumers, regulators, or investors. While, as Mr. Becker points out, there have been some improvements, the whole system leaves much to be desired. I am convinced that the only solution is the reflection of actual market values (or the best estimates thereof) along lines such as those outlined in the paper.

## BASIC MODEL

Let me turn to the basic formulation of the article. Becker notes that in an arbitrage-free world (and I would add in a world without information or transactions costs), we can price any asset by its risk-neutral value as follows:

$$\text{MVA}(i_0) = \sum_{p=1}^{P} \varphi_p \left[ \sum_{t=1}^{N} \frac{\text{ACF}_{p,t}}{\prod_{j=1}^{t-1}(1+r_{p,j}+\text{OAS}_A)} \right]$$

where

$\text{MVA}(i_0)$ = market value of asset with a given term structure at the time of valuation
$i_t$ = index of term structure at time $t$ ($t=0$ is the time of valuation)
$p$ = index of probability state (ranging from 1 to $P$)
$\varphi_p$ = probability of state $p$ occurring
$t$ = index for time (ranging up to $N$ = final maturity)
$j$ = index for payment (within $t$)
$\text{ACF}_{p,t}$ = asset cash flow (at $t$, given state $p$)
$r_{p,t}$ = riskless interest rate (at $t$, given state $p$)
$\text{OAS}_A$ = option adjusted spread on asset (adjustment for risk)

A similar equation can be created for the value of liabilities (MVL and $\text{OAS}_L$ substituted for MVA and $\text{OAS}_A$). Likewise, Becker creates a similar equation for the value of the firm. However, rather than using the traditional definition of MVE = MVA − MVL, given the legal restrictions of free cash flow, he looks at the value of the firm (or of a book of business) as the market value of the distributable cash flow. In the latter, MVDE or OAVDE and $\text{OAS}_{DE}$ are substituted for MVA and $\text{OAS}_A$). I will return to this point later. The nomenclature is a bit complicated, but the idea is clear. Indeed, these various models can all be classified as slightly simplified versions of the Arrow–Debreu model of state-contingent payoffs, only rather than having securities with state-dependent payoffs (one per time/state combination), complex assets are allowed to span the different states.

BASIC MODEL: INFORMATION REQUIREMENTS AND
UNDERLYING ASSUMPTIONS

While the above equation is intuitively pleasing and not incorrect for a theoretical point of view, it is important to take a close look at its information requirements and underlying assumptions. In order to directly solve the equation and obtain the risk-neutral estimate of the market value, the analyst must be able to (a) list each and every possible path and the interest rates associated with each path; (b) determine the probability of each path; (c) evaluate the cash flows associated with each point of time on each path; and (d) identify the fixed option adjusted spread that takes account of the risks inherent in the asset. I have to question whether this can be done to a degree that we can feel comfortable with the analysis.

I don't mean just to bring up the standard criticism of the Arrow–Debreu state-contingent models that it is impossible to name all the states. The structure merely requires that we are able to do so in a probabilistic sense. Thus, the problem at hand is not the listing of paths and their probabilities, but the identification of a stochastic process that will generate the paths and probabilities. We would then test these against the riskless government term structure to test if the model fits. There are a number of mathematical techniques for generating these paths and probabilities. The simplest is to assume that volatility $= 0$ and that the future looks just as today's term structure would predict. This naive model will properly price all government bonds, but it is tautological as it is asked to price the very instruments that were used to construct it (and would assign a zero value to all options on these riskless assets.) A more complex process, using historical or implicit volatilities is needed. Nevertheless, just as the naive model would properly value government bonds, we can create a stochastic process that may be correct today but which is incapable of predicting the future.

If we are to use these kinds of models, we need to be very careful regarding the robustness of the models. We have to ask whether the process being used has been able to solve the valuation problem for a large number of time periods. Moreover, since we are talking about relatively long-term assets and liabilities, we need to test the stability of the process. Is it sensitive to exogenous events (oil shocks, changes in inflationary expectations, changes in Fed policy, judicial rulings on insurer liability, etc.)? If not, the model will add a great deal of mathematical sophistication without adding economic understanding. If we are looking at consensus prices to test the model, does this mean that all market participants have the same consensus estimates of the paths and probabilities? If not, it is more likely that the process will not prove stable. Moreover, as Barr Rosenberg pointed out early in the development of the far simpler capital asset pricing model, when we need to rely on consensus, the consensus itself often leads to the model collapsing on itself.

Even if we are able to accept that the stochastic process is stable (at least within a short period of time), can we really assume that the OAS is constant across all paths and independent of the path? If not, the valuation that we obtain today will have value once the economy starts moving on a specific path or as volatility changes. Also, the problem is far more complicated as we move from the asset to the liability side of the insurer. We are only able to test the OAS on the asset side of the insurer. Here we can argue that we are looking at consensus prices, but this is far more difficult on the liability side, where information is more limited and markets less perfect. The low level of liquidity in secondary insurance markets will severely restrict the ability of the model to gage the liability OAS.

I am certain that one can find an appropriate stochastic process, undertake the needed empirical tests, and make the model work by incorporating a series of ongoing adjustments. I worry, however, that this kind of constant readjustment does not generate confidence. Rather, it is likely to result in the creation of a 'black box' type of model that few understand or appreciate. I recall when starting my career as a banker that we had a black box consisting of a duration-adjusted minimum spread that was used to generate prices on our international lending portfolio. As far as I could tell, none of the account officers understood the purpose of the black box or what it was trying to accomplish. It was just one more bureaucratic step that was needed in the approval process. No one bothered to explain duration or how the spread adjust for duration, and the account officers were unable to incorporate a risk adjustment into the model (which resulted in the bank taking a much higher exposure than was prudent in several high-risk developing countries). I firmly believe that it is not enough for the actuarial staff or investment staff to understand the model, it is critical that it can be explained to other decision makers.

Before going on, I would like to note that while I am skeptical about the implementation of the model due to the instability of the stochastic processes, especially those on the liability side of the insurer, this does not mean that the appropriate application of the model cannot be used to generate a better understanding of the problems that are faces in asset-liability management. This is especially so when the asset and liability portfolios incorporate significant amounts of optionlike characteristics. The fourth main section of David Becker's paper is an ideal example of how the model can be used as a tool to identify key sensitivities and present a graphical indication of the potential results of a specific strategy. I suspect that actuaries and investment professionals often think in terms of distributions of values rather than in terms of fixed values. The application of the OAVDE model to the decision of the appropriate investment strategy, the appropriate commitment of resources, etc., is welcome. I would like to see the resulting distribution printed rather than just the high-low graph (showing minimum, maximum, average, and OAVDE values), although these are far better than giving a single number.

## OAVDE AND THE ROLE OF CAPITAL STRUCTURE

It is important to note that the capital structure of an insurer is just as important as asset risk in determining the risk charge that should be incorporated into the liabilities. It is useful to model the insurer as a financial intermediary. Equity holders invest equity. The insurer then effectively borrows by issuing insurance policies which incorporate an implicit interest rate). Both equity and net premium are invested. The insurer is required to used these assets to pay all losses to the policyholders and all remaining assets belong to the equity holders. Let me look at a simplified version of this structure in Figure 1.

Since the assets are risky, there is some risk that the policyholders will not be paid in full. Thus, their payoff looks like a 45 degree line between the origin and the level of losses. Above this level, policyholders are paid in full. The equity holders have a zero return if assets are worth less than the level of

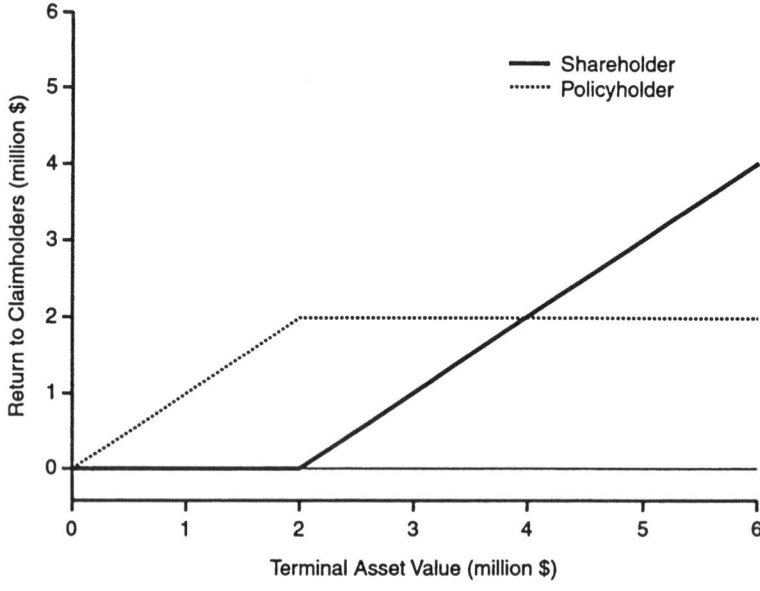

*Figure 1.* The insurance contract as a set of options. Claim against assets of insurer: policyholders vs. shareholder.

policyholder claims but receives the difference between the asset value of policyholder claims when assets are above this level (the 45 degree line from the face value of policyholder claims). The equity holders, in effect, own an option on the value of the assets with a striking price equal to the face value of the policyholder claim.

As the value of an option increases with volatility, the equity holders have the incentive to increase the overall riskiness of assets. However, if risk is high, policyholders will pay less for their claim (effectively increasing the interest rate paid by the insurer on their premium). Policyholders (or the regulators that represent their interests) will also try to limit any unilateral increase in risk once the policies are written, by insisting that a higher capital cushion is kept. If insurance contracts were riskless (because of some kind of government insurance), the OAS spread on insurance liabilities could be set to zero. Nevertheless, insurance is not riskless, and the implicit spread demanded by the insured should therefore be the number incorporated into the oas analysis. This may have nothing to do with the risk on the assets, as very low-risk assets with very high leverage can increase the risk to the policyholders, while risky assets combined with high levels of capital may result in a low level of policyholder risk. The paper notes the problem with obtaining an estimate of this spread, but I believe that more effort should be directed in this area.

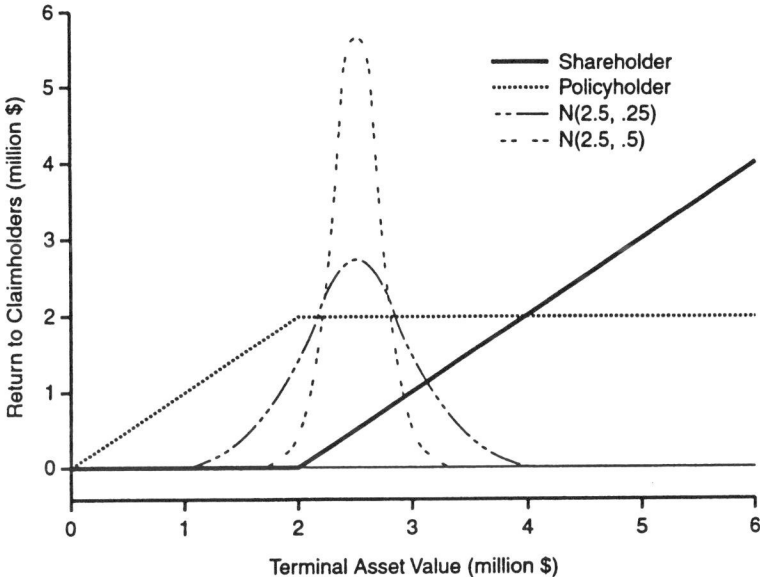

*Figure 2.* The effect of changing asset volatility. Claim against assets of insurer: policyholders vs. shareholder.

## Modeling of behavioral variables in OAVDE

The final area that I would like to comment on is the importance of incorporating the behavioral variables into the sensitivity analysis. This was briefly noted by Mr. Becker as one of the difficulties in using and OAVDE-like analysis, but I think that more emphasis needs to be placed on this area. One of the greatest problems involved in the pricing of mortgage-backed securities is accounting for prepayment behavior. Insurance policies are full of these kind of behavioral variables (lapse, exercising borrowing options, etc.) that have significant impacts on the value of the business to the insurer. A better appreciation for the impact of these kind of variables needs to be incorporated into the analysis. The OAVDE structure may also be important in determining nethods to reduce the volatility of policyholder behavior.

## Conclusion

Let me end at this point after congratulating Mr. Becker on his thorough analysis. I believe that the path he is on will continue to lead to important insights into the management of risk.

ALLAN BRENDER
*William M. Mercer Limited*

## 8. The cash flow method for valuing liabilities in Canada

*Comment: This paper was not presented at the conference nor was it even submitted in response to the Society of Actuaries Call for Papers. The topic was raised at the meeting and since it is a method, transparent in its logic and actually in use, it seems appropriate for it to be described in this volume. The method may very well not be useful in the US environment because there tend to be more options in the US than Canadian Life Insurance Contracts. – Ed.*

A number of the questions which have arisen at this conference have been answered by many Canadian actuaries. The answers we have arrived at are not quite the same answers that you might have expected to hear if you were just working in the USA. For example, we have had to ask ourselves the question 'If you have a demand liability, perhaps a cash value, is it acceptable to value the liability of a policy as anything less than the amount of this possible demand?" We have come to the conclusion that the answer is 'yes.'.

In all of our valuation work in Canada we factor lapse rates in; lapse rates trigger payment of cash values. So the expected payout of cash values is included in our reserves. If that then produces a reserve which is itself less than the cash value, so be it. We do calculate the difference if there is a deficiency and we report the deficiency, but that difference is not a liability.

Similarly, this method will often produce values for SPDAs (single premium deferred annuities) which are less than the actual book value of deposit. People are becoming more and more comfortable with that. The Canadian Institute of Chartered Accountants, which in this respect is acting similar to FASB, has a project just beginning to look at the valuation of financial instruments in general. Financial instruments are defined as all securities, all promises to pay. That includes all instruments which we normally think of as assets. But, it also includes insurance contracts. One question they could consider is whether a bank's deposits should be valued in by a method similar to or consistent with that used for insurance company deposits. Perhaps they should.

Now I want to talk about the cash flow valuation method. This is the content of Valuation Technique Paper #9 of the Canadian Institute of Actuaries, which we developed in the early 1990s and it came into effect on January 1, 1994. It is now required for the valuation of liabilities for all single premium annuities, whether they are in accumulation funds or payout annuities. Our latest draft standards for group insurance liabilities also anticipate that the cash flow valuation method will be used for this line of business. In general, there is an anticipation that the method will be used eventually for almost all products. Our new draft consolidated standards of practice talks about the use of the CFVM for all lines. As a matter of fact, I know one insurance company which writes business only in Canada, and which values all of its of its business this way.

It is important to note that the CFVM is a method which gives a value for the liability of an entire portfolio. One of the questions that was asked earlier had to do with loss of detail. We do not believe, at least for these products, that it makes a terrible amount of sense to come up with a liability for each contract. The traditional way of looking at the valuation of annuities takes into account the interest rate guaranteed in each particular contract. That interest rate could vary depending upon the week in which the contract was issued. The argument is that insurance companies, in fact, do not invest that way. They do not match contract for contract and they do not get interest rates which match what was in effect each week. As the CFVM was being developed, it was seen that it didn't make too much sense to insist upon valuation to the rate in each contract. When you look at how insurance companies really behave, we should look at analysis of an entire portfolio of business.

Another point which is implicit in a lot of what we do, a philosophical point which was also raised earlier this morning, is the matter of the extent to which things should depend upon the company as opposed to being standardized across the industry. In Canada, I think we are pretty set on having everything being company dependent. The appointed actuary has complete freedom in choosing valuation assumptions. There is no such thing as statutory assumptions. There is also no such thing as statutory vs. GAAP accounting; they're the same. There has been a lot of close work between regulators, industry, actuaries and accountants to develop one system which works for all.

One of the things that the actuary has to say in the opinion is "I have used assumptions which are appropriate to the nature of the business and to the circumstances of the company." So inherent in the actuary's certification is the philosophical point that your assumptions and your valuation depends upon the company circumstances, the company's way of doing business, and the company's way of investing.

We are assuming here with the cash flow valuation method, that there is a great deal of asset segmentation. The company to which I referred, which does business just in Canada in a single currency, operates 21 different asset segments. Every single asset is physically tagged on the computer record as belonging to one or another of the segments and there is very little movement of assets between segments. The cash flow valuation method is dependent upon doing some fairly sophisticated cash flow projections and being very upfront with all the assumptions.

How do we define the Method? This goes back to Actuarial Science 101. What is a reserve? We have stopped using the word 'reserve' because accountants think of a reserve as being a piece of surplus. We now use the term 'actuarial liability' or 'policy liability'. What is a reserve, or what is a policy liability? In an introductory course, we often start off by telling students that if insurance was a pay-as-you go business, where incidence of income was equal to incidence of expenses, then basically you wouldn't have any liability. For example, most of group insurance operates that way; there is usually some IBNR reserves, but there is very little in the way of real policy reserve. So, how do we explain the existence of reserves? We have them because there is a difference in timing. Particularly in the case of long term coverages such as whole life, the timing is such that the income comes first and the benefit payments come later. The reserve is the amount of assets that we have to have on hand today such that those assets plus the future premiums and future investment income will be sufficient to meet contractual obligations. That's the traditional way that we define liabilities.

The whole idea behind the CFVM is to take this explanation quite literally. You find that portion of total assets which you think is exactly sufficient to meet your obligations. Whatever that pot of assets is, that's the reserve. The physical assets are really the reserve. Now when you come to accounting, you have to assign a value to the reserve. So you ask what value does the accounting system assign to those assets? We happen to be using book value accounting, so we assign the book value as the value of the reserve or actuarial liability. But if we ever move to market value accounting, we will assign the market value of the assets as the actuarial liability.

We see that essentially everything is wrapped up in the assets. This is also true when you sell business. I happen to be part of the liquidation team of Confederation Life. When you sell off pieces of business, the fundamental question for the insurer that is going to take over the business is which assets are they going to take, assuming that you have assets for them to take. Again, it comes down to value of the assets. So the whole question then comes down to how do you find the assets?

Valuation Technique Paper #9 sets out a sequence of steps. We assume that you can do cash flow projections. We also assume you know all the details about your products and the underlying asset portfolio. We are assuming that you are using mortality tables and projecting expected payments and the expected maturing of deposits. Project lapses and payment and cash values, the payment of expenses, taxes, whatever physical financial transactions impact the business line.

We project all cash flows, to the time of the last liability payment. Now, the asset cash flows might go on beyond that time. If there are any remaining asset cash flows, discount them back to the time of the last liability payment. We assume that in all of this work, you will have made some assumptions about what interest rates are going to be in force at various times. Assuming that you have some sort of interest rate curve over time, you do have rates which you can use to discount all future asset cash flows to the time of the last liability payment. What the paper then suggests you do is to project all over again with one additional dollar of assets. Look at the difference that this makes in the value of asset cash flows discounted to the time of the last liability payment, the final surplus position. Once you have that difference, then you know exactly how many additional assets you have to add or subtract so that you have a final surplus of zero.

At Confed, we project with the assets we actually have and determine how much additional cash has to be added at time zero to meet the policy obligations. That is reasonable because there are all kinds of assets in the estate which we are not using in our calculations, and those assets happen to be invested in government bonds. We are using basic government yield curves for our interest rates. Our calculation of required cash and the interest rate assumptions we use to generate it is quite consistent with saying our future investments are restricted to government bonds. So, it works out pretty well.

Basically, using the process I've just described, we have the actuarial liability or reserve. Of course, the projections were based on a scenario created by a certain set of assumptions. What were the assumptions? Are they my best guess about everything, or am I using margins, allowing for adverse deviations and so on?

As I said, actuaries in Canada are responsible for setting all valuation assumptions. The methodology for this is that first of all, you pick your best guess estimate about everything. You relate mortality studies to standard tables to obtain a best guess estimate. Then you add margins for adverse deviation; we have professional guidance, technique papers and things of that sort, to give you some ideas about reasonable ranges for margins that you would add to your best guesses. Our guidance provides a specified range, a minimum and a maximum, for each margin. The minimum is a positive value, something to keep our naturally conservative actuaries and regulators happy. There is also a maximum margin that you can add; that's because we want to use these liabilities for realistic income reporting. Our statement is supposed to also be a GAAP statement and you're not supposed to go overboard on conservatism. Our statement is not intended to be a solvency statement at all. Solvency considerations not wholly addressed in the statutory statement. We address them in other ways, such as through required the risk based capital, and dynamic solvency testing

Getting back to the projections for the CFVM, you have to build in some provision for plausible adverse deviations. Now the word plausible is a really difficult word. What does plausible mean? Does it mean, assuming you have a probability distribution, that you want to cover off to the 99th percentile? Does it mean you want to cover off to the 70th percentile or, for everyone who believes that everything is Normal, two standard deviations or one standard deviation?

Some of the people who were involved with the authorship of the method tend to think that we are looking more within liabilities for something closer to the one standard deviation idea. The provision for adverse deviations is supposed to cover misestimation of the mean and a possible shift in the mean; it's not supposed to cover catastrophic things. That's what surplus is for. The question then is, how do you factor these margins into the cash flow valuation method? If the direction of the margin is clear, then we would say build them into your basic rates. This works for mortality rates and expenses.

Interest rates are much more complicated. There are also some other assumptions which are extremely complicated and the determination of margins for which is difficult and I think largely unappreciated. I think the most difficult one, particularly for life insurance is the lapse assumption. It turns out that sometimes in the early years of a policy, when reserves are lower than cash values, margins should be negative while at later durations, the margins should be positive. Finding these crossovers and they may not be unique, is an extremely difficult thing. It's a recursive problem because if you change the margin, you change the reserves and you change the relationship between the reserve and the cash value. It can be quite messy. I think that this is one place where eventually we will want to look at stochastic distributions for lapse rates.

In the CFVM we do projections under a variety of interest rate scenarios. The problem then is, what level of scenario do we want to use and how do we generate these scenarios? There really aren't good interest rate scenario generators out there. Most of the ones in the literature tend to come from option pricing papers and they are appropriate for option pricing. There is not enough emphasis in those distributions, I think, on variability, which is really what we are concerned with here. When you're looking towards pricing, variability is not really the main concern. So I think that we have a lot to do on scenario generators.

One last remark is that even though we are using book value accounting, now that this method has been used for a couple of years, we find that there is an interesting market value effect which is disturbing to a lot of insurance people in Canada. From quarter to quarter, the yield curve shifts; most interest rates generators which people are using begin with the current yield curve. Even if nothing happened in your portfolio, the mere shift in the yield curve will cause some shift, which might be 20–30 basis points, in your CFVM reserves. Many people, particularly insurance company presidents, do not like to see this in a book value environment that they've always lived in. A shift in interest rates when nothing has happened to their business can cause their reserves to go up or go down. This it affects their profit even though the assets are on a book value basis. They're finding that a little bit disturbing. But they'll get used to it.

C.D. O'BRIEN
*Royal Life Insurance*

## 9. The derivation and application of accounting standards to the market value of liabilities*

*Comment: The O'Brien paper, a version of which had previously appeared in the Journal of the Institute provides a carefully developed view of the accounting standards underlying any approach towards the calculation of the value of profits on a business. The McLaughlin paper takes a very careful look at the question of the method of discounting used in all these various approaches. The Ostaszewski paper provides a different and philosophical look at the problem. It raises the question of the value of the liability depending upon the identity of the grantor. The Lamm-Tennant discussion brings all this together, and perhaps this is a good place to end. – Ed.*

### INTRODUCTION

The purpose of this paper is to derive a set of accounting standards to be used in assessing the liabilities of a life assurance company, consistent with the assets being at market value, and set out how the suggested standards can be applied in practice.

Life assurance has lagged behind other industries in the development of generally accepted accounting principles. There are some complications: in particular, the long-term nature of the life assurance contract, the degree of uncertainty present, and the way in which high initial expenses are recouped from subsequent revenue. Furthermore, financial reporting has often been focused on statements designed to check solvency, as distinct from a presentation consistent with accounting principles. However, GAAP has been developed and refined in the USA for stock and subsequently mutual life companies. There have recently been developments in Australia, Canada, New Zealand and South Africa with the aim of producing accounts-oriented rather than solvency-based reports.

In the European Union, implementation of the Insurance Accounts Directive means that life assurance companies will in 1995 be required for the first time to prepare accounts which conform to applicable accounting standards and show a 'true and fair view'. In the UK there has been a fierce debate on how

---

*This paper is based in part on 'Profit, Capital and Value in a Proprietary Life Assurance Company', previously published by the Journal of the Institute of Actuaries (JIA 121, 1995, 285–361), and is included with permission of the Institute of Actuaries.

this is to be implemented, and different accounting bases are likely to be used for some time. The true and fair view requirement in the EU is in the context of assets being shown at market value, although UK practice has involved use of market values for some years already. In the USA, FAS 115 (*Accounting for Certain Investments in Debt and Equity Securities*) produces effectively the valuation of assets at market value. Hence there is a strong incentive to resolve how to assess the market value of the liabilities of a life assurance company.

## Accounting standards

### Standard setting

Accounting bodies have established standards for the preparation of accounts. There are many users or potential users of accounts, including shareholders, investment analysts, creditors and lenders, employees and public bodies. The standards are designed to produce accounts to meet these users' needs, although it is accepted that in some respects these needs may differ (e.g. a lender may prefer a higher degree of prudence when assessing future liabilities).

Countries have developed their own bodies with the responsibility for setting standards, such as the Financial Accounting Standards Board in the USA, and the Accounting Standards Board in the UK. This paper refers in particular to the work of the International Accounting Standards Committee (IASC). IASC's objective is for national bodies' standards to be consistent with its own.

From the work of these bodies we can consider:
1. the framework for assessing assets and liabilities which has been put forward;
2. general principles commonly applicable, e.g. prudence;
3. some principles applicable in a number of particular situations, e.g. discounting;
4. practices for the circumstances of particular industries (not well-developed for life assurance except in the USA).

### Assets, liabilities and value

We need to consider assets and liabilities together and hence it is useful to set out the definitions contained in the IASC's *Framework for the Preparation and Presentation of Financial Statements* (IASC, 1995):
- an asset is a resource controlled by the enterprise as a result of past events and from which future economic benefits are expected to flow to the enterprise;
- a liability is a present obligation of the enterprise arising from past events, the settlement of which is expected to result in an outflow from the enterprise of resources embodying economic benefits.

The excess of the firm's assets over its liabilities is its equity. It should be emphasized that this is the equity value in accounting terms rather than the value which the purchaser of a firm's shares may be prepared to pay.

The increase in the equity over a period comprises:
- new capital injected minus dividends paid;
- profits made in the period;
- other gains minus other losses, which are regarded as movements in the shareholders' reserves rather than profits.

One possibility is to restrict 'profits' to the excess of revenue over expenses from the 'ordinary activities' of the company. Gains resulting from the revaluation of assets would fall within 'other gains minus other losses'. However, a number of practices are applied. A key issue is that the determination of (assets and) liabilities is to be done in accordance with accounting standards. It is therefore helpful to consider in more detail certain elements of the IASC's framework and standards.

### International accounting standards

*Introduction*
It is worth setting out the objective given in the IASC's framework: "The objective of financial statements is to provide information about the financial position, performance and changes in financial position of an enterprise that is useful to a wide range of users in making economic decisions." The following sections consider issues arising from the IASC framework, and some particular standards which will be helpful when we examine life assurance later.

*Accruals basis*
One of the underlying assumptions is the accruals basis. The effect of transactions should be recognized when they occur rather than when cash is received or paid. Hence, by 'matching' revenue and costs to the appropriate period, the accounts can be helpful to users in making decisions. In particular, liabilities include obligations to pay cash, or its equivalent, in the future as a result of past transactions or other events.

*Going concern*
Accounts are normally prepared assuming that the firm is a going concern and will continue in operation for the foreseeable future.

*Prudence in the context of uncertainty*
We have to acknowledge that liabilities may be uncertain. The IASC comments: "Prudence is the inclusion of a degree of caution in the exercise of the judgements needed in making the estimates required under conditions of uncertainty, such that assets or income are not overstated and liabilities or expenses are not understated" (IASC, 1995). However, this does not allow the creation of

hidden reserves or excessive provisions, or the deliberate overstatement of liabilities.

*Comparability*
Comparability means that the measurement and presentation of like transactions must be carried out consistently throughout a firm and over time for that firm and in a consistent way for different firms.

*Reliability*
Reliability is particularly important: "Information has the quality of reliability when it is free from material error and bias and can be depended upon by users to represent faithfully that which it either purports to represent or could reasonably be expected to represent" (IASC, 1995). Reliability can be considered under the following headings:
- **faithful representation:** information must represent faithfully the transactions and other events it either purports to represent or could reasonably be expected to represent;
- **substance over form:** accounting should be in accordance with substance and economic reality and not merely legal form;
- **neutrality:** information should be free from bias;
- **prudence:** as referred to above;
- **completeness:** information should be complete within the bounds of materiality and cost.

*Understandability and relevance*
The IASC framework considers the qualitative characteristics of financial reports which are needed, and adds understandability and relevance to comparability and reliability.

*Timing of recognition of items*
We need to consider at what point in time we include items such as assets, liabilities and revenue in the accounts. It is especially important to consider how liabilities are established and subsequently released, since this directly impacts on the profit which is reported. The IASC framework indicates that a liability should be recognized "when it is probable that an outflow of resources embodying economic benefits will result from the settlement of a present obligation and the amount at which the settlement will take place can be measured reliably" (IASC, 1995). Timing is especially important for firms which offer long-term contracts. It is useful to refer to International Accounting Standard (IAS) 18, 'Revenue', and the sections on the rendering of services. The standard specifies that it does not apply to insurance contracts of insurance companies. However, studying the principles does assist the design of standards for life assurance.

IAS 18 explains that revenue associated with a transaction for services should be recognized by reference to the stage of completion of a transaction, provided that the outcome can be estimated reliably (the "percentage of completion method"). It states: "Under this method, revenue is recognized in the accounting periods in which the services are rendered. The recognition of revenue on this basis provides useful information on the extent of service activity and performance during a period." This standard also gives a useful example, where the selling price of a product includes an identifiable amount for subsequent servicing. In such a case the firm would defer an amount of revenue to cover the expected costs of the services under the agreement, together with a reasonable profit on those services.

The implication of the above is that profits for a period should reflect the profits made from services provided during that period. It is wrong to take credit for expected profits from services to be provided in the future. If a payment in advance has been received for future services, then the correct recognition of profit over time can be achieved by establishing a liability for the revenue relating to those future services. Such revenue encompasses both the expected costs of and profit from those future services. The logic would then follow through as follows. As those future services are provided, the liability (= cost + profit = revenue) is replaced by the costs incurred. In this way the profit emerges as those services are provided, if, of course, expenses are in line with expectations.

These principles are consistent with the reference in the IASC framework to "the requirement that revenue should be earned." This helps confirm the proposition that the presentation of assets and liabilities must ensure that profits from the provision of future services are not capitalized in advance. We also note that the EU Directives refer to profits which have been 'made' and the Companies Act in the UK which refers to 'realized' profits. The use of the past tense is significant. It is also useful to look at IAS 11 on Construction Contracts since this is particularly concerned with how to recognize financial items over the period of a long-term contract. The percentage of completion method is again applied, with the result that liabilities are adjusted over time so as to let profits emerge as the services are provided. IAS 11 also requires that when it is probable that total contract costs will exceed total contract revenue, the expected loss should be recognized immediately. More generally, costs that are not probable of being recovered are treated as an expense immediately.

Consider now a long-term contract where the firm receives a payment of $10 000 in year 1. In return, it provides services in each of years 1 to 4. The expenses incurred in providing such services in year 1 are $2000. It expects that there will be $2000 expenses in each of the remaining 3 years (inflation should be taken into account but is ignored for simplicity, as is discounting). Divide the total expenses between 'ordinary expenses', being those incurred in the year, and an increase in future liabilities being the expected future expenses of $2000 p.a. We then have the following at the end of the first year:

| Revenue | 10 000 | Ordinary expenses | 2000 |
|---|---|---|---|
|  |  | Increase in future liabilities | 6000 |
|  |  |  | 8000 |
|  |  | Profit | 2000 |
|  | 10 000 |  | 10 000 |

On this basis, the profit in years 2, 3 and 4 is expected to be zero. However, this calculation capitalizes all the profits on the contract into year 1, and is incorrect. What is required is to assess the expected revenue from the services provided in each of years 2 to 4, such revenue encompassing both expenses and profits. Say such revenue were $2500 p.a. Then the future liabilities are valued at 2500 × 3 = 7500 and the accounts would show:

| Revenue | 10 000 | Expenses | 2000 |
|---|---|---|---|
|  |  | Increase in future liabilities | 7500 |
|  |  |  | 9500 |
|  |  | Profit | 500 |
|  | 10 000 |  | 10 000 |

The profit in years 2, 3 and 4 would be expected to be the excess of the market value of the services over the expenses incurred, i.e. 2500 − 2000 = 500.

It may help to give the following explanation of revenue from IAS 18: "Revenue should be measured at the fair value of the consideration received or receivable." "Fair value is the amount for which an asset could be exchanged, or a liability settled, between knowledgeable, willing parties in an arm's length transaction." This means that in determining the value of liabilities on long-term contracts we should be considering the fair value of the services to be provided in the future.

Some authors have referred to a 'critical event' as being the time when revenue should be recognized (Myers, 1954). This can be a useful practical rule to apply in some circumstances. However, the argument above implies that it is not suitable where the firm is continuing to provide services throughout a long-term contract.

*Contingent gains and losses*
It is useful to consider IAS 10 (*Contingencies and Events Occurring after the Balance Sheet Date*) since while life assurance is excluded from its scope, it illustrates the principles of accrual, reliability and prudence. The term 'contingencies' relates to conditions or situations where the ultimate outcome in terms of gain or loss will be confirmed only on the occurrence or non-occurrence of one or more uncertain future events.

The standard indicates that if it is probable that future events will confirm a liability then, if a reasonable estimate can be made, such loss should be accrued. There may be a range of the possible amounts of loss, in which case the best estimate of the loss is accrued. Contingent gains are not accrued since this may result in recognizing revenue which may never be realized. If the realization of a gain were virtually certain, then the gain is not a contingency and accrual of the gain is appropriate. The standard also indicates that if the uncertainties are common to a large number of similar transactions then the amount of contingency may be based on the group of similar transactions.

*Discounting*

The IASC framework discusses possible ways of valuing assets and liabilities in the accounts, and accepts that the historical cost basis is that most often used. Accordingly, liabilities would be valued at the undiscounted amount of cash or cash equivalents expected to be paid to satisfy the liability in the normal course of business. However, the framework acknowledges the possible use of 'present value' accounting, where the liabilities are assessed as the present discounted value of the future net cash outflows to settle the liabilities. Indeed, there are two standards where present value accounting is specifically applied in calculating the liabilities: IAS 17 (*Accounting for Leases*); and IAS 19 (*Accounting for Retirement Benefits in the Financial Statements of Employers*), which refers to the actuarially determined value of benefits. Correspondingly, IAS 18 (*Revenue*) refers to cases where consideration is deferred, and the calculation of fair value requires the discounting of future receipts.

PRINCIPLES OF LIABILITY MEASUREMENT IN LIFE ASSURANCE

*The nature of liabilities*

We usually consider the 'main' liabilities under a life assurance policy as being the monetary amounts contractually payable to policyholders in specified circumstances, e.g. survival, sickness and death. The payments are at uncertain dates in the future, depending on, for example, rates and timings of deaths. The amounts payable may also be uncertain, depending on, for example, future investment performance. The liabilities will also be affected by policyholders exercising options, e.g. to surrender the policy early. However, life assurance is a long-term contract under which there is also a continuing obligation of the company to provide future 'services'.

*The nature of life assurance services*

Consider the services which a life assurance company provides to its policyholders. These are: advising, administration, investment and insurance. Such services make up the output of the company (see O'Brien, 1991), although they would not usually be legally distinct parts of a policy or paid for separately. Advising is part of the process whereby the policy is effected; administration includes informing the policyholder of the ongoing value of his policy; the investment service means that the insurance company rather than the policyholder is managing the investments. The 'insurance' service is exemplified by the insurance company paying the full sum assured on death immediately after the first premium is paid, or by annuity instalments continuing until death however long that means the payments are made. Incidentally, note that the supply of capital by shareholders is not a service to policyholders; it is a means by which the services can be arranged.

### Revenue from life assurance services

We have to place a value on the liability of the life assurance company to provide services. This liability is valued as the expected revenue from, or 'fair value' of such future services (not their expected cost). It is therefore useful to consider what we mean by the revenue from life assurance services.

The premiums and investment return, net of tax, receivable by a life assurance company can be (notionally) considered as comprising:
1. Amounts which are apportioned to policyholders for the payment of claims: economists would refer to these amounts as transfer payments rather than transactions reflecting an economic activity. Part is payable as claims in the current year, the remainder increases the amount set aside for payment of future claims ('cumulative policyholders' apportionment').
2. Payments for life assurance services: this is what constitutes revenue in economic terms.

By investment return we are including not only investment income but also capital appreciation (and depreciation).

Hence policyholders pay for life assurance services by receiving claim payments which are lower than the accumulated value of premiums paid. The difference is the price they are paying for the advising, administration, investment and insurance services.

### The application of accounting principles

*Introduction*
The objective of this section is to apply the accounting principles described earlier to the specific nature of life assurance to derive appropriate standards for valuing liabilities of life assurance companies. The basis for calculating liabilities should be consistent with the basis for valuing assets. IAS 25 (*Accounting for Investments*) excludes consideration of life assurance companies. Nevertheless, it can be noted that the standard refers to varying practices whereby investments may be held at market value or at historic cost (perhaps with revaluations to market value from time to time). 'Specialized investment enterprises' would normally use market value. The author's view is that life assurance company assets are most appropriately valued at market value, although there is an argument for assets used in the operation of the business (e.g. computers, premises used by staff) to be at historic cost.

*Accruals basis*
Life assurance is characterized by high expenses, including commission, in year 1, being matched by revenue (payments for life assurance services) in subsequent years. The accounts need to contain an adjustment in order to match costs and revenues. This may be either an addition to the value of assets or a deduction from the value of liabilities. What we are concerned with is ORMAC (outstanding revenue matching acquisition costs). In other words we consider what, at the balance sheet date, are the payments for life assurance services (revenue) which match acquisition costs and have not yet been received. Note:
- the payments for life assurance services are that part of premiums and investment income not apportioned to the policyholder;
- in placing a value on ORMAC we derive the present value of what are future cash receipts by discounting for interest;
- in assessing the future revenues in ORMAC we adjust for the expectation that some policies will be discontinued (e.g. through lapse or death) and the revenues not received.

Say we compare ORMAC with the acquisition costs which have not yet been recovered. Then if ORMAC is greater, we can divide it between unrecovered acquisition costs, i.e. a 'deferred acquisition cost' (DAC) asset, and the profit element relating to such costs which is included in ORMAC. However, if ORMAC is the lower figure, this means that the DAC asset is limited to the amount of ORMAC, and that acquisition activity has not made a profit.

Possible approaches in the presentation of assets and liabilities are:
- treat the whole of ORMAC as an asset;
- treat the whole of ORMAC as a deduction from liabilities;
- treat the profit element in ORMAC as an asset, treat that part which is unrecovered acquisition costs as a deduction from liabilities.

The ORMAC calculation is carried out on a prudent basis, and it may be reasonable for a company to decide not to recognize any profit element. This is consistent with the comments in IAS 18 (*Revenue*) where, during the early stages of a transaction, the outcome cannot be estimated reliably but it is probable that costs will be recovered. Revenue is then recognized to the extent of costs incurred but no profit is recognized.

*Going concern principle*
This principle implies that the firm will continue to write new as well as maintain existing business. New business may well have the effect of spreading overhead expenses and possibly reducing taxes. The value of future liabilities for expenses and payments to policyholders can therefore be assessed by assuming that future expenses and taxes will be at levels warranted by new business remaining at its current level.

However, the author's view is that there is another interpretation which would be acceptable. Because of the difficulty in making judgements extending over a long period, then if the result of some reduction in new business some years hence would be higher expenses or taxes, this can be assumed if it would be prudent to do so.

*Prudence in the context of uncertainty*
The benefits payable to policyholders are a liability which is uncertain. The value of the liability to provide services may also be difficult to estimate. Accounting standards require prudence. This implies we must build in a provision for adverse deviations. There is also a requirement to avoid 'hidden reserves' and hence the provision should not be excessive. Exercising judgement on this is not easy.

*Comparability*
While the consistency principle should be followed, this ought not to prevent appropriate changes in the basis used. Indeed, the basis for valuing liabilities should be amended from time to time to ensure that it is appropriately related to the market value of assets.

*Reliability*
The financial statements must faithfully represent the operations of the company. This means that the liabilities should be accurate and complete, subject to considerations of cost-effectiveness. This is demanding in an industry where estimates of future experience have to be made, and this may mean that particular attention has to be given to disclosing the basis of the liability calculation in the accounts.

Neutrality implies freedom from bias. Now users of life assurance company financial statements may have different objectives. A regulator concerned with solvency may wish to see greater prudence in the calculation of liabilities than does a shareholder. Hence the suggested principles for the calculation of liabilities in the accounts may be inappropriate for regulatory purposes.

*Timing of recognition of items*
We have seen previously that life assurance can be considered to encompass transfer payments (apportionments to policyholders) and life assurance services. Hence, noting that services are included at fair value not cost in order to avoid capitalizing future profits, the liabilities can be considered as: value of expected payments to policyholders minus value of expected future premiums plus the fair value of (revenue from) future life assurance services on business in force. However, in order to capitalize any future losses, we replace fair value (above) by expected cost if the latter is higher.

*Contingent gains and losses*
The need for prudence in the calculation of liabilities has already been recognized. Insurance is very much concerned with contingent risks. IAS 10 was drafted on a more general basis. Clearly the comments in the standard regarding grouping similar transactions can be applied: we should use prudent probabili-

ties applied to the large number of possible events. When considering a business risk which is not specifically an insurance risk, then even if this is not regarded as a probable contingent loss, the actuary may be more prepared than the accountant to assess the probability of an adverse outcome and hence calculate a liability being the expected value of a loss. The author's view is that this is perfectly proper. Indeed, IAS 10 is arguably imprudent by not requiring a liability to be established unless the future liability is 'probable'.

*Discounting*
Since we are concerned with future liabilities, it is right that they be discounted. This is consistent with the principles discussed earlier. The author's view is that it is appropriate to discount at the rate of return expected to be earned on the relevant assets. The rate of return used should incorporate capital gains, and is net of tax as appropriate.

## Conclusion

The author's conclusion is that it is appropriate to have a standard set of principles for the calculation of liabilities of a life assurance company. The following are suggested:
1. Liabilities are assessed as the value of benefits to policyholders plus the expected revenue from future life assurance services (or expected costs if greater), minus future premiums.
2. Liabilities are assessed prudently, but not excessively so, including a provision for adverse deviations.
3. Liabilities are assessed on a going concern basis (but some reduction in the size of activities could be assumed, with some resulting increase in the value of liabilities).
4. The liabilities are discounted to their present value, at the rate of return expected to be earned on the relevant assets.
5. The liabilities should be reduced, or the assets increased, by the outstanding revenue matching acquisition costs, where revenue is the amount not apportioned to policyholders.
6. The calculation should be made consistently, and should reliably and faithfully represent the operations of the company, without bias.

The above principles are consistent with the suggested accounting standards specifically applicable to life assurance proposed by O'Brien (1994).

## APPLICATION: THE EARNED PROFITS METHOD

### Introduction

The 'earned profits' method is a method of calculating assets and liabilities, and recognizing profits, set out by O'Brien (1994). It was designed to produce

314   C.D. O'Brien

a 'true and fair view' in insurance companies' accounts in accordance with the EU Insurance Accounts Directive. It uses assets at market value and liabilities in accordance with the principles discussed earlier. Since revenue plays an important part in the calculation of liabilities it is helpful to set out the framework in which the earned profits method works (Figure 1). Note that for this purpose investment income includes capital appreciation and depreciation, and is net of tax. Key points in Figure 1 are:

1. We divide premiums and investment income between what is apportioned to policyholders for payment of benefits and revenue, being what is forgone by policyholders, which is their payment for life assurance services.
2. Of the apportionment to policyholders part is used for payment of claims in the current accounting period and part is added to the amount set aside for payment of claims in the future (cumulative policyholders' apportionment).
3. The excess of revenue over expenses is the earned profit.
4. The earned profit may exceed the amount transferred to shareholders, especially if there are statutory solvency constraints affecting the latter. The excess is the amount added to the shareholders' accrued interest, i.e. the cumulative amount accrued for but not transferred to the shareholders.

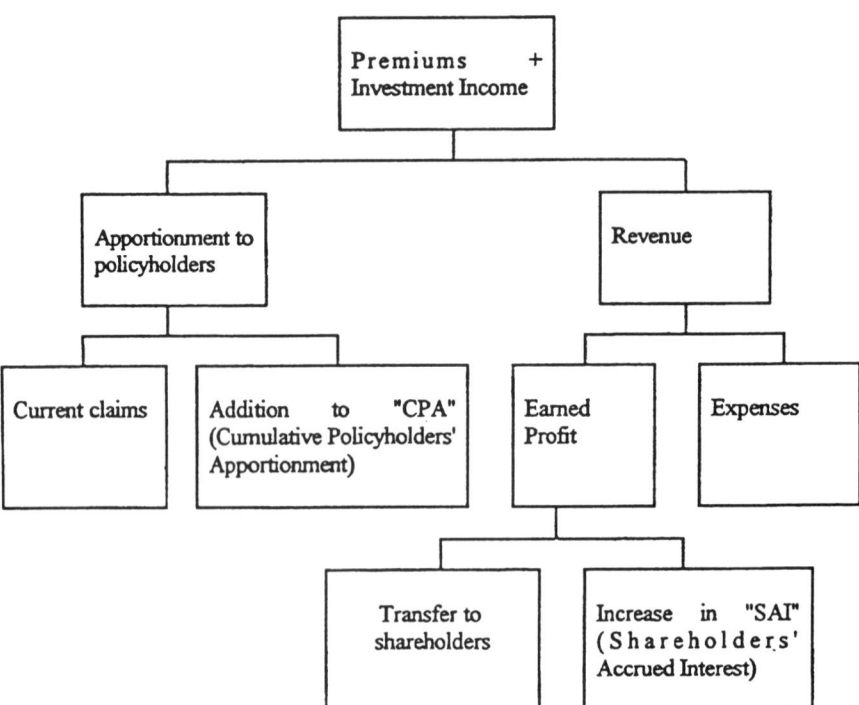

Figure 1.

## The 'current price approach'

In accordance with the foregoing we calculate liabilities as follows: value of expected payments to policyholders minus value of expected future premiums, plus expected revenue from future services, plus excess of future expenses over revenue from future services, if positive. Note that in placing a value on the obligation to provide future services, we use 'fair value', or revenue: this prevents capitalization of future profits. However, in order to meet the requirement that future losses should be capitalized, we use expenses instead of revenue for future services if that would give a higher liability. We are effectively asking a question very similar to what payment would have to be made to the policyholder to relieve the insurer of his obligations under the policy. The policyholder could then find another life assurance company to make the requisite payments and provide the future services, for which it would require appropriate compensation.

There is not generally an established market for the sale and purchase of life assurance policies. This means that this approach is difficult to apply in practice. However, it may be possible to develop some guidelines about the valuation of certain policies for this purpose. By 'revenue' we could equivalently say 'price', and hence assessing the actuarial liabilities in this way can be termed the 'current price approach'. One possibility is to consider the single premium which the life office would require, in addition to future premiums, for providing, on a new policy, the requisite benefits and services. This calculation would have to be adjusted to exclude that part of the premium ordinarily charged which relates to the services applicable at the acquisition of such policy, i.e. advising and initial administration; such adjustment may have to be on an approximate basis only.

It may be asked what amount would another insurance company, or reassurer, require to take over the office's obligations for benefits and services. However, the company acquiring the obligation may also be gaining resources or new business opportunities which can be used to develop its business, and therefore this line of enquiry may not be satisfactory in determining the value placed by the policyholder on the benefits and services. In any event, to devise a calculation basis on these lines for use in a company's accounts is quite difficult in practical terms.

The current price approach may be practicable for certain single premium policies such as immediate annuities. The office could consider the single premium which it would charge, at the balance sheet date, for the future annuity instalments then due, deducting that part of the premium which corresponds to commission and other initial expenses. In practice, the office would be placing a value on the annuity liabilities by means of assumptions of future experience which correspond to those which it uses in pricing immediate annuities at the balance sheet date.

It is quite difficult to apply the current price approach to other policy types. This is especially true where the policy benefits are secured by regular premiums.

However, this discussion does indicate that we would not ordinarily expect the liability to be less then the current surrender value of the policy. The policyholder would not relieve the insurer of his obligations for a lower amount. The only possible exception is where such surrender value is 'generous', discussed further below.

### The 'provisions approach'

We can re-express the liabilities using the following identities:

Value of expected payments to policyholders
= cumulative policyholders' apportionment (CPA)
+ value of future apportionments to policyholders

Expected revenue from future services
= value of future premiums
− value of future apportionments to policyholders

Value of excess of future expenses over revenue from future services
= value of future expenses
+ value of future apportionments to policyholders
− value of future premiums

Therefore the liabilities are: CPA + value of future expenses − (value of future premiums minus value of future apportionments to policyholders) if positive.

The key question here is how to determine the CPA. For this purpose we need to consider the type of policy and the benefits it provides.

Where the policy provides unit-linked benefits, then it is a logical starting point to say that the CPA is the current value of units. However, if the surrender value of the policy were this current value minus a deduction (other than one representing the cost of administering the surrender transaction), then the surrender value is a more appropriate reflection of what has actually been apportioned. To complete the liability calculation we need to make a projection of future financial flows under the policy. If future expenses exceed the premiums not allocated to policyholders then an addition is made to the liabilities. Such projections would be made on an appropriately prudent basis. The author's view is that they should avoid taking credit for profits which may arise on future surrender, since that means making an assumption that the policyholder will exercise an option which benefits the company. Some such profits may reliably be expected but the author's view is that they should be credited when the surrender actually takes place and the profit emerges and can be regarded as 'made'.

Consider 'participating', or 'with-profit' policies, which provide benefits, to which bonuses are added, being the policyholders' share in the profits of the company. The liability calculation needs to consider the office's policy in determining bonuses. For example, its practice may be to declare annual bonuses on a prudent basis, together with a final bonus on maturity such that the policyholder receives a payment approximately equal to his or her 'asset share', i.e. an accumulation of premiums paid with the investment return earned by the office, minus expenses, death claims and the shareholders' share of profits. In such a case the CPA is based on the asset share to date. To make the calculations merely with reference to the prudent level of bonuses declared to date may understate the liabilities. It may also be the case that the surrender value on a participating or with-profit policy is the asset share at the balance sheet date. In that event the CPA, being based on the asset share, would also be about equal to the surrender value. We also note that under such policies what is apportioned to policyholders in the future (using asset share methodology) will be the premium and investment return, less expenses, less the shareholders' profit. Hence there is no further liability for future expenses which cannot be met from future margins.

It may be helpful now to establish a general methodology. This can then be applied to determine the liability under a non-profit non-linked endowment assurance. We start from the position that the CPA on maturity is the projected maturity value. Then consider the CPA a year previously. This is the greater of the surrender value then payable and the amount which, together with the final year's premium, reduced by the final year's expenses and the amount apportioned to the policyholder for current year claims will, with interest, give the CPA (i.e. the maturity value) a year hence. In this way we determine the CPA a year from maturity. We can then deduce what is the revenue in the final year. Where the second situation above applies the revenue is the (prudent) estimate of expenses in the final year. We can then calculate what is the revenue in each year between the balance sheet date and maturity and the CPA at the balance sheet date.

This approach aims that the profit recognized at the balance sheet date does not exceed the greater of the profit which would be made if the policy were then surrendered, and the present value of the profit expected to be made if the policy continues. However, we need to modify the above stance since it is closely dependent on the surrender value, and this can be inappropriate. The surrender value on a policy may be:
1. guaranteed as a nominal amount;
2. guaranteed by the application of a stated rule to then current conditions, e.g. unit prices;
3. at the discretion of the company.

There may be instances where the surrender value is determined by the company on a discretionary basis, at a level in excess of what is 'reasonably expected' by the policyholder. For example, the company may use a formula to determine surrender values which in ordinary circumstances is acceptable and produces a modest profit. Say the market value of assets falls sharply and the granting of an unchanged surrender value would produce a loss to the life office. Such a surrender value may be above what the policyholder could reasonably expect. However, the office knows that only a small proportion of policyholders surrender in practice and it considers that asset values are likely to recover shortly. It does not feel it would be beneficial to incur the cost of changing its surrender value basis. Hence a 'reasonably expected' surrender value could be used in determining the liability, provided that the loss in granting generous surrender values (assessed using prudent assumptions) is also included.

It is also useful to make a comparison with the 'minimum actuarial reserve', where the liability is calculated using future expenses instead of revenues. We are deriving the minimum amount which, with future premiums, is expected to meet the requisite benefits and provide future services. The liability should not be less than this amount. The minimum actuarial reserve is:

> Value of expected payments to policyholders
> + value of future expenses − value of future premiums
> = liability − excess of revenue from future services over future expenses (if positive)
> = liability − profit from future services (if positive)

Consider a temporary assurance policy where no surrender value is payable. We are able to apportion to policyholders the whole of future premiums not needed to pay expenses, and hence revenue from future services equals the value of future expenses. Hence the minimum actuarial reserve is an adequate reflection of the liability. This is the same situation as that described earlier. Since the policyholder who surrenders will not receive any future services, he or she will not expect to pay for them, and we would not expect that the surrender value will be as low as the minimum actuarial reserve given that this has a deduction for profits from future services (the temporary assurance policy is an unusual case). Note also the example in Bangert's (1973) paper, where the surrender values are indeed higher.

Another constraint is that the liabilities should not be negative (with one exception). Negative liabilities imply that the policyholder has a debt to the life assurance company, this debt relating to past services. The one area where this can apply is where there is outstanding revenue matching acquisition costs.

*Assumptions*

In using the current price approach, the office would be expected to use assumptions regarding future experience which it uses in pricing the product as currently applicable, provided this a reasonable reflection of 'fair value'. In using the provisions approach the assumptions need to be prudent, incorporating a margin for adverse deviations which should not be excessive. It would be wrong to include a liability for general non-specific contingencies which would amount to 'hidden reserves'.

The going concern assumption is used. In particular, this means that:
- the future assumptions regarding expenses and taxation are made accordingly;

- we should not include any liability for additional expenses which may be payable if the office were closed to new business.

The rate of discount used is the rate of return assumed to be earned, net of tax. The calculations should be realistic, faithfully representing the company's operations. The assumptions should be based on current data and estimates as at the balance sheet date. This is consistent with use of the market value of assets which reflects current economic conditions. It would be wrong in calculating the market value of liabilities to use historic assumptions used in pricing of the products when sold some years ago.

### Deferred acquisition costs

We can reduce the liabilities by either:
1. ORMAC (outstanding revenue matching acquisition costs), or
2. DAC (deferred acquisition costs), being the unrecovered acquisition costs subject to a maximum of ORMAC.

The revenue we use in ORMAC has to be consistent with the concept of revenue used in the calculation of liabilities, i.e. that part of premiums and investment return not apportioned to policyholders. We then need to determine over what future period do the future revenues match acquisition costs. This can be expressed as using revenues up to a point in time which we can term the 'A' date of a policy. This is in contrast to the revenues beyond that date which relate to the services provided to policyholders in the future. One approach is to say that 'A' date is the point in a policy where the CPA first becomes positive. After that point, it is arguably not easy to justify an ORMAC asset (or deduction from liability) because the existence of ORMAC effectively implies that the policyholder is still 'owing' monies to the company from the acquisition. However, a positive CPA implies that the company has apportioned monies to the policyholder. Hence, ORMAC is calculated as the present value of revenue up to 'A' date, discounting for interest, at the rate of return assumed to be earned on the assets, net of tax, and withdrawals, covering the contingencies where premiums cease, i.e. incorporating not only lapses, surrenders and policies being made paid-up, but also death or other circumstances leading to premium cessation. The rates of withdrawal used should be assessed prudently.

In the ORMAC calculation we derive revenue by excluding, from premiums up to the 'A' date, the amount apportioned to policyholders for the payment of current claims. However, we also need to exclude that part of the revenue which matches the services being provided between the balance sheet date and 'A' date. Such revenue incorporates the cost of renewal administration and the profit relating thereto. While the costs can be estimated reasonably, the profits are not easy to determine since they are not identifiable as such. In practice, an estimate can be made by a projection for the period immediately following 'A' date of the revenues, renewal administration costs and profits; it may be reasonable to assume that the revenue prior to 'A' date is similar.

Now it may be that the design of products is such that the CPA becomes positive before acquisition costs have been recovered. In that case it makes sense to extend 'A' date up to the point where the present value of revenues is sufficiently high as to result in a DAC asset (or deduction from liabilities) which avoids the reporting of a loss at the outset of a policy but without crediting any profit. However, it may be prudent to limit 'A' date to some point which may be between say 4 and 10 years from the commencement of a policy on the grounds that revenue beyond that point is not sufficiently reliable to be taken into account and, in any event, it may be difficult to regard 'late' revenues as matching acquisition costs.

In practice the calculations could proceed along the following lines:

1. Consider policies of a certain type effected in a particular calendar year (say 1994).
2. Calculate the acquisition costs, including commission, for the policies in question.
3. Calculate the revenues relating to such policies which were received before the balance sheet date (say 31st December 1995). Hence if, for example, the whole of premiums to date has been forgone by policyholders, all premiums received to date on the policies (less the renewal administration costs up to 31st December 1995 and any associated profit) is the deduction from (2), the result being 'unrecovered acquisition costs'.
4. Calculate ORMAC by carrying out a projection of the policies up to 'A' date (which may be, for example, 2 years after the commencement date of the policies) and hence determine the future surpluses which we can match with acquisition costs.
5. If ORMAC is less than the unrecovered acquisition costs, then the former is the maximum asset or deduction from liabilities.
6. If ORMAC exceeds the unrecovered acquisition costs, then the former may be regarded as an asset or deduction from liabilities; or the unrecovered acquisition costs may be regarded as the DAC and deducted from liabilities, the excess being treated as an asset.
7. The results are aggregated across policy types and years of commencement.

There may be a number of other issues arising in the calculation. For example, if the acquisition costs incurred exceed those loaded for in premium rates, then one possibility is to regard the expense overrun as a loss, on the grounds that the overrun has no future matching revenues. The company's systems need to be able to identify the revenues received relating to a block of policies.

*Conclusion*

The 'earned profits' approach distinguishes between the premium and investment return which are apportioned to policyholders and the revenue which is what policyholders forgo in order to receive life assurance services. We consider liabilities in relation to payment of policyholder benefits and the revenue from future life assurance services (or cost, if higher). It is the use of revenue which avoids the capitalization of future profits. The 'current price approach' may be used in some circumstances, effectively being the price payable by the policyholder to secure the benefits and future life assurance services. However, this is quite difficult to apply in practice. Alternatively, we can apply the 'provisions approach' where the liability is the sum of the CPA amd the value of future expenses over that part of premiums not apportioned to policyholders.

We need to consider particular policy types when applying the 'provisions approach'. However, we have the following rules:
1. The liability should not be less than the current surrender value (except that if the surrender value is determined on a discretionary basis and exceeds the reasonably expected surrender value, the latter may be substituted).
2. The liability may not be negative, prior to any deduction for DAC or ORMAC.
3. The liability may not be less than the 'minimum actuarial reserve', where the cost of future life assurance services is used rather than revenue.

We can characterize the approach by saying that we calculate the liability as a 'prudent realistic reserve'. A deduction from liabilities may be made for DAC or ORMAC, where revenue is assessed consistent with the 'provisions approach'. The excess of assets over liabilities is the shareholders' accrued interest (SAI). The increase in SAI is the earned profit. It may be necessary to make a provision for deferred tax on the SAI, depending on the definition of profit for tax purposes.

SOME ALTERNATIVE APPROACHES

*Statutory solvency valuation*

Regulators of the life assurance industry have focused on ensuring that companies are solvent, i.e. have sufficient assets to continue in business and make the due payments to policyholders. This led to the making of regulations which prescribed that the assets and liabilities be calculated on a suitable basis to confirm that the solvency position of the company was satisfactory. Such investigation has been termed a 'statutory solvency valuation'. The importance of being able to continue payments to policyholders is such that this investigation is usually carried out on a basis which allows for a wide range of possible future conditions. Hence the calculation of liabilities in the statutory solvency valuation typically contains a greater degree of prudence than is consistent with accounting principles discussed earlier. Indeed, pressure for accounts of life assurance companies to be consistent with accounting principles rather than the more demanding regulatory requirements has come from stock companies concerned that the emphasis on solvency led to the value of their shares being understated. Some accountants have also been keen to take this opportunity to put the accounts of such companies onto a basis in line with traditional accounting standards.

Examples of the way in which liabilities may be given a higher value in the statutory solvency valuation than in the accounts are:
- use of investment, expense and mortality assumptions which contain margins for adverse deviations which amount to a degree of prudence too large to be consistent with faithful representation (in accounts this would be regarded as holding 'hidden reserves');
- increasing the liabilities so that policyholders' entitlements are secure even if the company is closed to new business;
- inclusion of a 'general contingency reserve';
- no allowance, or an inadequate allowance, being made for deferred acquisition costs.

However, there is an important reason which may justify the liabilities having a lower value in the statutory solvency valuation. This is because the accounts include a liability for the revenue from future life assurance services so that profit can arise over time as the services are provided. However, the main purpose of the statutory solvency valuation is arguably to check whether the assets are more than sufficient to pay the policy benefits and pay for the expenses expected to be incurred. From the viewpoint of the statutory solvency valuation it does not matter if the company fails to make any profits for its shareholders in the future; it is the policyholders on whom we are focusing. Nevertheless, it is usually regarded as inappropriate for the statutory solvency valuation liability to be (significantly) below the current surrender value, although there can be different views on what is meant by 'significantly' in this context, and whether the test is carried out in aggregate or on a policy-by-policy basis. Hence we could say that the statutory solvency valuation liability is typically the minimum actuarial reserve, but with a more prudent provision for adverse deviations, and subject to a minimum surrender value test.

This argument is different from the basis under which liabilities have to be calculated in statutory solvency valuations in the European Union. The EU Third Life (Framework) Directive requires: "The method of calculation of technical provisions ... shall be such as to recognize the distribution of profits in an appropriate way over the duration of each policy." This implies that the calculation uses revenue rather than expenses for future life assurance services. There is a separate requirement to provide for expenses so that the position should expenses exceed revenue is covered.

Clearly we have different requirements for the financial reports of life assurance companies. Do we need a degree of prudence consistent with accounting principles (A1) or greater than this to protect policyholders (A2)? Do we wish to see profits emerging over time as services are provided (B1) or do we have reason to omit future profits from the liabilities (B2)? The development of different sets of reports for these different purposes is right and proper.
- A1 and B1 lead to the accounting principles discussed earlier;
- A2 and B2 mean that we have a higher provision for adverse deviations, and we substitute costs for revenues in the liabilities, subject to a minimum

surrender value test. This can be appropriate for a statutory solvency valuation (but may be inconsistent with the EU requirement);
- A2 and B1 means that we use accounting principles subject to a higher provision for adverse deviations, and is consistent with the EU requirement.

Consider a policy where $A$, $E$ and $P$ represent the breakdown of future premiums into the apportionment to policyholders, expenses and profits. CPA is the cumulative policyholders' apportionment.

Then the accounting liability:

$= \mathrm{CPA} + A$    [benefits to policyholders]
$- (A + E + P)$    [future premiums]
$+ (E + P)$    [revenue from future services]
$= \mathrm{CPA}$

| CPA | A |
|---|---|
|  | E |
|  | P |

The statutory solvency valuation liability, if using future expenses (rather than revenues):

$= \mathrm{CPA} + A$    [benefits to policyholders]
$- (A + E + P)$    [future premiums]
$+ E$    [future expenses]
$= \mathrm{CPA} - P$

but using greater prudence in the calculation and in any event possibly subject to a minimum of the surrender value (which may be the CPA).

If the future expenses were not covered by revenue, then the premium is made up of $A$ and $R$ being the amounts apportioned and revenue respectively, while expenses equal $R$ (revenue) plus $L$ (loss).

Then the accounting liability and statutory solvency valuation liability both use future expenses:

$= \mathrm{CPA} + A$    [benefits to policyholders]
$- (A + R)$    [future premiums]
$+ (R + L)$    [future expenses]
$= \mathrm{CPA} + L$

| CPA | A |
|---|---|
|  | R |
|  | L |

but the statutory solvency valuation typically uses greater prudence.

The above argument has been developed on the basis that the assets in the statutory solvency valuation are at market value, which is being introduced throughout the EU, and has been present in the UK for some time (some deduction from asset values may be made in certain circumstances, e.g. where assets are not widely distributed). What is clear is that it is quite wrong to assume that the results of the statutory solvency valuation are necessarily appropriate for accounts prepared in accordance with generally accepted accounting principles and give a 'true and fair view'.

## Embedded values and PVP

When assessing the value of a life assurance company it is common to calculate its 'embedded value', being the present value of profits (PVP) expected to arise in the future, from business already written. In calculating the embedded value, estimates are needed of future experience, for example the investment return, tax, expenses, withdrawal and mortality rates, and charges. These are usually best estimates, where the margin for uncertainty is less than the prudence in accordance with accounting standards. To the projected profit stream is applied a discount rate reflecting the deferral of income and the risk relating to the emergence of income as judged by the shareholders. There is another method of calculating the embedded value. Instead of using best estimates we can build in margins for prudence in accordance with accounting standards, in conjunction with a discount rate which is the rate of return expected to be earned on the assets, net of tax. We can also calculate the embedded value as the difference between the market value of assets and a new calculation of liabilities (the 'embedded value reserve'). This would be similar to the minimum actuarial reserve, where the liability for future life assurance services is at cost rather than revenue. We also note the following, which would lead to the embedded value reserve being typically lower than the minimum actuarial reserve:

- the degree of prudence is in accordance with accounting principles rather than the statutory solvency valuation;
- no minimum surrender value test is included;
- it is assumed that some policies will be surrendered (or lapse, or be made paid-up), and the liabilities for policy benefits and future expenses are calculated (typically reduced) accordingly;
- a deduction is made for ORMAC.

We note that the embedded value is the value of all profits expected to arise under the statutory solvency valuation in future. This consists of two parts:

1. The shareholders' accrued interest, i.e. profits already made but not yet transferred to shareholders, because statutory solvency regulations do not permit such transfer, or because the company wishes to retain surplus, and
2. The present value of profits expected to be made from services to be provided in the future (on business already in force).

Hence we can see that the embedded value cannot be considered to be profits which have already been earned, made or realized. It is the inclusion of item (2) above which is contrary to accounting principles which do not permit the inclusion of profits to be made in the future. The inclusion of profits to be made in the future on existing business highlights the significance of the (uncertain) estimates of future experience to a greater degree than where we are concerned (in ordinary accountancy) with profits which have already been made. Notwithstanding the above comments, the practice in the UK of certain companies which own insurance companies has been to include in their consolidated accounts a profit equal to the increase in embedded value.

## A 'margins' basis

### The UK 'accruals method' proposals 1990-94

The Association of British Insurers (1992) issued draft proposals for a method of recognizing profits in stock companies called the 'accruals method'. The proposals were originally issued for comment in 1990. The method contains a calculation of the shareholders' accrued interest. We can derive the liabilities of the company as the market value of assets less the SAI. A key point in the proposals was the use of 'planned profit margins'. We can think of this as adding such margins so as to substitute revenue for costs in relation to life assurance services.

There were a substantial number of objections to the use of planned profit margins. Such margins were intended to be applied to each of the different services provided, e.g. renewal administration, mortality risks. A choice was made of how the margin was to be decided, e.g. by adding 20% to renewal expenses. However, in practice, these were very subjective estimates, more like guesses. Companies typically price their products on the basis of an overall profit target rather than a profit on each individual element. Furthermore, it is not possible to apply controls to verify that the (assumed) planned profit margins happened in practice. The policyholder pays for all his or her services in one (single or regular) premium: profits on individual services cannot be identified. The way in which parameters were chosen to calculate the planned profit margins caused several problems. Say one margin is 20% of renewal expenses. If expenses increase, does the profit margin increase? This is illogical: higher expenses are usually associated with lower not higher profits.

The theory of planned profit margins indicates that they should be applied only to the services provided to policyholders (advising, administering, insuring, investing). Profit then reflects the excess of what the policyholder pays for that service over the cost to the company (the profit margin on that service). Such profit should be sufficient to compensate the company for the risks it runs, for example that surrenders might be high, or that tax rates might increase. However, the accruals method applied planned profit margins not only to services but also to some business risks such as surrender rates: that is quite wrong.

A number of other issues which also caused problems, including certain aspects of with-profits business and the need to meet the newly prescribed accounts formats. Also, there was no attempt to calculate the planned profit margin on services provided at the commencement of the policy, and there was much concern that a profit at the outset was determined as a residual after planned profit margins in the future (on an arguably subjective basis) had been allowed for.

The accruals method proposals received support from only a few companies. Accordingly, the proposals as originally published, using planned profit margins, are no longer going ahead. Instead there is a proposal termed the 'achieved profits method' which is currently under discussion. Effectively this requires a calculation of the present value of future statutory solvency profits, using so-called 'risk margins'. The outcome may be the embedded value; or a lower amount if the risk margins are such as to remove some future profits. The inability to validate risk margins is a key concern, as is the wide variety of results which could be produced: a disappointing preference for pragmatism instead of using soundly-based principles.

*The margins approach generally*
The use of profit margins in respect of individual services will inevitably cause difficulties since policyholders do not in practice pay for services individually and hence it is not possible to verify what an actuary might postulate regarding such margins.

## Other approaches

*Deferred acquisition costs*
One approach to deferring acquisition costs is to spread the deferral over the lifetime of the policy. This may be done by making assumptions about the rate at which costs are recovered, using some formula; or Zillmerization, particularly where a net premium method of valuation is used. However, such approaches may not identify precisely what are the revenues matching acquisition costs, where revenue has the meaning used in this paper, to enable an appropriate matching to be carried out. Sometimes the distinction between 'premiums' and 'revenues' is not made appropriately. Furthermore, in many product designs, it is wrong to think of acquisition costs being recovered over the lifetime of the policy. For a policy where the surrender value in the first 2 years is low, with the office explaining that it has had high initial expenses to meet, this implies that those costs are being recovered in the early years rather than evenly over the lifetime of the policy.

*Other overseas developments*
This chapter is unable to review other overseas developments in detail. However, a 'margin on services' method has been developed in Australia, which has some similarities to (and also several differences from) the way margins were used in the accruals method which was proposed in the UK. In Canada, the policy premium method has been introduced, with both the statutory solvency valuation and the accounts based on this.

CONCLUDING COMMENTS

*Comparisons*

Table 1 is a comparison of the valuation of assets and liabilities of a unit-linked company using the statutory solvency valuation and the earned profits method in the accounts. ORMAC is shown as an asset, although it could instead be a deduction from liabilities.

In this example, it is seen that the Shareholders' Accrued Interest, being the excess of assets over liabilities, increased from 71 on 1st January (after the transfer to shareholders) to 86 on 31st December (before the transfer). Hence the earned profit is 15. Alternatively, we can calculate the SAI after the transfer to shareholders of 7 has been made, i.e. it reduces from 86 to 79. Then the increase in SAI is 79 − 71 = 8, and to this we add the statutory solvency profit

*Table 1.*

|  | 1st January (after transfer to shareholders) |  | 31st December |  |
|---|---|---|---|---|
|  | Statutory solvency | Earned profits | Statutory solvency | Earned profits |
| *Value of assets* |  |  |  |  |
| Linked assets | 1000 | 1000 | 1100 | 1100 |
| Other assets | 110 | 110 | 130 | 130 |
| ORMAC | 0 | 20 | 0 | 22 |
| Total | 1110 | 1130 | 1230 | 1252 |
| *Value of liabilities* |  |  |  |  |
| Unit liabilities | 1000 | 1000 | 1100 | 1100 |
| Future expenses not met from future premiums (excluding premiums needed for ORMAC or apportioned to policyholders) | 70 | 52 | 80 | 59 |
| AIDS | 8 | 5 | 8 | 5 |
| Options | 4 | 2 | 4 | 2 |
| Resilience test | 3 | 0 | 4 | 0 |
| Fund closure | 5 | 0 | 6 | 0 |
| General contingency | 10 | 0 | 10 | 0 |
| Total | 1100 | 1059 | 1212 | 1166 |
| Surplus (statutory solvency) |  |  | 18 | n/a |
| SAI (earned profits method) pre-transfer |  |  | n/a | 86 |
| Transfer to shareholders' fund [= statutory solvency profit] |  |  | 7 | 7 |
| Surplus carried forward (statutory solvency) | 10 | n/a | 11 | n/a |
| SAI (earned profits method) post-transfer | n/a | 71 | n/a | 79 |
| Earned profit = statutory solvency profit (7) + increase in SAI (79 minus 71) |  |  |  | 15 |

of 7 to give the earned profit of 15. For a mutual office writing participating business, there is no earned profit for shareholders, provided we are assuming that all the remaining assets are being apportioned to policyholders. For a stock company writing participating business, the statutory solvency valuation may place a value on the liabilities including (prudently calculated) bonuses declared to date. There then may be surplus assets, referred to as the 'estate' which are not analysed further. The Earned Profits method requires a calculation of what part of the estate can be apportioned to policyholders and the remainder which is included in the shareholders' accrued interest.

*Total value and rate of return*

We can also use the approach in this paper to analyse the value of the company. In particular, we distinguish between SAI and the embedded value: the latter includes future profits not yet made on existing business. We also distinguish between embedded value and total value: the latter includes the profits expected from new business to be written in the future.

The company's value can hence be shown as in Figure 2. The 'prudent realistic' basis uses the liability calculation in the earned profits method, ignoring ORMAC (which is shown separately in Figure 2).

Note: in the UK there is a practice of holding a separate shareholders' fund. The net assets of such fund are part of the company's value.

We can use an example of a unit-linked company as follows, where items (1) to (3) are consistent with Table 1:

|     |     | 1 Jan | 31 Dec |
| --- | --- | --- | --- |
| (1) | Statutory solvency surplus carried forward in long-term fund (after transfer to shareholders) | 10 | 11 |
| (2) | Excess of prudent realistic liabilities over statutory solvency liabilities | 41 | 46 |
| (3) | ORMAC | 20 | 22 |
| (4) | Value of expected profits on future services on existing business | 110 | 114 |
| (5) | Value of expected profits on future new business | 120 | 121 |
|     | Shareholders' accrued interest = (1) + (2) + (3) | 71 | 79 |
|     | Embedded value = (1) + (2) + (3) + (4) | 181 | 193 |
|     | Total value = (1) to (5) | 301 | 314 |
|     | Earned profit = statutory solvency profit |   | 7 |
|     | + increase in SAI |   | 8 |
|     |   |   | 15 |

We then calculate the rate of return of the company by dividing the earned profit by the shareholders' accrued interest (which is effectively the capital base of the company):

$$\text{Rate of return} = \frac{\text{earned profit}}{\text{SAI}} = \frac{15}{71} = 21.1\%$$

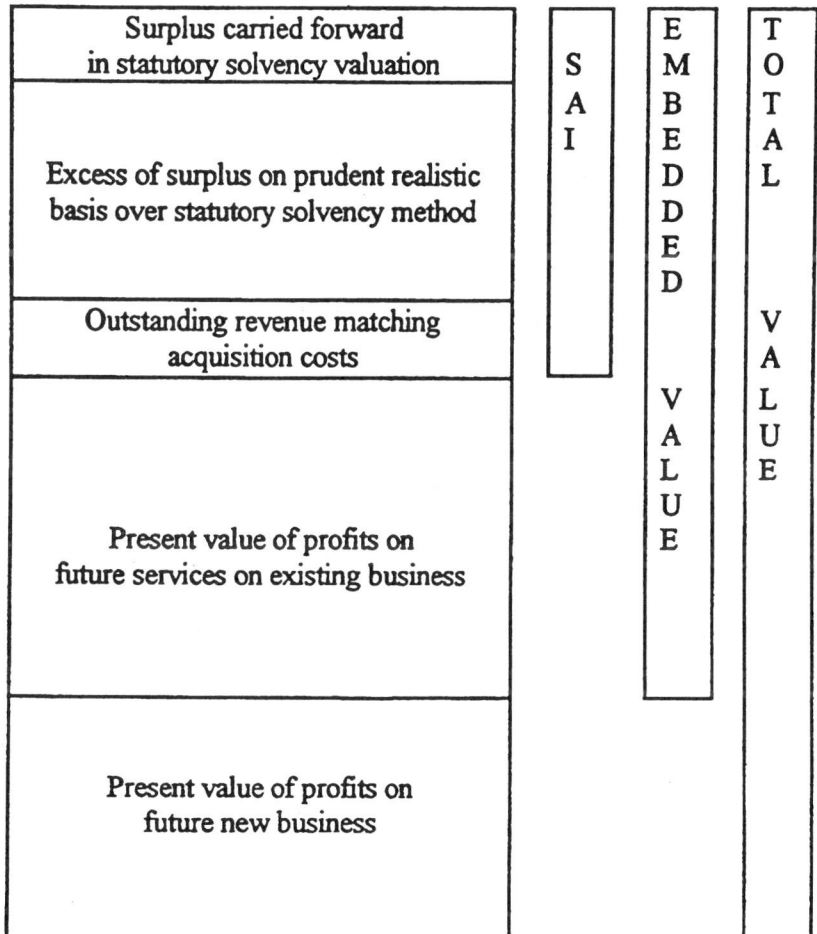

Figure 2.

## Summary

This chapter has considered how accounting principles can be applied to the specific circumstances of life assurance companies to develop a set of principles which can be used to determine the market value of liabilities. The earned profits method of calculating profits adopts these principles and can be used by companies to prepare accounts which in normal circumstances would meet the requirements for a 'true and fair view' and can be considered to be in accordance with generally accepted accounting principles.

The methodology avoids the capitalization of future profits by using the revenue from future life assurances services. It uses economic principles to distinguish revenue from what is apportioned to policyholders for the payment of policy benefits. By using the concept of the CPA it avoids the problems inherent in estimating (and verifying) the profits on individual activities. The calculation of deferred acquisition costs focuses on matching costs and revenues, and uses the concept of ORMAC (outstanding revenue matching acquisition costs). The approach can be used to present a new analysis of the value of a life assurance company, and the rate of return which the company is making.

## REFERENCES

Association of British Insurers (1992). Draft proposals on accounting for shareholders' profits in long-term insurance business.
Bangert, R.M. (1973). Valuation of a life assurance company for purchase. *Journal of the Institute of Actuaries*, **99**, 131–152.
International Accounting Standards Committee (1995). International Accounting Standards 1995. London: IASC.
Myers, J.H. (1959). The critical event and the recognition of net profit. Accounting Review.
O'Brien, C.D. (1991). Measuring the output of life assurance companies. Geneva Papers on Risk and Insurance, Issues and Practice, 59.
O'Brien, C.D. (1994). Profit, capital and value in a proprietary life assurance company. *Journal of the Institute of Actuaries*, **121**, 285–339.

S. MICHAEL McLAUGHLIN
*Ernst & Young LLP*

# The indexed discount rate method for fair valuation of liabilities

### Abstract

The indexed discount rate method for fair valuation of liabilities calls for projections of liability cash flows using realistic assumptions as to future experience. Multiple scenarios are projected covering the range of options that might be exercised by contract holders and by the company, and the range of different levels of experience that might be observed. The projected cash flows for each scenario are discounted at the Treasury spot rate appropriate to the duration of the cash flow. No adjustment spread is added to the Treasury rates because that would inappropriately make further adjustment for risk. The fair value is selected as the mean of the range of present values. The discount rate is determined objectively as of the date of valuation.

This method reflects the uncertainties in the cash flows, and determines their value based on the current yield curve in an objective manner. Actuarial judgment is necessary in developing the various assumption scenarios, but not the discount rate. The fair value of liabilities so determined is consistent with the market value of the supporting assets, but is not derived directly from them. Specific assets may be modeled in order to test assumptions, but the fair value of liabilities is not dependent on any current or future portfolio of assets.

### Introduction

The fair value of most financial assets is easily determinable, based on recent prices paid in an active secondary market. This is called market value. The book value of financial assets is also easily determinable, based on cost or amortized cost. For financial reporting, either value might be acceptable – the choice is a philosophical one. The view favoring market value might argue that it is more realistic as it reflects the dynamics of the market; the view favoring book value might argue that it is more stable thus better suited for use in comparing to long term liabilities. Whichever philosophical choice is made, implementation is easy because either value can be determined in a straightforward manner.

The fair value of most liabilities, on the other hand, is less easily determinable. Many financial liabilities are not actively traded in a market. For example, while the holder of a corporate bond has an asset that is easily traded, the issuer of that same bond may have much less flexibility in increasing or decreasing its liability incrementally. Similarly, life insurance contract liabilities can not easily be traded after their issue. Withdrawals or surrenders may occur at the option of the contract holder, but sale of the entire contract in most circumstances is not possible. The issuer may be able to sell a group of contracts, but such sales are relatively infrequent and the price of each transaction is negotiated separately. Further, the value is known only when the sale is consumated. Thus for liabilities, a pure philosophical discussion of the appropriate choice of book versus fair value for financial reporting is stymied by the difficulty of determining market value. Thus one might see liabilities held at book value for the sake of expediency, even when assets are held at fair value. However, it is difficult to understand the meaning of a balance sheet with this inconsistency.

Accordingly, it is very desirable to find an alternative method for determining fair value for financial liabilities, specifically insurance contracts. The fair value of liabilities will move over time in approximate synchronicity with the market value of assets, thus reducing balance sheet distortions. Of course equity will rise and fall with changing interest rates, but the changes in equity will be representative of asset and liability mismatches, not the idiosyncrasies of the accounting method. Actuarial methods already exist for determining the value of a group of insurance contracts that is proposed for sale. These 'appraisal' methods involve discounting future cash flows at an appropriately selected risk rate of return. The methods have been validated, in broad terms, by final settlement prices of actual transactions. Several variations of actuarial appraisal methods are possible. The method proposed in this paper is one variation. It attempts to make the approach as objective and as easily understood as possible, given that in the absence of an active market some subjectivity and complexity inevitably remain.

## Criteria

Prior to defining the approach, a set of criteria was developed that a fair value method for liabilities should meet. The shape of the proposed method was developed from the criteria, which were established based on a concept of the important elements of fair valuation of both assets and liabilities. A fair valuation method for liabilities should meet the following criteria: (i) it must be independent of the specific assets used to support the liabilities; (ii) it must be objective, as far as possible; (iii) it should be consistent with other actuarial methods in common use; (iv) it should be general enough to deal with the wide range of insurance contracts in existence; and (v) it should be simple to understand.

### Independence of the assets

The fair value of liabilities must be independent, as far as possible, of the specific assets used to support the liabilities. The fair value of assets in an insurance company are able to be determined independent of the liabilities, and of course independent of each other. This characteristic is highly desirable and perhaps is intrinsic to a definition of 'fair' value. Likewise, the fair value of liabilities should be independent of the specific supporting assets, as well as the presence or absence of other liabilities.

It seems essential that this criterion be met. The assets supporting the liabilities as of the date of valuation will not be held indefinitely. One day later the assets could be traded, at fair value, for new assets with different characteristics. Should the value of the liabilities change as a result of such turnover? We think not. In company acquisition situations, provided that the portfolio of assets is liquid and can be marked to market, the value of the liabilities is little if at all dependent on the specific assets themselves. The purchaser is not likely to regard the asset portfolio as a permanent characteristic of the insurance contracts. Instead the purchaser feels free to determine a price in the knowledge that the portfolio can be turned over, if desired, in a reasonable length of time.

If the company being sold has an illiquid asset portfolio, or one whose market value is uncertain, the transaction may appear unattractive to the purchaser. The purchase price would tend to be lower than it would be otherwise. This is reflective of the value of the assets as seen by the purchaser, and is not an impairment or reflection of the value of the liabilities.

Thus it seems that an appropriate method of determining fair value of liabilities is one that is independent of the asset portfolio; hence the fair value will not change when the asset portfolio changes. Much that comes later depends on adherence to this criterion.

As a corollary, we also propose that the fair value of one liability, or group of liabilities, should not be dependent on the existence of other liabilities. The existence of multiple liabilities (e.g. traditional life insurance business and deferred annuities) may indeed reduce overall risk to the enterprise (the covariance of risk phenomenon) but that does not affect the value of the liabilities themselves. If the enterprise is subject to lower overall risk, that fact will presumably be reflected in lower capital requirements.

Of course, the fair value of the liabilities will be dependent on the characteristics of the liabilities themselves. The cash flows that are likely to emerge over time will be dependent on the terms of the contract, future mortality, lapsation, and other factors. Thus all 10-year Treasury notes of a given coupon and maturity are alike, but not all SPDAs with identical issue ages are alike. This is due to the different behavior of different groups of SPDAs. Some are pension qualified, others are issued to schoolteachers, others are distributed through licensed brokers. Different groups of contracts will behave differently and thus will appropriately have different fair values.

*Objectivity*

The choice of the discount rate for the valuation must be objectively determinable. The present value of future cash flows is sensitive to the discount rate assumption, which in turn can be a subjective choice unless clearly defined. Typically the discount rate is based on an earned interest rate and a risk adjustment spread. Subjectivity arises in selection of both the earned rate and the spread. In some cases even the direction of the spread is subjective. To reduce subjectivity the preferred method is one in which the choice of discount rate is not based on judgment. The discount rate is therefore proposed to be based on an external index, or rate. This criterion also facilitates compliance with other criteria, namely independence, consistency and simplicity.

It is true that many other assumptions are necessary in discounted cash flow methods, and many of those assumptions involve judgment in their determination. Nonetheless the interest rate for discounting is unique, because it is the only assumption shared with the asset valuation. Other assumptions (mortality, lapse rates, etc.) are specific to the liabilities. To preserve maximum objectivity and consistency with the market value of assets we propose that judgment in establishing this sole 'shared' assumption be eliminated.

*Consistency*

The method should be consistent with existing actuarial methods, specifically those relating to actuarial appraisals of insurance company values, gross premium valuations, and option pricing. Meeting this criterion enhances the method's credibility and simplicity, and avoids the need for new methodologies to be developed.

Consistency is also important in other respects. The method should be capable of consistent application at all companies. Different asset portfolios and different choices of discount rate would reduce consistency of liability valuation. Standardization in these areas will improve comparability of financial reporting across companies. The method also should be consistent with (although not dependent on) the value of the supporting assets. The market value of the assets is itself based on market conditions, which for financial assets means primarily the level and shape of the interest rate yield curve. Thus the fair value of liabilities, to be consistent, must also depend on the same yield curve as that underlying asset market values. For this reason, as mentioned above, the discount rate is based on an objective external index.

*Generality*

The method should not vary in its fundamentals due to different specific contract provisions. The same approach should apply to traditional and interest sensitive life insurance, deferred and immediate annuities, and health and property/casualty reserves. The method should be applicable internationally, although it need not be consistent with existing accounting conventions in all countries. The method also should not be defined in terms of specific modeling tools.

*Simplicity*

The method must be easily explainable and understandable to its intended audience. The audience comprises relatively sophisticated professionals and investors, thus this criterion is not a very demanding one. Yet a method that is understandable only to a minority of experienced professionals or academics is rejected by this criterion. The indexed discount rate method as proposed in this paper meets all the above mentioned criteria.

## METHOD

The indexed discount rate method is a discounted cash flow approach. It is contemplated that multiple realistic projections of future liability cash flows are made, which are then discounted at an objectively determined rate of return. The cash flows projected should be those which are likely to occur, taking into consideration the future behavior of contract holders and the company and other risks. The discount rate is a risk free rate; no adjustment spread is added or subtracted because uncertainties in future cash flows are already reflected in the projections. The present value of each projection of cash flows is found using the same discount rate for all projections. The fair value is selected as the mean of the present values so determined.

### Cash flows

In projecting cash flows, it is appropriate to estimate future benefits to be paid and the likelihood of continuance of the contract. Thus, assumptions are needed as to future mortality rates, morbidity rates, (more generally, the frequency and severity of claim), interest and dividends paid, expenses, contract lapse rates, and withdrawals of funds, either through surrenders or policy loans. However, both parties to the contract have choices that they may make over time. For certain contracts, withdrawals or deposits may be made by the contract holder after issue. Simply paying the next premium (where necessary for contract renewal) is the contract holder's option. The company also has options – it may elect to reduce the rates of interest credited to the contract in order to increase profitability, subject of course to competitive considerations. In addition to uncertainties in cash flows due to options that may be exercised, there are risks that are not under the control of either the contract holder or the company.

A single projection of cash flows therefore may not be adequate. Multiple projections would most likely be needed to evaluate the range of choices that may be made and the uncontrolled risks that might influence cash flows. It is envisioned that several reasonable alternatives would be explored, with varying sets of assumptions as to future experience. Both optimistic and pessimistic views would be considered. Unlikely or extreme outcomes would not be used.

### Interest rate for discounting

The market value of financial assets is dependent on the yield curve of interest rates for the highest quality government securities (Treasuries) applicable on the date of valuation, plus a spread to reflect the risk of the asset cash flows being realized. The question arises whether a spread relative to Treasuries is appropriate here in the choice of a discount rate for valuation of liability cash flows.

The risks to the holder of an asset are that future cash flows will be received in smaller amounts, or later than expected. To reflect this, when discounting future cash flows an adjustment spread is added to the risk free interest rate. The risks to the holder of a liability are that future cash flows will be necessary in larger amounts, or sooner than expected. Thus it may seem appropriate to reflect this by using a discount rate based on a risk free rate reduced by an adjustment spread.

Although either risk-adjustment spreads or multiple scenarios may be used to evaluate risk and uncertainty, the use of both devices together may be redundant. It is proposed here that the use of multiple scenarios to evaluate the likelihood of receiving the projected cash flows is sufficient consideration of risk. No adjustment to the risk free discount rate is necessary, because there are no known risks that were not already considered. Thus the discount rate for each cash flow is the duration-appropriate Treasury spot rate on the date of the fair value determination. This single set of rates fully reflects the yield curve, is totally objective, and is easily determinable on any given date from published information.

It could be argued that there is an inherent inconsistency in projecting multiple future interest rate paths but discounting at current yield curve rates. However, all future paths are derived from and consistent with the current yield curve. Multiple paths are used to create a range of assumptions. Using the current yield curve gives equal weight to all sets of assumptions, instead of lower weight to high interest rate scenarios, and vice versa. The same discount rates are applied to all cash flows averaged across all scenarios.

### Selection of central value

A range of present values will be available, based on the multiple projections of cash flow, each discounted at the same discount rates. Presumably all outcomes are possible and reasonable, although the relative likelihood of each arising is unknown. One fair value must be selected. We propose that the mean value is the preferred approach, although the median value may be more appropriate in some situations. There is a rough analogy with the operation of securities markets. Many participants evaluate the attractiveness of an asset, each from their own perspective. Some participants view the asset as expensive, others view it as cheap. A transaction occurs when two parties feel that the price is attractive, each for their own purposes. The market price is a reliable indicator of value because such transactions occur frequently. If the market is fairly efficient, the market price should lie near the center of a range of reasonable values that might be determined by many participants. Each scenario can be regarded as a separate possible determination of value. Either the mean or median of many different but reasonable values may be a fair method of determining value.

The mean value reflects all projection values equally, whether high or low, to a greater extent than the median. Thus the mean is the preferred approach where there is a skewed distribution of values. The validity of using the mean does depend on the assumption that each scenario is equally probable. While this may not be exactly true, a weighted mean is not suggested due to its potential subjectivity. Instead, distortions on this account are minimized by using a large number of scenarios. If the mean value is influenced significantly by one or two extreme scenarios, this may indicate that too few scenarios have been tested. Either a larger number of scenarios should be explored, or the extreme values should be reexamined for plausibility. Outcomes that are only remotely likely should be excluded. In some cases the multiple outcomes may be widely dispersed, or a few extreme outcomes can not be eliminated. In these cases the median value may be more representative than the mean. Judgment is needed in making this selection. It should be noted that the use of the median versus the mean for selecting the central fair value may have an impact on the relative conservatism of the fair value.

## Assumptions

In this section we will discuss the major assumptions as to future experience that are needed, in the context of the indexed discount rate method.

### Contract structure

The projections should clearly reflect the nature of the contract, namely its date of inception, date of expiry if applicable, the conditions for its renewal, the type and amount of benefits payable, and the existence or absence of premium or other guarantees.

### Premiums and deposits

Flexible premium contracts will require a range of assumptions consistent with the projected interest rate environment. For example, deposits would tend to be larger when credited rates are high and spreads are thin. The projection models used should allow reasonable assumptions to be set and reviewed.

### Mortality

For life insurance and payout annuities, mortality rates are easily available from experience or published sources. Nonetheless, for some types of coverage, perhaps a range of mortality rates should be considered. For example, stochastic testing of mortality rates may be more important for term life insurance with large net amounts at risk than varying interest rates.

## Morbidity

For disability or medical insurance, the range of claim costs can be much wider than for life insurance. Here, it would seem extremely desirable for multiple projections of liability cash flows to be made, using a range of probabilities as to frequency of claim and its continuance or severity. The effect of varying morbidity on the range of cash flow results could be much more significant than the effect of varying interest rates.

## Lapsation

The contract holder generally has the right to terminate the contract merely by discontinuing payment of future premiums, where necessary for contract continuance, or by requesting surrender. Benefits may be payable at the time of lapsation, but of course the contract ceases to exist and no future cash flows need be projected from that point. A range of lapse rates should be considered. The rates used should take into account the economic incentives to lapse, such as disintermediation or self selection against the company.

## Withdrawal of Funds

We use this term to mean full or partial surrender of the fund balance or cash value of the contract, or policy loan borrowing. Experience studies can be relied on as an indicator of possible future experience, but it will usually be necessary for the actuary to consider how future experience may differ. The range of variation could be considerable for highly interest sensitive contracts.

## Credited interest rates

Many contracts have policyholder funds or contract reserves to which the insurance company credits accruing interest. A clear and objective approach for establishing this assumption is important. We will use a universal life contract as an example. The credited rate for a universal life contract will vary over time within a given projection scenario, and will also vary between different projection scenarios. Policyholder choices will be based heavily on credited rates and their relation to marketplace and competitor rates. It is important to use multiple scenarios to estimate these effects. Present projection methods often estimate the credited rate based on the rate earned by the asset portfolio. The difference is typically a pricing or target spread, modified as necessary by competitive conditions. Competitive conditions are typically described in terms of external indices, for example the 5-year Treasury rate plus some margin. We suggest that in large part credited rates are determined by the competitive market. Therefore credited rates could be defined directly from models of the external competitive marketplace for similar products, instead of from an asset portfolio rate.

As an alternative approach, the credited interest rate could be set using a projected earned interest rate less a spread. The earned rate could be projected independently of the company's specific asset portfolio. To express this another way, in projecting multiple cash flow scenarios, the company could examine a wide range of possible investment spreads that might be obtained. The spreads should bear a reasonable relationship to external market interest rates and typical asset portfolio rates at the projected date, widening and narrowing realistically.

Present tools and methods could continue to be used. It would seem acceptable to model a typical asset portfolio using its performance under a range of future interest rate assumptions to develop the range of investment spreads that might be attained, or to validate a range of assumed spreads. The company's existing asset portfolio might be the basis of one estimate, or range of estimates of future earned interest rates, but it need not (perhaps should not) be the only basis. The use of a model of assets to establish a reasonable range of spreads and hence credited rates does not violate our criterion that the fair value be independent of the specific asset portfolio of the company.

*Expenses*

Realistic assumptions are appropriate here. All expenses which the company is contractually obligated to pay (i.e. commissions), as well as costs of administration are liability cash flows and should be considered. Ideally a range of assumptions should be explored. There is likely to be some relationship between the level of interest rates and the level of inflation of expenses, and this should be considered. It seems reasonable to assume that, for an ongoing company, new business will continue to be sold which will aid in covering overhead expenses. Thus expenses need not escalate rapidly as the number of contracts in force declines over time.

Taxation at the level of the contract should be considered. Examples include premium taxes and real estate or property taxes. Taxes at the enterprise level should be excluded, consistent with the valuation of assets. Thus profit taxes (for example US Federal income tax) and equity or wealth taxes would be excluded.

*Dynamic and interdependent assumptions*

Many of the assumptions required for projection are interdependent with each other. For example, if the credited interest rate falls too low relative to competitors (as it might when interest rates are rising rapidly) there is increased likelihood of contract lapsation, as the contract holder seeks better deals elsewhere. On the other hand, when interest rates fall, the company may be able to widen its spread. Similarly, capital gains or losses might arise as interest rates move. They should be allowed for in the projections even absent the modeling of specific assets.

The projections should consider all such interdependence between assumptions and maintain internal consistency among them. Present modeling tools are capable of establishing assumptions by formula such that consistency is preserved automatically across multiple scenarios. Certain assumptions are dynamic in the sense that they describe behavior, either of the company or the contract holder. Caution is needed to avoid undue optimism, but conceptually the contract holder will tend to act to maximize contract value, and the company will tend to act to minimize it. The assumptions should reflect the balance between these forces.

*Other assumptions*

Examples may include policyholder dividends, options to purchase additional coverage, cost of living benefit increases, and the like. All such assumptions should be established using similar principles, namely that realistic estimates should be developed and included in each projected scenario. To the extent feasible, each assumption should be varied appropriately in each multiple scenario. As far as possible, the set of assumptions used in each scenario should be internally consistent with each other.

As mentioned above, a range of assumptions should be used wherever possible. All assumptions used should be in a reasonable range, and should not be biased in the direction of either optimism or pessimism. No new techniques are necessarily involved in the setting of assumptions, although new tools may be created in future that will automate the process.

### OTHER CHARACTERISTICS OF THE METHOD

The fair valuation of liabilities as suggested herein is applicable to the full range of financial liabilities associated with insurance contracts. Thus liabilities presently characterized as life reserves, contract reserves, fund balances, active life reserves, claim reserves, and unearned premium reserves are all amenable to valuation by this method. Of course, the shorter the term and the more certain the receipt of the cash flows is the less the difference between fair value and book value.

The method proposes no explicit adjustment for cost of capital. Projections of liability cash flows will not, for example, include investment income on target surplus or allocated capital. Capital that is necessary to be tied up to support the liabilities does not increase or decrease the liabilities; it affects the profitability and even solvency of the enterprise as a whole, but not the fair value of the liabilities. Capital can be regarded as necessary to support the variability of future cash flows, but the proposed indexed discount rate method already reflects variability of cash flows. Therefore no further adjustment for cost of capital is necessary.

It could be argued that insurance contract liabilities cannot be held without supporting capital, and that the fair value determination should reflect the cost of that capital as a necessary business expense. It is true that reflecting cost of capital is appropriate when the discount rate includes a substantial risk premium (i.e. realistic earned investment rates are well below the discount rate). In the indexed discount rate method, risk is reflected in the projection assumptions, not the discount rate. A risk free discount rate is used. The investment income rate earned on real assets supporting capital is closely comparable, and includes any appropriate risk premium. Thus there is no additional cost of capital relative to the risk free discount rate used in this method.

The fair value of liabilities may, in some cases, be much smaller than account value, or cash surrender value. The proposed method makes no specific adjustment for this. For some contract holders the surrender benefit may exceed the fair value of the liability, and vice versa for others. Recall that, unlike GAAP reserves, the fair value of the liability is not gross of a deferred acquisition cost (DAC) asset.

### RELATIONSHIP TO APPRAISAL METHODS

Appraisal methods are used to determine the value of future earnings. This can be regarded as valuation of asset and liability cash flows combined, as distinguished from separate valuation of assets and liabilities. Large spreads are added to risk free interest rates to obtain a discount rate. This large positive spread is appropriate because the stream of future earnings is uncertain. The spread is also appropriate because the value typically relies on a single projection scenario. (Sensitivity testing is often used to provide more information on varying assumptions.)

Gross premium valuations determine the value of liabilities using a discount rate based on asset portfolio earned rates. Thus assets and liabilities are valued at the same discount rate. Appraisal methods and gross premium valuation methods are internally consistent because of use of the same rate for discounting asset and liability cash flows. The value of equity (i.e. the present value of future earnings) using appraisal methods generally will be lower than using gross premium valuation methods, on account of the higher discount rate used for appraisals.

The indexed discount rate method also develops a fair value for liabilities that is consistent with the fair value of assets. Both values are based on risk free rates with adjustment for risk. Risk adjustment is made for assets by directly reflecting market values and for liabilities by using multiple scenarios to evaluate the range of values. The indexed discount rate fair value of liabilities will be appropriately somewhat conservative relative to the gross premium valuation, because of reflecting more risk. Thus the value of equity using indexed discount rate methods will also be somewhat lower than using gross premium valuation methods. Although general rules are difficult to define, it appears that indexed discount rate equity should be relatively close to appraisal value. The simple example in the Appendix bears out this expectation.

## Relationship to Option Pricing Methods

Option pricing methods are methods that attempt to quantify the costs of options in financial instruments. When selling a deferred annuity or buying a mortgage-backed security, the insurance company needs to know the cost of options that may be exercised by the other party. If an adequate price can be charged, or if a sufficient spread is earned, the risk of the transaction is tolerable. In option pricing, future cash flows are projected, then discounted back initially at a risk free rate. An adjustment spread may be necessary to equate the discounted present value with the market price. It is possible to solve for this spread when the market price is known. The spread reflects the uncertainties in the projected cash flows. The uncertainties include credit risk, i.e. risk of default on payment of cash flows, the risk of volatility in future interest rates, and the resulting variations in cash flows themselves which are dependent on future interest rates. Having determined this spread it may be used to value other instruments with similar risk characteristics. The value so obtained is an option adjusted price, which should be highly consistent with market values if they can be obtained directly.

Option pricing methods commonly rely on multiple scenarios or stochastic processes, based on different interest rate yield curves over time. An interest rate generator is used to create multiple randomly different future yield curves. Constraints are used to avoid extreme fluctuations, and also to ensure that the future yield curves are not inherently inconsistent. Current option pricing approaches can be classified as either scenario or lattice methods. Scenario methods project cash flows such that, at each stage, a determination is made of the amount of cash flow, based on its dependence on interest rates. The present values of cash flows in each scenario are discounted at interest rates projected in that scenario. Scenario methods are most appropriate for insurance contracts and mortgage related instruments where each cash flow is dependent on preceding events. Lattice methods determine the value, if any, of options directly by determining the worth of the option at each future date, assuming that interest rates have either moved up or down in increments.

Option adjusted pricing methods have been reasonably validated for many financial assets. However, the methods are subject to some limitations. Modeling errors may occur because of the difficulty of ensuring that future yield curves are arbitrage free, i.e. do not allow inconsistent levels of interest rate to coexist on the yield curve. Different tools are used to generate multiple random future yield curves, and there is no consensus that any one of these tools is best. Also, true market values are the result of many different viewpoints and some inherent market inefficiency.

The inclusion of some level of option pricing based adjustment spread to the risk free rates proposed in this paper was considered but rejected. Instead, it was felt that the use of multiple assumption scenarios, including variations in interest rates, adequately reflects uncertainties inherent in the cash flows. An additional adjustment spread would reduce fair values which is inappropriately optimistic when evaluating liability cash flows. Similarly, the use of multiple sets of projected interest rates for discounting was considered but rejected, based on the objectivity criterion.

## CONCEPTS OF PROFIT, RISK

As mentioned above, there is no provision in the choice of assumptions for margins of conservatism or provisions for adverse deviation. All future cash flows, including expected gross premiums, are projected using a range of realistic assumptions. Thus there is no explicit allocation for future profits in the liability cash flows. However, credited rates are in fact based on realistic expected spreads. If the asset portfolio is not invested solely in Treasuries, spreads will be earned over the risk free rate. We regard this spread as associated with the choice of assets, not the liabilities. The spread is the expected reward to the company for choosing a particular set of assets. No additional spread is attributed to the liabilities.

Nonetheless, the indexed discount rate method should work well in practical financial reporting. By using a risk free discount rate, the method produces a fair value that is somewhat conservative, relative to a gross premium valuation, but not unreasonably so. The fair value is likely to be less conservative than present book value methods, at least in certain interest rate situations. The indexed discount rate method fair value is also somewhat conservative relative to an option pricing method, which would include an adjustment spread in the discount rate. We rejected this approach as inappropriately producing a lower 'fair' value. Another effect would be that future profits would be lower than with the indexed discount rate method.

Past profits are not taken into account, and do not affect the fair value of liabilities. The initial price is reflected however to the extent that actual experience is used as the basis for assumptions used in the projection of future cash flows. Thus a group of insurance contracts will have certain characteristics that reflect, in part, the original price paid. To the extent that past profits have arisen, they reside in surplus, or retained earnings. Surplus of course may also have increased due to capital infusions and investment income, and may have decreased due to policyholder or shareholder dividends.

We considered but rejected an approach that would use initial contract purchase price to determine an adjustment spread to apply to risk free rates. This approach would create profit breakeven at issue, which may be inappropriate, or unduly conservative reserves based on negative adjustment spreads. In many cases also the initial price is not representative of the long term performance of the contract. It was felt that the initial pricing spread should not be 'locked in'.

## US GAAP AND DEFERRED ACQUISITION COSTS

The deferred acquisition cost asset (DAC) is a peculiarity of US GAAP. DAC can be regarded as a portion of future profits whose present value is included in GAAP equity. To the extent that costs have been incurred in the acquisition of insurance contracts, such expenses are not considered a loss, or a sunk cost. Instead an asset is held which is gradually recovered using all or a portion of future profits.

There are different approaches to determining DAC, depending on the nature of the product. For margin-based products such as universal life contracts, DAC is amortized in proportion to the future stream of gross profits (ignoring acquisition expenses) that is expected to arise over time. Future gross profits arise because the liability, or reserve held, together with future premiums and investment income, is more than sufficient to pay future benefits and expenses. As time passes the reserve releases and gross profits emerge. The DAC is amortized using all or part of the gross profits. The DAC can be regarded as an offset to the reserve. DAC may not exceed future profits. One test for DAC recoverability is to compare the net GAAP liability (i.e. reserves less DAC) to the gross premium valuation reserve. If the net GAAP liability is the greater, then some conservatism still remains and some future net profits will emerge.

The indexed discount rate method, as proposed, develops a fair value liability which combines future benefit and expense reserve components. While the fair value of liabilities is reasonable, if the method were to be used for GAAP it may be preferable (although not necessary) to modify the proposed approach. One modification could be to unbundle the fair value into two components, an account value and a 'new' DAC, such that the net liability equals fair value. Alternatively, a new DAC could be defined as the market value, using an external index rate, of future book profits (i.e. cash flows adjusted for the release of benefit reserves in each projected year). It is felt to be outside of the scope of this paper to propose further details of GAAP financial statement presentation. Deferred tax adjustments will continue to be appropriate under GAAP for temporary differences between the GAAP value of assets and liabilities and the value for tax purposes.

APPLICATION TO VARIOUS TYPES OF CONTRACTS

The indexed discount rate method can be applied to all current types of insurance contracts.

*Universal life, deferred annuities, and other interest-sensitive policy contracts*

For these contracts, discounted cash flow methods may arrive at fair values quite different from fund value. As mentioned above, this has implications for future profit patterns and the appropriateness of holding DAC. There is a numerical illustration of the application of this method to a universal life contract, attached as an Appendix.

### Traditional non-participating life and health

For these contracts relatively few contract options exist. It seems likely that relatively few scenarios would suffice to explore an adequate range of assumptions.

### Traditional participating life insurance

For these contracts, policyholder dividends are paid in a manner similar but not identical to interest rate credits on universal life contracts. The projections would need to take care to preserve reasonable relationships between earned interest rates and the rate used to set dividends, as well as between mortality and expense experience assumptions used in setting policyholder dividends.

### Variable life insurance and annuities

These products are currently reserved at the market value of policyholder funds. While the indexed discounted rate method could be applied, it would not seem necessary nor likely to generate a more appropriate fair value than the market value of the contract funds. For variable products, therefore, no change in fair value of liabilities is proposed. DAC would continue to be held where appropriate.

### Property/casualty

Most property/casualty liabilities are currently undiscounted. The indexed discount rate method would require discounting, but it may also require fuller exploration of the range of outcomes, some of which are adverse. When a mean value is taken, including some adverse scenarios, the fair value may be fairly consistent with or more conservative than the present single best estimate approach.

## Acknowledgments

The author gratefully acknowledges assistance and advice from several individuals, who have made many valuable suggestions and criticisms. However, any errors or omissions remain solely the responsibility of the author. The opinions expressed in this paper are those of the author and do not necessarily represent the opinions of his employer.

## References

Asay, Michael R., Peter J. Bouyoucos and Anthony M. Marciano (1989). An economic approach to valuation of single premium deferred annuities. *Financial Institutions Research*, April.

Griffin, Mark (1989). The excess spread approach to pricing and designing the SPDA. *Fixed Income Research*, December.

APPENDIX: NUMERICAL ILLUSTRATION OF FAIR VALUE OF A
UNIVERSAL LIFE CONTRACT

A simple model was used to generate comparisons between current US GAAP accounting results and the results of the indexed discount rate (IDR) method. This simplified example is intended to be typical but not necessarily representative of all universal life contracts currently inforce. The example is a universal life contract issued to a male aged 45, with face amount of $100 000. There is a total first year deposit of $30 per unit followed by lower target premiums of $10, annually. Front end loads of 5% are deducted, plus $60 per policy per year. Surrender charges begin at 100% of target premium, and decline uniformly over 10 years. COI charges are based on the 1980 CSO table.

Expenses in the first year include commissions at 75% of target premium and 2% of the excess, plus issue expenses of $60 per policy, $0.10 per unit and 15% of premium. Mortality is based on 75% of the 1975–80 Males table.

In the 'median' scenario (Table 1) investment income was assumed at 9% and the credited rate was 7%, thus the interest spread was 200 basis points in all years. Spread, mortality margins and expense loads all contribute to book profits. The present value of future cash flows is taken at the risk free rates at the time of valuation, namely a yield curve of 5% for 5 years followed by 7% thereafter.

GAAP results under Statement of Financial Accounting Standards No. 97 are shown for comparison. Account value, DAC and the net GAAP liability are shown per unit inforce, consistent with the fair value as determined by the indexed discount rate method. For this example, a 20 year DAC amortization period was used. Gross premium valuation (GPV) results are also shown. These results are the present value of future cash flows discounted at 9%.

As can be seen, in this example the fair value liability is lower than the net GAAP liability under SFAS 97 in all years. Thus using the IDR method will result in higher equity than under present methods for a given asset portfolio assuming consistent asset valuation. The IDR method is somewhat conservative relative to a gross premium valuation, in which equity would be still higher.

For a given asset portfolio, profit emergence is slowest under GAAP and fastest using a gross premium valuation. With GAAP no profit emerges at

Table 1. Universal life contract example: GAAP, fair value and gross premium valuation

| Year | Account value | DAC | Net GAAP liability | IDR method fair value | GPV |
|---|---|---|---|---|---|
| At issue | 28.11 | 13.40 | 14.71 | (0.98) | (9.64) |
| 1 | 36.66 | 12.34 | 24.32 | 15.08 | 6.30 |
| 2 | 45.36 | 11.24 | 34.12 | 23.74 | 14.67 |
| 5 | 72.44 | 7.97 | 64.47 | 49.11 | 40.51 |
| 10 | 119.22 | 3.52 | 115.70 | 96.03 | 85.68 |
| 15 | 161.21 | 1.15 | 160.06 | 142.37 | 132.92 |

issue, while using a gross premium valuation all profit is recognized immediately. Using the IDR method, profits would emerge at an intermediate rate, i.e., partly immediately and partly over time. The profits that would emerge over time will consist of a spread on the assets supporting the IDR reserve plus variances where actual experience differs from that assumed in the liability cash flow projections.

In this example, the appraisal value at 13% is $1.07, which falls close to the IDR fair value at issue.

### ADDENDUM TO APPENDIX A: THE INDEXED DISCOUNT RATE METHOD FOR FAIR VALUATION OF LIABILITIES

In this addendum, all scenarios generated in the simple model are presented. The scenarios were generated deterministically using judgment. The intent is to show how the actuary might explore the full range of options exploring the different types of risk to which the liabilities are exposed. Both favorable and unfavorable variations to best estimated assumptions were used. Both wide and narrow assumption deviations were selected. In most cases only a single assumption was changed; however, in a few scenarios combinations of assumption changes were used. No attempt was made to bias the set of scenarios toward liberalism or optimism as to future experience. All scenarios are intended to represent realistic possibilities. The scenarios used are summarized in Table 2.

As discussed in the paper, cash flows were projected for each scenario's assumptions. Each scenario's cash flows were then discounted at the same

Table 2.

| No. | Description | At issue | 1st year | 5th year |
|---|---|---|---|---|
| 1 | Base assumptions | (0.98) | 15.08 | 49.11 |
| 2 | (Credited rates) pop up 1.5% | 7.56 | 23.93 | 61.51 |
| 3 | Gradual up 1.5% | 6.39 | 22.72 | 59.97 |
| 4 | Pop down 1.5% | (8.21) | 7.60 | 38.68 |
| 5 | Gradual down 1.5% | (7.31) | 8.53 | 39.84 |
| 6 | Mortality up 20% | 2.61 | 18.74 | 53.26 |
| 7 | Mortality down 20% | (1.57) | 11.43 | 45.04 |
| 8 | Lapse rates up 2% | 0.22 | 16.29 | 50.39 |
| 9 | Lapse rates down 2% | (2.54) | 13.53 | 47.66 |
| 10 | (Admin.) expenses up 50% | 0.63 | 16.75 | 50.61 |
| 11 | Expenses up 10% | (0.66) | 15.42 | 49.42 |
| 12 | Expenses down 10% | (1.29) | 14.76 | 48.82 |
| 13 | Expenses down 50% | (2.57) | 13.44 | 47.64 |
| 14 | Extra premium, year 3 | (0.44) | 15.64 | 60.50 |
| 15 | Mortality down 10% | (2.74) | 13.29 | 47.10 |
| 16 | Lapse rates up 1% | (0.36) | 15.71 | 49.77 |

*Continued*

Table 2. Continued

| 17 | (Credited rates) pop up 75 bp | 3.11 | 19.32 | 55.05 |
| 18 | Gradual up 75 bp | 2.56 | 18.75 | 54.34 |
| 19 | Pop down 75 bp | (4.74) | 11.19 | 43.68 |
| 20 | Gradual down 75 bp | (4.26) | 11.69 | 44.31 |
| 21 | Pop up 75 bp and lapses up 1% | 3.38 | 19.60 | 55.42 |
| 22 | Pop up 75 bp and lapses up 1%, plus extra premium deposit | 4.44 | 20.70 | 67.63 |
|  | Mean | (0.82) | 15.25 | 49.38 |
|  | Median | (0.98) | 15.08 | 49.11 |

Treasury rates used in the example to produce the fair value of liabilities. The values were determined at three different dates, namely at issue, one year later at the first policy anniversary, and at the fifth anniversary. The results are shown in both tabular and graphical form in Figures 1–3

Given the relatively small number of scenarios, the distributions are not perfectly smooth; however, their general shape is consistent with what one might expect. There is a concentration of values in the center of the distribution, with a lower frequency of occurrence of very high and low values. None of the scenarios would be described as producing an extreme result. The histograms appear reasonably symmetrical, but at all three dates the mean is slightly higher than the median, indicating a slight skewness of the distribution of results to the right (higher values).

Although the model is admittedly simple, the results seem to support the validity and practicability of the IDR method. The range of values is fairly

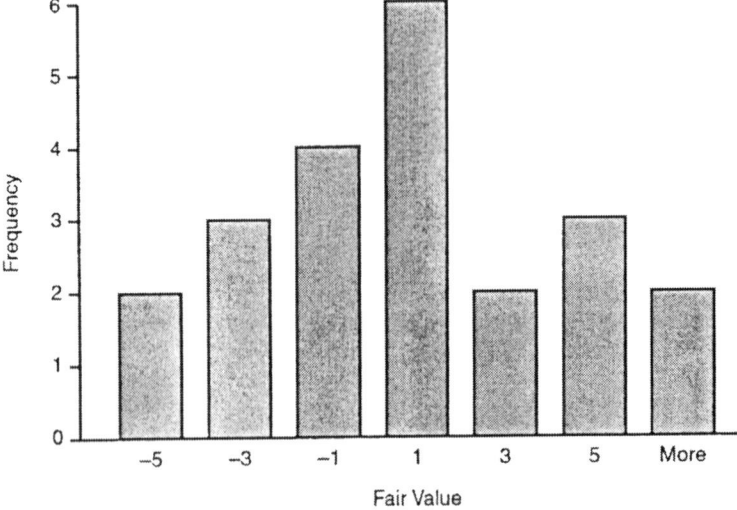

Figure 1. IDR method at issue.

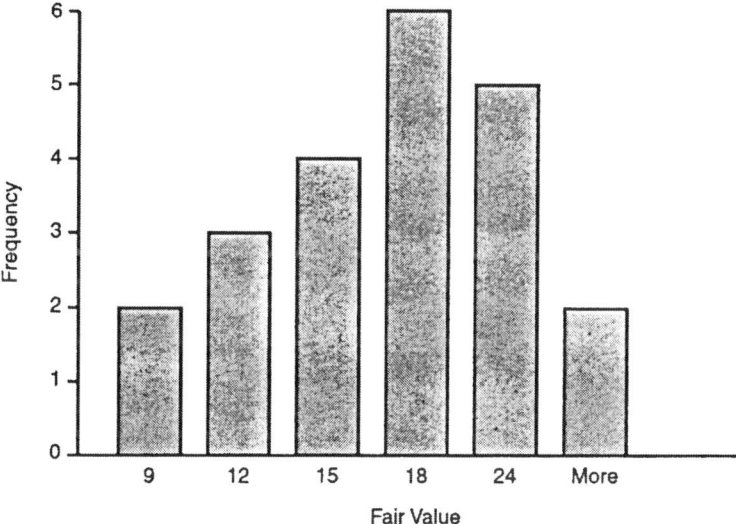

*Figure 2.* IDR method, year 1.

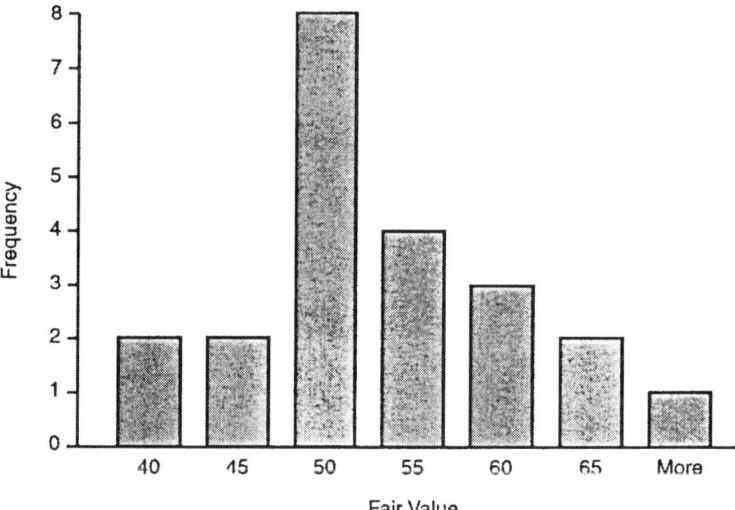

*Figure 3.* IDR method, year 5.

wide but this appears realistic, and the distribution of results seems well behaved. Hence, a choice of either the mean or median should be a good indication of fair value.

KRZYSZTOF M. OSTASZEWSKI
*University of Louisville*

# Is Paul v. Virginia dead?

## Abstract

In this work, we articulate the case for values of insurance liabilities being company dependent. In the process, we identify main factors determining market values of such liabilities, analyze them from the perspective of dependence on the company issuing them, and follow this with a suggested regulatory approach allowing for company independent valuation. Such regulatory approach is in conceptual agreement with the emerging risk-based capital paradigm.

## Introduction

Early life insurance companies, especially Friendly Societies, were troubled by unpredictability of their death benefit disbursements. As the principles of actuarial sciences developed, and mortality tables were published, this unpredictability gave in to a better understanding of death related cash flows. This contributed to the growth and success of the life insurance industry. The Golden Age (Black and Skipper, 1994) of the US insurers, the 1950s and 1960s, was characterized by nearly complete knowledge of death related cash flows because of actuarial knowledge; and predictability of other cash flows (i.e. lapses, surrenders, new business, investment returns) because of an economic environment providing stability of those factors. One could say that Golden Age was the 'quiet before the storm'. Subsequent developments (Sametz, 1987), such as:

- Unprecedented levels of inflation, and unpredictability of inflation rate;
- Unprecedented levels of volatility of financial markets, especially interest rates;
- Unprecedented deregulation, consumerism, and competition, leading to greater efficiency in consumer behavior, disintermediation, and change in the industry position versus other financial institutions,

resulted in the life insurance industry experiencing what is common in those three factors, i.e. 'the unprecedented', which first and foremost meant unpredicability of liability cash flows, or even a complete makeover of the nature of those liabilities. Any hopes of greater stability after inflation decline were quite successfully removed by the tumultous years of 1993 and 1994.

This historical process was, in our opinion, not just a result of a change in the economic environment, but also a change in the very nature of life insurance business (within the given economic environment, of course). The factors of inflation, interest rates, or deregulation, are external to a life insurance contract. Yet we believe that in addition to those external considerations, a historic change in what life insurance is, is occuring. To explain that, let us bring a quote from the 1868 *Paul v. Virginia* Supreme Court ruling (per Black and Skipper, 1994): "Issuing a policy of insurance is not a transaction of commerce. (...) These contracts are not articles of commerce in any proper meaning of the word. They are not subject to the trade and barter. (...) They are like personal contracts between parties which are completed by their signature and the transfer of the consideration."

When the significance of this decision is discussed, the subject is usually state versus federal regulation of insurance. Nevertheless, this was also a decision concerning valuation of insurance liabilities. The decision stressed that insurance liabilities, when viewed from the perspective of the policyowner, are not marketable assets, and as such, exhibit, first and foremost, characteristics of a completely private transaction between two parties. The value of a policy asset (i.e. insurance liability) is determined solely by the original transaction, and expressed by the consideration extended. Thus book value accounting is fully justified.

The 1944 *United States v. South-Eastern Underwriters Association, et al.* decision of the Supreme Court (per Black and Skipper, 1994) overturned *Paul v. Virginia*. This meant the end of the sole state domain over insurance, even if that domain was extended by the 1945 McCarran–Fergusson Act. The part of *Paul v. Virginia* concerning implications for insurance liabilities valuation was overturned less rapidly, but probably in a more decisive fashion, in the marketplace.

In this chapter we concentrate on life insurance liabilities. We do agree that many issues raised here apply to insurance in general. Nevertheless, this concentration allows us to use some specific examples, or point out specific policy implications.

To the extent that a life insurance policy is a private transaction between the insurer and the insured, its value is given by the actuarial valuation employed by the insurer. To the degree that the policy is a traded asset, or a commodity easily replaced in the marketplace, its value is easily given by the market. We claim here that at the time of its pronouncement, the *Paul v. Virginia* decision, in the part concerning valuation, quite adequately represented reality, then. However, as the insurance marketplace developed, the traditional life insurance policy was 'peeled off', those parts of it which repesent tradeable assets, or commodities, became unbundled, and either traded, or purchased separately. In fact, less and less of a traditional policy is a private transaction. In this sense the *United States v. South-Eastern Underwriters Association* also represented a recognition of reality. We claim, however, that a life insurance policy remains, to a degree, to be specified later, an financial instrument, whose value is partly outside of the framework of market valuation.

We claim that the 'financial storms' of the 1970s, 1980s and 1990s may have precluded us from noticing that the process which was then happening was quite a natural phenomenon of establishing market values of those insurance liabilities which are properly valued by the market, and separating them from those which are not valued by the market. Sippel (1993) discusses the emerging paradigm of financial intermediation. He points out that in view of rapid changes in the nature of financial intermediation, it is natural to analyze financial products from first principles. This leads him to identify the following four elements of a financial product:
- Method of making money: bear risk, manage spread, process information, aggregate, distribute;
- Legal form: bank, property/casualty insurer, life insurer, thrift, etc.;
- Market definition: size, geography, demographics, etc.;
- Needs/wants met: uncertainty reduction, advice/information, record-keeping, access to money.

The traditional life insurance was very much a result of evolution out of medieval guilds, or other fraternal or mutual societies: it kept some of the bones of its predecessors, even though it was barely using them at all. It had a clearly defined legal form, and the market (protection and hedging of human capital value of the family breadwinner), but it bundled the functions of bearing risk, managing spread, and aggregation, while meeting the needs of uncertainty reduction in human capital value and in securities market value, as well as advice and financial planning. Sippel (1993) points out that the new paradigm calls for financial intermediaries to use capital, information, and brains, to establish products which offer any possible combination of the four elements of a financial product, often in the most refined version. One example given by Sippel is Fidelity Investments which offers aggregation of securities in such most refined version to the most widely defined market, under the legal form of private ownership, most carefully separating numerous needs and wants met. Of course, market values of Fidelity's liabilities are clearly established, as it was precisely Fidelity which worked on 'peeling off' various pieces of traditional life insurance product, in order to establish them as separate products in the marketplace.

One important part of the valuation of life insurance liabilities is whether they are company-dependent. Is life insurance protection a commodity which can be easily replaced by switching to another company? More precisely, there are two major parts of traditional life insurance:
- Death protection;
- Savings accumulation and disbursement.

These are, of course, supplemented by a bundle of human capital and financial options (we will return to this subject, also see Smith, 1982). The industry itself has successfully managed to unbundle these two products, by offering term

insurance and annuities (with these products being high growth areas). Our question can therefore be rephrased as follows:
- Do the consumers purchase death protection without any regard for the company used?
- Do the consumers accumulate and disburse their savings without regard for the company used?

If both questions are answered to the affirmative, we will have made a very strong case for identical, company independent, market value accounting of life insurance liabilities. If, on the other hand, the answer is 'no', we may have to become careful in assigning market values to those liabilities.

One more important issue to raise is the fact that the homogeneouity of the product is precisely one of the defining characteristics of a competitive market. Pritchett and Wilder (1986) point out that especially cash-value life insurance products and disability income products, and, to the lesser degree, term insurance and annuities, lend themselves naturally to the product differentiation strategy. This does not imply complete monopoly power, but leads to what Pritchett and Wilder call workable competition. Nevertheless, different life insurance companies' products are not necessarily perfect substitutes for each other, and being company dependent, may lead to difficulties in establishing market values for liabilities given by them.

## THE NATURE OF LIFE INSURANCE LIABILITIES

Saunders (1994) analyzed the financial intermediaries specialness and points out that the economic role of financial intermediaries lies in matching the needs of the saving public (households) with those of economic investors (corporations). This results in financial intermediaries having liabilities which are someone else's securities. In fact, their role lies precisely in transforming the primary securities (corporate bonds and stocks, and other direct forms of debt and equity) into secondary securities, or better yet, derivative securities, i.e. securities whose cash flows are derived from other, underlying, securities. The term 'derivative security' has been reserved for more exotic creations, such as options, futures, swaps, and mortgage derivatives, yet one can clearly see that, for example, a single premium deferred annuity, is also a derivative security, as it transforms the cash flows of the insurance firm's investment portfolio into those flowing to the firm's clients.

Thus financial intermediaries provide the service of crafting derivative securities which match the supply of savings from the household sector with the demand for those savings in the corporate sector. However, the demand for savings expresses itself in the form of supply of securities, and those securities may not be the ones demanded by the suppliers of savings, herein lies the role of the financial intermediaries, who transform bonds and stocks into securities demanded by the saving public.

The key point here is that derivative securities crafted by financial intermediaries must be valued in a manner analogous to other derivative securities. In particular, we must note that the market valuation of a portfolio of life insurance liabilities is determined by the following factors:
- Existing investment portfolio;
- Baseline investment strategy;
- Existing liability portfolio;
- Baseline crediting strategy;
- Management's policy regarding new business and departures from existing baselines;
- Customers characteristics expressed in deaths, withdrawals, lapses, and terminations.

When valuing existing liabilities, we may allow ourselves to make a simplifying (yet not necessarily true) assumption that their value is indeed independent of any new business produced in the future, and of any departures from existing policies. Given that, we can now treat the remaining factors as a package of cash flows and options. Black and Scholes (1973) analysis implies then that the value of such a package can be determined by risk-neutral valuation (see also Hull, 1993, Chapter 12), as the discounted expected value in the risk-neutral world. Practically, this means averaging present values obtained along sample interest rate scenario paths. Samples such are generated by a stochastic process assumed to govern the yield curve evolution. This valuation process assumes, of course, that derivative securities valued are dependent solely on the interest rates (yield curve).

All of the above ideas are currently a standard part of actuarial valuation, especially cash flow testing. What we do want to bring into this framework is an identification of the composition of the underlying derivative securities, especially the ones which are company dependent.

It is quite clear that the contract wording, especially nonforfeiture rights, give the policyholder in a life insurance, or an annuity, policy, a set of options (Smith, 1982). In addition to that, however, we have other pieces to the combined option package, which are less obvious. First, within any possible guidelines in the policy, or regulatory guidelines, the company receives an option to set its investment policy and, in relation to it, its crediting strategy. Secondly, the company has an option to default. It is important to note that the default option is not policy specific, but extends to all of its liabilities. This means that the combined package of options can be divided into the following pieces:
- Investment baseline of the insurance company;
- Crediting strategy of the insurance company;
- Option to default by the insurance company;
- Policyowners options, including nonforfeiture rights.

These do, in fact, correspond to the identified above factors relating to valuation of life insurance liabilities.

If valuation is performed by the firm, it is quite natural to exclude the option to default. This results in a lower risk-adjusted discounting rate, or higher value of the liabilities. However, the market value, if determined by the reinsurance price, or other price required for liabilities transfer, may indeed include that option. If a weak company transfers its liabilities to a strong one, generally the strong one requires a payment. This clearly is compensation for the increase in the market value of liabilities at the moment of transfer.

We see therefore, that there are parts of the valuation of life insurance liabilities, and all insurance liabilities at that, which are company dependent. We will now proceed to illustrate this phenomenon and to analyze it by the use of a simple example. Then we will analyze the implication of this observation.

## ONE COMPANY, SEVERAL BALANCE SHEETS?

Imagine an insurance firm engaged in life insurance business. Let us call it Realife Mutual Life Company. We will study Realife's market balance sheet under very simple assumptions. We will, however, incorporate various options involved in the asset/liability portfolio. Realife issues a one-year policy promising to pay 5% on a $1000 deposit made today in a year from now. The 5% credited rate matches the current one-year Treasury rate. Let us now consider Realife's baseline investment strategy.

Merton (1974) developed an option-based model of the risk structure of interest rates which we consider applicable to this situation. As we had indicated, it is the portfolio of options which puts a financial intermediary in business. A true market-value balance sheet must consider that. Merton's methodology is rooted precisely in that approach. It assumes that the purchaser of a bond holds a risk free note and sells a put option to the bond issuer, for which the bondholder receives the yield spread of the bond over the corresponding Treasury.

The market value of a risky loan is, in Merton's model, given by

$$F(t) = Be^{-it}[(1/d)N(h_1) + N(h_2)]$$

where the symbols have the following meanings:

$B$ = Maturity amount of the loan,
$A$ = Total assets of the borrower,
$i$ = Risk free rate of interest,
$t$ = The length of time remaining to loan maturity (here $t = 1$),
$d$ = The borrowers leverage ratio equal to $Be^{-it}/A$,
$N(h)$ = Cumulative distribution function of the standard normal distribution,
$h_1$ = $-[0.5\sigma^2 t - \ln(d)]/(\sigma t 0.5)$,
$h_2$ = $-[0.5\sigma^2 t + \ln(d)]/(\sigma t 0.5)$,

$\sigma^2$ = Volatility (measured by the standard deviation) of the assets of the borrower.

Merton's model also implies that the market yield $k$ of a risky loan is given by:

$$k = i + (-1/t) \ln[(1/d)N(h_1) + N(h_2)]$$

Realife's baseline investment strategy is to buy bonds of the corporation named High Yield Inc. with leverage ratio of 0.7, and volatility of assets of 30%. The bonds sell at the yield of 7.063%. Realife sells a one-year single-premium deferred annuity (SPDA) with no early withdrawal privilege crediting one-year Treasury rate at $1000 face (today). We will assume that Realife has a 5% of liabilities surplus requirement, with $50 of company's capital invested in the project. If all of $1,050 is invested as baseline states, and surplus requirements and default options are ignored, Realife's market balance sheet is:

| | $ |
|---|---|
| **Assets** | |
| High Yield Inc. zero-coupon bonds due one year hence | 1050.00 |
| **Liabilities** | |
| SPDA | 1000.00 |
| **Surplus** | 50.00 |

Without any default occuring, one year hence, Realife will develop the following market balance sheet:

| | $ |
|---|---|
| **Assets** | |
| High Yield Inc. zero-coupon bonds maturing at | 1124.16 |
| **Liabilities** | |
| SPDA maturing at | 1050.00 |
| **Surplus** | 74.16 |

This represents a 48.32% return on capital, clearly a rather extraorbitant rate. Realife may be inclined to modify its crediting strategy, by becoming more generous to its SPDA customers, and thus expanding its market share. Before we elaborate on the implications of that, let us reconsider the initial balance sheet of Realife. Merton's model implies that market value of $1000 face of High Yield's bonds is $979.58. Thus the true initial market balance sheet should read:

| | $ |
|---|---|
| **Assets** | |
| High Yield Inc. zero-coupon bonds due one year hence | 1028.56 |
| **Liabilities** | |
| SPDA | 1000.00 |
| **Surplus** | 28.56 |

As it turns out, Realife is failing its capital requirements, by holding only 2.86% capital. Let us now imagine that Realife decides that it no longer needs to credit as a risk-free company, but rather decides to credit 6%. It might be interesting to note that the model of Merton implies that Realife, with its 5% capital ratio, has 7.08% volatility of assets, if it credits 6%.

If the options on the balance sheet are ignored, initial market values are:

| | $ |
|---|---|
| **Assets** | |
| High Yield Inc. zero-coupon bonds due one year hence | 1050.00 |
| **Liabilities** | |
| SPDA | 1000.00 |
| **Surplus** | 50.00 |

The ending balance sheet becomes:

| | $ |
|---|---|
| **Assets** | |
| High Yield Inc. zero-coupon bonds maturing at | 1124.16 |
| **Liabilities** | |
| SPDA maturing at | 1060.00 |
| **Surplus** | 64.16 |

The return on capital drops to 28.32%, but the company's competitive position is enhanced immensely. On the other hand, the Merton model states that the customer holding the SPDA actually had a $990.05 note, not a $1000.00 note, with the difference of $9.95 effectively being paid by the state's Guaranty Fund.

The analysis given in this simple example is in no way exhaustive. In addition to that there are many factors influencing market values of liabilities which do not remain directly under company's control. Let us say some words to that issue now.

- Product market value does depend on the product type. Every insurance product carries numerous options, either sold or bought by the company, which cause the generic Treasury yields to be adjusted for discounting by the spreads paying for those options;
- Insurance firms operate in the capital market environment which causes them to have cost of funds provided for asset purchase to be influenced by both product fund costs, and capital fund costs. The process of intermediation provides a payment to purchasers of insurance product which must meet the competition for their funds, while the owners of the insurance firm must be paid for their capital enough to compensate for the additional risk undertaken.
- Despite variability of the investment baseline, the company can only do so much. Returns in the capital markets are effectively described in Markowitz' Efficient Frontier, which plays the role of 'price list of capital': it gives the effective rate of return for the degree of risk accepted.

Thus the full analysis of the appropriate market value of insurance liabilities will, first and foremost, include those factors independent of the insurance firm, i.e. cost of funds (capital and customer funds), capital market returns, and product marketplace. However, as we do point out here, even in a competitive modern insurance marketplace, it is possible to 'customize' firm's market value of liabilities by quietly purchasing one's default option from the consumers.

## Implications for Management and Regulation of Life Insurance Enterprises

Thus we conclude that Paul v. Virginia is not all dead yet. Life insurance liabilities do indeed include portions which are company dependent, and a life insurance contract is not merely a commodity traded in a perfectly competitive market, but it still holds some properties of a 'simple handshake agreement'.

*Two questions naturally arise:*  *The answers suggested here are:*
- Should management do something about it?
- No.
- Should regulators do something about it?
- Yes.

Let us explain. One of the major reasons why the Statement of Financial Accounting Standards No. 115 has set upon us is that book values of liabilities are subject to subjective factors, and do not fully correspond to objective reality, here given by the market. This clearly suggests that company-specific options, such as the option of insolvency, should be excluded from the liabilities valuation. If the liabilities were perfectly company-independent, valuation would be established quite easily, via comparison. Since some degree of dependence on the company issuing policies does exist, we consider the following approach most appropriate.

First, management should consider only the company-independent portion of the liabilities in valuing them. Two major company-dependent portions can be identified. One is the insolvency option. This one must be excluded in valuation. It is quite reasonable to expect that the company does not assume that it will not perform its obligation to customers. The other one is the investment baseline and the crediting strategy as a function of investment performance. Despite regulatory guidelines, significant variations in life insurance companies' portfolios do exist. Here, the differences among companies, in view of diversification of their portfolios, can mostly be attributed to the degree of market risk of those portfolios. The increased riskiness of the investment portfolio should be represented, however, in the insolvency option, not in the discount rate of liabilities. The option-adjusted spread of liabilities should, in fact, equal zero over that of appropriate Treasuries. The reason for that is also the regulatory framework of the insurance industry – the main reason regulation exists is to prevent market failures related to insolvencies (hopefully without harm to the market process, i.e. without promoting moral hazard).

Second, company-dependent portions of valuation of liabilities is therefore mainly expressed in the insolvency option. The company receives this option, and pays for it with additional spread credited. From the regulatory standpoint, no such spread should exist, and the option should not be created. One way to prevent that is to collect the additional spread in taxes or mandatory reinsurance. This would most likely result in a further adjustment in the price of liability, as the company would continue to trade with its customers. A better way then seems to be to simultaneously lower the value of the option, and remove portion of the spread by requiring a portion of the assets to be placed in lower risk, lower return assets. This is precisely the risk-based capital approach. However, the existing framework calls for rather rigid computation according to asset classes. From the point of view presented in this work, it seems quite natural to view risk-based capital as an adjustment for the value of the insolvency option, effectively the only company-dependent portion of the market value of insurance liabilities.

REFERENCES:

Black, Fisher and Myron Scholes (1973). The pricing of options and corporate liabilities. *Journal of Political Economy*, **81**, 637–654.

Black, Kenneth Jr. and Harold D. Skipper, Jr. (1994). *Life Insurance*, 12th edn. Englewood Cliffs, NJ: Prentice Hall.

Hull, John C. (1993). *Options, Futures, and Other Derivative Securities*, 2nd edn. Englewood Cliffs, NJ: Prentice Hall.

Merton, R.C. (1974). On the pricing of corporate debt: the risk structure of interest rates. *Journal of Finance*, **29**, 449–470.

Pritchett, Travis and Ronald P. Wilder (1986). *Stock Life Insurance Company Profitability and Workable Competition*. Philadelphia: S.S. Huebner Foundation for Insurance Education.

Sametz, Arnold W. (1987). The 'new' financial environment of the United States. In Edward I. Altman (ed), *Handbook of Financial Markets and Institutions*, 6th edn. John Wiley and Sons, New York.

Saunders, Anthony (1994). *Financial Institutions Management: A Modern Perspective*. Burr Ridge, IL: Richard D. Irwin, Inc.

Smith, Michael L. (1982). The life insurance policy as an options package. *Journal of Risk and Insurance*, **45**, 583–601.

Sippel, Erich W. (1993). One system of financial intermediation: a new paradigm. American Council of Life Insurance, Chief Investment Officers Conference, March.

JOAN LAMM-TENNANT
*Villanova University*

# Comments on *'Earned profit method'*, *'Indexed discount rate method'* and *'Is Paul vs. Virginia dead?'*

Michael McLaughlin presented the case for the indexed discount rate method for fair valuation of liabilities using realistic assumptions as to future experience. McLaughlin states that multiple realistic scenarios covering the range of feasible options should be observed. The projected cash flows for each scenario are discounted at the Treasury spot rate appropriate for the duration of the cash flow. McLaughlin argues that no adjustment should be added to the Treasury rate because it would inappropriately overcount risk and optimistically reduce fair value of liabilities. In essence, McLaughlin shifts the complications imputed in the discount rate decision to the estimation of the cash flow.

Christopher O'Brien develops the earned profit method for fair valuation of liabilities. The approach is a method of calculating assets and liabilities, and recognizing profits. He begins by considering the accounting standards and the interactions between assets, liabilities and profits. After reviewing the nature of the life assurance, O'Brien derives a suggested set of standards specifically for the calculation of liabilities. It begins by distinguishing the portion of premium and the investment return which is revenue versus an apportionment to policyholders for payments of benefits. The apportionment to policyholders can further be divided between the part which is used for payment of claims in the current accounting period versus the part added to the amount set aside for payment of future claims. Revenue less expenses becomes the 'earned profit'. Liabilities are then considered in relation to payment of policyholder benefits and revenue from future life assurance services or cost, if higher. It is the use of revenues which avoids the capitalization of future profits. O'Brien provides us with a set of accounting standards to be used in assessing the liabilities of a life assurance company consistent with the assets being valued at market value.

Krzysztof Ostaszewski articulates the case for company specific values of insurance liabilities. He identifies the factors that determine the market value of liabilities as follows: investment portfolio and strategy, liability portfolio and crediting strategy, management policy regarding new business and changes in business, and company characteristics such as lapse and withdrawals. I believe he has a consensus on this issue as the conference participants have either directly or indirectly implied your thesis. What a great way to wrap up the conference, that is on a point of agreement. Hohmann and Reitano explicitly state that except for the discount spread, any attempt to standardize the underlying assumptions would probably defeat the objective of establishing a 'fair value'. Assumptions regarding premiums, mortality, profits, credit rates and surrender behaviors must take into account product and company specifics to capture fair value. Ostaszewski and Vanderhoof tend to agree that insurance companies may be 'derivative peddlers'. Ostaszewski defines financial institutions as providing the service of crafting derivative securities which match the supply of savings from household sector with the demand for those savings in the corporate sector. It is this simple but clever perspective of what appears to be a confounding industry which makes his paper a notable addition to the literature.

# List of contributors

## DAVID F. BABBEL

**David F. Babbel** joined the Wharton School Faculty in 1984. He teaches in the graduate program primarily in the areas of insurance finance and investment management. Prior to joining Wharton, he was on the finance faculty for seven years at the University of California at Berkeley, where he taught principally in the areas of international financial management, corporate finance, and investments. A former vice president and director of research in the Pension and Insurance Department at Goldman, Sachs & Co., Professor Babbel is a financial consultant for several of the larger insurance companies. He has published prolifically in the academic and professional literature on asset/liability management, insurance, fixed income investments, and foreign exchange risk management. He is co-author of *An Insurance Primer: A Review of the Insurance Industry, Market Structure, Products, Asset Needs; The World Bank Primer on Reinsurance*; a Society of Actuaries monograph entitled *Valuation of Interest-Sensitive Financial Instruments*, and a McGraw-Hill textbook entitled *Financial Markets, Instruments and Institutions*. Currently he is completing a book entitled *Investment Management for Insurers*. He received his undergraduate training in economics at Brigham Young University, and his graduate training at the University of Florida in finance. His postdoctoral education in insurance was undertaken at the University of Pennsylvania's Wharton School.

## DAVID N. BECKER

**David N. Becker** is Vice President, Chief Actuarial Officer and Appointed Actuary for Lincoln National Life Insurance Company. His research interests include stochastic modeling, option pricing, cash flow testing and profitability/value based measurement methodologies. He is a frequent speaker at Society and industry meetings and professional seminars. Mr Becker has served on several committees and task forces of the Society of Actuaries and the American Academy of Actuaries. He is a past chairperson of the Society's Individual Life Insurance and Annuity Product Development Section Council and chairperson of the Society's Investment Section Council. His papers have appeared in *Best's Review, Reinsurance Reporter*, newsletters of the Society's Product Development, Financial Reporting and Investment Sections and the *Transactions*, of which 'A Generalized Profits Released Model for the Measurement of Return on Investment for Life Insurance' (TSA, XL), won the Annual Prize of the Society of Actuaries.

## PHELIM BOYLE

**Phelim Boyle** did graduate work in theoretical physics in Dublin before becoming an actuary. He worked in Liverpool for two years and moved to the University of British Columbia in Vancouver, Canada in the early 1970s. Professor Boyle has had a strong research interest in financial economics. A number of his papers use the ideas developed in financial economics to tackle problems in actuarial science and insurance. For example, he and his colleagues used option pricing theory to value maturity guarantees under investment linked contracts. He has also used stochastic interest rate models to analyze interest rate risk measurement for insurance companies. Professor Boyle has also published papers in insurance economics and mathematical demography. Many of his papers deal with the numerical aspects of financial economics. He was one of the first advocates of using Monte Carlo methods and this is one of his current research interests. Professor Boyle is on the editorial board of nine academic journals in the fields of financial economics and insurance. He has been an invited Visiting Professor at several universities throughout the world. Professor Boyle is a Fellow of the Institute of Actuaries (UK), as well as a Fellow of the Canadian Institute of Actuaries. Professor Boyle is currently Director of the Centre for Advanced Studies in Finance at the University of Waterloo and a faculty member in the School of Accountancy.

## ARNOLD A. DICKE

**Arnold A. Dicke** was Executive Vice President and Product Actuary at USLIFE Corporation in New York. He recently completed a term as Vice President, Life Insurance, for the American Academy of Actuaries and has also served as the Society of Actuaries' Vice President in change of the life practice area. Mr. Dicke's interest in market-value accounting issues began when he was chair of the Academy's Committee on Life Insurance Financial Reporting, during which time he visited FASB on several occasions. More recently, he has served as chair of the working group on liabilities of the ACLI Task Force on Market Value Accounting.

## MARK GRIFFIN

**Mark Griffin** is an Executive Director with Goldman Sachs International, where he heads the Pension and Insurance Strategy Group in the London office. Mr. Griffin has worked with insurance companies and pension funds on asset/liability and asset allocation matters across North America and Europe. After graduating from the University of Waterloo in 1982, Mr. Griffin worked with the Metropolitan Life Insurance Co. in their Ottawa, Toronto, and New York offices. In 1986 he joined Morgan Stanley in New York, transfering to the London office in 1992. In 1994 he joined Goldman Sachs' London office. Mr. Griffin has authored a number of papers for both the Society of Actuaries and AFIR as well as various financial periodicals including the *Journal of Portfolio Management*.

## JOAN LAMM-TENNANT

**Joan Lamm-Tennant** is a Professor of Finance at Villanova University, Pennsylvania. As a member of the graduate faculty, she instructs Portfolio Theory and Management, and Security Analysis. Dr. Lamm-Tennant has published and lectured extensively on investment policies and practices of the insurance industry. Her publications include articles in journals such as *The Journal of Business, Journal of Banking and Finance, Journal of Risk and Insurance, Review of Research in Banking and Finance*, and *Journal of Insurance Regulation*. She has published working papers for Goldman, Sachs and Co., SEI Co., Chalke Inc., Arthur Andersen & Co., KPMG Peat Marwick, and is author of the book *Mutual Funds: Analysis, Allocation and Peformance Evaluation* and co-editor of *Financial Management of Life Insurance Companies*. Her research has received awards sponsored by the International Insurance Society, State Farm Insurance Company, Chicago Board of Trade, Chartered Property–Casualty Underwriter Foundation, Huebner Foundation at the University of Pennsylvania and the Academy of Financial Services. As an invited lecturer, Dr. Lamm-Tennant has presented to many academic and industry groups including the Board of Directors of international insurance companies. Her presentations focus on asset allocation, asset-liability management and investment performance benchmarking. Technology which she has developed is currently utilized by US property–casualty insurers for managing and benchmarking investment portfolios. Dr. Lamm-Tennant serves on the Board of Directors for Selective Insurance Group, Inc., Focus Trust Fund and the Financial Analysts of Philadelphia. Dr. Lamm-Tennant received a BBA degree in Accounting and a MBA degree in finance from St. Mary's University, Texas, and a PhD in finance, investments and insurance from the University of Texas at Austin.

## S. MICHAEL MCLAUGHLIN

**S. Michael McLaughlin** is a Partner of Ernst & Young LLP and Director of National Life Actuarial Services. Mr. McLaughlin is a Fellow of the Institute of Actuaries, an Associate of the Society of Actuaries, and a Member of the American Academy of Actuaries. In his 24-year career in the insurance industry, he has gained wide experience in all areas of insurance. He has spent 11 years in the public accounting arena preceded by 13 years with life and accident and health insurers. He has worked on reserving, financial reporting, product development, re-pricing, and experience monitoring. His clients include life, health and annuity insurance companies, Blue Cross Blue Shield plans, and HMOs. Most recently he has been heavily involved with Mutual Company GAAP implementations and demutualizations. Mr. McLaughlin has served on various professional committees, including the Academy's Committee on Life Insurance Financial Reporting and the Society's State Health Committee. He has also spoken on many occasions at meetings of the Society of Actuaries and at the Valuation Actuary Symposium. Mr. McLaughlin is author of several published articles, and was awarded the Society of Actuaries Annual Prize in 1987, for his *Transactions* paper *A Comparison of Alternative GAAP Methodologies for Universal Life*.

## Shyam J.B. Mehta

**Shyam J.B. Mehta** holds an MA in mathematics from Jesus College, Cambridge University. He joined Bacon & Woodrow in 1975, and qualified as a Fellow of the Institute of Actuaries in 1978. In 1986, Shyam went to stockbrokers Shearson Lehman Hutton as Associate Director. He undertook detailed research into the UK life assurance as well as the worldwide property/casualty industries. Shyam joined Tillinghast – Towers Perrin, consulting actuaries, in 1988 as Research Officer and Consultant. His special areas of expertise are asset/liability stochastic modeling, the pricing and design of retail products for financial institutions, pricing of primary asset classes and derivatives, and valuation of life and non-life insurance companies. He is particularly interested in the analysis and pricing of risk, not just for financial/insurance products and institutions, but also in the sphere of property appraisal and capital projects. He reads widely around the subjects of modern financial theory and corporate finance. Shyam is widely known for his many presentations, papers and speeches on financial issues pertaining to the insurance industry. He is chairman of two Institute of Actuaries working parties, one investigating the financial management and control of unit trusts, and the other examining the construction of stochastic asset models. He is on two other working parties, relating to the economic impact of introducing solvency standards for UK pension funds and to developing actuarial involvement in capital investment projects.

## Christopher D. O'Brien

**Christopher D. O'Brien** graduated with a degree in Economics from Cambridge University in 1972, and then qualified as a Fellow of the Institute of Actuaries in 1975. He became an Associate of the Society of Actuaries in 1991. Mr. O'Brien was a member of the Institute of Actuaries Working Parties on Disclosure of Information and Profit Recognition. In 1994 he presented a paper to the Institute of Actuaries on Profit, Capital and Value in a Proprietary Life

Assurance Company. Mr. O'Brien is Appointed Actuary of Royal Life Insurance in Liverpool, England. He is a Vice-President of the Liverpool Economic and Statistical Society, and of the Manchester Statistical Society.

## KRZYSZTOF M. OSTASZEWSKI

**Krzysztof M. Ostaszewski** is a Professor of Mathematics and the Actuarial Program Director at the University of Louisville. He is an Associate of the Society of Actuaries, a Member of the American Academy of Actuaries, and a Chartered Financial Analyst. Mr. Ostaszewski holds a Ph.D. in Mathematics from the University of Washington. Mr. Ostaszewski's main areas of interest are asset/liability management, privatization of social insurance, and applications of fuzzy sets methods in actuarial science. He authored a monograph, *Possible Applications of Fuzzy Sets Methods in Actuarial Science*, published by the Society of Actuaries in 1993, as well as research monographs and papers published by the American Mathematical Society and in journals such as *Journal of Risk and Insurance, American Economic Review*, and many others. He has worked in asset/liability management at Hartford Life Insurance Companies and Providian Capital Management. During the first half of 1995, Mr. Ostaszewski studied actuarial aspects of free market reforms in Poland under a Fulbright Research Fellowship.

## ROBERT R. REITANO

**Robert R. Reitano** is Vice President of the Investment Policy and Research department of John Hancock Mutual Life in Boston, is a board member and Chairman of the Committee of Finance for John Hancock Variable Life Company and John Hancock Life Insurance Company of America, and board member of several other John Hancock subsidiaries. His current research interests include integrating risk capital objectives with investment policy, the market valuation of liabilities, and yield curve risk management. This latter interest has led to the development of new duration measures which reflect the risk of general non-parallel yield curve shifts, as well as an investigation of immunization and management strategies in this general context. Mr. Reitano has been a member of several industry task forces and committees, he has spoken at a number of industry seminars and events, and has presented several two-day educational seminars on his research for the Society of Actuaries. His papers have appeared in the Journal of Portfolio Management, the Transactions of the Society of Actuaries, and the Actuarial Research Clearing house. His papers have won an Annual Prize of the Society of Actuaries, and two biennial Redington Prizes awarded by the Investment Section of the Society of Actuaries. Mr. Reitano has a PhD in Mathematics from Massachusetts Institute of Technology, is a Fellow of the Society of Actuaries, a member of the American Academy of Actuaries, and a member of the International Actuarial Association.

## KIM B. STAKING

**Kim B. Staking** received a BA in economics from Brigham Young University, an MBA (finance concentration) from the University of California, and a PhD in Managerial Economics (concentration in risk and insurance and secondary emphasis in finance) from the Wharton School of the University of Pennsylvania. For the past six years, he has worked at the Inter-American Development Bank where he is Senior Financial Economist in the Infrastructure and Financial Markets Division. At the Bank, he concentrates on the development of financial institutions and markets.

Prior to joining the Inter-American Development Bank, Mr. Staking taught and conducted research in the areas of risk management and financial markets in the Finance Department of the Institut Européen d'Administration des Affaires (INSEAD) in Fontainbleu, France. He has also taught at the Wharton School of the University of Pennsylvania, the Université de Lausanne and California State University (courses in Risk Management and Insurance, Investment and Portfolio Theory, and International Finance). He has extensive experience in international banking having worked at Crocker National Bank in San Francisco, California and Santiago, Chile. He has consulted on asset-liability management and insurance issues for the World Bank, Continental Insurance Corporation, the US General Accounting Office, and the American Institute for Property–Liability Management, among others. His publications have appeared in the *Journal of Finance*, the *Journal of Risk and Insurance*, and *Financial Institutions Research* (Goldman Sachs).

## ROBERT C. WILKINS

**Robert C. Wilkins** (AICPA, IMA) joined the Financial Accounting Standards Board (FASB) in 1978 as a project manager on its research staff. He has managed projects addressing a variety of technical issues, including in-substance defeasance, compensated absences, and various leasing issues. He was responsible for the Board's consideration of expanding the use of fair value measurements in accounting for investments in debt and equity securities, which resulted in the issuance of FASB Statement No. 115. His current efforts are focused on the accounting for derivatives and hedging activities. Mr. Wilkins has also worked on improving various aspects of the FASB's communication of its accounting guidance. He developed the parameters for issuing FASB Technical Bulletins, which are used to provide timely guidance on emerging issues and implementation problems, and, as the project manager, he was instrumental in the Board's decision to establish the Emerging Issues Task Force (EITF). In addition, he developed the *Current Text*, which is the FASB's encyclopedia of the authoritative accounting literature, and *EITF Abstracts*, which provides a concise summary of EITF issues and their resolution.

Prior to joining the FASB, Mr. Wilkins was in the accounting research department of Deloitte & Touche (formerly Deloitte Haskins & Sells) in the New York executive office and was also an audit manager in the Cincinnati office.

Mr. Wilkins received a BSBA degree in accounting and an MBA in finance from Xavier University. He is a member of the American Institute of Certified Public Accountants and the Institute of Management Accountants.

# Index

AAA corporate model, adjustment spread 101–2
ABC bonds 204–5
accounting equation xvii
accounting principles
  history vii–x
  life insurance x–xii, 310–13
accounting principles x–xi
accounting spreads 205
accounting standards 303–30
  *see also* Statements of Financial Accounting Standards
  application to life assurance 310–13
  Australia and Canada 326
  deferred acquisition costs 319–20, 326
  earned profits method 313–21
  embedded values and present value of profits 324–5
  international standards 305–9
  margins approach 325–6
  standard setting 304
  statutory solvency valuation 321–4
  total value and rate of return 328–9
accounting systems 8, 216–22
  market-value accounting 201–13
  Merrill Lynch Life 138
accruals method 305, 311, 325–6
accumulations 130–1, 134, 273
ACF *see* asset cash flow
actuarial appraisal 14, 56–61, 98, 122–3
  *see also* appraisal method
  assumptions 61
  definition 56
Actuarial Standards Board (ASB) 56n2
adjustment spread 94–6, 342
  ARM Financial Group 130
  company perspective 96–100
    average cost of debt 96–7
    cost of funds 99–100
    dedicated assets 97–9
  public perspective 101–3
after-tax returns 153
American Academy of Actuaries, Task Force 22
American Institute of Certified Public Accountants (AICPA) 218, 220, 221, 222
American options 79, 90
amortization, DAC 9, 10, 218, 219, 220

Analytical Risk Management *see* ARM Financial Group
annuities, 6/4 254, 255
applicable treasury rate 202, 203
Appointed Actuaries 201–2
appraisal method 28, 29, 56–61, 211, 332, 341
  base case 58
  comparison 69
  definition 56–7
  statutory capital requirements 60
appraisal value (AV) 28–9, 56
  definition 57, 58
  discount rate impact 58–9
  interest rate impact 59–60
  option adjusted 267–8
arbitrage pricing theory (APT) 182, 225–6
ARM Financial Group 127–32, 133, 134
Arrow Debreu securities 197–8
asset cash flow (ACF) 228, 233, 291, 299–300
asset managers 128
asset matching 167
asset pricing models 148–9, 178, 181–3
  arbitrage pricing 182
  capital asset pricing 148, 153, 181–2, 199
asset risk
  life company valuation 143–80
  non-par products 154–5
asset valuation reserve (AVR) 240–1, 267, 275, 277
assets 357–8
  definition 304
  independence 332–3
  portfolio 29
  segmentation 298
  spreads 204–6
  valuation 28–9
  volatility 294, 295
assurance *see* insurance
AV *see* appraisal value
AVR *see* asset valuation reserve

Babbel, D.F. 115–26, 212, 363
bail out feature (BO) 254, 255
balance sheet
  ARM Financial Group 128–9, 131
  Merrill Lynch Life 138–9

371

## 372  Index

balance sheet (*continued*)
  option-based model  356–8
balance sheet  xvii
Becker, D.N.  29n1, 215–87, 363
behaviour
  insurance companies  111–13
  policyholders  104–11
benchmarking  266–7
beta ratios  176–7, 181–2
binomial model  75–7, 89
Black model  200
Black-Scholes model  75, 91–2, 149, 182–3, 198
BO *see* bail out feature
bond prices  242
bond valuation method  13
bonus smoothing policy  165–6
book profits  273, 274
book value accounting  11–12, 18, 19, 201, 299, 301
book value earnings  283
Boyle, P.  197–200, 212, 364
Brender, A.  297–301
broker distribution, with-profit company  173–4
business risk, life company valuation  143–80
Butsic, R.P.  21–113

call options, SPDA  155–6, 189–96
callable bonds  74, 83–5, 87–8
Canada, valuation methodology  297–301
capital asset pricing model (CAPM)  148, 153, 181–2, 199, 262–3
capital gains  240
capital ratios  201
capital structure  293–5
Carr, D.  127–32
cash flow ratio method  15
cash flow testing  15
cash flow valuation method (CFVM)  15, 298–301
cash flows  25–6, 241–2
  discounted  94–5
  indexed discount rate method  335
cash matching  233, 235
CDF *see* cumulative distribution function
central value selection  336
CFVM *see* cash flow valuation method
Choi, F.D.S.  xvii–xviii
collateral management obligations (CMO)  246
commutativity  80, 82, 91
company attributes  31

company dependence  298, 353–6, 359–60, 361–2
company perspective, adjustment spread  96–100
comparability  306, 312
Confederation Life  299, 300
consensus forecasts  187
conservatism  207, 217
consistency  334
constructive methods  24–9, 120, 126
  *see also* option pricing method
contingent gains and losses  308–9, 312–13
cost of funds method  236
counting  viii
Cox-Ross-Rubenstein model  75–9, 91–2
  American options  79
  binomial model  75–7
  European options  75–9
  multi-step lattice  77–8
CPA *see* cumulative policyholders' apportionment
credit risk
  definition  26–7
  spread  27
credited rates  338–9
  resetting  39, 111–12
  single premium deferred annuity  36, 39–41, 42
creditworthiness spread  125
Crowne, J.E.  127, 137–42
cumulative distribution function (CDF)  251, 252
cumulative policyholders' apportionment (CPA)  316, 317, 319, 323
current price approach  315–16, 320

DAC *see* deferred acquisition costs
DE *see* distributable earnings
death benefits, unpredictability  351
debt securities  xii, 1
deductive methods  24, 28–30, 120, 131
  *see also* appraisal method
default option  355
default spread (DS)  231
deferred acquisition costs (DAC)  218, 219, 222, 224, 270
  amortization  218, 219, 220
  assets  9, 10, 11, 67–8, 71, 131, 141
  calculation  320
  earned profits method  319, 321, 326
  indexed discount rate method  343–4
  offset method  67–9
deposit liabilities  3
derivatives  6, 354–5

Dicke, A.A. 7–20, 364
direct salesforce, with-profit company 173
discount rates 143–4, 150, 157, 178
    gross investors 189
    impact on actuarial value 58–9
    indexed discount rate method 335–6
    net investors 188–9
    unit-linked products 163
    variable life policies 161–2
    with-profit (par) business 164–6, 169–70
discounted cash flows 16, 26, 33, 130, 309, 313, 334
discounting spread 94–104
    *see also* adjustment spread
    company perspective 96–100
    public perspective 100–3
    schedule of rates 94–5
disintermediation 107
distributable earnings (DE) 241, 243, 244, 268
double entry bookkeeping ix
DPAC *see* deferred acquisition costs
DS *see* default spread
Duran, J.P. 127, 133–5
dynamic behaviour *see* behaviour

earned profits method 313–21
    appraisal 361
    assumptions 318–19
    current price approach 315–16, 320
    deferred acquisition costs 319–20
    example 327–8
    provisions approach 316–18, 321
economic rents 116
economic surplus *see* net worth
efficiency model, option pricing 73–4, 85–6
EGM *see* expected gross margins
EGP *see* expected gross profits
Elam, C.P. 21–113
embedded options 27, 28, 30
embedded values 324–5
enterprise total return (ETR) 269
equation of value 149–50, 161
equity
    definition 304–5
    returns 185–7
    with-profit (par) business 163–4
ETR *see* enterprise total return
EU
    Insurance Accounts Directive 303, 314
    Third Life (Framework) Directive 322
European options 75–8, 90
examples
    indexed discount rate method 346–7

market-value accounting 202–4
option adjusted value of distributable earnings 246–64, 246–71
single premium deferred annuity 34–48, 108–9, 112–13, 189–96
Universal Life policy 48–56, 109–11, 113
existing structure value 170–4, 179
expected asset cash flows 59
expected future earnings 56
expected gross margins (EGM) 67, 68
expected gross profits (EGP) 67, 68
expected present value (EPV) 76, 77, 78, 79
expenses 307–8, 339
Exposure Draft 4, 21–2

fair value accounting 1–6, 270
fair value of assets (FVA) 28, 57
fair value of liabilities (FVL)
    *see also* valuation methodology
    changes 95–6
    comparison of methods 7–20
    definitions 4–5, 7, 28, 57, 64–5
    determination difficulties 2–4, 6
    implementation 127–42
    Task Force 22
fair value reserves 95, 96, 100, 103
FASB *see* Financial Accounting Standards Board
federal income taxes 273, 274, 287
Feldblum, S. 12–113
Fidelity Investments 353
Financial Accounting Standards Board (FASB) 1–2, 304
financial economics 197–200
financial intermediaries 353, 354–5
financial product, characteristics 353
firm
    accounting systems 216–17
    value of the 215–95
fixed income securities 62, 225, 226–7, 286
    analysis 233
    cash flows 227
    pricing 80–5
flexible premiums 107–8
franchise value 115–18, 119, 212
free capital 167–9
free cash flows 240, 241, 242, 277
future premiums 146, 147, 208
FVA *see* fair value of assets
FVL *see* fair value of liabilities

GAAP *see* generally accepted accounting principles

generally accepted accounting principles
    (GAAP)   xi, 7, 8, 277, 278
  see also Purchase GAAP models
  deferred acquisition costs   343–4
  equity   11–12, 128, 131
  interest maintenance reserve   223
  liability valuation   223
  summary of development   218–22
GIC see guaranteed investment bond
going concern principle   305, 311–12
goodwill see existing structure value
government bond yields   147, 154, 157, 164
GPV see gross premium value
Griffin, M.W.   201–9, 364
gross investors   153
  discount rates   178, 189
gross premium value (GPV)   219
guaranteed investment bond (GIC)   73, 83–5, 260
guaranty funds   101

Heath, Jarrow, Morton (HJM) interest rate model   92–3
hedge strategies   5, 256–60
  interest rate caps   256–8
  portfolio hedge   257, 258–9, 260
hedge trade-offs   261–4
historic returns   186–7
HJM model see Heath, Jarrow, Morton interest rate model
Ho-Lee fixed income model   80–5
  callable bonds and GICs   83–5
Hohmann, J.E.   21–113, 211–12

IASC see International Accounting Standards Board
IDR see indexed discount rate method
illiquid assets   206
IMA see interest maintenance adjustment
immediate annuities   18, 315
immunization   234, 235–6, 237
implementation, fair value of liabilities   127–42
IMR see interest maintenance reserve
income statement   xvii
independence of the assets   332–3
indexed discount rate (IDR) method   331–49
  applications   344–5
  appraisal   361
  assumptions   337–40
  comparison with GAAP accounting   346–7
  concepts of profit, risk   342–3
  cost of capital   340–1
  criteria   332–7
  deferred acquisition costs   343–4
  example   346–7
  methodology   334–7
  relationship to other methods   341–2
  scenarios   347–9
indexed valuation method   69–71
  see also appraisal method
  definitions   69, 70
industry approach, adjustment spread   102
inflation, life companies   185, 186
insolvency guarantee programs   124
insolvency option   359
instability, life insurance industry   351–2
insurability   105
insurance companies
  see also life companies
  behaviour
    credit rates resetting   111–12
    crediting strategy   112
    SPDA example   112–13
    UL example   113
  flow diagram   247
insurance stock, market value   115, 116, 118
interdependence   339
interest maintenance adjustment (IMA)   14–15
interest maintenance reserve (IMR) method   14, 62–4, 223, 275
  definition   62
interest rate caps   256–8
interest rate paths   206
  calculation of   227–8
  generator model   30–1, 32
interest rates   301
  discounting   335–6
  impact on appraisal value   59–60
  real short-term   184
interest-sensitive liabilities   206–7
international accounting standards   305–9
International Accounting Standards Board (IASC)   304–6, 307, 309
International Accounting Standards (IAS)
  No.10 (Contingencies)   308, 312
  No.11 (Construction contracts)   307
  No.18 (Revenue)   306–7, 308, 309, 311
inventory, valuation   viii
investment income   286
investment returns
  equity returns   186–7
  life companies   148, 151–2
  real short-term interest rates   184
  term premiums   184–5

investment returns (*continued*)
  volatility 187–8
investment strategies 247–53
  benchmarking 266–7
  invest long 247, 248, 251
  ladder strategy 248–50, 251–2
investors, life companies 144, 153
issuance 98, 99, 100, 102

Keating, J.M. 21–113
Kirkland 127
Kolsrud, D.S. 21–113

ladder strategy 248–50, 251–2
Lamm-Tennant, J. 211–13, 361–2, 365
lapsation 338, 339
lapse assumption 301
lapse rates 159–60, 297
lapse risk 159–61, 170–1
lattice-based models 30, 72, 77–8, 80–92, 342
  complex contracts 87–9, 90
  HJM model 92–3
  pre-payment models 88
  yield curve scenario 89
law of one price 22–3
LCF *see* liability cash flow
lender viii, ix
liabilities
  *see also* market value of liabilities
  definition 304
  design 253–6
    risk adjusted value 255
    spread analysis 254
    yield analysis 254
  duration 63
  principles of measurement 309–13
liability cash flow (LCF) 229, 285
liability risk, life company valuation 143–80
liability spread (LS) 232, 236, 237
life companies 143–80
  after-tax risk and return 153
  asset pricing models 181–3
  balance sheets 356–8
  beta ratios 176–7, 181–2
  discount rates 188–9
  existing structure value 170–4
  investment return assumptions 151–2, 183–8
  management implications 359–60
  non-par business 154–7
  par (with-profit) business 162–70
  profit characteristics 145
  risk of failure 175–6
  summary 177–9
  target surplus 174–5
  taxation 152, 188–9
  valuation methodology 145, 146–50
  variable life policies 158–62
life insurance
  company dependence 353–4
  evolution 351–4
  financial product 353
  functions 8
  liabilities measurement 309–13
  nature of services 309–10
  private transaction 352
  profit characteristics 145–6
  revenue 310
life insurance liabilities
  accounting standards 8–10
  characteristics 7–8, 354–6
  company specific values 351–60
  valuation factors 355–6
liquidation value x, 115–18
liquidity risk 27–8
long-term inflation assumptions 185
long-term liabilities 62, 63, 70
LS *see* liability spread

MacDonald, K.A. 21–113
McLaughlin, S.M. 21–113, 331–49, 365–6
management, insurance companies 359–60
management accounting systems xi, 8
mandatory securities valuation reserve (MSVR) 275
manufacturing business, profit characteristics 146
margins approach 325–6
market price viii–ix
market to book adjustment method 66–7
market value analysis 233–4
  comparison with OAVDE 280–7
    convergence 281–2
    two paradigms 282–7
  limitations 237–9
  modified approach 281, 282
market value of assets (MVA) 269, 291
  examples 202–3
  value of the firm 228–9, 232, 234, 237
market value of earnings (MVE) 283, 291
market value of liabilities (MVL) 22, 202, 203, 269, 282, 292
  accounting standards application 303–30
  asset management applications 232–7
  background viii–ix, xii, xiv
  balance sheets 356–8
  calculation methods 230–2
  definitions 4, 5, 118, 119, 120

# Index

market value of liabilities (MVL) (*continued*)
   equations 118, 119
   insurance stock 115, 116, 118
   limitations 239
   option pricing structure 225–30
   proposals 222–4
   risk 117–18
market value of surplus (MVS) 203, 224, 232, 234, 269
market yield 357
market yield adjustment method 64–6
   definition 64–5
market-value accounting
   appraisal 211–13
   asset spread considerations 204–6
   conservatism 207
   conversion procedures 209
   example 202–4
   illiquid assets 206
   interest-sensitive liabilities 206–7
   stress tests 207–8
market-value accounting xii, 201–13, 216
marketable securities project 1–2
Markowitz Efficiency Frontier 250, 358
mean value 336–7
mean/variance diagram 250
measurement, liabilities 309–13
measurement technology xviii
Mehta, S.J.B. 143–80, 212, 366
Merfeld, T.J. 21–113
Merrill Lynch Life 137–42
   balance sheet 138–9
   development 137–8
   policy liabilities 140
Merton, R.C. 356–8
methodology *see* valuation methodology
migration methods 213
minimum actuarial reserve 318
mismatching, free capital 168
Monte Carlo simulation 92
morbidity 337
mortality 337
mortgage-backed securities 88
MSVR *see* mandatory securities valuation reserve
multi-point option pricing 242
mutual company, discount rates 164–5
MVA *see* market value of asset
MVE *see* market value of earnings
MVS *see* market value of surplus

National Organization of Life and Health Guarantee Associations 122, 123, 124, 125

negative market value 284
net GAAP liabilities (NGL) 67, 68
net investors 153
   discount rates 178, 188–9
net premium value (NPV) 69
net present value 276
net worth 118–19
new business
   risk 171
   sales subsidy 173–4
NGL *see* net GAAP liabilities
NOLHGA *see* National Organization of Life and Health Guarantee Associations
non-par business 19, 20
   asset risk 154–5
   existing structure value 171–3
   lapse rates 171–2
   liabilities valuation 154, 317
   modelling issues 156–7
   put and call options 155–6, 189–96
NVP *see* net premium value

OAAV *see* option adjusted appraisal values
OAC *see* option adjusted convexity
OAD *see* option adjusted duration
OAE *see* option adjusted equity
OAI *see* option adjusted income
OAS *see* option adjusted spread
OATR *see* option adjusted total return
OAV *see* option adjusted value
OAVA *see* option adjusted value added
OAVDE *see* option adjusted value of distributable earnings; option-adjusted value of distributable earnings
OAY *see* option adjusted yield
objectivity 333
O'Brien, C.D. 303–30, 366
option adjusted appraisal values (OAAV) 267–8, 270
option adjusted convexity (OAC) 228–9, 238
option adjusted duration (OAD) 228–9, 238
option adjusted equity (OAE) 293–4
option adjusted income (OAI) 268, 269
option adjusted spread (OAS) 31, 292, 294
   distribution 248–9, 253
   value of the firm 227, 228, 230–1, 243–5, 253, 255, 271
option adjusted total return (OATR) 268, 269
option adjusted value added (OAVA) 268–71
option adjusted value of distributable earnings (OAVDE) 211–12, 239–87
   alternative strategies 245–6
   applications 264–71

option adjusted value of distributable earnings (OAVDE) (*continued*)
  appraisal 289–95
  basic model 290–1
    assumptions 291–3
  behavioural variables 295
  comparison with market value analysis 280–7
  examples 246–64
  formula 244
  hedge strategies 256–60
  hedge trade-offs 261–4
  investment strategies 247–53, 266–7
  liability design 253–6
  objections to 276–80
  portfolio restructure 260–1
  present values 249, 250
  price of security 239–45
  pricing 272–6
  role of capital structure 293–5
option adjusted value (OAV) 264, 268, 269, 270
  surplus 262, 264
option adjusted yield (OAY) 243–4, 245–6
  distribution 249–50, 253, 254, 255
option pricing method 22, 23, 26, 30–56
  *see also* constructive methods
  assumptions 31
  definition 30–1
  discounting spread 94–104
  dynamic behavioural assumptions 104–13
  multipoint 242
  relationship to indexed discount rate method 341–2
  scenario approach 30–3
  valuation approach 33–56
option pricing theory 72–92
  Cox-Ross-Rubenstein model 75–9
  definitions 72–3
  efficiency model 73–4, 85–6
  Ho-Lee fixed income model 80–5
  insurance company examples 73
  lattice-based models 30, 72, 80–92
  life companies 149, 170, 182–3, 199
  replicating portfolio 75, 82
  scenario-based models 89, 90–1
  structure 225–30
  volatility 84
  von Neumann-Morgenstern theorem 74–5
  yield curve models 89
option risk 30
options 355
ORMAC *see* outstanding revenue matching acquisition costs

Ostaszewski, K.M. 351–60, 367
outstanding revenue matching acquisition costs (ORMAC) 319, 320, 321, 324, 327
  calculation of 311

P-GAAP models *see* Purchase GAAP models
par (with-profit) business 162–70
  *see also* non-par business
  asset matching 167
  broker distribution 173–4
  direct sales force 173
  discount rates 163, 164–6, 169–70
  equity 163–4
  existing structure value 173–4
  free capital 167–9
  liability calculation 316–17
  required surplus 166–7
  statutory valuation basis 167
paradigms 197–200, 211, 282–7
paths *see* interest rate paths
Paul v. Virginia (1868), insurance contract 352
payout liabilities 129–30, 134, 135
pension plan 279
policy loans 105–7
  preferred loan 106
  tax implications 107
  UL policy 106
policyholders
  behaviour
    assumptions 108
    flexible premiums 107–8
    policy loans 105–7
    prediction 238
    SPDA example 108–9
    surrenders/withdrawals 104–5
    UL example 109–11
  put options, SPDA 191–6
pool of risk 74
portfolio hedge 257, 258–9, 260
portfolio restructure 260–1
present value balance (PVB) 244
present value of distributable earnings (PVDE) 244, 259, 261
present value of liabilities (PVL) 119, 120
present value of profits (PVP) 324
present value of the statutory net income (PVSNI) 256
price of security 239–45
pricing 272–6
  accumulation formula 273
  paradigms 23–4, 211

profits
  accumulation 273
  book profits 273, 274
  indexed discount rate method 343
  realized 307
proprietary company, discount rates 165
provisions approach 316–18, 321
prudence 305–6, 312, 316–17, 322, 323
public perspective, adjustment spread 100–3
pump project 276
Purchase GAAP (P-GAAP) models 131, 134–5
put options 155–6, 189–96
  value 115–17, 212
put-call parity 79
PVB *see* present value balance
PVDE *see* present value of distributable earnings
PVP *see* present value of profits
PVSNI *see* present value of the statutory net income

RAPV *see* risk-adjusted present value
RAV *see* risk adjusted value
real economic growth 185–7
real short-term interest rates 184
realized return (RR) 237
recognition, timing of 306–8, 312
Reddy, S.D. 21–113
reinvestment 233
Reitano, R.R. 21–113, 121, 211–12, 367
reliability 306, 312
replicating portfolio 75, 82
required return (RQ) 237
required spread on assets (RSA) 236
required surplus 166–7, 274
reserve 299
return on capital employed 186
return of premium (ROP) 253, 254, 255
revenue 306–7, 308
  life assurance services 310
risk
  components of value 117–18
  lapse 170–1
  new business 171
  systematic 148, 171
  unsystematic 178
risk adjusted present value (RAPV) approach 25–6, 29
risk adjusted value (RAV) 251, 255
risk free discount rate 343
risk/return diagram 250
risky loan, market value 356
Robbins, E.L. 21–113
Robertson, R.S. 21–113

Rogers, D.Y. 21–113
Roman merchant viii–ix
ROP *see* return of premium
RQ *see* required return
RR *see* realized return
RSA *see* required spread on assets

SAI *see* shareholders' accrued interest
sales distribution capacity, free capital 168–9
SAP *see* statutory accounting principles
scenario-based methods 30–1, 89, 90–1, 342, 347–9
securities 9–10
  *see also* Arrow Debreu securities
security, price of 239–45
separate account variable annuities 131
SFAS *see* Statements of Financial Accounting Standards
shareholder dividends 277
shareholders
  variable life policies 158–9
  wealth 240
shareholders' accrued interest (SAI) 327, 328, 329
Siegel, H.W. 21–113
sign changes 275
similarity principle 22, 23, 24
simple cash flows 147–8
simulations 92–3, 121
single premium deferred annuity (SPDA) 32, 33, 73, 87, 130, 200
  acquisition costs 37
  balance sheet 357–8
  call option results 155–6, 196
  cash flow valuation method 35–6, 297
  credited rates 36, 39–41, 42
  hedge strategies 256–60
  insurance company behaviour 112–13
  interest rate volatility 47–8
  investment strategies 247–53
  lapse rates 43–4
  liability design 263–6
  mortality rates 35, 37
  number of paths 45–7
  option statistics 191
  policy characteristics 189–90
  policyholder behaviour 108–9
  present value 42
  product specifications 34
  put option results 155–6, 191–6
  renewal expenses 41–2
  simplified model 190
  surrenders 34, 38–9, 42–4
  testing horizon 44–5
  yield curve characteristics 190–1

Index 379

SPDA *see* single premium deferred annuity
spot rate discount approach 132
spreads 227, 230–2
   analysis 254
   spread-to-Treasuries 227, 248–9
Staking, K.B. 115n1, 118, 289–95, 367–8
state regulation 352
Statements of Financial Accounting Standards (SFAS)
   No.60 70, 219, 222
      characteristics 218
      impact of 4, 9, 10, 16
   No.97 71, 140, 141
      characteristics 219–21
      impact of 9, 10, 16, 222
   No.107 4, 6, 16, 133
   No.115 65, 66, 142, 221–2
      background 1–6
      impact of 9–10, 11–12, 15, 17, 21
      problems xii–xiii
   No.120 9, 10, 16, 218
statutory accounting
   adjustments xi
   changes 278–9
statutory accounting x–xi, xiii, 8, 217–18, 283
statutory book value earnings 283
statutory solvency valuation 321–4
   example 327–8
stress tests 207–8
surplus 273, 274–5, 357–8
   definition 279
   interpretations 279–80
   option adjusted value of 258
   value of 224
surrender value 4, 317–18
surrenders 34, 38–9, 42–4, 104–5
   charges 38–9, 105, 130
SWAP 261, 262, 263
systematic risk 148, 171, 178

tangible assets 120–1, 122
target surplus 174–5
Task Force
   appointment 22
   report 21–113
      comments 115–26
      summary 22–30
tax accounting 8
tax implications, policy loans 107
taxation 152, 188–9
term premium 184–5
testing horizon 33, 44–5
third party market 280, 284, 285, 286

timing of recognition 306–8, 312
total value and rate of return 328–9

UK
   Accounting Standards Board 304
   accruals method proposals 325–6
UL *see* Universal Life
understandability 306
unit-linked policies *see* variable life policies
United States v. South-Eastern Underwriters Association, et al (1944) 352
Universal Life (UL) policy 32, 33, 73, 87, 88
   cash flow valuation 48–9
   expenses and surrender charges 50–1
   flexible premiums 49–50
   indexed discount rate method 346–7
   mortality rates 51–2
   policy loan utilization 48, 53
   policyholder behaviour 106, 109–11
   product specifications 48
   surrenders 53–4
unpredictability, death benefits 351
unrealized gains and losses 9–10, 67
unsystematic risk 148, 178
US Treasury approach, adjustment spread 99, 100–1

valuation approach 33–56
   evaluation 55–6, 125–6
   examples
      SPDA 34–48
      UL policy 48–56
   summary 54–5
valuation methodology 7–20
   appraisal method 14, 56–61
   ARM Financial Group 127–32, 133–5
   asset pricing models 148–9
   bond valuation 13
   cash flow valuation method 297–301
   catalogue 12–13
   company specific values 351–60
   constructive methods 24–8, 120, 126, 211
   critique 211–13
   DAC offset method 67–9
   deductive methods 28–30, 120, 211
   discounted cash flow surrogates 12, 13–14, 18, 19
   earned profits method 313–21
   equation of value 149–50
   evaluation 17–19
   existing methods adaptation 12–13, 16–17, 19, 20
   Heath, Jarrow, Morton interest rate model 92–3

valuation methodology (*continued*)
   indexed discount rate method 331–49
   indexed valuation method 69–71
   interest maintenance reserve method 62–4
   interest-rate risk management 12, 13, 14–16
   life companies 146–50
   market to book adjustment method 66–7
   market yield adjustment method 64–5
   Merrill Lynch Life 137–42
   option pricing method 22, 23, 26, 30–56, 149
   simple cash flows 147–8
value, components 117, 118
value of the firm 215–95
   *see also* market value of liabilities
value of insurance inforce (VIF) 131, 132, 134
Vanderhoof, I.T. vii–xv
variable life policies
   cash flow risk characteristics 159
   discount rates 161–2
   equation of value 161
   lapse risk 159–61
   non-unit reserves and surplus 159
   product characteristics 158–9
VIF *see* value of insurance inforce
volatility 10
   assets 292, 294, 295
   investment returns 187–8
von Neumann-Morgenstern theorem 74–5

wealth, maximization 240
Wilkins, R.C. 1–6, 368–9
with-profit business *see* par (with-profit) business
withdrawal function 207
withdrawals 104–5, 208, 338

yield curve 301
   characteristics, SPDA 10–11
   models 80, 89–90
yields, analysis 254

zero-coupon bonds 226

# The New York University Salomon Center Series on Financial Markets and Institutions

1. I.T. Vanderhoof and E. Altman (eds.): *The Fair Value of Insurance Liabilities.* 1997
   ISBN 0-7923-9941-2
2. R. Levich (ed.): *Emerging Market Capital Flows.* 1997　　ISBN 0-7923-9976-5
3. Y. Amihud and G. Miller (eds.): *Bank Mergers & Aquisitions.* An Introduction and an Overview. 1997　　ISBN 0-7923-9975-7

KLUWER ACADEMIC PUBLISHERS – DORDRECHT / BOSTON / LONDON